Gabriele Anderl, Linda Erker, Christoph Reinprecht (eds.)
Internment Refugee Camps

Histoire | Volume 192

Gabriele Anderl (Dr.) is a freelance researcher in Vienna. She worked for the Austrian Historical Commission and for the Austrian Commission for Provenance Research and is vice president of the Austrian Society for Exile Research (öge). She published numerous books and articles in the field of contemporary history, especially on the National Socialist era, on flight, rescue and exile.

Linda Erker (Dr.) is a historian and postdoc researcher at the Department of Contemporary History at Universität Wien. In her postdoc project she focuses on the migration of knowledge and the migration of scholars from Austria to Latin America between 1930 and 1970 (especially to Argentina and Chile). She is a board member of the öge.

Christoph Reinprecht (Dr.) is a professor for sociology at Universität Wien and president of the öge. His research interests are migration and city, social inequality and political sociology as well as the history of sociology, in particular the constitution of the social field of empirical sociology in Vienna.

Gabriele Anderl, Linda Erker, Christoph Reinprecht (eds.)
Internment Refugee Camps
Historical and Contemporary Perspectives

[transcript]

Paul Grüninger Stiftung, St. Gallen (Switzerland)

Bibliographic information published by the Deutsche Nationalbibliothek
The Deutsche Nationalbibliothek lists this publication in the Deutsche Nationalbibliografie; detailed bibliographic data are available in the Internet at http://dnb.d-nb.de

This work is licensed under the Creative Commons Attribution-Non Commercial 4.0 (BY-NC) license, which means that the text may be may be remixed, build upon and be distributed, provided credit is given to the author, but may not be used for commercial purposes.
To create an adaptation, translation, or derivative of the original work, further permission is required and can be obtained by contacting rights@transcript-publishing.com
Creative Commons license terms for re-use do not apply to any content (such as graphs, figures, photos, excerpts, etc.) not original to the Open Access publication and further permission may be required from the rights holder. The obligation to research and clear permission lies solely with the party re-using the material.

First published in 2023 by transcript Verlag, Bielefeld
© Gabriele Anderl, Linda Erker, Christoph Reinprecht (eds.)

https://www.transcript-verlag.de/

Cover Design: Juma Hauser / www.jumahauser.net
Editing: Philip Parr
Coordination: Lena Coufal
Printed by: Majuskel Medienproduktion GmbH, Wetzlar
https://doi.org/10.14361/9783839459270
Print-ISBN 978-3-8376-5927-6
PDF-ISBN 978-3-8394-5927-0
ISSN of series: 2702-9409
eISSN of series: 2702-9417

Printed on permanent acid-free text paper.

Contents

Introduction
Gabriele Anderl, Linda Erker and Christoph Reinprecht 9

Part I
The polysemic function (character) of camps

Internment practices during the First and Second World Wars
A comparison
Matthew Stibbe and Kim Wünschmann 29

Austrians in Trinidadian internment during the Second World War
The case of the Stecher family
Christian Cwik 47

Rehabilitation through labour
Welfare or control in a postwar Austrian internment camp
Rachel Blumenthal 59

United Nations versus the Federal Agency
The recognition of asylum-seekers in West German camps after 1949
Michael Mayer 73

Can camp life create a common world?
Michel Agier 87

Part II
(Dis)empowering role of humanitarian intervention

Interventions by non-governmental organisations in state-run internment camps in France
The rescue of Jewish children from Rivesaltes as told through the example of Vivette Hermann
Lilly Maier 99

Reconstructing Lives, Creating Citizens
The role of the American Jewish Joint Distribution Committee (JDC) in the rehabilitation of detainees on Cyprus, 1946–49
Anat Kutner 111

Civilian internees, common criminals or dangerous communists?
The International Committee of the Red Cross, the United Nations Command and internment in South Korea, 1950–53
Jean-Michel Turcotte 125

Vicious circles of disempowerment
The social dynamics of contemporary German refugee shelters
Birgit Behrensen 137

Enhancing agency and empowerment in refugee camps as total institutions – real or illusory?
Maximiliane Brandmaier 147

Part III
Strategies of coping and resistance

Undesirable asylum-seekers from National Socialist Germany in France
Horst Rosenthals' comics in Gurs Camp
Pnina Rosenberg 161

Singing and dancing for freedom of movement
Enacting citizenship and resisting forced confinement in "hotspot" refugee camps in Thessaloniki, Greece 2016
Ioannis Christidis 177

Room(s) for children?
Children's everyday practices in a "community shelter" in Switzerland today
Clara Bombach 193

Part IV
Pathways and transitions

Cycles of incarceration
From the "Third Reich" through British Mandatory Palestine to Mauritius
Roni Mikel-Arieli 209

Forced to flee and deemed suspect
Tracing life stories of interned refugees in Canada
during and after the Second World War
Andrea Strutz 229

Filling the gap
Displaced Persons and émigré scholars
in the post-slavery society of the US South
Andreas Kranebitter and Peter Pirker 251

The life and afterlife of a twentieth-century French camp: Gurs
Christoph Jahr 269

Hard time in the Big Easy
The unique role of New Orleans in Second World War
enemy alien internment
Marilyn G. Miller 287

Annex

Index of names 305

Short biographies of contributors and editors 309

Introduction

Gabriele Anderl, Linda Erker and Christoph Reinprecht

The global map of forced migration in its myriad forms, causes and circumstances is testament to the extent of refugee flight and exile in the world today. The planet is covered with a network of lines – a familiar image for the visualisation of global migration, representing not only escape routes but also nodes where the movement of fleeing people has been delayed or brought to a halt. Whereas the lines represent migration paths between countries of origin and receiving nations, the nodes represent places of (often forced) accommodation and detention in camps. There are some striking regional differences within this map: some of the lines are broken, others end abruptly, seemingly in the middle of nowhere; some of the nodes are densely clustered, others stand in isolation. Yet, overall, the map leaves no doubt that we are living in an age of forced migration, a "century of camps." (Zygmunt Bauman)[1].

The detention, often through force, of refugees and asylum-seeking individuals in camps is not a recent phenomenon: states have long used the practice to regulate and control the movement of humans across borders. During the First World War, for example, tens of thousands of so-called "enemy aliens" were kept in internment camps. Before and during the Second World War, Jewish refugees and other individuals persecuted by the National Socialist regime were subjected to even worse treatment. Shortly after the end of that war in 1945, countless camps for Displaced Persons – including Jewish survivors of the Shoah – were established. Since then, camps of various types have been used to restrict and control the movement of refugees.

Indeed, the internment of refugees and asylum-seekers continues to this day. Both inside and outside Europe, the authorities are currently discussing, trialling and establishing different types of camps on a massive scale. Yet, the objective is always the same: to detain refugees. Historical and contemporary immobilisation and "encampment"[2] practice reflects the fact that states and governments often perceive individuals who seek protection and asylum as potential sources of danger. It is for

---

1 Zygmunt Bauman, "A Century of Camps?", in *The Bauman Reader*, edited by Peter Beilharz (Malden, MA: Blackwell, 2001), 230–280.
2 Michel Agier, *Managing the Undesirables. Refugee Camps and Humanitarian Governance* (Cambridge: Polity 2010).

this reason that the incarceration and subsequent forced deportation of refugees and Displaced Persons have become so commonplace around the world, even though such measures often violate fundamental human rights and hinder NGOs' efforts to support and help refugees.

The origins of this book can be traced back to December 2020, when the Austrian Society for Exile Research (öge) held a conference that addressed both the history and recent developments in state-organised (forced) accommodation of refugees. The society is an independent association of people who work in the field of exile research.[3] Although its original focus was on exile from Austria during Austro-Fascism and National Socialism, it has since broadened its remit to encompass current forms of flight and exile. Therefore, the conference aimed to bring historical and contemporary experiences and perspectives into dialogue with one another. This volume presents a selection of thoroughly revised contributions to the conference, including in-depth analyses of local phenomena, case studies and comparative discourses from an international and historical perspective. All of the papers have undergone a rigorous two-step internal and external peer-review process.

From a variety of disciplinary angles, the articles in this book explore the organised, state-led and forced placement of past and present refugees and ask how their fates have unfolded within internment camps. They draw parallels – and highlight contrasts – between different types of detention while also considering each camp's unique historical context. Moreover, they investigate the social, relational and organisational context that characterise these camps in their function as transitory spaces.

Any book that attempts to bring historical and contemporary analyses into dialogue requires clear, unequivocal definitions. Hence, all of the articles in this collection construe "camp" solely as a place where refugees and asylum-seekers are held in custody; they do not discuss forced labour camps, re-education camps, concentration camps, or extermination camps. This distinction is crucial given the ongoing debate over the term in the historical and social sciences. With reference to Hannah Arendt's famous article "We Refugees,"[4] a prominent argument describes camps "as the hidden matrix and nomos of the political space in which we are still living."[5] According to Giorgio Agamben, camps represent a state of emergency, based on a blurring of demarcation lines between right and wrong, inclusion and exclusion, legitimacy and exception. Far beyond the use and function of camps in colonial warfare, the role played by concentration and extermination camps under National Socialism

---

3   https://exilforschung.ac.at.
4   Hannah Arendt, "We Refugees", in *Hannah Arendt, The Jewish Writings*, edited by Jerome Kohn and Ron H. Feldman (New York: Schocken Books, 2007), 264–274.
5   Giorgio Agamben, *Homo Sacer. Sovereign Power and Bare Life* (Stanford: Stanford University Press, 1998), 166.

and the Soviet Gulag, the refugee camp has become a means of biopolitical control in modern world. This is why, following this argument, every single camp, in whatever form, carries the potential to become a concentration (and extermination) camp.

However, from the editors' perspective, it is imperative to draw a distinction between refugee camps, on the one hand, and forced labour and concentration camps, on the other. Although a clear differentiation may be difficult in some cases, especially as some camps may transition from one form to the other, in general they can be distinguished on the basis of their respective underlying agendas. All camps represent an organizational arrangement, tracing back to military origins, that are evident in their spatial, legal and organisational structure. However, whereas imperial, colonial and totalitarian regimes have long used camps as instruments for the imprisonment, submission, deportation, or even extermination of their own and other populations, refugee camps are committed to a specific humanitarian agenda, established during the First World War and institutionalised after the Second through international law (most notably the Geneva Conventions and the UN Declaration of Human Rights). This embeddedness in international law and humanitarian action is crucial when studying and comparing historical and current examples of refugee internment.

Refugee camps perform a dual function: they provide emergency aid and a minimal level of care for fleeing people and/or Displaced Persons, yet they are also state-led surveillance centres that endeavour to control those people. Various aspects of this Janus-like character are addressed in this book. One interesting example, from both historical and sociological perspectives, refers to the creation of new categories of state-driven and humanitarian intervention. In their article on internment practices during the First and Second World War, *Matthew Stibbe* and *Kim Wünschmann* describe the coining of the term "enemy aliens." This category became particularly significant for Jewish and political refugees from National Socialist Germany who were often detained in camps in isolated regions, such as the Isle of Man, a British Crown Dependency lying in the Irish sea, roughly halfway between Great Britain and Ireland, which became one of the emblematic places of this experience. In his article, *Christian Cwik* investigates another such place, the British colony of Trinidad, where 500 Austrian citizens were interned as "German enemy aliens" after the so-called "Anschluss" in 1938. Similar examples in this book – such as *Rachel Blumenthal*'s paper on the Displaced Persons camp in Bad Gastein and *Michael Meyer*'s article on asylum-seekers who arrived in Germany after 1945 and were placed under the mandate of the United Nations Relief and Rehabilitation Administration (UNRRA) and then the International Refugee Organisation (IRO) – underline the (ambivalent and shifting) relations between categories formulated by state (mostly securitarian) and humanitarian logics. Many of the cases discussed in this book demonstrate that this tension also frames the behaviour of the internees themselves. For instance, according to *Michel Agier*, internment camps for refugees and Displaced People are characterised by ever-increasing contradictions that open up new opportunities for bottom-up processes of collective action and solidarity.

Research into refugee camps has identified three key structural features that have varied historically according to political and/or legal context:[6] specific territorial situation (refugee camps are often established in liminal areas that are difficult to access); exceptional legal status (protection by international law but outside the legal framework that applies in the state where the camp is located); and social exclusion (regulation and control of external contacts). Throughout the world, refugees, asylum-seekers and Displaced People have testified that detention in a camp brings only short-term relief as their supposedly temporary status becomes permanent, their hopes of a free life in exile are frustrated and their human rights are ignored.

Both autobiographies and historical and ethnographic research indicate that support from outside the camps is an important means of overcoming the always difficult and often hopeless plight of stranded internees. Such support may be provided by voluntary organisations (as *Lilly Meyer* demonstrates in her paper on social workers who lived within the French camp of Rivesaltes), local (Jewish) advocacy groups, transnational non-governmental organisations (see the articles by *Anat Kutner* and *Jean-Michel Turcotte*), or professional refugee aid and care networks (see the contributions of *Birgit Behrensen, Maximiliane Brandmaier* and *Clara Bombach*). Some of the articles focus on specific groups (e.g. children: see *Lilly Meyer* and *Clara Bombach*), others concentrate on a particular task (e.g. rehabilitation and integration in the local labour market: see *Rachel Blumenthal* and *Anat Kutner*), while still others explore the internees' self-organisational activities (see *Michel Agier* and *Ioannis Christidis*). Decisive factors for self-organisation are sociocultural and/or political homogeneity, access to and control of communication, the nature and extent of formal regulations, and the wider local environment. While some detainees have expressed their resistance through theatre, music, art, or even handicrafts (see the papers of *Pnina Rosenberg* and *Ioannis Christidis*), a politically hostile environment, such as that of South Korea in the early 1950s, may thwart such activities (see *Jean-Michel Turcotte*'s article). External refugee and care workers may gain an empowering role if they display a commitment to partisanship (see *Clara Bombach*), although this may equally bring them into conflict with their professional or societal environment.

---

6   Michel Agier, *Un Monde de Camps* (Paris: La Découverte, 2014); Bettina Greiner and Alan Kramer (eds.), *Die Welt der Lager. Zur "Erfolgsgeschichte" einer Institution* (Hamburg: Hamburger Edition, 2013); Christoph Jahr and Jens Thiel (eds.), *Lager vor Auschwitz: Gewalt und Integration im 20.Jahrhundert* (Berlin: Metropol Verlag, 2013); Joël, Kotek and Pierre Rigoulot, *Das Jahrhundert der Lager. Gefangenschaft, Zwangsarbeit, Vernichtung* (Berlin/München: Propyläen, 2001).

Refugee camps can vary significantly in terms of form and function: organised and permanent; informal and mobile; socially isolated and woven into the urban fabric. From the perspective of the refugees, too, each camp establishes a different reality: between protection and deprivation of rights, marginalisation and self-assertion, recognition and rejection. However, analysing internment from a time-comparative angle reveals changing conceptualisations of refugees and Displaced People depending on the prevailing political system and the dominant migration/asylum and welfare regime. Since the end of Second World War, there is evidence of increasing differentiation (also in legal terms) between "refugees," "asylum-seekers," "people under subsidiary protection", "returnees", "unlawful migrants", "undocumented foreigners" etc. Today, in a context where the erratic circulation of "wandering strangers"[7] is challenging the world's migration and refugee regimes, those categories are eroding and becoming arbitrary in the use. While state agencies respond with ever more restrictions, increased surveillance and/or militarised border control, humanitarian action and social assistance have become entangled in a vicious cycle of disempowerment (see the articles by *Birgit Behrensen* and *Maximiliane Brandmaier*).

While the term "refugee detention centre" suggests a static institution with a stable function, several of the contributors describe a more dynamic reality for both the internees and the places where they are detained. For many of the Jews and other refugees who fled persecution and extermination in the 1930s and 40s, the weeks or months they spent in refugee camps were relatively brief interludes during their journeys to new lives in exile (see *Andrea Strutz*'s article on refugees in Canada). For others, detention ended with deportation to a German concentration camp (see *Christoph Jahr*'s exploration of Jewish refugees and volunteers who fought on the side of the Republic in the Spanish Civil War and were subsequently interned in Gurs Camp in southern France). Gurs exemplifies the way in which a refugee camp's function may change over time: in this case, from a detention centre for members of the International Brigades (including many Jewish left-wing activists from Germany and Austria), to a prisoner-of-war camp and a prison for Vichy collaborators, and finally to a "lieu de memoire" – a place of Holocaust remembrance – today. Other papers discuss the societal context of the detention of Jewish refugees, for example under colonial regimes (see the articles by *Roni Mikel-Arieli* on Mauritius, *Andrea Strutz* on Canada and *Christian Cwik* on Trinidad) or in the Deep South of the United States (see the contribution of *Andreas Kranebitter* and *Peter Pirker*). Finally, many of the articles address the long-term impacts of refugee internment practices. As *Marilyn G. Miller* puts it in her paper, "With the benefit of hindsight […] it is clear that the Enemy Alien Control Program […] set a precedent for subsequent US policies

---

7   Didier Fassin, *Life, A Critical User's Manual* (Cambridge: Polity Press, 2018), 40.

and practices that have routinely treated non-citizens arriving from Latin America as dangerous criminals."

The articles in this book touch upon a wide range of interesting topics that merit further historiographical, sociological and anthropological investigation,[8] including: living conditions, hygiene and medical provision within detention centres; mortality rates among Displaced Persons; the specific issues faced by refugee women, children, and ethnic and sexual minorities; conflicts and struggles between different social and political groups; the fear of spies and "fifth columnists," especially in times of war; camp administration and security management; the ongoing tension between accommodation and regulation; the roles played by external support agencies, self-organised cultural and political activities, and vocational training in terms of helping refugees cope with the pressures of internment and preparing them for post-camp life; the prevalence of camps under colonial administrations and during the Cold War; and, finally, "Alija Bet" – the highly organised yet illegal migration of hundreds of thousands of Jews from Europe to the British Mandate of Palestine between 1938 and the founding of the state of Israel in 1948.

The articles in this collection

Part I: The polysemic function (character) of camps

The article by historians Matthew Stibbe and Kim Wünschmann is a cross-temporal exploration of internment in the first half of the twentieth century. In their analysis, they demonstrate that the mass incarceration of non-combatants, including "enemy aliens," deportees, refugees, internally Displaced Persons, political suspects and social outcasts, began in earnest during the First World War. Under the guiding principle of national security, imperial states (especially Great Britain and France) implemented internment policies that were coordinated throughout their metropolitan, dominion and colonial territories, and across their land and sea borders. Internment thus became an integral part of a global war culture and laid bare global class, race and gender inequalities.

The authors then focus on the lessons "learned" from the practice of detaining "enemy aliens" between 1914 and 1918 and their impact on policy-making during the century's second major conflict. In particular, they stress the much greater scale of exile, expulsion and flight that characterized the Second World War, while also

---

[8] See also the volume edited by Gabriele Anderl, Hinter verschlossenen Toren. Die Internierung von Geflüchteten von den 1930er Jahren bis in die Gegenwart (Wien: Verlag der Theodor Kramer Gesellschaft 2022).

highlighting a significant change in the application of the term "enemy alien" itself. As ever more people were categorized in this way, it became increasingly necessary to differentiate between "real enemy aliens" and "technical enemy aliens." The latter, much larger group consisted of (mostly Jewish) refugees who had fled National Socialist persecution. In Great Britain, tribunals were established to distinguish "friendly enemy aliens" from "dangerous enemy aliens." At first only the latter were interned. However, the official policy took a sharp turn after the German invasion of the Netherlands, Belgium and France in the late spring of 1940 brought the threat of invasion ever closer. A state of panic and heightened anxiety over national security not only supplanted careful attempts to separate enemy agents from refugees but also had a direct impact on internment policy as unprecedented numbers of men, women and children were detained in civilian internment camps, and over 7,000 men were deported to Canada and Australia. Yet the option of detaining all or nearly all "enemy aliens" was only practiced for a relatively short period (a few months at most), and many "loyal" refugees were subsequently released from internment or given the option of enlisting in the Pioneer Corps, a unit in the British armed forces.

Finally, Stibbe and Wünschmann show that the internment of white German and Austrian settlers in the colonies led to racial role reversals similar to those that had taken place in the First World War. Indeed, their detention challenged a well-established colonial order that was otherwise firmly based on white "European" dominance.

In his case study, historian and Latin America specialist Christian Cwik explores the integration and internment of European émigrés on Trinidad from the so-called "Anschluss" until the end of the Second World War. More than 500 Austrian citizens – most of them Jews from Vienna who had arrived on the Caribbean island prior to the beginning of the war – were interned in camps as "German enemy aliens" between 1940 and 1945. Among their number were members of the Stecher family. In 2013, Cwik interviewed Hans Stecher about his escape from the National Socialists, arrival in Trinidad, eventual detention and post-war life on the island. His article not only chronicles the fate of Hans and the rest of the Stecher family but places their experiences within a broad historical context. Supplemented with research conducted in Britain's National Archives, the author explains how and why many emigrants from Central Europe ended up in Trinidad, their pre-war integration within island society and the British colonial administration's subsequent introduction of its internment policy. Furthermore, he looks at the topic from a global perspective, with reference, for example, to migration from China and Syria during the 1920s and 30s due to the increasing importance of the oil industry and the proposal to use Trinidad as a reception centre for evacuees from war-torn Malta and Gibraltar.

In her article, the historian Rachel Blumenthal uses the example of everyday life in an internment camp for Jewish Displaced Persons in the Austrian spa town of

Bad Gastein between 1945 and 1948 to illustrate the contradictions that characterise so many refugee camps: on the one hand, they are places of sanctuary, welfare and care; on the other, they are sites of surveillance and control. Blumenthal sketches the working and living conditions within the camp as well as the inmates' relationships with the inhabitants of Bad Gastein, which at the time was in the US occupation zone. Forced labour was not official policy for interned non-repatriable residents in this zone. Moreover, the US government specifically exempted Jewish refugees from the local requirement that able-bodied Displaced Persons must accept any offer of employment. Nevertheless, the military governor and the camp administrator strongly encouraged the camp's residents to work, as officers and relief workers alike viewed this as an essential component of their rehabilitation. Consequently, UNRRA established workshops within the camp to "inculcate workmen to disciplined, high-quality work and honest shop conduct." In order to maintain a high rate of employment, the welfare organisation also stipulated that only workers would receive extra food rations – a policy that ignored the fact that many Jewish survivors were still recovering from years of forced labour during the war. Blumenthal thus traces the lines of conflict that ran between the internees' personal and often traumatic war experiences and their desire to re-establish independent lives, on the one hand, and the UNRRA's determination to oversee the residents' rehabilitation through tight control and hard work, on the other.

The historian Michael Mayer also investigates the complexity of the asylum issue in the chaotic aftermath of the Second World War. Many asylum-seekers who reached West Germany at that time had been victims of the National Socialists; others had been collaborators. Those who arrived prior to 30 June 1950 were placed under the mandate of UNRRA and its successor organisation, the IRO (founded in 1946). However, the IRO officially ceased all operations in West Germany at the beginning of 1952, at which point the Federal Republic assumed full responsibility for the recognition process, establishing the Federal Agency for the Recognition of Alien Refugees (Bundesdienststelle für die Anerkennung ausländischer Flüchtlinge) the following January. This state-run asylum system obliged all new arrivals to report to a camp for political screening purposes. In addition, the government initially intended to institute a second recognition process for those who were already in the country (many of whom were still under IRO mandate), although that scheme was later abandoned. Previously, around 75 per cent of the country's refugees had lived outside of the country's camps. Now, though, Camp Valka in Bavaria was chosen as the sole location for implementation of the new policy. Guided by the requirements of the Geneva Refugee Convention, every case had to be individually considered.

Mayer highlights the contrasting approaches of the IRO and the West German authorities towards the processing of asylum-seekers and the granting of asylum. The former organisation – which was founded primarily to provide social benefits to foreign refugees and, if possible, prepare them for resettlement abroad – saw no need to investigate whether any refugee's claims of persecution were genuine. It was usually sufficient for the applicant simply to declare their opposition to the government of their home country. This approach, which was backed by the Western Allies, has to be seen in the context of mounting East–West tension, when numerous people sought protection under the IRO's mandate by claiming to be anti-communists after fleeing from the Soviet sphere of influence. By contrast, the West German authorities felt that the arrival of ever more refugees was placing an intolerable burden on the still war-stricken country. Moreover, they often perceived foreign refugees as a security problem. As a result, whereas the IRO had viewed camps simply as a means to accommodate people who would otherwise lack shelter, the West German government initially saw an opportunity to utilise them as a control mechanism. However, there was a gradual realisation that the disadvantages of enforcing mandatory internment – most notably the high costs – outweighed the supposed security "benefits." This eventually led to a change of policy that not only allowed but actively encouraged refugees to find alternative accommodation.

The anthropologist Michel Agier views refugee camps as places of socialisation and politics, and thus as potential sites for the creation of a "common world." Based on extensive ethnographic research in numerous camps in contemporary Europe and Africa, he develops an understanding of these institutions that is marked by three dualisms: that between the camp as heterotopia and place of refuge; that between securitarian and humanitarian logics; and that between urgency and endlessness (the camp as a waiting zone). The fact that camp life is characterised by uncertainty, undesirableness and precarity should not lead to the conclusion that such places are doomed to anomie and destructive disintegration. According to Agier, most camps struggle with two opposite perspectives: the demolition and eradication of their facilities; or their transformation into permanent urban neighbourhoods. The latter transformation is possible because refugees are not passive objects of custody. Rather, they actively engage in creating new forms of autonomous self-governance, especially when their efforts are reinforced by support from civil society actors, NGOs, associations and volunteers.

Part II: The (dis)empowering role of humanitarian intervention

The historian Lilly Maier explores the international non-governmental aid organisations that sent social workers, doctors and nurses to internment camps in the south of France during the Second World War, and especially the role played by one remarkable young woman – Vivette Hermann – in these relief efforts. From 1941 onwards, Rivesaltes served the Vichy government as a state-run internment camp for refugees, political opponents (such as communists), Sinti, Roma, and especially Jews, many of whom had been deported from Baden and the Palatinate in Germany. It was considered as a "family camp," since the majority of Vichy France's child internees were sent there with their parents. A shortage of supplies and inadequate sanitation meant conditions in the camp were catastrophic from the very beginning, and many of the detainees died. Then, in April 1941, most of the Jewish inmates were transferred to a separate section, where the living conditions were even worse.

The volunteers lived inside the camp to offer as much assistance as they could to the internees. They were engaged in a daily battle against hunger and malnutrition, struggled to improve sanitary conditions, started kindergartens and schools and provided medical and psychological assistance. Vivette Hermann arrived as a social worker in Rivesaltes in November 1941 and shortly thereafter started to coordinate the liberation of over 400 Jewish children from the camp. Initially, this involved persuading the parents to grant permission for their children's removal and preparing the children themselves for the separation. Later, with the blessing of the French Jewish humanitarian organisation Oeuvre de Secours aux Enfants (OSE), Hermann liberated about a dozen extra adolescents by falsifying their ages on the official forms.

In the summer of 1942, after Hermann had completed her mission, the camp became an "antechamber of Auschwitz" when the Vichy authorities started arresting Jewish families and sending them to Rivesaltes prior to transferring them to the SS-run Drancy internment camp and, from there, to the extermination camps.

In her paper, the historian Anat Kutner tells the story of survivors of the Shoah who were arrested on arrival in the British Mandate of Palestine in the summer of 1946 and forcibly transferred to camps on the island of Cyprus. Most of them were Displaced Persons who wished to start a new life in a Jewish state that they would help to establish less than two years later. Between August 1945 and July 1946, the British authorities had responded to the arrival of thousands of illegal immigrants on the coast of Palestine by holding them captive in the Atlit detention camp, near Haifa, and Latrun Prison, near Jerusalem. However, as these holding areas continued to fill, they decided to establish new camps on Cyprus, partly in the misguided hope that this would dissuade other potential illegal immigrants from making the trip. The internments on Cyprus symbolised the burgeoning conflict between the British officials in Mandate Palestine – who wanted to control immigration and therefore the demographic composition of the population – and migrating survivors of the Shoah who viewed settlement in the region as their natural right. Support for the detainees was provided primarily by the American Jewish Joint Distribution Committee (JDC), as only an organisation with no political affiliation could hope to resolve the complex humanitarian crisis that the British authorities had created. It was allowed to operate freely as it was not perceived as a Zionist organisation, and it had the means and organisational ability to provide desperately needed basic humanitarian aid as well as cultural and educational programmes that not only gave life in the camps some meaning but also helped the detainees to prepare for their future lives in Israel. In addition, it negotiated improvements in medical supplies and extra food rations, which the British had severely restricted.

Many children and teenagers were housed in the camps as they generally comprised a significant proportion of the illegal immigrants, and a "youth village" was established to house orphans who had travelled alone. The British authorities did not grant any special privileges to this children's camp, but the JCD was granted permission to import study materials. Many of the children were illiterate because they had been deprived of a proper education during the war years. In the camps, they were taught solely in Hebrew and the school promoted Zionist values. Further educational programmes were established for adults in the other camps, and some of them received vocational training (although the primary purpose was simply to keep them occupied). Finally, in this period of escalating violence, mobilisation of the people and the economy for the war effort – and ultimately the transition from Jewish community to statehood – was paramount for the leaders of Jewish Palestine. The detainees on Cyprus played their part in this by donating thousands of valuable items – often of great sentimental value – to the cause.

In his contribution, the historian Jean-Michel Turcotte examines the role of international organisations in South Korean internment camps between 1950 and 1953. During the early Cold War, the efforts of the International Committee of the Red Cross (ICRC) to provide relief to non-military captives in South Korea were frustrated by deep-rooted hostility towards the detainees' alleged political ideology as well as the complexity of the internment system. The government and international aid agencies played significant and often overlapping roles. However, throughout the conflict, the ICRC's attempts to deliver assistance to internees, refugees and political prisoners were hampered by the fiercely anti-communist policies of South Korean and US military and political authorities and the United Nations Command (UNC). Indeed, the UN authorities were unwilling to adhere to the Geneva Convention on the treatment of civilians; instead, the internees were considered as common criminals. As a result, they were held captive in South Korea's prisons and prisoner-of-war camps, where they remained until the very end of the Korean War and sometimes far beyond.

The sociologist Birgit Behrensen addresses the current accommodation of refugees in so-called "community shelters" – facilities that have become increasingly commonplace in Germany since 2008. These institutions come under the jurisdiction of the country's federal states, so they are organised and managed in a variety of different ways. Often, however, they impose restrictions such as entry controls, bans on overnight visits and attendance checks that hinder the residents' ability to lead independent lives. The article presents the results of a qualitative survey of refugees and social workers in the federal state of Brandenburg (eastern Germany) and compares them with the findings of an earlier study conducted in Lower Saxony (western Germany), with a particular focus on the psychosocial consequences of living in shared accommodation. As Behrensen points out, the residents have to cope with the traumatic experience of escape, negotiate a path through the labyrinthine asylum procedure and address the challenges of life in a new society and an uncertain future. At the same time, the centralised accommodation system forces them into increasing dependency on the social (support) services by consolidating and deepening existing power asymmetries. One important consequence of these power asymmetries and related inequalities is that it has become increasingly difficult to establish alliances between social workers and refugees. The results of the survey also suggest that these negative dynamics are more prevalent in the post-socialist context of eastern Germany, where the effects of disempowerment are evident on individual and collective levels. A key aspect of this seems to be the lack of any tradition – or recognition – of migrant organisations, which has significant societal repercussions in terms of refugees' immobilisation, disempowerment and exclusion.

The social psychologist Maximiliane Brandmaier explores the long-term consequences of detention in a refugee camp today, with particular reference to the residents' mental health. Based on the findings of a qualitative social-psychological research project conducted in Austrian communal reception centres, the author discusses refugees' and asylum-seekers' capacity to manage their everyday lives in these institutions. In interviews, the residents were asked about their living conditions, how they were dealing with their uncertain status and the restrictions they faced (e.g. in relation to accessing the labour market and experiences of racism and discrimination). Three coping strategies emerged in their responses: adaptation; "meaningful action" (e.g. establishing a daily routine or defining and accomplishing self-imposed goals, such as language acquisition); and protest and resistance.

Informed by Erving Goffman's concept of "total institution," the author pays special attention to the social workers who operate within the reception centres. What sort of (social and/or professional) support do the refugees receive, and how is it perceived? Brandmaier points out that the social workers have to perform a delicate balancing between help and control in order to fulfil their "double mandate": while many of them seek to empower their clients, they also act on behalf of the state. In turn, this generates a sense of ambivalence among the refugees: their appreciation for the practical support they receive stands in stark contrast to an assumed lack of solidarity and commitment. Therefore, the asylum regime itself hampers the detainees' emancipation and restricts their individual (and collective) agency.

Part III: Strategies of coping and resistance

The historian Pnina Rosenberg explores daily life in Gurs Camp in France, where, among others, former Republican fighters from the Spanish Civil War and members of the International Brigades as well as many Jewish and non-Jewish refugees and deportees from National Socialism were interned during the Second World War. The history of this camp, including the role played by the many artists who were interned there, has been well researched, but Rosenberg makes a valuable contribution to the literature with her study of the German-born artist Horst Rosenthal's satirical comic books *A Little Guide through Gurs Camp 1942*, *Mickey Mouse in Gurs Camp* and *A Day in the Life of a Resident*. Along with many other inmates of Gurs Camp, including fellow artists, Rosenthal was deported to Auschwitz in 1942 and became a victim of the Shoah. However, his comic books were preserved by the Swiss nurse Elsbeth Kasser, who worked in Gurs and supported the inmates by acquiring their art. These works now form part of the Elsbeth Kasser Collection in Zurich's Archive for Contemporary History.

Rosenberg convincingly argues that comic books can shed new light on camp life under the Vichy regime, with particular reference to Rosenthal's satirical view of the political situation and conditions within Gurs. His works are suffused with critical irony due to his deft use of omnipotent narrators and the tension he creates between text and image, both of which are placed into historical context through Rosenthal's allusions to cultural life in pre-war Berlin and French anti-Semitism.

The ethnomusicologist Ioannis Christidis presents a case study on singing and dancing as a form of resistance in a twenty-first-century camp in Greece. When calls were made to "shut down" the Balkan migration route in the spring of 2016, many of the migrants who were trying to cross the border between Greece and North Macedonia found themselves trapped close to the village of Idomeni. Over the course of the next few weeks, Greek police forcibly transferred some 15,000 people into hastily erected refugee camps. As the author demonstrates, these so-called "hotspot" camps soon became sites of resistance.

EU anti-migration measures and the manifold regulations of migration and asylum regimes explicitly target forced migrants. They are pushed into a limbo state where the absence of basic human, civil and political rights renders them completely subject to state power and leaves them susceptible to unaccountable institutional violence. However, these processes of victimisation and dehumanisation constitute only one aspect of the complex experience of forced confinement. Based on his ethnographic fieldwork and engagement with activists, Christidis highlights the important role played by music and musical practice in challenging the inhuman conditions in the hotspot camps of Thessaloniki. Whereas traditional protest techniques were strictly limited within the camps, a number of migrants – mostly from Syria – started to foster political participation, enthusiasm and empathy through music and dance performances. In this way, they succeeded in shifting the narratives around refugees from vulnerability and victimisation towards individual agency and collective resistance.

Social anthropologist Clara Bombach's article is based on field research she conducted in a "community shelter" that houses families of asylum-seekers in modern-day Switzerland. In contrast to mainstream research that tends to emphasise the negative aspects of life in this type of accommodation (forced communities in a confined space with restricted privacy), the author highlights the ways in which the centre may enhance social integration and recognition, with particular reference to the roommates' interactions with one another: speaking the same language and coming from the same country of origin constitute basic elements for a supportive environment and the cultivation of friendships.

The article focuses on families who wish to leave the "shelter" as soon as possible and explains that their fates rest entirely on decisions made by the Swiss authorities. How do they cope with their lack of agency in this situation? And how are their children adapting to life in asylum accommodation? Bombach describes them as strong and proactive protagonists. Far from feeling any shame about their lack of resources or attempting to protect their privacy, these families welcomed the researcher into their accommodation, defined the centre as their "house" and talked candidly about their temporary, uncertain circumstances. According to Bombach, their routines enabled them to maintain family practices in a confined space, while the family room became a protected space of retreat for family members and friends alike. Although the children's scope of action and activity increased with age, the author emphasises that they all had at least some capacity to adapt it to their needs. The conclusion is that a camp may become a life world in which children learn to deal with restrictive circumstances without losing the dream of finding a new home that they can call their own.

Part IV: Pathways and transitions

In her article, the historian Roni Mikel-Arieli discusses the British authorities' deportation of around 1,500 Jewish refugees from Mandate Palestine to the island of Mauritius and their subsequent internment in a former prison that was hastily converted into a detention camp. Mikel-Arieli focuses specifically on a group of internees who were released from the National Socialist concentration camps of Dachau and Buchenwald on condition that they would leave the "German Reich" with immediate effect. Since most countries had already closed their gates to Jews who were attempting to flee from Central Europe, the British Mandate territory of Palestine became an increasingly important place of refuge. In response, the British authorities introduced ever-tighter restrictions on Jewish immigration, mainly for geostrategic reasons. The White Paper of May 1939 imposed a rigorously restricted quota on new arrivals prior to the introduction of a complete ban and the categorisation of Jewish refugees from "German Reich" territories as "enemy aliens" following the onset of the Second World War. Nevertheless, Zionist organisations and the Viennese Jewish businessman Berthold Storfer continued to organise illegal ship transports to Palestine on a large scale. The British response was so robust that it ran the risk of triggering a "war within the war." The punitive deportation of Jewish refugees to Mauritius – a remote outpost of the British Empire in the Indian Ocean – represented the culmination of that response. Although conditions in the Beau-Bassin detention camp were harsh and a significant number of the detainees died – mostly of tropical diseases – Mikel-Arieli acknowledges that the National Socialist concentration camps were far worse. Nevertheless, she highlights the paradox of hundreds of people from Central Europe being forced to live as internees in a society shaped by colonialism.

In her contribution, the historian Andrea Strutz investigates the life stories of refugees deported from Great Britain to Canada as "enemy aliens" during the Second World War. First, she describes the organisational framework of British and Canadian domestic policies. Then she explains that the internees dealt with the situation in which they found themselves in different ways. About two-thirds of the interned refugees were expellees from Germany, while the remaining third had fled Austria. The majority were Jewish in origin, unmarried and relatively young.

Strutz focuses on three members of this group: Joachim (Jim) Lambek (1922–2014), Fritz (Friedrich) Rothberger (1902–2000) and Gustav Reinhold Jacoby (1875–1965). Although their lives before their expulsion by the National Socialists had been very different, they were united by the challenges that followed: the traumatic experience of forced eviction from their homeland and their efforts to assert themselves both privately and professionally in Canada (or eventually admit defeat and return to Europe).

On the basis of these refugees' biographies, Strutz demonstrates the important roles played by age, education and individual agency during and especially after their forced internment in Canada. She traces their life stories, explores the problems that arose during the integration process (e.g. encounters with anti-Semitism and a lack of job opportunities, especially for older refugees) and demonstrates the cultural, academic and professional contributions that former interned refugees eventually made to their new home.

In their contribution, the social and political scientists Andreas Kranebitter and Peter Pirker ask how European Displaced Persons adapted to life in the post-slavery society of the American South after 1945 and assess the impact of their resettlement on that society. In addition, they explore how these immigrants' experiences in National Socialist forced labour and concentration camps, and subsequently in refugee camps, shaped their personal biographies.

Kranebitter and Pirker focus on two academic studies of Displaced Persons in three southern US states: *Displaced Persons in Georgia*, written in 1954 by the émigré Viennese social scientist Gregor Sebba, which supplemented statistical analysis of secondary data with in-depth interviews with selected individuals; and Rudolf Heberle's New Americans: *A Study of Displaced Persons in Louisiana and Mississippi* (1951). After summarising Sebba's and Heberle's biographical experiences and outlining their contrasting approaches to their work, the authors address the epistemological breaks and blind spots in the social-scientific research into European Displaced Persons after the Second World War. In addition, they highlight the fact that Heberle's upbeat, "positivist" assessment of the resettlement programme was warmly received, while the academic and political establishment ensured that Sebba's far more critical report remained unpublished. Finally, they link the two researchers' contrasting perspectives to their respective immigration experiences: whereas Heberle's story was one of "successful" integration, Sebba never considered himself as a fully acculturated US citizen.

In the collection's second exploration of Gurs Camp in southern France, the historian Christoph Jahr explains that all camps have a "life" and often an "afterlife," that they serve different purposes in different periods and that they are frequently "reused" in different contexts. For him, one of the main features of the "modern camp" is its adaptability, with changes repeatedly made to size and structure to meet the current needs of the camp authorities. The operational history of Gurs illustrates this point perfectly, as Jahr demonstrates before turning his attention to the camp's commemoration since the end of the war. For six and a half years – from early 1939 to late 1945 – Gurs fulfilled a variety of functions under three very different political regimes. It was a "cosmopolitan" place that housed internees from a number of different countries. At first, it was populated by political refugees (mostly members of the International Brigades and anti-fascists) who fled to southern France from February 1939 onwards in the wake of Franco's victory in the Spanish Civil War. The camp's second phase was heralded by the German–Soviet Non-Aggression Pact of August 1939 and the start of the Second World War the following month. By November, France was firmly in the grip of anti-communist hysteria, anti-Semitism and xenophobia, which prompted the mass internment of political opponents (including domestic communists) and especially "enemy aliens," many of whom were German or Austrian Jewish refugees. Following the German invasion in the spring of 1940, the French government interned as many as 15,000 so-called "indésirables" – unwanted foreigners and domestic political opponents – in Gurs. Then, in October 1940, after the collapse of the democratic Third Republic and the installation of the collaborationist Vichy regime in southern France, some 6,540 Jews from Baden and the Palatinate were deported from Germany and partly accommodated in Gurs. Living conditions were extremely harsh from the outset, due to poor sanitation, a constant risk of disease and perpetual food shortages. Nevertheless, the camp became a vibrant centre of intellectual and artistic activity, with classes for the children and lectures for the adults, a theatre group and an orchestra. In its fourth phase, between August 1942 and March 1943, almost 4,000 Jewish internees were handed over to the Germans, with the majority of them subsequently transported to death camps, primarily Auschwitz, via the Drancy transit camp, near Paris.

Gurs closed for the first time in November 1943. However, after the Allies liberated France in August 1944, they arrested and then needed to find accommodation for tens of thousands of actual and alleged collaborators as well as Italian and German civilians. As a result, they reopened the camp on a temporary basis. It ceased operations for the second and final time towards the end of 1945. Decades later, the site was transformed into a place of remembrance, which led to some discussion over whether the final group of internees (prisoners-of-war and collaborators) should be included in the commemoration or whether that would signal a lack of respect for the earlier inmates who had been victims of terror and anti-Semitism.

Marilyn G. Miller's article addresses the internment of non-citizen "enemy aliens" in New Orleans, Louisiana, during the Second World War. As Miller explains, these internees, most of whom were German or Austrian émigrés, were categorised as "Pro-Nazi," "Anti-Nazi," or "Jew" in a November 1944 report. Using this document as her starting point, Miller, an expert in Latin American literature and culture, sheds new light on a little-known and largely unexplored aspect of US internment policy: namely, New Orleans' unique role in the processing of European nationals who were deported from Latin America to the United States as part of a Washington-led hemispheric security initiative following the bombing of Pearl Harbor. In stark contrast to its famed reputation as the fun-loving "Big Easy," Miller demonstrates that the city was not only a "Gateway to the Americas" through which thousands of "enemy aliens" traversed en route to other internment camps throughout the country but also boasted its own "anti-Nazi" facility – Camp Algiers – where Jewish and other "problem" internees were detained for the duration of the war and beyond.

***

The editors would like to thank various people and institutions whose cooperation and support made the publication of this book possible: the authors of the individual contributions; the academic reviewers for their expertise and time; Kerstin von Lingen and Nora Walch for their invaluable cooperation and support while preparing the conference that preceded this publication; Juma Hauser for her sophisticated cover layout; Lena Coufal for her willingness, and enthusiasm, in carrying out administrative work and coordination; Philip Parr for his attentive, careful and accurate language editing; the transcript Verlag for an excellent support and cooperation; and finally, the institutions whose financial contributions facilitated the printing of this volume and subsequent open access, namely the Österreichische Gesellschaft für Exilforschung (Austrian Society for Exile Research), the Zukunftsfonds der Republik Österreich (Future Fund of the Republic of Austria), the Paul Grüninger Stiftung (St. Gallen, Switzerland), the Österreichische Forschungsgemeinschaft, and the Institut für historische Sozialforschung of the Arbeiterkammer Wien.

Part I
The polysemic function (character) of camps

Internment practices during the First and Second World Wars
A comparison

Matthew Stibbe and Kim Wünschmann

The First World War was the first international conflict to witness the mass incarceration of non-combatants on a prolonged, multilateral basis. With at least 800,000 civilians detained in camps in Europe, and a further 50,000 to 100,000 throughout the rest of the world, internment became part of a global war directed against "enemy aliens," deportees, refugees and "internal enemies." Internment processes often involved movement over significant distances within and across international borders. Imperial Britain, for instance, developed a number of internment hubs across the world, from the Isle of Man, Gibraltar and Malta to Canada, Australia, South Africa, Egypt, Bermuda, the Caribbean and India. France similarly had hubs in Tahiti, Indo-China, Madagascar, Dahomey, North Africa, Corsica and along its Atlantic and Mediterranean coastlines. In terms of where they could intern enemy civilians, the Central Powers were largely limited to Europe, or in the case of Ottoman Turkey, the Middle East, but detainees could still be moved over vast areas. Meanwhile, Latin American countries were either pressured into interning German vessels and their crews by Allied countries or did so as a matter of state policy. China, which joined the Allied side in 1917, did not order an immediate mass internment of Germans, but nonetheless carried out expulsions in 1919. This followed similar moves by Siam in 1918.[1]

---

[1] For the worldwide picture, see Matthew Stibbe, Civilian Internment during the First World War: A European and Global History, 1914–1920 (London: Palgrave Macmillan, 2019); and Daniela L. Caglioti, War and Citizenship: Enemy Aliens and National Belonging from the French Revolution to the First World War (Cambridge: Cambridge University Press, 2021). On British "hubs," see Stefan Manz and Panikos Panayi, Enemies in the Empire: Civilian Internment in the British Empire during the First World War (Oxford: Oxford University Press, 2020); and on their French equivalents, Mahon Murphy, Colonial Captivity during the First World War: Internment and the Fall of the German Empire, 1914–1919 (Cambridge: Cambridge University Press, 2017). On Chile, Argentina and neutral (pre-1917) Brazil, see Stefan Rinke, Latin America and the First World War (Cambridge: Cambridge University Press, 2017), 52.

In other ways, too, First World War internment helped forge a new world order. From 1917 onwards, and again at its first post-war conference in 1921, the International Committee of the Red Cross (ICRC) campaigned for an end to civilian internment and a convention banning its use in future wars. Having failed in this ambitious aim, the ICRC's second post-war conference, held in Geneva in October 1925, merely suggested that "any civilian who is detained by an enemy state" in a future conflict "should, as a bare minimum, benefit from the protections then in force for prisoners of war."[2] In spite of this, the revised Geneva Convention of 1929, which included new safeguards for military prisoners of war, contained no explicit provisions in relation to their civilian counterparts.[3] True, a draft agreement regulating the treatment of "civilians of enemy nationality" was tabled at an ICRC conference in Tokyo in 1934. However, it was not adopted by the League of Nations or at interstate level.[4] It was only under the 1949 Geneva Convention that civilian prisoners of war were finally given explicit protections in international law.

This failure to "update" international treaty law before 1949 is striking but obscures other potential continuities between the two world wars and perhaps overstates the importance of the legal at the expense of the political and cultural realms. It suggests that the experience of civilian internment and its use as an instrument of war by belligerent and neutral states between 1914 and 1920 was largely forgotten in the inter-war years, especially by diplomats, League of Nations officials and international jurists. However, in this article, we contend that "lessons" learned from First World War internment did have a significant – if previously overlooked – impact on decisions made by state actors and international policy-makers during the Second World War. We examine this on three levels. First, we look at instances in both conflicts where the principle of reciprocity (*Gegenseitigkeitsprinzip*) worked, or failed to work, to prevent or at least minimise the abuse of civilian prisoners. Second, we address continuities and ruptures in the cultural meanings ascribed by state and non-state actors to internment. And third, we explore the ongoing connections between internment and global inequalities based on class, race and gender. Our conclusions are necessarily tentative, given the disparity that has emerged in recent years between what is now a very rich historiography on First World War internment and the less well-developed state of research on the Second World War. Nonetheless, we see our findings as a useful starting point for uncovering patterns of continuity as well as rupture between 1914–20 and 1939–45.

---

2 "Résolutions et voeux votés par la XIIe Conférence internationale de la Croix-Rouge, Genève, 7–10 octobre 1925," Revue Internationale de la Croix-Rouge 82 (1925): 814–31, at 824.
3 Stibbe, Civilian Internment, 295.
4 Gunner Lind, "Genesis of the Civilian in the Western World, 1500–2000,", in Civilians at War: From the Fifteenth Century to the Present, edited by Gunner Lind (Copenhagen: Museum Tusculanum Press, 2014), 47–82, at 70; see also Caglioti, War and Citizenship, 313–19.

Reciprocity as a means of protecting civilian internees in the two world wars

The lack of formal, codified safeguards in international law for "enemy alien" civilian detainees did not mean that they had no protection at all. Rather, it meant that the protections they did enjoy relied more on political considerations and cultural factors than on universal principles. After 1914, those internees who experienced the least abuse – and, in relative terms, the best conditions – did so largely on the basis of their nationality, although as we will see later, class, gender and race could also play a role. Captor states were unlikely to mistreat the nationals of an enemy state that was holding similar or higher numbers of their nationals. Britain (including its empire) was especially well placed to benefit from the *Gegenseitigkeitsprinzip* as by 1917 it held 36,000 Germans and 11,000 Habsburg subjects, compared to just 3,500 and 200 British subjects held in Germany and Austria-Hungary, respectively.[5]

Until the chaos of the last few weeks of the war, if reciprocity broke down between *powerful* belligerent states, neutral diplomats and international bodies like the ICRC were likely to intervene to de-escalate the situation, and they enjoyed some success when doing so. Neutral states might also broker exchange agreements for particular categories of civilian and military prisoners (such as those with certain health conditions or those of a certain age), as in an Anglo-German agreement signed at The Hague in July 1917 or the even broader Franco-German exchange agreed at Bern in April 1918.[6]

The reverse side of this was that civilian internees from *weaker* states, including countries that had effectively collapsed due to military invasion, enemy occupation and accompanying mass population displacement (e.g. Serbia and Romania), or states that, for other political or economic reasons, were not so invested in the welfare of their interned citizens (e.g. Italy), enjoyed few, if any, protections under the *Gegenseitigkeitsprinzip*. Hundreds of thousands of other civilians, including refugees and deportees, were detained by their own governments and did not even appear on lists of prisoners sent to the ICRC.[7]

Even if it protected some internees before the end of the war, reciprocity as a mechanism for regulating internment broke down completely in November 1918, when the defeated Central Powers were forced to return all Allied military and civilian prisoners in their hands, while Britain, France, Portugal, the United States and

---

5 Matthew Stibbe, "Civilian Internment and Civilian Internees in Europe, 1914–20," Immigrants and Minorities, 26 (2008) 1–2: 49–81, at 73.
6 Richard B. Speed III, Prisoners, Diplomats, and the Great War: A Study in the Diplomacy of Captivity (New York: Greenwood Press, 1990), 37–42.
7 Alan Kramer, Dynamic of Destruction: Culture and Mass Killing in the First World War (Oxford: Oxford University Press, 2007), 44–68, 151–2.

a host of other victor powers continued to hold German and Austro-Hungarian nationals both in Europe and around the world. Furthermore, when they were eventually released in 1919–20, many of the German and Austro-Hungarian internees were forcibly expelled from the countries that had detained them, even if they had been residents for years or even decades prior to 1914. Indeed, expulsion was the norm everywhere except the United States, Canada and Brazil, all three of which permitted their ex-internees to remain unless they were identified as threats to national security.[8] Article 220 of the Treaty of Versailles also required that the "German government undertake to admit to its territory without distinction all persons liable to repatriation," thereby absolving the Allies of any responsibility for making such *Auslandsdeutsche* ("Germans abroad") homeless or stateless.[9] Similar provisions were written into the Treaty of St Germain with Austria (Article 166), the Treaty of Trianon with Hungary (Article 150), the Treaty of Neuilly with Bulgaria (Article 111) and the Treaty of Sèvres with Turkey (Article 213).[10] By contrast, Allied states faced no such obligations in relation to their nationals released from internment in territories of the former Central Powers. Nor could they be repatriated without their express consent.

Reciprocity, then, was a far from perfect or consistent mechanism for the protection of civilian prisoners in the First World War. So how did it function in the Second World War? In this conflict, reciprocity remained the guiding principle of the belligerents' policies. It informed the treatment of internees and negotiations about their exchange and repatriation, which again depended on the mediation of protecting powers, most importantly Switzerland, Sweden, Spain, Portugal and, until its own entry into the war, the United States. When it came to humanitarian protection of civilian internees, the ICRC also continued to play a central role. Like the envoys of the protecting powers, the organisation's representatives conducted camp inspections and compiled reports that, in turn, informed the belligerents' reciprocal actions. Compared to the First World War, the ICRC now had a stronger mandate as its role in organising humanitarian relief work had been explicitly inscribed into the 1929 Geneva Convention. The same convention also gave the protecting powers, whose good offices had hitherto been based on custom, a formal and universally recognised status.[11]

---

8   Matthew Stibbe, "A Forgotten Minority: The Return of the Auslandsdeutsche to Germany in 1919–20," Studies on National Movements 5 (2020): 144–83.
9   The Treaties of Peace, 1919–1923 (New York: Carnegie Endowment for International Peace, 1924), Vol. 1, 118.
10 Ibid., Vol. 1, 323, 514 and Vol. 2, 689, 857.
11 "Geneva Convention Relative to the Treatment of Prisoners of War 1929," Articles 79, 86–88 <https://ihl-databases.icrc.org/ihl/INTRO/305> (13 May 2021). See also Index of Protecting Powers Mediating between the Different Enemy States, undated, R 41393, Politisches Archiv des

Although the codification of a civilian convention had to be shelved for the time being, the ICRC campaigned for the provisions of its 1934 Tokyo draft to be respected nonetheless. A first call to do so was sent to the governments of the warring states on 2 September 1939. An ICRC memorandum followed on 21 October 1939.[12] The belligerents, however, preferred to fall back on the 1929 Geneva Convention and negotiated bilateral agreements to observe it in their treatment of enemy civilians as well as POWs. As a result, this convention, which was much more detailed than the 1907 Hague Convention IV respecting the Laws and Customs of War on Land, became the key legal text with regard to civilian internment during the Second World War. For example, copies of it were distributed by the US Justice Department to the Immigration and Naturalization Service (INS), which initially administered the country's civilian internment camps, along with a reminder to officials that

> [t]he minimum standards of treatment which have been established and which must prevail throughout this Service are based upon the provisions of the Convention between the United States of America and forty-six other Powers [...] The government of the United States has agreed with the belligerent powers to apply those provisions to civilian alien enemy internees wherever applicable.[13]

Moreover, the convention became an important yardstick for states to assess an enemy's treatment of their nationals, and as such it also served as a propaganda tool. Belligerents referred to the laws of war not only to justify their policies towards enemy civilians but also to denounce their opponents' alleged violations.[14] There was nonetheless a certain asymmetry here, as liberal democratic states were politically much more beholden than authoritarian regimes to international conventions, not least because of pressure from their own citizens and elected parliamentarians to comply with them. A state's political system mattered, in other words. Adherence to the Geneva Convention could be entirely neglected under dictatorships, as was seen, most strikingly, in the war between National Socialist Germany and the Soviet Union on the Eastern Front between 1941 and 1945.

Auswärtigen Amts, Berlin (PAAA); H. S. Levie, "Prisoners of War and the Protecting Powers," American Journal of International Law 55 (1961) 2: 374–97.

12 German Consulate in Geneva to Foreign Office, 20 November 1939, R 41390, PAAA; List of Belligerents that Agreed on Treating Civilian Internees on the Basis of the 1929 Geneva Convention, 15 January 1944, R 41393, PAAA; President of the ICRC to Dutch Foreign Minister, 5 August 1941, 2.05.80, No. 665, National Archives [NA], The Hague.

13 US Department of Justice Memorandum to INS, 28 April 1942, quoted in Tetsuden Kashima, Judgement without Trial: Japanese American Imprisonment during World War II (Seattle – London: University of Washington Press, 2003), 195–6.

14 See Kim Wünschmann, "'Enemy Aliens' and 'Indian Hostages': Civilians in Dutch–German Wartime Diplomacy and International Law during the Second War," German History 39 (2021) 2: 263–83.

For the US government, reciprocity was of utmost importance vis-à-vis Imperial Japan. By the end of 1942, while the number of US civilians in German captivity was comparatively small (a mere 1,491 internees – 788 men and 703 women), almost ten times as many (between 12,000 and 13,000, some of whom were not interned) found themselves in territories under Japanese control.[15] The total number of US internees had already been reduced through exchanges in July 1942 (over 1,300 repatriated) and October 1943 (approximately 1,240, plus 260 Canadian nationals and citizens of various Central and South American republics sent home), but according to one estimate about 6,000 Americans were still in internment camps in 1944, "most of them located in the Philippines (four camps), in Shanghai (two camps), or in Weihsien in North China (one camp)". Another 1,000 civilians were "said to be in hospitals or interned in their own homes."[16] The total number of Allied civilian nationals in Japanese hands in the Asia-Pacific region is estimated at more than 130,000, including over 40,000 women.[17] The US government included a long list of "deprivations of rights, cruelties, wanton neglect, mistreatment and hardships" in an official complaint it lodged with the Swiss protecting power on 27 January 1944.[18]

Cultural meanings of internment

Both contemporary supporters and critics of First World War internment located its meaning in concerns about "public safety." For its supporters, it was a necessary tool against internal subversion and espionage. It also prevented captured men of military age from returning home to join their respective armies and helped to control the flow of refugees. Critics of internment such as the Canadian John Davidson Ketchum, on the other hand, saw it as a reflection of the "ruthless inhumanity of the modern armed state" that practised all manner of "cruelties" in the name of "'national

---

15 Robert R. Wilson, "Recent Developments in the Treatment of Civilian Alien Enemies," American Journal of International Law 38 (1944) 3: 397–406, at 397–8, 401. The number of US internees in Germany remained largely unchanged over the next twelve months. An official German report from 31 December 1943 counted 1,494 US internees. See Strength Report of North American and British Nationals in German Civilian Internment Camps, 31 December 1943, R 41393, PAAA. The same report records 10,274 British civilian internees. A year later, numbers had fallen to 632 US and 5,813 British internees. See Strength Report, 31 December 1944, R 41393, PAAA.
16 Wilson, "Recent Developments," 397–8, at 397 n. 3. Cogan counts over 5,000 American internees in the Philippines. See Frances B. Cogan, Captured: The Japanese Internment of American Civilians in the Philippines, 1941–1945 (Athens: University of Georgia Press, 2000), 1–2.
17 Christina Twomey, "Double Displacement: Western Women's Return Home from Japanese Internment in the Second World War," Gender and History 21 (2009) 3: 670–84, at 670.
18 Department of State Bulletin, 12 February 1944, quoted in Wilson, "Recent Developments," 399.

security.'" While state governments were the principal culprits, in Ketchum's view, internment operations also relied on the "passive acquiescence" of majority populations, who thereby displayed a lack of "imagination, [and an in]ability to feel with and for [their] fellow-men."[19]

Recent studies by Arnd Bauerkämper and Matthew Stibbe have nonetheless juxtaposed considerations of "security" with those of "humanity." The prolonged internment practices of the First World War certainly gave rise to new ways of conceptualising what it meant to be human, and new ways of advocating for humanitarian polices in the sphere of international politics. Non-state actors, such as the ICRC, the Quakers and various Swiss and Dutch philanthropic groups, saw their interventions in humanitarian terms and became increasingly skilled at fundraising and garnering publicity for their causes. Neutral states like Switzerland and the Netherlands also projected themselves as pursuing a humanitarian agenda when they agreed to intern certain categories of severely ill prisoners and provide appropriate healthcare. In Spain, King Alfonso XIII ordered the establishment of a European War Office, run by his private secretary from the Royal Palace in Madrid, to assist families in locating missing relatives, including those held in captivity. More loosely, the global medical profession shared knowledge about the psychological harm caused by long-term internment, and transnational actors devised new forms of relief that treated internees as rational beings with free will, not as "objects" of charity, still less as "security risks."[20]

While humanitarianism was to some degree professionalised and redefined during the war, so too was national security. One aspect of this was the effort that imperial states put into devising internment policies that were coordinated across their different metropolitan, dominion and colonial territories. Imperial Britain, for instance, treated Germans, Austro-Hungarians, Turks and Bulgars in all parts of the British-ruled world as "enemies of the empire" and transferred groups of prisoners across land and sea borders, including from East Africa to India, the Caribbean to Canada, Palestine to Egypt and Singapore to Australia.[21] The French

---

19 John Davidson Ketchum, Ruhleben: A Prison Camp Society (Toronto: Toronto University Press, 1965), xviii.
20 Arnd Bauerkämper, "National Security and Humanity: The Internment of Civilian 'Enemy Aliens' during the First World War," Bulletin of the German Historical Institute London 40 (2018) 1: 61–85; Arnd Bauerkämper, Sicherheit und Humanität im Ersten und Zweiten Weltkrieg: Der Umgang mit zivilen Feindstaatenangehörigen im Ausnahmezustand, 2 Vols. (Berlin: De Gruyter, 2021); Stibbe, Civilian Internment, 183–237. On the hitherto little-known European War Office in Spain, see Marina Pérez de Arcos, "'Finding Out Whereabouts of Missing Persons': The European War Office, Transnational Humanitarianism and Spanish Royal Diplomacy in the First World War," The International History Review, The International History Review 44 (2022) 3: 497–523.
21 Manz and Panayi, Enemies, 100–10.

government similarly moved civilian prisoners between colonies in West and North Africa and metropolitan France.[22] Finally, there is the question of informal empires or spheres of influence. Britain put pressure on various South American countries, Siam, Greece, China and Portugal (with respect to its African colonies) to treat Germans within their borders as "suspect" populations. The United States did the same with respect to Panama and Haiti, and actually arranged the deportation of Germans from Panama to New York in 1918.[23] Thus, internment reflected new demographic concepts of national and imperial security, merging into and becoming entangled with even more violent land and population policies in the German, Habsburg, Russian and Ottoman spheres.[24]

Comparisons of civilian internment and its cultural meanings in the two world wars were drawn almost as soon as the second conflict had begun. Legal scholars, in particular, grappled with questions of terminology as well as continuities and breaks in the treatment of civilian internees. The German-born, US-based lawyer Robert M. W. Kempner, for example, observed in 1940 that "the usual legal concept of the term 'enemy alien,' as it was known in the war of 1914–1918" had reappeared in international discourse since the start of the Second World War. There was, however, "one essential change in its application as compared to previous wars: a totally different circle of persons seen from a political and sociological viewpoint is affected." During the First World War, those targeted by restrictive measures included a number of "unwilling subjects of their country," such as "natives of Alsace-Lorraine, Poles, Czechs, Greek, Armenian and Syrian subjects of the Ottoman Empire." Now, in the Second World War, policy-makers of the belligerent states had to distinguish more sharply between what Kempner – himself a refugee from Nazi Germany living in the United States – termed "real enemy aliens" and "technical enemy aliens." The "second[,] much larger group" consisted of refugees who had fled National Socialist persecution. Precisely because individuals in this category had often been labelled "enemies" by their country of origin and were in the process of renegotiating (national) belonging, Kempner saw that "[i]n this war [...] it is more important to inquire into the fundamental spiritual loyalties of a person rather than the formal facts concerning his national origin and previous residence."[25]

---

22   Murphy, Colonial Captivity, 161.
23   Stibbe, Civilian Internment, 36–7.
24   Kramer, Dynamic, 47–9, 140–52; Vejas Gabriel Liulevicius, War Land on the Eastern Front: Culture, National Identity and German Occupation in World War I (Cambridge: Cambridge University Press, 2000); Christin Pschichholz (ed.), The First World War as a Caesura? Demographic Concepts, Population Policy, and Genocide in the Late Ottoman, Russian, and Habsburg Spheres (Berlin: Duncker & Humblot, 2020).
25   Robert M. W. Kempner, "The Enemy Alien Problem in the Present War," American Journal of International Law 34 (1940) 3: 443–58, at 443–4, 458. On terminology and the desirability of discontinuing the use of the term "enemy alien" as a designation for all persons from the

Kempner was not the only one detecting "new factors" guiding the belligerents' policies towards enemy civilians after 1939.[26] Both contemporary and present-day analysts have linked the unprecedented number of refugees among civilian internees in Western Allied captivity to the increasingly important role of political ideologies at work in the Second World War era. Indeed, National Socialist Germany's expansionist drive for new "living space" and its destructive racial/antisemitic worldview shaped the conduct of this war in ways that were different from the ideological clashes of the earlier conflict.[27] For political opponents, social outsiders and those deemed racial enemies of the "Third Reich," in particular, these ideologies were life-threatening. The image of the detention site iconic to the Second World War is first and foremost that of the National Socialist camp system or the Soviet "Gulag archipelago." Their origins preceded the war and, in the case of the Soviet Union, outlived it.[28] However, their entanglement with the civilian internment camp – a phenomenon of the First World War that reappeared in 1939 and exhibited its own lines of continuity with the recent past – is still under-researched in histories of the camp universe of the Second World War.

The much greater scale of exile, expulsion, denationalisation and flight distinguishes the Second from the First World War. National Socialist Germany's policy of interning some enemy nationals, as well as many of its own citizens, in concentration camps added to the previously experienced trauma – while reinforcing the strongly held anti-fascist convictions – of many refugees who made it to the relative safety of non-German-controlled territory. All three major Western Allied powers attempted to take this into account when devising their internment practices. Tribunals to distinguish "friendly enemy aliens" from "dangerous enemy aliens" were set up, and the option of securing release from internment by enlisting in the armed forces was established. Both policies show that the traditional test categories of nationality and domicile – already surrounded by ambiguities in the practice of internment during the First World War – were of even less use when assessing foreign civilians' loyalties or enmities during the Second World War.

---

territory of the enemy, see Charles Gordon, "Status of Enemy Nationals in the United States," Lawyers Guild Review 2 (1942) 6: 9–20.

26   Robert R. Wilson, "Treatment of Civilian Alien Enemies," American Journal of International Law 37 (1943) 1: 30–45, at 36.

27   Ibid., 30. See also Arnold Krammer, Undue Process: The Untold Story of America's German Alien Internees (London: Rowman & Littlefield, 1997) 13; Rachel Pistol, Internment during the Second World War: A Comparative Study of Great Britain and the USA (London: Bloomsbury, 2017), 5.

28   See Dan Stone, Concentration Camps: A Short History (Oxford: Oxford University Press, 2017), 34–79.

Among the three million aliens residing in France in September 1939 there were an estimated 45,000 Germans and Austrians.[29] As it had done in 1914, France started to intern civilian "enemy aliens" in large numbers immediately after the start of the war. Initially, the French government had planned to review each case and conduct a "sieving" (*criblage*) to release harmless refugees and émigrés. On 17 September 1939, however, the Ministry of the Interior ordered that political refugees should not be released but kept under guard, albeit separately from other groups of internees.[30] As in the previous conflict, internment also targeted "internal enemies" – so-called *indésirables français*. Most of these French citizens were left-wing political activists, while others were convicts or ex-convicts. Some of the political *indésirables* were forcibly evacuated to camps in the south in the wake of the German advance in June 1940.[31] By the time of the 22 June armistice, more than 35,000 persons of German and Austrian origin had also been (temporarily) detained: between 15,000 and 18,000 *sujets ennemis* had been rounded up immediately after the outbreak of war, while a further 20,000 had been arrested after 10 May 1940. Civilian internment camps that originally were not too different from those of the First World War now mutated into holding pens from which foreign Jewish internees were deported in 1942–3, most of them via Drancy to Auschwitz, where they were murdered.[32] The example of French camps under Vichy jurisdiction, such as Gurs, Les Milles and Rivesaltes, and in particular agreements to house around 7,000 German Jews deported from Baden and the Palatinate in October 1940 at Gurs, and then to transport them and others via Drancy to the death camps from July 1942, alerts us to the fact that the institutional borderline between civilian internment camps and the National Socialist camp system was sometimes blurred.[33]

Compared to France, three times as many refugees from Germany, Austria and Czechoslovakia – an estimated 80,000 people – had been admitted to Great Britain before the outbreak of war. Most of them – perhaps 70,000 – were Jews.[34] Instead

---

29   Kempner, "The Enemy Alien Problem," 449. See also Christian Eggers, Unerwünschte Ausländer: Juden aus Deutschland und Mitteleuropa in französischen Internierungslagern 1940–1942 (Berlin: Metropol, 2002), 50; Denis Peschanski, La France des camps: l'internement, 1938–1946 (Paris: Gallimard, 2002); Claude Laharie, Petite Histoire des camps d'internement français (Morlaas: Cairn, 2020).

30   Eggers, Unerwünschte Ausländer, 48–9.

31   Ibid., 48, 221; Kempner, "The Enemy Alien Problem," 452; Peschanski, La France des camps, 90–4, 155.

32   Eggers, Unerwünschte Ausländer, 234–5; Bauerkämper, Sicherheit, Vol. 2, 784–91.

33   See Peschanski, La France des camps, 146, 345–55; Claude Laharie, Gurs 1939–1945: Un Camp d'internement en Béarn (Morlaas: Cairn, 2020). See also Maier, Rosenberg and Jahr, this volume.

34   See Louise London, Whitehall and the Jews 1933–1948: British Immigration Policy, Jewish Refugees and the Holocaust (Cambridge: Cambridge University Press, 2000), 12; Pistol, Internment, 15.

of ordering immediate mass internment, the Home Office instituted tribunals to distinguish between refugees and potentially dangerous "enemy aliens" among the Germans and Austrians on a case-by-case basis. Within six months, some 120 alien tribunals interviewed more than 70,000 individuals and classified enemy civilians into three categories: A, B and C, with A the most dangerous group, who required immediate detention. The overwhelming majority of cases, an estimated 64,000, were classified as C and thus remained at liberty for the time being.[35]

British internment policy took a U-turn when the attack on the Low Countries and France brought the threat of a German invasion of the British Isles much closer to home. Patterns of mass internment from the previous war re-emerged. The "May panic" overthrew careful attempts to distinguish between dangerous persons and refugees, and tribunal classifications ceased to make much difference when it came to official decisions on whom to intern. What is more, approximately 4,100 Italians, interned after Mussolini had declared war on Britain on 10 June 1940, were not granted the right to tribunal hearings.[36]

The events of summer 1940 set in motion a global mass movement of civilian internees similar to that seen during the First World War. Once again, Britain used its empire to transport enemy civilians between different locations. Between 21 June and 10 July 1940, five vessels were used to deport over 7,000 men to Canada and Australia.[37] In the Asia-Pacific region, British India became an important internment hub, with a number of camps established there, including a site at Ahmednagar that had been used in the First World War and held about 1,200 Germans by September 1942.[38] In 1941–2, Britain's success in persuading neutral Iran (Persia) to allow the transfer of 800 Germans on its territory to captivity in Australia provided a pretext for Germany's deportation and internment in camps at Biberach, Wurzach, Laufen and Liebenau of 2,200 or so UK-born residents of the German-occupied Channel Islands.[39]

---

35   Kempner, "The Enemy Alien Problem," 445–6. Kempner calculates 74,233 examined cases within six months: 62,244 Germans and 11,989 Austrians. See also Miriam Kochan, Britain's Internees in the Second World War (London – Basingstoke: Macmillan, 1983), 10, 18; Pistol, Internment, 17–18.
36   Pistol, Internment, 19, 33.
37   Louise Burleston, "The State, Internment and Public Criticism in the Second World War," in The Internment of Aliens in Twentieth-Century Britain, edited by David Cesarani and Tony Kushner (London: Frank Cass, 1993), 102–24, at 115.
38   Bauerkämper, Sicherheit, Vol. 2, 904. On the little-researched history of the almost 2,700 Japanese civilians and colonial subjects interned in British India, see Christine de Matos and Rowena Ward, "Forgotten Forced Migrants of War: Civilian Internment of Japanese in British India, 1941–6," Journal of Contemporary History 56 (2021) 4: 1102–25.
39   Bauerkämper, Sicherheit, Vol. 2, 770–4.

The Second World War also saw inter-state transfers of civilian internees. Under pressure from the Roosevelt administration, fifteen Latin American states deported over 6,500 men, women and children categorised as "dangerous enemy aliens" to the United States for internment.[40] Faced with the looming threat of a Japanese invasion of its colonies, the Dutch government, exiled in London, reached an agreement with the British and transported almost 2,000 male civilians from the Dutch East Indies to British India.[41] Civilian internment of white settlers in the colonies led to racial role reversals similar to those that had taken place in the First World War. Internment in overseas possessions challenged a colonial order otherwise based on white "European" dominance. In the British West Indies, for example, the authorities removed a black matron from the Hanover Street women's camp in downtown Kingston, Jamaica, in response to a German protest about the deployment of non-white guards.[42]

Internment and global inequalities

During the First World War, internment laid bare global inequalities of class, race and gender as well as some of the intersections between them. White, male, literate civilian prisoners of military age were often treated well. Those who deviated from this supposed norm were either ignored or recategorised as "refugees," "deportees," "stateless persons" or various types of "internal enemies."[43] Captor powers sought to maintain class distinctions both by establishing "privilege camps" and lighter forms of internment (e.g. in private accommodation) for those with the ability to pay and by ensuring that destitute "enemy aliens" were the first to be detained and the last to be released. Several hundred black and South Asian civilians were held in Germany and Austro-Hungary, most but not all of them merchant sailors and most of them British or French nationals. They often faced discrimination from white fellow-pris-

---

40 The exact numbers are 4,058 classified as Germans, 2,264 as Japanese and 288 as Italians. Among the deportees were more than 80 Jewish refugees. See Max Paul Friedman, Nazis and Good Neighbors: The United States Campaign against the Germans of Latin America in World War II (Cambridge: Cambridge University Press, 2003), 2, 11. See also Miller, this volume.
41 See Wünschmann, "'Enemy Aliens,'" 275.
42 Joanna Newman, Nearly the New World: The British West Indies and the Flight from Nazism, 1933–1945 (New York and Oxford: Berghahn, 2019), 206. See also Cwik, this volume.
43 On the increasingly blurred but still partly functioning lines drawn between these groups, see Peter Gatrell, "Minorities in and at War: Exposure, Persecution, Reaction," in Nations, Identities and the First World War: Shifting Loyalties to the Fatherland, edited by Nico Wouters and Laurence van Ypersele (London: Bloomsbury, 2018), 177–95.

oners, guards and other camp personnel.[44] The ICRC's International Prisoner of War Agency held information on each prisoner's nationality, gender, date of birth and profession, but not their race, which remained hidden from view on its index files.

Officially, belligerent powers did not hold enemy women as internees, so where women were discovered behind barbed wire by ICRC inspectors, it was often claimed that they had "volunteered" to stay in camps rather than accept expulsion/deportation so that they could be with their husbands. Even Britain, which did not intern enemy women in Europe, did so in India and Africa.[45] Imperial Germany held enemy women from occupied territories as hostages, suspected illegal fighters and unregulated prostitutes. In the army staging areas, where ICRC officials were not allowed, German troops sometimes rounded up women and teenage girls as well as men for forced labour.[46] It was in the Austro-Hungarian camps for domestic political suspects and internally Displaced Persons that the highest numbers of women and children were interned, however. Death rates in some of these camps reached catastrophic proportions in 1914–15 and again in 1918.[47]

The wives and children of male internees also suffered in numerous, largely hidden ways. Internment of family breadwinners could mean immediate destitution for some, and a gradual descent into poverty for others. Women who married foreign men automatically lost the nationality of their birth; then, if their husbands became "enemy aliens" on the outbreak of war, they did too.[48] Women internees were less likely to appear on lists sent to the ICRC yet were more likely to be poor and/or to belong to a minority ethnic group, as Stefan Manz and Panikos Panayi have recently shown in the case of at least 663 "refugee" German women and children who were deported to South Africa from German and other African colonies after 1914.[49] In May 1919 the Women's International League for Peace and Freedom (WILPF), meeting in Zurich, was one of the few organisations to bring to light the abuse of female deportees as a key aspect of the internment question. Point 34 in its list of demands to the Allied peacemakers in Paris (all of which were ignored) read:

---

44   Stibbe, Civilian Internment, 50–2.
45   See Manz and Panayi, Enemies, 198–204, 215–23, 238.
46   Kramer, Dynamic, 222–4; Matthew Stibbe, "Gewalt gegen Zivilisten: 'Arbeitsverweigerer' im von Deutschland besetzten Nordfrankreich und im südlichen Bayern während des Ersten Weltkrieges", in Gewaltgemeinschaften? Studien zur Gewaltgeschichte im und nach dem Ersten Weltkrieg, edited by Sven-Oliver Müller and Christin Pschichholz (Frankfurt am Main – New York: Campus Verlag, 2021), 75–104.
47   Matthew Stibbe, "Gendered Experiences of Civilian Internment during the First World War: A Forgotten Dimension of Wartime Violence," in Gender and Conflict since 1914: Historical and Interdisciplinary Perspectives, edited by Ana Carden-Coyne (Basingstoke: Palgrave Macmillan, 2012), 14–28.
48   Ibid., 21.
49   Manz and Panayi, Enemies, 203.

Mass deportations have become a worldwide phenomenon since 1914 and inflict suffering and death in many forms upon innocent people [...] [T]his subject should receive attention at the earliest possible moment. The expulsion of thousands of innocent people cannot be treated as an internal affair of any of the nations concerned.[50]

The scale of female detention clearly distinguishes the Second from the First World War. During the later conflict, all major belligerent powers interned women who, in many cases, also brought children to the camps. The authorities usually established separate detention sites for women and children. The total number of civilian aliens interned in Great Britain is estimated at around 27,000 people, including some 4,000 women.[51] Female internees were initially held in London's Holloway Prison, and separated from their children. Later, women and children were deported together to the Rushen Camp in Port Erin and Port St Mary on the Isle of Man. In 1941, Port St Mary was turned into a "married persons" camp to unite families.[52]

The largest number of women and children were interned in the United States, where restrictive measures against civilians had a clear racial bias. While the country pursued a policy of "selective internment" for enemy civilians from Europe, men, women and children of Japanese ancestry were targeted collectively on the basis of their ethnic origin.[53] After the attack on Pearl Harbor, initial arrests were conducted on the basis of "ABC" lists prepared by the FBI and the Office of Naval Intelligence (ONI).[54] While the majority of those arrested were Germans and Italians, fewer than half of them were interned after their hearings; "[i]n contrast, more than two-thirds of the Japanese aliens remained in internment camps during the war."[55] Overall, more than 30,000 men, women and children of enemy nationality were held in internment camps overseen by the Department of Justice.[56]

---

50   WILPF, "Resolutions Presented to the Peace Conference of the Powers in Paris," May 1919 <http://wilpf.org/wp-content/uploads/2012/08/WILPF_triennial_congress_1919.pdf> (10 November 2021).
51   David Cesarani, "An Alien Concept? The Continuity of Anti-Alienism in British Society before 1940," in The Internment of Aliens, edited by Cesarani and Kushner, 25–52, at 45. For female internees, see Pistol, Internment, 33; Bauerkämper, Sicherheit, Vol. 2, 725, 976.
52   Pistol, Internment, 35, 43, 45.
53   The term "selective internment" is borrowed from Pistol, Internment, 50.
54   Wilson, "Treatment of Civilian Alien Enemies," 42; Charles W. Harris, "The Alien Enemy Hearing Board as a Judicial Device in the United States during World War II," International and Comparative Law Quarterly 14 (1965) 4: 1360–70; Jörg Nagler, Nationale Minoritäten im Krieg: "Feindliche Ausländer" und die amerikanische Heimatfront während des Ersten Weltkriegs (Hamburg: Hamburger Edition, 2000), 678 n. 31; Pistol, Internment, 31.
55   Peter Irons, Justice at War: The Story of the Japanese-American Internment Cases (Oxford: Oxford University Press, 1983), 24.
56   Krammer, Undue Process, x; Pistol, Internment, 52; Bauerkämper, Sicherheit, Vol. 2, 818.

A special case in the history of civilian detention during the Second World War is that of the almost 120,000 men, women and children of Japanese ancestry who were driven from their homes on the Pacific coast to camps in the interior of the country. These camps were administered by the War Relocation Authority. The term "internment," which resonated with international legal thinking about the treatment of civilians in wartime, was not used by the authorities for these detention sites. Rather, the repressive measures were described as "evacuation" and "relocation." They did not target the approximately 58,000 Italians and 22,000 Germans living on the West Coast.[57] About two-thirds of those affected by the eviction, which started in late March 1942, were *Nisei* – American-born children of Japanese immigrants (*Issei*), who, as US citizens, had a constitutional right not to be treated as "enemy aliens."[58] Although other countries also detained "internal enemies" and "suspect" citizens of neutral or friendly nations – aside from the above-mentioned French measures, almost 2,000 British citizens accused of fascist sympathies were held in the United Kingdom,[59] as were six alleged international communists among the country's Czech and Slovak political refugees[60] – the scale of racial discrimination in the treatment of Japanese-Americans was unprecedented and eventually resulted in similarly unprecedented post-war restitution for the detainees.

Inevitably, the German regime's inherent racism and antisemitism created stark inequalities in its application of internment. The outbreak of war in September 1939 turned foreign civilians from enemy states into "enemy aliens," among them an estimated 40,000 Jews of (former) Polish nationality. The National Socialists either expelled or interned these people, in contrast to their treatment of civilians of Western Allied nations. Some 2,000 Polish or stateless Jews were imprisoned in the SS concentration camps of Sachsenhausen and Buchenwald in 1939.[61] In February 1940, Himmler ordered the release of "enemy alien" Polish nationals from the internment

---

57 Pistol, Internment, 7; Arnold Krammer, "Feinde ohne Uniform: Deutsche Zivilinternierte in den USA während des Zweiten Weltkrieges," Vierteljahrshefte für Zeitgeschichte 44 (1996) 4: 581–603, at 588.
58 See Irons, Justice, 81–103.
59 See A. W. B. Simpson, In the Highest Degree Odious: Detention without Trial in Wartime Britain (Oxford: Clarendon Press, 1992); Aaron L. Goldman, "Defence Regulation 18B: Emergency Internment of Aliens and Political dissenters in Great Britain during World War II," Journal of British Studies 12 (1973) 2: 120–36; Pistol, Internment, 135; Bauerkämper, Sicherheit, Vol. 2, 724.
60 National Council for Democratic Aid, Morrison's Prisoners: The Story of the Czechoslovakian Anti-Fascist Fighters Interned in Britain (London: Marston Printing Co., 1941).
61 Yfaat Weiss, Deutsche und polnische Juden vor dem Holocaust: Jüdische Identität zwischen Staatsbürgerschaft und Ethnizität 1933–1940 (Munich: Oldenbourg, 2000), 212–13; Kim Wünschmann, Before Auschwitz: Jewish Prisoners in the Prewar Concentration Camps (London – Cambridge, MA: Harvard University Press, 2015), 225.

camps run by the Wehrmacht. However – in a move that clearly distinguished Germany from the other belligerent countries – he transferred all Poles considered to be threats to national security as well as "all Polish Jews and all stateless Jews of former Polish nationality" from internment camps to the concentration camp system.[62] With the German attack on the Soviet Union in June 1941, Soviet civilians were likewise detained. Even those who were fortunate enough to stay out of the SS-run concentration camp system faced harsh and discriminatory treatment that was often in conflict with the spirit of the 1929 Geneva Convention. For example, British, Dutch, French and Belgians interned in the Wehrmacht-run Wülzburg Camp in Bavaria in the early years of the war fared relatively well and did not have to work. By contrast, when Soviet internees took their place from the summer of 1941 onwards, they had to perform forced labour for local businesses.[63]

In what constitutes a remarkable deviation from Germany's otherwise heavily ideologically driven internment practice, individual Jews who were considered valuable bargaining chips in negotiations to repatriate non-Jewish German nationals in Allied hands were exempt from the National Socialists' genocidal project of exterminating every Jewish man, woman and child in Europe. About 2,500 Jews were traded in this way, although implementation of the scheme was anything but consistent. While a few hundred Dutch Jews with dual nationality or Palestine certificates were exchanged for non-Jewish German nationals, around 1,800 Polish Jews who held Latin American identity papers were deported from Bergen-Belsen to their deaths in Auschwitz in October 1943.[64] During the Holocaust, all attempts to administer aid and relief initiated by Jewish organisations, the protecting powers and

---

62 Governmental District Executive Aussig to County Executives and Police Offices, 16 February 1940, 1381, Finding Aid 1, File 7, Russian State Military Archives (RGVA). Thanks are due to Jörg Osterloh for pointing us to this source.

63 See Walter König, Flüchtlingslager Wülzburg: Ankunft und Integration der Heimatvertriebenen in Weißenburg (Weißenburg: Lühker, 1990), 73; Rainer Kammerl, "Der 'Russische Friedhof' im ehemaligen 'Fallgarten,'" Villa Nostra – Weißenburger Blätter: Geschichte, Heimatkunde, Kultur 3 (2010): 19–27, at 19–20.

64 For numbers, see Beate Meyer, "Protected or Persecuted? Preliminary Findings on Foreign Jews in Nazi Germany," European Holocaust Studies 3 (2021): 87–114, at 111–12; Gisela Rothenhäusler, Reaching across the Barbed Wire: French PoWs, Internees from the Channel Islands and Jewish Prisoners from Bergen-Belsen in Schloss Wurzach (1940–1945) (Lindenberg: Fink and Jersey: Channel Island Publishing, 2012), 293. See also Yehuda Bauer, Jews for Sale? Nazi–Jewish Negotiations, 1933–1945 (New Haven, CT – London: Yale University Press, 1994); Alexandra-Eileen Wenck, Zwischen Menschenhandel und "Endlösung": Das Konzentrationslager Bergen-Belsen (Paderborn: Schöningh, 2000). Another remarkable exception occurred in the sphere of military captivity, where Western Jewish POWs were mostly protected from antisemitic mistreatment. See Raffael Scheck, Love between Enemies: Western Prisoners of War and German Women in World War II (Cambridge: Cambridge University Press, 2021), 219–20, 226–7, 338, 359.

the ICRC met their ultimate limits. Indeed, the moral authority of the ICRC in particular was deeply damaged by its failings in the Second World War. Consequently, efforts to re-establish its reputation as the chief guardian of international humanitarian values and provider of assistance to families separated by military conflict and genocide dominated almost all of its activities in the post-1945 period.[65]

Conclusion

Before the Second World War began, the "lessons" learned from the First World War seemed to have been clear. As early as 1923, Britain's Committee of Imperial Defence concluded that expulsion rather than the financially much more costly option of civilian internment should be government policy in the next conflict. Similarly, in the United States, Attorney General Francis Biddle "was determined to avoid mass internment, and the persecution of Aliens that had characterized the First World War."[66] When hostilities commenced in Europe in 1939, the US government duly called on the belligerents not to detain civilians and instead to implement "mutual release and repatriation."[67] However, noble intentions aimed at more humane treatment did not prevail and mass civilian internment re-emerged in 1939–45, albeit not quite on the same scale as in the previous conflict.[68] In Britain, it proved to be a temporary measure: by August 1942, the number of civilian internees had been reduced to about 5,000, while approximately 4,500 German, Austrian, Italian, Czech and Slovak men, some of them veterans of the International Brigades in the Spanish Civil War, had left the camps by virtue of enlisting in the Pioneer Corps.[69] Like mass release for military service, the tribunal system instituted in Britain and the

---

65   See Gerald Steinacher, Humanitarians at War: The Red Cross in the Shadow of the Holocaust (Oxford: Oxford University Press, 2017).
66   Francis Biddle, In Brief Authority (Garden City, NY: Doubleday & Company, 1962) 207. For the British Committee, see Tony Kushner and David Cesarani, "Alien Internment in Britain during the Twentieth Century: An Introduction," in The Internment of Aliens, edited by Cesarani and Kushner, 1–22, at 3.
67   US aide-mémoire, 2 October 1939, R 41390, PAAA.
68   Absolute numbers comparable to those established for the First World War are still missing for the Second World War. Counting only civilians in internment camps defined in the narrow sense – i.e. those camps that operated in line with customary standards for civilian internment, including inspections by international humanitarian organisations and the protecting powers – the numbers appear to be lower than during the First World War. However, if all the camps of the Second World War that held civilians are taken into account, there can be no doubt that the numbers were significantly higher than in 1914–20.
69   Kushner and Cesarani and Kushner, "Alien Internment," 14; Pistol, Internment, 80; Detlev Brandes, Großbritannien und seine osteuropäischen Alliierten 1939–1943 (Munich: Oldenbourg, 1988), 100.

United States during the Second World War was a new departure. It reflected both a greater willingness to distinguish between "real aliens" and "technical aliens" and the far greater number of refugees. To be sure, tribunal hearings were far from systematic and at best pseudo-judicial in practice. In particular, they contained inadequate domestic and international safeguards against discrimination on grounds of nationality, race, class and gender.

What, then, had changed between the two world wars? One thing that had clearly not altered was the role of reciprocity in determining the treatment of civilian prisoners.[70] If Britain no longer enjoyed all the advantages of leverage through higher numbers, at least vis-à-vis its new enemy after December 1941 – Imperial Japan – alongside the United States it still had the greatest say in how the international diplomacy of civilian internment in the West was managed. On the other hand – and cutting across the question of formal inter-state relations between enemies – the 1939–45 period did see some important shifts in the relationship between internment and both humanitarian and security agendas. Refugees from Central Europe, who comprised the majority of civilian prisoners in the West, were identified by their captors, at least after 1940–41, as potential supporters of the global war effort against the Axis powers. However, security concerns were increasingly entwined with racist agendas, as seen, albeit in very different ways, in the United States and Germany, in particular.

Across the world, women and children were much more likely to be found among civilian internment camp populations in the Second World War compared to the First, but in both conflicts the hidden suffering of those who struggled to survive on the outside while family members were in captivity remains under-investigated in most accounts of the camp universe. Above all, though, it is the internment camps' ever-increasing and often overlapping functions – from places where adherence to internationally agreed norms could be exhibited, through new forms of imperial, inter-state or continent-wide security, to spaces where genocide, mass purges and mass murder could be committed – that makes the period 1939–45 extraordinary, rather than the number of internees who were held within them.

---

70 Bauerkämper, Sicherheit, Vol. 2, 708, 736, 754, 980, 997, 1033–4.

Austrians in Trinidadian internment during the Second World War
The case of the Stecher family

Christian Cwik

Introduction

I first met ninety-year-old Hans Bernd Stecher in his house in Goodwood Park, several kilometres to the west of Port of Spain, Trinidad, in September 2013. Hans had arrived on the English-speaking Caribbean island as a fifteen-year-old boy together with his parents, an aunt and an uncle in late 1938.[1] They had fled from National Socialist persecution in Austria in the hope of reaching Maracaibo in Venezuela, where Hans's great-uncle Jakob had lived since the early 1930s, following his own flight from Romania.[2] Jakob had informed his relatives in Vienna that the British colonial government had recently opened its borders to refugees from the "Third Reich," which was why they had headed, in the first instance, to Trinidad. They had assumed that the final leg of the trip would be relatively straightforward, given the island's close proximity to Venezuela.

However, rather than travelling on to Venezuela, which in actuality was not a simple journey as it entailed crossing a tropical wilderness (the Gulf of Paria, the Orinoco Delta) in a region that had little public or private transportation, the Stechers decided to remain on Trinidad, not least because English was the official language, as opposed to Spanish. Until the outbreak of the Second World War, the island's 500 or so Austrian and German refugees either tried to integrate within Trinidadian society (few refugees had settled on neighbouring Tobago) or attempted to migrate to the United States or Latin America.[3] However, Great Britain's declaration of war on 4 September immediately transformed anyone with a German passport from refugee to "enemy alien." Thereafter, they were monitored closely by

---

1   Interviews with Hans Stecher, Goodwood Park, Trinidad and Tobago, 21 and 26 October and 9 and 29 November 2013, transcripts in author's private archive.
2   Interview with Stecher, 21 October 2013.
3   Nathan Eck, "The Rescue of Jews with the Aid of Passports and Citizenship Papers of Latin American States," Yad Vashem Studies 1 (1957): 125–52.

the colonial government, even though most of them had been victims of Hitler's inhumane policies and divided into three categories: Category A (immediate internment); Category B (subject to certain restrictions); and Category C (exempt from both internment and restrictions).[4] However, following the Wehrmacht's invasion of Denmark, Norway, the Netherlands, Belgium and ultimately France in the spring of 1940, the British government deemed it necessary to tighten its laws against "enemy aliens" on its territory, including its colonial possessions.

Consequently, in June 1940, the Trinidadian police arrested the now seventeen-year-old Hans Stecher in downtown Port of Spain and interned him with his father and his uncle Wilhelm on Nelson Island, about three kilometres from the main island in the Gulf of Paria. Meanwhile, his mother and aunt were sent to neighbouring Caledonia Island. The small islands' old quarantine stations served as internment camps for Trinidad's male (Nelson) and female and child (Caledonia) "enemy aliens" for the next three to four months, until they were all transferred to Camp Rented in the St James district of Port of Spain. Some of the 500 or so internees (mostly those of Austrian or German descent) remained in detention until the end of the war, while others were freed, often due to the support they received from Jewish aid agencies, such as American Jewish Joint Distribution Committee (JOINT) and the Hebrew Sheltering and Immigrant Aid Society (HIAS). Stecher and his family – along with many other Austrians – remained in Trinidad after the end of the war and eventually became British citizens. (Trinidad and Tobago remained a British colony until its independence in 1962.)

This paper provides a detailed account of the experiences of some of the Austro-Jewish refugees who were interned on Trinidad during the Second World War. It is based on research conducted in the National Archives in Kew, London, the National Archives of Trinidad and Tobago in Port of Spain, the Archives of the Jewish Community in Vienna, the Archives of the American Jewish Joint Distribution Committee,[5] the Archives of the United States Holocaust Memorial Museum (USHMM) and the National Archives of Gibraltar in addition to information provided by Hans Stecher in a series of interviews and meetings in fall 2013 and winter 2014. These investigations focused on the refugees' flight from Europe (juridical and political backgrounds, escape routes and acculturation processes), their daily lives until their detention in 1940 and, finally, their daily lives in the internment camps.

---

4   1914 Aliens Registration Act (4 & 5 Geo. V c.12) <https://blog.nationalarchives.gov.uk/collar-lot-britains-policy-internment-second-world-war/> (5 June 2021).
5   <https://archives.jdc.org/>.

Juridical and political backgrounds and escape routes

With the *"Anschluss"* in March 1938, the situation for Jews in Austria became dangerous and unbearable. Flight became the only option for many, but that still left the issue of where they might go, because a visa was needed for most of Austria's neighbouring countries, as well as a lot of money and/or a surety. Moreover, Italy was not a safe destination because of the cooperation between Berlin and Rome, and the same was true of Hungary, which was under the fascistic government of Admiral Horthy. Meanwhile, Switzerland's immigration laws were strict and rigorous, especially with respect to fleeing Jewish refugees, who were granted asylum only if they could prove they were under personal threat due to *political* activities; peril due to race, religion or ethnicity was considered insufficient grounds for admission.[6] Consequently, the only viable possibilities for most of Austria's Jews were Czechoslovakia and Yugoslavia. A much smaller number had the resources to reach the Americas, but they still had to travel to a European port city. Initially, even German ports, such as Hamburg and Bremen, as well as the likes of Amsterdam, Le Havre, Bordeaux, Marseilles and Lisbon, offered passages to New York, Havana, Veracruz, Barranquilla, Rio de Janeiro, Buenos Aires, Port of Spain and others. But the National Socialists changed the emigration rules frequently, imposing further restrictions each time. Austrian Jews could still travel on their Austrian passports in the immediate aftermath of the *"Anschluss,"* However, by the time the "Decree on passports for Jews" was issued on 5 October, 1938, at the latest, the German authorities only issued German passports and all passports held by Jews were declared invalid. Passports for travelling abroad became valid again only after the passport authorities had marked them with a stamp (a red "J") denoting that the passport holder was a Jew.

Prior to the Second World War, the main goal of National Socialist policy against Europe's Jews and other persecuted groups was to force them from the continent and seize their assets. However, many lower-class victims of this policy could not afford the visas, vaccinations, insurance, taxes (e.g. the Reich Flight Tax), train and shipping fares, accommodation and cash deposits they needed in order to flee. The most important of these prerequisites was a valid visa for a destination country. Demand for visas increased rapidly in the wake of the National Socialists' intensification of their expulsion policy in the late 1930s, which prompted US president Franklin D. Roosevelt to launch an initiative with the aim of mitigating the global refugee problem. Representatives from thirty-two countries and twenty-four voluntary organisations duly attended an international conference in the small French town of Évian-les-Bains from 6 to 15 July 1938. However, while most of the delegates expressed sympathy for the Jews and other persecuted victims of National Socialism, they failed to

---

6 Jean-Francois Bergier et al., Final Report of the Independent Commission of Experts Switzerland: Second World War (Zurich: Pendo, 2002).

find a solution. France and the United Kingdom, in particular, had received large numbers of refugees in the first half of 1938 and demanded a fairer distribution of the émigrés. Yet, of the thirty-two participating nations, only the Dominican Republic agreed to accept more Jewish refugees – 100,000 in total. However, in fact the country didn't even accept a thousand refugees.[7]

In the months leading up to the Évian Conference, the British Colonial Office had formulated several settlement proposals for refugees with particular skills and/or certain amounts of capital.[8] At the conference, the leader of the British delegation, Edward Turnour, 6th Earl Winterton, suggested the British colonies of Northern Rhodesia, Kenya and Tanganyika as possible host territories for Jewish refugees from Germany and Austria.[9] Enquiries about the British West Indies as alternative places of exile were ignored by the British delegation, even though the Colonial Office had previously considered British Guiana and British Honduras (Belize) for that purpose.[10] For instance, British officials felt that Guiana could be presented as an alternative to Palestine in order to counter US claims that Britain was not doing enough to solve the "refugee crisis."[11]

By contrast, the British colony of Trinidad and Tobago in the south-eastern Caribbean was rarely considered in these Colonial Office discussions for two main reasons: first, the islands were in a state of political unrest due to the activities of the Afro-Caribbean union leader Tubal Uriah Butler (1897–1977);[12] and, second, the

---

7   Allen Wells, *Tropical Zion: General Trujillo, FDR, and the Jews of Sosua* (Durham, NC: Duke University Press, 2009); Hans Ulrich Dillmann / Susanne Heim, Fluchtpunkt Karibik. Jüdische Emigranten in der Dominikanischen Republik, Berlin 2009.
8   Joanna Frances Newman, "Nearly the New World: Refugees and the British West Indies, 1933–1945," unpublished dissertation, University of Southampton, 1998, 59; Joanna Newman, Nearly the New World: The British West Indies and the Escape from Nazism, 1933–1945 (New York: Berghahn Books, 2019).
9   Frank Shapiro, Haven in Africa (Jerusalem – New York: Gefen, 2002), 35, 44.
10 Anthony Sherman, Island Refuge: Britain and Refugees from the Third Reich 1933–1939 (London: Elek, 2020); Bernard Wasserstein, Britain and the Jews of Europe, 1939–1945 (Leicester: Leicester University Press, 1999); Martin Gilbert, "British Government Policy towards Jewish Refugees (November 1937–September 1939)," Yad Vashem Studies 13 (1979): 127–69.
11 Louise London, "Jewish Refugees, Anglo-Jewry and British Government Policy, 1930–1940," in The Making of Modern Anglo-Jewry, edited by David Cesarani (Oxford: Blackwell, 1990), 163–90; Louise London, "British Immigration Control Procedures and Jewish Refugees 1933–1939," in Second Chance: Two Centuries of German-speaking Jews in the United Kingdom, edited by Werner E. Mosse (Tubingen: CB Mohr, 1991), 485–517.
12 Kirk Meighoo, Politics in a Half-made Society: Trinidad and Tobago, 1925–2002 (Princeton, NJ: Markus Wiener, 2003); Jerome Teelucksingh, Ideology, Politics and Radicalism of the Afro-Caribbean (New York: Palgrave Macmillan, 2016). See also: The Report of West Indian Royal Commission [The Moyne Report], Cmd 6607 (London: His Majesty's Stationery Office, 1945); Howard Johnson, "Oil, Imperial Policy and the Trinidad Disturbances 1937," Journal of Imperial and Commonwealth History 4 (1975) 1: 29–54; Howard Johnson, "The Political Uses

colony's oil and gas industry was crucial to the British military complex. However, it was precisely this second factor that made the islands so attractive to immigrants. Together with Venezuela, Mexico and Texas, Trinidad was in the vanguard of global oil production in the interwar period, which attracted a number of Chinese and Syrian immigrants to the island throughout the 1920s and early 1930s. These new arrivals prompted the colonial authorities to restrict access, as the British parliamentarian Arthur Creech Jones explained in a telegram to the under-secretary of state for Dominion affairs, Malcolm Macdonald, on 17 July 1938:

> As regards Trinidad, it is true that there are good many Chinese and a certain number of Syrians, most engaged in petty trade, small general stores and the like. In 1936 the immigration legislation was tightened up and an Immigration Ordinance passed, No. 4 of 1936. This Ordinance does not discriminate in term against any nationalities, but it is stated in a confidential despatch from Sir M. Fletcher of the 4th of March 1937, that the Ordinance is frankly designed for the purpose of preventing entry into the colony, and it is aimed more particularly at Chinese and Syrians.[13]

In his "confidential despatch," Arthur George Murchison Fletcher (the island's governor) had suggested that the problematic ordinance – which had triggered a protest from the Chinese ambassador in London – should be replaced with a quota system. He had also raised the possibility of "sheltering a number of people (900 German Jews) whose ultimate destination is America" on Trinidad.[14] This figure was greater than the total number of immigrants to the colony over the previous five years. In response, Norman Bentwich from the *Central Council of Jewish Refugees* (CCJR) in London had suggested turning the island into a "country of first refuge."[15] The government rejected that proposal on 12 December 1937 although it did confirm that Trinidad could continue to be a hub for German-Jewish refugees en route to the United States. This route was not cheap: the price of a transit visa for Trinidad was £ 52 (equivalent to about £ 2,135 today)[16] and all disembarking passengers were obliged to pay a deposit and had to be in possession of an onward steamer ticket.[17] Crucially for the Stecher family and others who could afford to make their way to

---

of Commissions of Enquiry (1): The Imperial Colonial West Indies Context: The Forster and Moyne Commissions," Social and Economic Studies 27 (1978) 3: 255–75.
13   CO 295/603/II, Immigration Restriction, 1938, Fol. 1a, 2r, National Archives, UK.
14   Ibid., Fol. 2a.
15   Ibid., Fol. 2r.
16   <https://www.nationalarchives.gov.uk/currency-converter/#currency-result> (10 September 2021).
17   Letter from the Colonial Office to Arthur Hilton Poynton, 18 November 1938, in CO 295/603/II, Fol. 3a.

Trinidad, however, on 1 December the Colonial Office had sanctioned some "small-scale settlement" on the island.[18]

Unfortunately, the island had an "acute shortage of all types of housing and employment throughout the colony,"[19] so it would be difficult for the German and Austrian refugees to find places to live, especially if ongoing discussions in London resulted in a host of evacuees arriving from Malta and Gibraltar, too.[20] This was one of the reasons why discussions were held regarding the construction of camps.

Ultimately, Trinidad's border remained open to refugees for a period of just three months, from 1 October to 31 December 1938. The deposit for entry was £ 50 (equivalent to £ 1,967 today)[21] per person, which the colonial authorities estimated was sufficient to cover living expenses for a year.[22] The scheme was so short-lived largely because Fletcher's successor, acting governor George Huggins, was against Jewish immigration to the island.

The Stechers' flight from Europe and their daily lives in Trinidad prior to detention

Hans Stecher could trace his family's origins to Czernowitz in Bukovina (now Chernivtsi in Ukraine) and Klausenburg (now Cluj in Romania) – two regions that formed part of the Habsburg Austro-Hungarian Empire at the time. His father Viktor (born in Czernowitz on 16 November 1884) left his hometown to study law at the University of Vienna around 1904, while his mother Sophie (née Baltinester, born in Czernowitz on 14 January 1898) moved to the city ten years later, shortly after the outbreak of the First World War. They were among hundreds of thousands of Jewish migrants who relocated from east to west in the Habsburg Empire in the first two decades of the twentieth century. However, many of their relatives remained in Ukraine, Poland and Romania.

Viktor and Sophie Stecher married in 1921, and Hans Bernd was born two years later. By then, Viktor had been working as a lawyer in Vienna for six years, and he would continue to do so until the *"Anschluss"* of March 1938.[23] However, from that

---

18   Ibid.
19   Telegram from the Officer Administering the Government of Trinidad to the Secretary of State for the Colonies, 1 December 1938, CO 295/603, No. 272, Fol. 9.
20   Trinidad was discussed as a possible destination for these evacuees alongside Ceylon, Mauritius, Ghana, South Africa and Jamaica. See CO 323/1799/1, Fol. 22a, National Archives, UK.
21   <https://www.nationalarchives.gov.uk/currency-converter/#currency-result> (04 November 2021).
22   Interview with Stecher, 21 October 2013.
23   H.Ä. Liste der Rechtsanwälte Wien, 19 April 1917, Hans Stecher's private archive.

moment onwards, he knew that he would face persecution due to his support for the recently outlawed Social Democratic Party, so escape seemed the only option.

The Stecher family reached Port of Spain on 13 October 1938,[24] then lived as "free aliens" in Trinidad until their internment, which began on 16 June 1940. Nevertheless, Hans and his immediate family – his parents, his aunt Wilhemina and his "uncle" Wilhelm (who was actually one of Viktor Stecher's cousins) – all feature on a list of 301 "enemy aliens" that the Trinidadian authorities compiled on 2 November 1939.[25] Also on the list are the Tauscher family – Erich (one of Hans's uncles, a Viennese merchant and watch repairer), his wife Bertha, and his two daughters Gertrude and Alice. Nationalities are not specified, but careful cross-referencing with the archives of the Austrian Jewish Community in Vienna,[26] the United States Holocaust Memorial Museum (USHMM), the archives of the Jewish Development Committee (JDC) and additional archives in Trinidad, Curacao, the United States, Germany, and Austria has revealed that these two families were far from the only Austrians on the island. For example, Gustav Freud (a relative of the famous Viennese neurologist Sigmund Freud), the Fischer family (Ernst Otto, Inge and Lucy), Otto and Irene Malameth and the Hammerman family (Esther, Helene and Baruch) were already on Trinidad. Another 200 Austrian refugees would join them after the list was compiled.

Hans and his parents, his second cousin Siegfried (a dentist who had trained at the University of Vienna) and his aunt Wilhemina had left Vienna's West Station and travelled via Nijmegen to Amsterdam in September 1938.[27] They were forced to leave "Uncle" Wilhelm behind on the platform because his immigration papers were not in order.[28] Hans remembered this moment vividly: "There stood Uncle Wilhelm, a very sad figure because he had to say goodbye to us and stay behind alone."[29] (Fortunately, though, Wilhelm's escape to Trinidad was merely delayed: he arrived on the island about a month after the rest of the family.) Everyone in Hans's party carried two to three suitcases that contained their most treasured possessions, including many books. When the train passed the border control in Nijmegen on 16 September,

---

24 Interview with Stecher, 21 October 2013.
25 "List of Enemy Aliens in the Colony of Trinidad," 2 November 1939, 6924/24, National Archives, UK.
26 Kartei zur Auswanderung, Auswanderungsfragebögen, Archiv der Israelitischen Kultusgemeinde, Wien.
27 Hans was a pupil at the Gymnasium Zirkusgasse in Vienna-Leopoldstadt until 7 May 1938. See Iris Franziska Meister, Die Judenschule. Nationalsozialistische Bildungspolitik am Beispiel des BG Wien II, Zirkusgasse (Frankfurt am Main: Peter Lang, 2011).
28 The terms under which Jews were permitted to travel are outlined in Viktor Stecher's passport, Hans Stecher's private archive.
29 Interview with Stecher, 21 October 2013.

"it was a fantastic feeling of freedom."³⁰ After arriving in Amsterdam, the Stechers rented an apartment for a week prior to the departure of their ship.

En route to Trinidad, the ship stopped in Madeira, where goods were offloaded, and several passengers disembarked. It then continued on to Suriname, which was the first true taste of the Tropics for many of the remaining passengers. In Paramaribo, the Stechers visited the famous Neve Shalom Synagogue on Keizer Street, built in 1723, and therefore older than any of Vienna's synagogues. The next stop was Georgetown, in British Guiana, where Siegfried left the ship. He had struck up a friendship with a rich British-Guianese couple during the voyage and they had invited him to stay on their estate in Berbice. However, he eventually left the colony because of work-permit issues (Austrian degrees were not recognised in the British Empire) and ended up studying medicine at Exeter University in the UK. Several years later, in the 1950s, he returned to the Caribbean to take up a position as a medical officer in Port of Spain's General Hospital.

Upon arrival in Trinidad in 1938, the remaining Stechers still intended to join Viktor's uncle Jakob in Maracaibo, Venezuela. However, Hans was the only member of the family who could speak Spanish, having learned it at school in Vienna, whereas Viktor and Sophie could both manage reasonably well in English and French, so they swiftly chose to remain on the island, even though their welcome had been lukewarm, at best. Hans recalled: "They were always afraid to admit people, always afraid to allow people to enter […] [I]t is a very short-sighted view."³¹ Similarly, in his first letter from the island, Otto Malameth wrote: "There are a lot of European diseases, of which I would like to name but two – unemployment and anti-Semitism […] [G]ood old acquaintances, albeit with a Trinidadian twist."³² Nevertheless, in spring 1939, Viktor Stecher helped Erich Tauscher to establish a watchmaker's shop – the Viennese Watchmaker – in downtown Port of Spain, and business was soon booming.

Even though most of the Austrian families on Trinidad were not especially religious, they tried to maintain their Jewish traditions and community life as best they could. For instance, in 1938, a small group rented a house in Victoria Street, Port of Spain, and converted it into a synagogue. After the war was over, they moved to larger premises on the corner of Edward Street and Park Street where they could

---

30 Ibid.
31 Ibid.
32 Roberto Kalmar Lachs's private archive.

hold more professional services and accommodate Jewish sailors from the nearby US naval base at Chaguaramas.³³

Because of the already mentioned course of war in spring 1940 (Blitzkrieg) the British government decided to establish an internment camp in St. James (Port of Spain) for all enemy aliens in the country. With the surrender of the French Army in June 1940 they reopened the old quarantine stations on Nelson and Caledonia Island as internment camps because the construction work on the camp in St. James was far to be over.

June 1940, when all of the island's Austro-Jewish "enemy aliens" were arrested and informed: "You are going to be interned at the governor's pleasure."³⁴ The Stechers' turn came in the early hours of 16 June. Each member of the family was allowed to pack just one suitcase before they were marched from their St Vincent Street apartment to the police headquarters on Sackville Street, although one of the officers did take pity on Hans and allowed him to take his pet dog, too. The Stechers were suspected of being "German Nazi spies" due to their apartment's close proximity to the police station, so they were kept under lock and key.³⁵ Hans recalled: "There was a terrible smell in the cell; we couldn't sleep."³⁶ During my interviews with him, he was always keen to stress that the arrests came as a profound shock to the whole family precisely because it was the first time that any of them had suffered discrimination since their arrival on Trinidad almost two years earlier.

Detention and daily life in the internment camps

Hans, Viktor, Wilhelm and Warry the dog were transferred by small boat from the fishing village of Carenage, to the west of Trinidad's capital, to Nelson Island on 18 June 1940, after a second sleepless night in the police cells. The same boat had already taken Sophie and Wilhemina to Caledonia Island, about 300 metres to the north, and therefore just about within shouting and waving distance. They would remain on their respective islands for about the next 100 days, while they waited for work to be completed on the permanent Camp Rented.

A total of 126 male internees³⁷ – including Erich Tauscher, who had been arrested a few days before the Stechers – were housed in buildings that had previously ac-

---

33   The United States established a naval base at Chaguaramas, west of Port of Spain, in 1942 as well as two airforce bases at Waller Airfield (close to Valencia) and Carlsen Airfield (Caguanas) as part of Churchill and Roosevelt's destroyers-for-bases deal of 2 September 1940. The naval base remained active until 1969.
34   Interview with Stecher, 21 October 2013.
35   Ibid.
36   Ibid.
37   Ibid.

commodated generations of East Indian indentured labourers while they served out their quarantine prior to starting work on Trinidad's sugar plantations. Hence there have been "camp construction" on Nelson Island as well as on the other five islands of the Mini-Archipelago (Craig, Lenagan, Pelican and Rock Island) opposite of Port of Spain. We can learn from a few texts by Trinidadian historians, such as Anthony de Verteuil, about the history of the five islands from the early British period at the end of the 18th century up to Decades later, in the 1970s, leaders of the local Black Power movement were incarcerated in the same buildings.[38] Hans recalled that the residents of 1940

> had to chip wood for the government, which was really hard work because it was really hot on the island during the day. Furthermore, we had to cook our own food. I remember boiling coffee in old iron kettles that had been used in the sugar industry. I also remember stirring eggshells into the coffee with an oar. I still don't know why I had to do that![39]

No all the enemy aliens arrived the two islands on the same day. The watchmaker Erich Tauscher (who has been a victim of the November Pogrom) has been detained some days earlier than the Stecher's. The old quarantine station on Nelson Island was already used as a prison.[40] The 126 internees lived in barracks that opened onto an internal courtyard, as opposed to cells, and they slept on plank beds in family groups. Moreover, there was no fear that their detention might be a precursor to eventual deportation back to the "Third Reich."

In addition to the Stechers and Tauschers, many other Jewish refugees from National Socialist Europe were interned on the Nelson and Caledonia Island, including Alfred, Wilhelm and Richard Bronner, Norbert, Resi and Heinrich Frisch, Bernhard Mahler, Emil Welwart, Kurt Seinfeld, and the aforementioned Ernst Otto Fischer, some of whom attempted to maintain a Jewish way of life within the camp. One of the few Christian internees whom Hans could remember was Karl Alfred, who befriended the Stechers and had no issue with the other residents' Jewish activities.[41]

When all of the internees – men, women and children – were finally transferred to Camp Rented in early October 1940, the Jews and Christians were housed in separate wooden barracks, but they could interact freely with one another. Most of the Christians were German Protestants. Some had been born on the island to nineteenth- and early twentieth-century German immigrants, while others had

---

38   Anthony de Verteuil, Western Isles of Trinidad (Port of Spain: The Litho Press, 2002).
39   Interview with Stecher, 21 October 2013.
40   Nelson Island did have one bona fide prisoner, however. The union leader Tubal Uriah Butler was kept in solitary confinement on the north-west tip of the island for the duration of the war.
41   Interview with Stecher, 21 October 2013.

migrated there between 1933 and 1938. Oscar Moser – a member of the former group – was the only known supporter of Hitler's government; as such, he had been interned before the others, in September 1939.

In June 1941, nine months after Camp Rented had accepted its first internees, the facility suddenly had to accommodate a further 751 refugees from the French steamer *Winnipeg*, which had been en route from Marseilles to Guadeloupe when it was intercepted by the Dutch warship HNMS *Van Kinsbergen* and redirected to Port of Spain. Of the new arrivals, 210 were German, 284 were Austrian, 27 were natives of other enemy nations and 72 were officially stateless. Extra tents had to be erected to house the hundreds of new internees. The rest of the ship's passengers were not classified as "enemy aliens," so the government quickly extricated them from the camp and facilitated their onward migration, mainly to the United States.[42]

German submarines attacked two British merchant ships in the Gulf of Paria in 1942, which prompted the colonial authorities in Port of Spain to tighten restrictions on the island because of the real military threat.[43] The colonial government ordered a complete curfew for Trinidad which also meant closing the schools.

Each day in Camp Rented was similar to the one before. After the morning roll-call, the wardens checked the barracks and the residents cleaned them until they were spotless. Then the agricultural and manufacturing work would begin and continue for the rest of the day. The Jewish internees kept Shabbat on Saturdays and organised cultural activities on Sundays. Only school-age children were allowed to go to school in town; the rest of the internees were obliged to remain within the confines of the camp. Seventeen-year-old Hans Stecher attended Queen's Park Savannah Public High School, where he fully integrated with his classmates. He would often purchase leather for a detained Hungarian Jew and smuggle it back into the camp when the school day was over. In return, his fellow-internee trained him to be a saddler.

Conclusion

Most of the Austro-Jewish refugees who were arrested in June 1940 remained in captivity for a total of three and a half years (including the initial three months on Nelson and Caledonia islands). Only a handful made successful applications for visas that enabled them to continue their journeys to the United States. One such was Erich Tauscher, who reached New York in 1941. When the other internees were finally released from the camp in 1943 and 1944, they were placed under a form of parole that

---

42 Eric Jennings, Escape from Vichy (Cambridge, MA: Harvard University Press, 2018), 46–51.
43 Gaylord T. M. Kelshall, The U-Boat War in the Caribbean (Annapolis, MD: United States Naval Institute Press, 1994).

obliged them to report to the police station each day and subjected them to travel and work restrictions as well as a night-time curfew. These measures continued until the end of the war.

As soon as the restrictions were lifted in 1945, Viktor and Hans opened a leather goods shop in downtown Port of Spain. Six years later, they applied for and received British citizenship.

Figure 1: Tombstone of Hans Bernd Stecher, Woodbrook Cemetery, Port of Spain, Trinidad and Tobago

Source: Christian Cwik, Private Archive, Port of Spain, 6 February 2018.

Rehabilitation through labour
Welfare or control in a postwar Austrian internment camp

Rachel Blumenthal

Introduction

In October 1945, Major Taylor of the US military government berated the "difficult behaviour" of Jewish Displaced Persons living in internment camps in Austria. It was impossible, he said, to persuade the "Jewish group" to accept employment in spite of the many opportunities available in Graz.[1] Taylor ignored the fact that members of this "Jewish group" had been recently liberated from German concentration camps or Soviet work camps. In their former lives, the Displaced Persons had been forced to perform hard, manual labour in inhumane conditions. An inmate in the Mauthausen camp, not far away, described how he had to "pick up a piece of rock, you know, carry it up [...] maybe like 50 stories, dump it, drop it."[2] Anyone who complained was either beaten or pushed 50 metres down the quarry to his death.[3] Others had spent the war years in the Soviet Union sawing trees from morning to night seven days a week, sometimes in minus 60 degrees.[4] Strangely, at the end of the war, Jewish refugees in Graz refused to "take employment," although according to Taylor, woodcutters were badly needed to provide fuel for the coming winter.[5]

In postwar Austria, labour, frequently unpaid, was an integral part of the lives of Displaced Persons. Austria, like Germany, was divided between the four Allied Powers, and policies varied between the different zones. For instance, in the US zone – namely the provinces of Upper Austria and Salzburg – forced labour for refugees was not official policy. Moreover, the US government specifically exempted Jews from the

---

1 Letter from Reuben Resnick to James Rice, October 1945, Joint Distribution Committee (JDC) Archive, Item ID # 661045.
2 Norman Belfer interviewed 31 May 1996, United States Holocaust Memorial Museum Archive, Item RG-50.030*0367, p. 38 of transcript.
3 Alan Levy, *Nazi Hunter: The Wiesenthal File* (New York: Carroll & Graf, 2002), 68.
4 Goldie Buch Jonas interviewed 5 May 2013, United States Holocaust Memorial Museum Archive, Item RG-50.030*0697, pp. 41–4 of transcript.
5 Resnick letter to Rice.

local requirement that able-bodied Displaced Persons accept employment. This exemption was based on the fact that during the six preceding years, Jews had been the victims of state-sponsored persecution, displacement and murder by Germany and its allies. The American policy contrasted with the practice in the British and French zones of occupied Germany and Austria, where all Displaced Persons were required to work.[6] Indeed, the French General Commandant of the military government issued an order in December 1945 stipulating that Displaced Persons who refused to work would be denied access to food and accommodation.[7] The actual practice in internment camps in the US zone of Austria did not always comply with the official exemption. The US military government and subsequently welfare workers of the United Nations Relief and Rehabilitation Administration (UNRRA) strongly encouraged all refugees to work.

Relief in return for labour echoes Victorian concepts of welfare. In 1832, the British government established the Royal Commission to Investigate the Poor Laws, which subsequently recommended that relief should be granted to able-bodied adults and their families only in well-regulated workhouses. The justification was that destitute people were idle by choice. Parliament adopted the commission's recommendations in the 1834 Poor Law Amendment Act. As a result, the supply of food and accommodation to homeless men and women depended on their willingness to work within the confines of the workhouse.[8]

This review of life in an Austrian internment camp is intended to clarify whether the object of employment of Holocaust survivors in workshops was to promote their rehabilitation or to attain order and control over them.[9] In other words, did the labour serve the residents' interests or was it part of a quid pro quo arrangement between the camp administrator and the Displaced Persons?

Compensation demands for work performed by foreigners during the Second World War have framed the boundaries of research on the connection between camps and labour. Most studies of foreign and forced labour in Central and Western

---

6   George Woodbridge, UNRRA: *The History of the United Nations Relief and Rehabilitation Administration* (New York: Columbia University Press, 1950), Vol. 2, 519–21; Laure Humbert, "French Politics of Relief and International Aid: France, UNRRA and Rescue of European Displaced Persons in Postwar Germany, 1945–47," *Journal of Contemporary History* 51 (2016) 3: 628–30.
7   Humbert, "French Politics of Relief," 628.
8   George R. Boyer, *The Winding Road to the Welfare State: Economic Insecurity and Social Welfare Policy in Britain* (Princeton, NJ: Princeton University Press, 2018), 38.
9   In this article, the term "survivor" is based on the definition of the United States Holocaust Memorial Museum, which refers to individuals who were displaced, persecuted or discriminated against due to the racial, religious, ethnic, social and/or political policies of the National Socialists and their collaborators between 1933 and 1945. See <https://www.ushmm.org/remember/holocaust-survivors> (27 September 2020).

Europe concentrated on Germany and reviewed the period up to its defeat.[10] One striking exception is Ulrich Herbert's *Geschichte der Ausländerbeschäftigung in Deutschland 1880 bis 1980*. Herbert describes how postwar West Germany viewed the use of forced labour between 1939 and 1945 as an exceptional, war-related case and failed to connect this experience with the subsequent mass employment of foreigners by German companies.[11] There is no comparable study of forced labour in Austria during and after the war. Instead, studies of Displaced Persons in Austria focused on the frequently violent encounters between locals and foreigners.[12] Another topic of interest is the temporary residence of Jewish Displaced Persons in Austria *en route* to redemption in Israel.[13] UNRRA and its relations with the refugees in Austria have attracted only limited attention, except for brief references to the "preferential treatment" the organisation allegedly afforded to Jewish Displaced Persons.[14]

Archives of the United Nations are the main source for my review of labour and internment camps. To date, limited use has been made of the organisation's documents relating to its operations in postwar Austria. My case-study is a camp for Displaced Persons at Bad Gastein in the Austrian Alps, which I selected because of the relatively comprehensive and so-far unexplored documentation of life at this site. Following a brief description of the camp, the rest of the paper presents a detailed analysis of the inmates' labour.

---

10 An early example is Benjamin B. Ferencz, *Less than Slaves: Jewish Forced Labor and the Quest for Compensation* (Cambridge, MA: Harvard University Press, 1979). A more recent study is Johannes-Dieter Steinert, *Deportation und Zwangsarbeit: Polnische und Sowjetischer Kinder in Nationalsozialistischen Deutschland und im besetzten Osteuropa, 1939–1945* (Essen: Klartext Verlag, 2013).

11 Ulrich Herbert, *Geschichte der Ausländerbeschäftigung in Deutschland 1880 bis 1980: Saisonarbeiter, Zwangsarbeiter, Gastarbeiter* (Berlin – Bonn: J.H.W. Dietz Nachf., 1986), 186. Michael Burri reviewed forced labour in Austria between 1939 and 1945 but did not discuss the continuation of the practice after the war. See Michael Burri, "Postwar Contexts and the Literary Legacy of Forced Labor in Austria," *New German Critique 93* (2004): 103–30.

12 See, for example, Margit Reiter, "'In unser aller Herzen brennt dieses Urteil.' Der Bad Ischler 'Milch-Prozess' von 1947 vor dem amerikanischen Militärgericht," in *Politische Affären und Skandale in Österreich. Von Mayerling bis Waldheim*, edited by Michael Gehler and Hubert Sickinger (Thaur: Kulturverlag, 1995), 323–45.

13 Thomas Albrich, *Exodus durch Österreich: Die jüdischen Flüchtlinge 1945–1948* (Innsbruck: Haymon-Verlag, 1987).

14 Norbert Ramp, "Prejudices and Conflicts between Locals and Jewish DPs in Salzburg and Upper Austria," *Journal of Israeli History* 19 (2008) 3: 62.

The camp for Displaced Persons at Bad Gastein

In the spring of 1945, the US Twelfth Army moved southwards from Bavaria into the Austrian Alps while Soviet forces advanced westwards into Vienna and the surrounding areas. The Allied occupation of Austria ended Germany's seven-year annexation of the country. US control drew refugees to Upper Austria and Salzburg and foreigners almost doubled the local population.[15] According to UN records, 36,704 Jewish refugees entered Vienna in one month alone (August 1946) and after registration, medical examination and "dusting" (with DDT) at the Rothschild Reception Centre, continued westwards to the Austrian Alps.[16] They joined non-Jewish inmates liberated from concentration camps, former forced labourers and ethnic Germans expelled from their homes in Eastern Europe.[17] The destination of the Jewish refugees (totalling approximately 200,000) was the Italian port of Trieste. They sought to start life anew far from the European continent. The British refusal to admit refugees to Mandatory Palestine and strict US immigration quotas thwarted their plans. Instead, they found themselves detained in Austrian Displaced Persons' camps for months or even years.

In October 1945, the US military government requisitioned five hotels in Bad Gastein, a town in the province of Salzburg that was renowned for its radon-rich thermal springs. Since Roman times, people with ailing health had sought cures in this grand spa. The trigger for the requisitions was a damning report by Earl G. Harrison, envoy of President Harry S Truman, which categorised the local refugees' living conditions as "deplorable."[18] Harrison also criticised the military government's policy of housing former perpetrators together with their victims and called for separate camps for Jewish refugees. The creation of a camp consisting of the five requisitioned hotels was one outcome of his report. It served as a temporary home for between one thousand and two thousand Jewish survivors, with the number fluctuating throughout the camp's existence due to the constant arrival and departure of refugees. In addition, it was impossible to establish a precise figure because many

---

15   See "Als Oberösterreich kurz zwei Millionen Einwohner hatte" <https://www.nachrichten.at/nachrichten/politik/70-jahre-zweiter-weltkrieg/Als-Oberoesterreich-kurz-zwei-Millionen-Einwohner-hatte;art173463,1788336> (27 September 2020).

16   Narrative and statistical report for August 1946, United Nations Archives, UNRRA File S-1253-0000-0032-00001. One explanation for this migration is the pogrom that took place in Kielce, Poland, on 4 July 1946. See Jan Tomasz Gross, *Fear: Anti-Semitism in Poland after Auschwitz* (New York: Random House, 2005).

17   Tara Zahra, "'Prisoners of the Postwar': Expellees, Displaced Persons and Jews in Austria after World War II," *Austrian History Yearbook* 41 (2010): 191.

18   The Harrison Report is cited at <http://germanhistorydocs.ghi-dc.org/pdf/eng/Harrison_Report_ENG.pdf> (27 September 2020). See also Albrich, *Exodus durch Österreich*, 45.

refugees avoided registration with the military or local authorities. Rooms in the hotels were crowded and sometimes there was no running water or heating.

The US military government authorised UNRRA to administer camps throughout the region, including Bad Gastein. A small, eleven-person unit (Team 322) supervised day-to-day life in the camp. The first camp director was Jacob Lomazow, a former US soldier who married one of the inmates and left the camp six months after his arrival.[19] The refugees played an active role in the camp's management. The residents of each hotel elected five representatives to a central committee headed by a survivor named Jakubowicz.[20] The central committee's mandate was to represent the interests of the Displaced Persons vis-à-vis UNRRA. Salzburg's military government retained and exercised ultimate control over the camp.

UNRRA policy on labour by Displaced Persons

UNRRA publications and documents outline three distinct and conflicting approaches to work by refugees. The initial position was that employment was voluntary but should be encouraged and stimulated by every possible means.[21] George Woodbridge, the organisation's historian, expressed this view when suggesting that the higher the level of employment in appropriate work, the happier the residents.[22] Less than a year after the commencement of operations in Austria, UNRRA adopted a resolution that undermined the voluntary nature of work by refugees. In June 1946, the organisation's central committee convened in Washington and resolved that able-bodied Displaced Persons in Austria, such as former soldiers or labourers from Eastern Europe who refused to return home, should accept suitable employment under conditions no less favourable than for the local population.[23] This resolution expressly excluded persecuted groups, including Jewish refugees. A pamphlet published by UNRRA in the following month on its operations in Austria advocated a third approach. It described the organisation's efforts to encourage full employment of Displaced Persons, particularly inside camps. The overall objective was "to employ all DPs in work for which they had training and enable untrained DPs to follow courses in trade or craft," and this time there was no explicit exemption for

---

19 Lomazow married Wanda Neumark from Łódź, who survived the war under a false identity. See the Wanda Lomazow Collection in the United States Holocaust Memorial Museum <https://collections.ushmm.org/search/catalog/irn162662> (27 September 2020).
20 Jakubowicz's first name does not appear in the UNRRA records.
21 Woodbridge, *UNRRA*, Vol. 2, 519–21.
22 Ibid., 519.
23 Minutes of the Thirtieth Meeting of the UNRRA Central Committee of the Council, 17 June 1946, Washington, DC, UN Archives, UNRRA File S-1536-0000-0239-00001.

Jewish refugees.[24] In conclusion, UNRRA advocated labour by Displaced Persons, but it remains unclear whether Jewish refugees were exempt from compulsory work.

Employment in the Bad Gastein camp

In January 1946, Team 322 at Bad Gastein published a programme detailing the establishment of twelve workshops in the camp for the refugee community.[25] The intention was to employ the inmates as carpenters, metalworkers, electricians, motor mechanics and plumbers. Workshops would also be set up for shoemaking, the production of upper and fancy leather goods slippers, hats and mittens, ladies' dresses and men's tailored garments. According to the programme, each workshop would elect a leader who would be responsible for acquiring tools and materials, overseeing their correct use, ensuring that work was completed on schedule, cleanliness and worker satisfaction. The team also proposed the creation of a workers' council composed of workshop leaders, UNRRA officials and Displaced Persons' representatives.

The workshops had three declared aims: (1) to produce high-quality goods for the camp itself and the local community; (2) to inculcate disciplined, high-quality work and honest shop conduct among the workers; and (3) to provide practical training facilities for those who wished to learn a trade.[26] Accordingly, the declared motivation was for the benefit of both the refugees (by providing them with useful training) and the authorities (by promoting discipline among the residents and producing much-needed goods). In contrast to Woodbridge, the authors of the programme did not claim that employment would result in happier residents.

The camp administrator and residents duly set up the workshops. A shortage of tools and materials limited the number of people they could employ. In response, the Joint Distribution Committee (JDC), a Jewish welfare organisation, supplied sewing-machines and carpentry tools (see Figure 1).[27] Jewish refugees also performed camp management functions, such as serving as policemen and working in the local People's Court, the camp store and the UNRRA office. In addition, they undertook "manual labour tasks concerned with the cleanliness and orderliness of the camp."[28] The UNRRA team set up a workers' council but almost immediately

---

24 *UNRRA at Work: UNRRA in Austria* (London: European Regional Office, 1946).
25 UNRRA Team 322, "Program for Badgastein Workshops," 15 January 1946 (unsigned), UN Archives, UNRRA File S-1509-0000-0020-00001.
26 Ibid.
27 See the JDC reports for US zone operations, 10 September 1946 and 4 October 1946, Center for Jewish History, YIVO Archives, RG 294.4.
28 Report by Leon Fisher, 12 March 1946, JDC Archives, Item ID # 660980.

disbanded it for overstepping its authority.²⁹ UNRRA submitted lists of inmates employed within and outside the camp to the Austrian regional authority, the mayor (*Bürgermeister*), who calculated wages for the labour performed and deducted a fixed amount to cover the cost of the refugees' maintenance.³⁰ The local authority then registered the balance for work performed in the camp to the account of UNRRA, rather than the worker.

Figure 1: Workshops in the Bad Gastein camp for Displaced Persons

Source: United States Holocaust Memorial Museum, Rabbi Eli A. Bohnen Photograph Collection, Accession Number 2015.458.1.

UNRRA documents attest to the fact that hundreds of Bad Gastein inmates worked during their time there, mainly inside the camp. There were more male than female workers, since many women in the camp were pregnant and/or looking

---

29 Letter of 1st Lt. Col. Thomas B. Giboney, 23rd Infantry Regiment, 12 January 1946, in UNRRA File S-1509-0000-0020-00001.

30 UNRRA Team 322, narrative report, 1–31 July 1946, UN Archives, UNRRA File S-1494-0000-0338-00001.

after small children.[31] In April 1946, a total of 495 residents of the camp worked including three individuals who were employed outside the camp by the military government.[32] Eight months later, the number of working refugees had declined to 276 (208 men and 68 women).[33] Nevertheless, these reports clearly contradict Ben Shepherd's assertion in *The Long Road Home* that Jewish Displaced Persons refused to work.[34]

Payment for inmates' labour

Payment for labour performed by the refugees in the workshops became a major bone of contention between the UNRRA team and the residents. The workshops produced goods of high economic value, including clothes, shoes, hats and furniture. Similarly, residents undertook many of the maintenance tasks around the camp, which obviated the need to hire local tradesmen. In addition, any work done in the camp formed part of the financial reckoning between UNRRA and the *Bürgermeister*. However, UNRRA did not pay the refugees wages for their work. Instead, it rewarded them with larger food rations and/or points. For instance, a working inmate was entitled to twice as much food as a non-worker in return for thirty-six hours' work. In view of the chronic shortage of food in the region and the very poor basic diet, this was a major incentive for participation in the workshop programme.

The second form of work motivation was a point system based on a pecking order. A shop leader received sixty points for a week's work, while an apprentice (at the bottom of the hierarchy) was entitled to just twenty-four. These points could then be exchanged for food, toiletries, cigarettes, clothing or shoes (provided in part by the Red Cross) in the camp store (referred to as the *"magazin"* or "PX" in the UNRRA documents).[35] The declared aims of this system were to encourage work in the camp, to

---

31 On the postwar baby boom see Atina Grossmann, "Victims, Villains and Survivors: Gendered Perceptions and Self-perceptions of Jewish Displaced Persons in Occupied Postwar Germany," *Journal of the History of Sexuality* 11 (2002) 1–2: 291–318.

32 UNRRA Austrian Mission, semi-monthly statistical report on DP Assembly Centre Administration, 30 April 1946, UN Archives, UNRRA File S-1494-0000-0372-00001.

33 UNRRA Austrian Mission, monthly statistical report on Displaced Persons, December 1946, UN Archives, UNRRA File S-1494-0000-0372-00001.

34 Ben Shephard, The Long Road Home: The Aftermath of the Second World War (London: Vintage Books, 2011), 278.

35 UNRRA Team 322, Program for Badgastein Workshops, 15 January 1946 (unsigned), UN Archives, UNRRA File S-1509-0000-0020-00001.

ensure the fair distribution of clothing and other goods and "to prepare members for a normal economic life."[36]

The points system failed to meet the expectations of the camp administrator. First, refugees charged money for the goods they produced in private workshops using the tools and raw materials supplied by UNRRA and the JDC. The camp welfare officer regarded this as dishonest.[37] According to a UNRRA resolution, charging money for goods or services amounted to black-market activities and would be reported to the military government. The organisation duly ordered the closure of the private workshops and threatened to report any future infringements to the military court.[38] A later memorandum jointly signed by the camp military commander and the UNRRA director reiterated (in German) that all work undertaken in the shoemakers' workshop must be remunerated with points, not cash.[39] Next, the administrator complained that too many residents were receiving the maximum number of points and workers were falsifying their worksheets. In response, a general staff meeting advocated stricter control of the residents' "wages."[40] In addition, UNRRA staff criticized the fact that non-working residents still received "all the comforts they require," while the meagre rewards afforded by the points system did not constitute sufficient incentive to work.[41] Team 322 suggested an alternative – "no work, no food"[42] – but there is no evidence that this system was subsequently adopted in the camp.

In response to rising dissatisfaction among the residents, Team 322 set up a "workers' café" in a local bakery (the well-known Sponfeldner pastry shop), where refugees could exchange points for sandwiches supplied by the *Bürgermeister* and coffee, tea or beer supplied by the JDC.[43] Any camp resident could purchase a two-week "café card" for ten points that entitled him or her to ten servings at the café,

---

36 "The Point System – Badgastein," 11 April 1946 (unsigned), UN Archives, UNRRA File S-1510-0000-0006-00001.
37 Memorandum from Fay Calkins to Mr Lomazow re "Control in the Café," 1 March 1946, UN Archives, UNRRA File S-1509-0000-0020-00001; Marguerite Pohek, "Welfare Programme," January 1946, UN Archives, UNRRA File S-1494-0000-0338-00001.
38 Resolutions of UNRRA team meeting with DP officer, 27 March 1946, UN Archives, UNRRA File S-1509-0000-0020-00001.
39 Memorandum from the camp commander and UNRRA director to the shoemakers' workshop, 5 April 1946, UN Archives, UNRRA File S-1510-0000-00001.
40 Minutes of General Staff meeting, 22 January 1946, UN Archives, UNRRA File S-1510-0000-0002-0001.
41 James Travis, acting deputy director, Bad Gastein Assembly Centre 46, monthly report, 1 February, UN Archives, UNRRA File S-1494-0000-0338-00001.
42 Ibid.
43 Report by Fay Calkins, undated, UN Archives, UNRRA File S-1510-0000-0005-00001.

whereas heavy workers received their ration in the form of a free "sandwich card."[44] The café was open every evening, with dancing to a live band twice a week. At first, the inmates greatly appreciated this new facility. According to the welfare officer, "workers seem to enjoy getting cleaned up and taking their girls out for a date."[45] This success proved short-lived. The supply of beer and workers' rations dried up after a month, and thereafter the café opened just twice a week for dancing, with no refreshments available.[46]

UNRRA staff made frequent changes to the points system. For instance, in April 1946, the camp administrator amended the pay scale and developed a new work-requirement system – he justified the changes on the grounds that residents were still reluctant to work.[47] The following month, a report advocated a total revision of the system to combat the falsification of timesheets and eliminate wage inequality.[48] Then, in June, the camp director listed the points system under the heading "problems and targets." He reported a reorganization of the system to ensure that only those who were actually working and making constructive contributions to the camp would receive points. However, this reorganisation proved unsuccessful due to a lack of merchandise to offer workers in exchange for points earned.[49] The next month, Team 322 admitted that the points system may have to be abandoned altogether due to a lack of stock in the storeroom and the depleted supplies of cigarettes provided by the Red Cross. This problem was compounded when UNRRA and the *Bürgermeister* agreed that workshop employees would not be paid but instead would receive extra food rations and preferential treatment in the distribution of clothing.[50]

Unfortunately, the archives contain no reports from the second half of 1946, so it is unclear what happened to the workshops during this period. UNRRA's frequent revisions of the points system highlight the problems associated with its efforts to impose its authority on the residents. The organisation attempted to regulate the refugees' labour, but the refugees refused to take orders.

---

44   The term "heavy workers" appears in the UNRRA report and presumably refers to inmates engaged in hard manual labour.
45   Report by Calkins.
46   Memo from Fay Calkins to Jacob Lomazow, 7 April 1946, UN Archives, UNRRA File S-1510-0000-0006-00001.
47   "Work Projects," 22 April 1946 (unsigned), UN Archives, UNRRA File S-1510-0000-0006-00001.
48   Report by Lee Hamburg of Team 322, 31 May 1946, UN Archives, UNRRA File S-1494-0000-0338-00001.
49   Report by Lee Hamburg of Team 322, 30 June 1946, UN Archives, UNRRA File S-1494-0000-0338-00001.
50   Narrative report, 31 July 1946, UN Archives, UNRRA File S-1494-0000-0338-00001.

Relations between the administrator and the inmates

The relationship between the camp administrator and the inmates was characterised by a complete lack of trust. From the outset, the UNRRA welfare officer attempted to lay down the rules. In response, the residents' central committee explained that they were responsible "for the whole economic system and can change any personnel they deem dishonest, at any time."[51] Team 322 rejected this claim, but at the same time advocated more self-government and a greater sense of responsibility for the elected committee.

Tensions between UNRRA and the central committee came to a head in March 1946. The latter filed three complaints against the points system in the workshops.[52] First, they demanded that all inmates should be provided with one packet of cigarettes each week and one cake of soap each month, without these items being included in the points system. Lomazow, the camp director, rejected this demand on the grounds that "any exception to the point system would disturb its effectiveness."[53]

In the second complaint, the central committee accused the camp store staff of favouritism and contended that they reserved many of the better goods for their friends. It suggested that the store management should be replaced. In addition, it demanded a special shopping hour for the camp's teachers.

The subject of the third complaint was control of the goods supplied by the JDC. This Jewish organisation distributed food, religious items and clothes to camps throughout Europe, including Bad Gastein. The central committee demanded the right to appoint a representative to manage the JDC storeroom and keep an accurate record of all incoming articles and their distribution.

The central committee threatened strikes and walkouts if these three complaints were not addressed. A visiting JDC representative eventually negotiated a compromise between the two sides. This included a reduction in the number of points required for a packet of cigarettes (although not for a bar of soap), replacement of the camp store manager and disclosure of the supplies sent by the JDC to the camp and their distribution.

At the end of February 1947, UNRRA ceded control of the Bad Gastein camp to the military government. This may be seen as part of the process of winding up UNRRA,

---

51   Letter from Fay Calkins to Captain Levy, 29 November 1945, UN Archives, UNRRA File S-1510-0000-0006-00001.
52   Report by Leon Fisher, 12 March 1946, JDC Archive, Item ID # 660980 and Bad Gastein Assembly Centre 46, monthly report, 31 March 1946, UN Archives, UNRRA File S-1494-0000-0338-00001.
53   Ibid.

which ceased all operations a few months later.[54] However, the local team attributed it to "a series of alleged black-market incidents" in the camp.[55] In September, the military government closed the camp and moved the remaining inmates to the Magen David (Star of David) camp in Ebelsberg, Linz. By the end of 1948, the vast majority of Jewish refugees had left Austria for the newly created state of Israel, the United States, Canada, Australia and other countries.

Conclusion

Labour was an essential feature of the UNRRA programme for the administration of Displaced Persons who were caught in a state of limbo in postwar Austria. In his review of refugees and individuals without documents, Gérard Noiriel suggests that assistance is simultaneously an instrument of control over the beneficiaries.[56] The case-study of the Bad Gastein camp for Displaced Persons confirms this view. It illustrates how UNRRA perceived employment as both a means of control and a form of welfare.

There was a consensus between the UNRRA team and the residents of the Bad Gastein camp regarding the benefits of work. The staff viewed it as rehabilitation, while the residents welcomed the opportunity to keep themselves occupied with meaningful, productive work that was very different from the slave labour that many of them had endured during the war. Nevertheless, disputes broke out repeatedly. The workshops and camp maintenance formed part of the survivors' attempts to regain control of their lives. They wanted the freedom to choose particular vocations and trade. They expected to receive payment in cash – or a cash equivalent that actually had some value – for their efforts. They set up their own workshops and charged cash for the products they made. In response, UNRRA restricted the forms of labour residents could undertake, prohibited trade and insisted on paying for work with points rather than cash. Indeed, the organisation refused to allow cash payments even when the points system collapsed due to a shortage of resources.

UNRRA reports and memos repeatedly emphasised the need to teach refugees discipline and obedience (or "honesty" in UNRRA jargon). As part of this policy, the organization viewed any activity that generated cash as black-market profiteering and prohibited it. Order and control were the guiding principles of labour in the

---

54   Jessica Reinisch, "'Auntie UNRRA' at the Crossroads," *Past and Present 218* (2013) 8: 71 <https://doi.org/10.1093/pastj/gts035> (21 October 2021).

55   Letter from the Office of the Commanding Officer to the UNRRA director, 10 February 1947, UN Archives, UNRRA File S-1492-0000-0068-0002.

56   Gérard Noiriel, *Réfugiés et sans-papiers: La République face au droit d'asile XIXe–XXe siècle* (Paris: Hachette Littératures, 1998), 12.

Bad Gastein camp and the chief beneficiary was the camp administrator – namely UNRRA – not the refugees.

The notion of rehabilitation through labour for the benefit of the organisations that administer refugee camps persists to this day. Immigrant detention centres in the United States are a striking example of the double-speak on camp labour. Under the Trump administration, the Immigration and Customs Enforcement Agency (ICE) operated an allegedly voluntary work programme for detainees. The declared goal was to provide detainees with opportunities to work and earn money. Another aim was to reduce the negative impact of confinement by combating idleness.[57] However, reports in the media revealed that some privately run detention centres coerced detainees into working for just one dollar a day.[58] Many detained immigrants did not even receive these wages.[59] Contrary to the declared aims of the voluntary work programme, labour by detainees was a means of control. ICE was the main beneficiary of the fruits of the immigrants' work.

---

57 <https://www.ice.gov/doclib/detention-standards/2011/5-8.pdf> (27 September 2020).
58 <https://www.nytimes.com/2019/01/29/opinion/forced-labor-immigrants.html> (27 September 2020). The Thirteenth Amendment to the Constitution exempts prisons from the minimum-wage requirement.
59 See the American Civil Liberties Union's research report on the detention of immigrants under the Trump administration <https://www.hrw.org/sites/default/files/supporting_resourc es/justice_free_zones_immigrant_detention.pdf> (27 September 2020).

United Nations versus the Federal Agency
The recognition of asylum-seekers in West German camps after 1949

Michael Mayer

Introduction

Zwetan M.[1] was born in Bulgaria in 1926. In 1943, he moved to Rottweil in southwest Germany to work in I. G. Farben's chemical plant. Two years after that, in November 1944, he volunteered for the Waffen-SS and subsequently fought in the area of Prague, where he was taken prisoner in May 1945.[2] In 1949, he was released from a prisoner-of-war camp in the Soviet Union and travelled to Austria. Three years later, he illegally crossed the border into West Germany and eventually arrived at Camp Valka, which was one of the main camps for foreign refugees in the Federal Republic. Once there, he applied for asylum, which was granted in 1953.[3] This story is presented to demonstrate the complexity of the asylum issue in post-war West Germany. Many asylum-seekers who reached the Federal Republic had been victims of the National Socialists; others – like M. – had been collaborators.[4]

Asylum-seekers who reached West Germany after the end of the Second World War and before 30 June 1950 were placed under the mandate of the United Nations

---

1   All asylum-seekers' names are anonymised to protect their privacy.
2   See his registration card for the city of Rottweil (in which his employer and his recruitment by the SS are both mentioned), International Tracing Services [ITS], Bad Arolsen, Document 73590787. See also the affidavit of his former battalion commander, Hauptsturmführer Johann Schulzer, 28 January 1957, ITS Document 79452864. The documents do not indicate whether M. moved to Germany "voluntarily."
3   See, in the context of a retrial, the notice of the Federal Agency for the Recognition of Alien Refugees, 1 October 1958, ITS Document 79452861. The story is much more complicated because M. had used a false name on his application. However, he was able to remain in West Germany after gaining recognition for a second time in 1958.
4   For more on former collaborators who claimed asylum in the Federal Republic after 1949, see Michael Mayer, "Asyl für Kollaborateure in der Bundesrepublik? Die Gewährung eines Asylstatus für Ausländer in den Diensten des Nationalsozialisten," Zeitschrift für Geschichtswissenschaft 69 (2021) 9: 729–50.

Relief and Rehabilitation Administration (UNRRA) or – after the UNRRA's dissolution – the International Refugee Organisation (IRO), if they were eligible. Many were subsequently resettled, but a significant number remained in the Federal Republic. The Allied High Commission insisted that the West German government must grant these people asylum as *heimatlose Ausländer* (homeless foreigners).[5] From 1953 onwards, following a period of transition, the West German authorities had responsibility for recognising all foreign refugees who had reached the Federal Republic after 30 June 1950. Therefore, it is important to differentiate between the IRO's and the West German administration's recognition processes in various refugee camps throughout the country. The aim of this article is to analyse how these two authorities carried out their respective recognition processes and to describe their interactions with each other. Furthermore, the article explores the federal reception camp for foreign refugees, Camp Valka, close to Nuremberg, the only camp where interrogations of asylum-seekers were conducted from 1953 on.[6]

Previous researchers have investigated the UNRRA's and IRO's interrogation of Displaced Persons.[7] By contrast, foreign refugees who arrived in West Germany after 1949 and were placed under IRO mandate have received less attention.[8] The same is true for the interconnections between the IRO's recognition process, which continued until 1952, and the way in which the West German Federal Agency for the Recognition of Alien Refugees (*Bundesdienststelle für die Anerkennung ausländischer Flüchtlinge*), founded in January 1953, defined persecution.[9]

The next section will explain how foreign refugees falling under the auspices of the IRO were recognised as people who were entitled to legal and material assistance provided by the United Nations. The second section focuses on the transfer of authority over foreign refugees from the IRO to the West German administration. Thereafter, as the third section explains, the German authorities seemingly

---

5   See para. 1 of the Gesetz über die Rechtsstellung heimatloser Ausländer im Bundesgebiet, 25 April 1951, Federal Law Gazette [BGBl.] I, 269–71, at 269. This law officially introduced 30 June 1950 as the retroactive effective date.

6   In 1955, Camp Zirndorf was founded close to Nuremberg-Fürth, which, after the closure of Camp Valka in 1960, was the only camp where interrogations of foreign refugees took place in the Federal Republic.

7   See, for instance, Anna Holian, Between National Socialism and Soviet Communism: Displaced Persons in Postwar Germany (Ann Arbor: University of Michigan Press, 2011), 56–77. See also other papers in this volume.

8   François Crépeau, Droit d'asile. De L'Hospitalité aux contrôles migratoires (Brussels: Editions de l'Université de Bruxelles, 1995), 73, states that the IRO, which was mainly responsible for Displaced Persons, was less inclined to provide assistance to refugees arriving after 1945 (i.e. persons who had not been displaced by the war). However, ITS documents show that this continued on a large scale.

9   The author is currently working on a habilitation thesis on West German asylum policy between 1949 and 1970.

perceived the refugees as a security threat that could be solved only by interning them in the repurposed Camp Valka for the duration of the recognition process. The final section analyses various aspects of that recognition process. This framework highlights the IRO's and West German authorities' contrasting approaches towards persecution and the granting of asylum.

The article focuses on Bavaria for two important reasons: first, it received more refugees from the Soviet sphere of influence than any other German state; and, second, it was the location of both Camp Valka and the Federal Agency for the Recognition of Alien Refugees.

The IRO and its recognition of asylum-seekers in West German camps

Following its establishment in 1946, the IRO was responsible for refugees fleeing persecution and reaching the occupied zones of the Western Allies in Germany.[10] This continued even after the founding of the Federal Republic of Germany in May 1949. Asylum-seekers who reached the West German border might be sent to Camp Valka, close to Nuremberg, or any other camp for foreign refugees, after which the IRO would question them to determine whether they should be placed under IRO mandate.[11]

A person was deemed eligible for consideration for asylum if they had suffered from "persecution, or fear, based on reasonable grounds of persecution because of race, religion, nationality or political opinion."[12] However, the IRO did not attempt to verify each individual claim of persecution. It was usually sufficient for a person simply to claim that they were opposed to the government in their home country, whereupon the IRO agents would note "political reasons" on the application form and place the person under their mandate.[13] In practice, only people fleeing from the Soviet sphere of influence or claiming to be anti-communists were placed under the mandate of the IRO. Thus, the IRO – which was backed by the Western Allies and vehemently criticised by the USSR – became a significant manifestation of the East–West divide.[14]

---

10   The IRO was the successor of the UNRRA. See the Constitution of the IRO: UN General Assembly Resolution No. 62, 15 December 1946, United Nations Resolutions I, 97–121.
11   For the US zone, see the letter from US Commissioner for Bavaria George N. Shuster to Bavarian Minister President Hans Ehard, 19 November 1951, Bavarian Main State Archive [BayHStA], Munich, MInn 88406.
12   Part I, Section C, No. 1 of UN General Assembly Resolution No. 62, 15 December 1946, United Nations Resolutions I, 97–121, at 113.
13   See, for instance, the case of Petar P. from Yugoslavia: ITS Document 79604311.
14   See Greg Burgess, Refugees and the Promise of Asylum in Postwar France, 1945–1995 (Basingstoke: Palgrave Macmillan, 2019), 154f.

The West German authorities were regular critics of the IRO's work. For instance, on 15 February 1952, the secretary of state for refugees in the Bavarian Ministry of the Interior, Theodor Oberländer, claimed:[15] "The IRO commissions never reached a decision whether to grant asylum." Rather, they only checked if the people who were sent to the camps by the German authorities after crossing the border "could be recognised as international refugees according to the IRO statutes."[16] In other words, the IRO merely had to decide who should be placed under its mandate and therefore become eligible for assistance and possible resettlement. If resettlement of an individual refugee failed, the IRO would maintain assistance and then (until the end of 1951) transfer the person to the care of the West German authorities, who were obliged to afford them asylum if they had entered the country prior to 30 June 1950. Thus, IRO mandate status was a de facto guarantee of asylum in a country that had no opportunity to conduct its own investigations into the applicant. The West German authorities were keen to overhaul this system as part of the process of regaining sovereignty following the partial end of the Allied occupation.

The case of Tihomir M. – a Yugoslav, born in 1924 – typifies the IRO's approach to refugees in post-war Germany. Arrested by German forces in his home town of Belgrade in November 1941, M. subsequently worked as a forced labourer in a gas plant, a flour mill and a scrap-iron shop in Bremen. The UNRRA – the predecessor of the IRO – registered him as such on 13 June 1945, then repatriated him to Yugoslavia.[17] Almost five years later, on 1 May 1950, M. left his home country and enlisted in the French Foreign Legion in the Austrian city of Innsbruck. However, in Lyon, en route to Marseilles, from where he was to be shipped overseas, he took flight. Later, during an interview with West German police officers, he explained: "I didn't want to be trained in Africa to be sent to Indochina to die for France."[18] Over subsequent months, he worked in a coal mine in Mons, Belgium, before illegally crossing the border and entering the Federal Republic on 24 June 1951.[19] M. expressed a wish to work for the British forces in West Germany, but he was refused permission to do so and sent to the IRO in Hannover, where he was registered and questioned. M. claimed that he had travelled to the Federal Republic "because I didn't agree with

---

15   For more on his National Socialist past and the debate about him after 1959, see Philipp-Christian Wachs, Der Fall Theodor Oberländer (1905–1998) (Frankfurt am Main: Campus Verlag, 2000).
16   Letter to the Federal Ministry of the Interior, Bonn, German Federal Archives [BArch], Koblenz, B106/47453.
17   See his IRO application, 3 July 1951: ITS Document 79438435.
18   Interrogation by the police in Camp Friedland, 12 July 1951: ITS Document 79438432.
19   See his IRO application, 3 July 1951.

the political and economic conditions in Yugoslavia [...] I didn't feel well under that political system. I preferred to return to Germany."[20]

M. was placed under IRO mandate on 3 July 1951, so from that moment his asylum in West Germany was effectively guaranteed. The IRO did not ask for any evidence of persecution. Instead, the IRO agent simply noted as reason for M.'s flight from Yugoslavia: "Because of bolshevism there."[21] Therefore, as was the case in most IRO interrogations, it was sufficient for a refugee fleeing the Soviet sphere of influence merely to express his opposition to the regime in his home country. Proof of individual persecution by state actors was not required.[22] This was because the IRO's primary concern was the social welfare and resettlement of foreign refugees.[23] Therefore, the organisation's first task was to decide who was eligible for welfare benefits. When refugees requested resettlement in the United States or other countries, each applicant's potential "economic benefit" to the country in question was a more important factor than proof of persecution.[24]

Especially from 1951 on (following the founding of West Germany in 1949), the IRO started to wind down its operations, to such an extent that it added only sixty-eight refugees to the 240,000 people who were already living under IRO mandate in the Federal Republic in the first ten months of 1951.[25] Despite this lack of activity, the Western Allies continued to resist a full transfer of responsibility for the country's refugees to the West German authorities. Nevertheless, in the autumn of 1951, they finally agreed that the Federal Republic's own agents should be able to interrogate foreign refugees,[26] on condition that the interrogators would consult with either the Allied authorities or the IRO if they concluded that an asylum-seeker's claims were unfounded.[27] Shortly thereafter, on 15 January 1952, the IRO officially ceased opera-

---

20 Interrogation by the German police in Camp Friedland, 12 July 1951.
21 IRO application, 3 July 1951.
22 This gave refugees "strong incentives [...] to overemphasize the political nature of their flight": Gerard Daniel Cohen, In War's Wake: Europe's Displaced Persons in the Postwar Order (Cary, NC: Oxford University Press, 2012), 51.
23 See Annex 1 of the Constitution of the IRO, UN General Assembly Resolution No. 62, 15 December 1946, United Nations Resolutions I, 97–121, at 110–15.
24 See Laura Stokes, "The Permanent Refugee Crisis in the Federal Republic of Germany," Central European History 52 (2019): 19–44, at 24.
25 For more on the sixty-eight refugees, see the letter from the Federal Ministry of the Interior to the Bavarian Ministry of the Interior, 1 January 1952, BArch, B106/47453. For more on the 240,000 refugees under IRO mandate, see the inter-ministerial meeting of West German Federal Ministries, 6 June 1955, BArch, B106/5340.
26 Letter from the Federal Ministry of the Interior to the Bavarian Ministry of the Interior, 1 January 1952.
27 See Günter Schoeppe, "Die Sammellager für Ausländer," in Heilsbronn-Colloquium 1963. Abgelehnte Asylbitten, edited by the Nansen-Society (Augsburg: Hofmann, 1963), 39–70, at 39.

tions,[28] even if IRO agents continued working on a smaller scale for another couple of months. Now the Federal Republic was left with sole responsibility for the recognition process, although the Western Allies remained in overall control of West German affairs until 1955 and continued to issue orders on how to proceed.[29]

The West German authorities establish a system to recognise asylum-seekers at Camp Valka

The start of West Germany's post-war asylum policy can be dated to 15 July 1950, as that was the day when the Western Allies instructed the Federal Republic to establish "foreigners' camps" (*Ausländerlager*) for refugees fleeing persecution in their home countries. This usually involved the repurposing of former UNRRA or IRO camps or sites that had previously accommodated German refugees or expellees. The IRO conducted interviews in these camps to determine the applicants' eligibility for asylum,[30] but this raised objections from the German authorities. For example, the Directorate of Border Police Departments in Bavaria – the state where the majority of West Germany's border crossings took place – complained that "every person arriving at the border and claiming political asylum had to be admitted regardless of their eligibility."[31] Six months earlier, US Commissioner for Bavaria George N. Shuster had instructed the Bavarian authorities that they could not reject refugees solely on the grounds that they had crossed the border from a non-persecuting country, such as Austria.[32] Nevertheless, the Bavarian secretary of state for refugees Oberländer told the Directorate, "[N]o asylum should be granted to foreigners who, coming from Austria, illegally cross the Bavarian borders because they are, as is generally known, not in danger of persecution there."[33] The Bavarian authorities thus tried to prevent refugees from entering the country amid ongoing fears that any who found their way to a camp were sure to gain recognition from the Allies.

After the IRO ceased to place foreign refugees under its mandate in 1952, the West German authorities attempted to implement their own asylum policy, which

---

28   See the letter from Secretary of State Oberländer to the Federal Ministry of the Interior, 15 February 1952, BArch, B106/47453.
29   For instance, the Allies were still responsible for the criminal persecution of refugees. This continued until 5 May 1955, when all restrictions on the Federal Republic's handling of foreign refugees were finally lifted.
30   See letter from the Allied High Commission for Germany to the Federal Government, 14 July 1950, BArch, B106/47453.
31   Letter to the Bavarian Ministry of the Interior, 15 May 1952, BayHStA, MInn 88345.
32   Letter to Bavarian Minister President Ehard, 19 November 1951, BayHStA, MInn 88406.
33   Letter, 31 May 1952, BayHStA, MInn 88345.

involved sending all new *and resident* refugees (many of whom were under IRO mandate) "to a camp to be politically screened."[34] Previously, 75 per cent of all refugees had lived outside of the country's camps,[35] but the Federal Council's Refugee Committee stressed that it was necessary "to reappraise debatable cases that were not definitively settled in the past."[36] In this way, the Federal Republic tried to undo the work of the IRO by initiating a second recognition process that would be conducted on its own terms.

Camp Valka was chosen as the location for the implementation of this new policy. Established to accommodate spectators at the Nuremberg Nazi party's rallies of the 1930s, it was later transformed into a forced labour camp. After coming under the auspices of the UNRRA in 1946, the first residents were refugees from Estonia and Latvia who named the camp after the city of Valka, which is situated on the border between the two Baltic states.[37] Four years later, the IRO placed Valka under the authority of the Bavarian government, which subsequently offered it to the federal government as the country's first "federal reception camp." By then, it could accommodate 330 inmates. Hence, from the autumn of 1950 onwards, every illegal immigrant into West Germany who claimed asylum was sent to Camp Valka for registration and a security screening.[38] However, for the time being, their applications for recognition were not processed there, even after the Western Allies gave West German agents permission to conduct interrogations in the autumn of 1951. This was due to fears that the Allied authorities would continue to overrule any rejected applications and insist that the refugees were granted asylum anyway. To avoid such an outcome, the plan was to hold the refugees in limbo at Camp Valka until such a time as the Federal Republic could make its own, independent decisions on asylum applications without any risk of Allied interference.

On 6 January 1953, after almost two years of sustained pressure from the Allied authorities,[39] the West German government finally passed a decree to regularise the recognition process for all asylum-seekers who had reached the country from the

---

34   Minutes of a meeting of the Federal Ministries, 11 January 1951, BArch, B106/47453.
35   See letter from the Federal Ministry of the Interior to the Federal Chancellery, 22 November 1950, BArch, B106/47453.
36   Minutes of a meeting of the Refugee Committee of the Bundesrat, 13 September 1952, BayHStA, MInn 90419.
37   See letter from Vello L. (a former inmate from Estonia) to the Bavarian Ministry of the Interior, 29 January 1954, BayHStA, MInn 88418.
38   See letter from the Bavarian Ministry of the Interior to the Federal Ministry of the Interior, 15 February 1952, BArch, B106/47453.
39   See Decision No. 10 of the Allied High Commission, 6 March 1951, Official Gazette of the Allied High Commission for Germany, 794f., at 795.

Soviet sphere of influence.⁴⁰ This gave the Federal Republic almost total responsibility for its foreign refugees,⁴¹ which meant it could not postpone the implementation of a thorough recognition process any longer. From now on, every person claiming asylum would be sent to Camp Valka, where the Federal Agency for the Recognition of Alien Refugees would process each application under the terms of the Geneva Convention. The final decision would rest with a Recognition Board that included representatives of the UNHCR.⁴² In the event that an application was rejected, the claimant could file an objection, which was discussed at a second meeting of the Recognition Board. In addition, claimants had access to an appeals procedure at three tiers of the administrative court system.⁴³

The new recognition regime's first order of business was to review the cases of the 5,000 foreign refugees who had entered the Federal Republic since 30 June 1950.⁴⁴ However, most of these people were already living outside of Camp Valka, so they would have to be either persuaded or compelled to return to the camp in order that their applications for asylum could be reassessed. This proved to be an impossible task, as we shall see in the next section.

The problem of mandatory residence in Camp Valka

All foreign refugees who claimed asylum in West Germany were required to register with the police and surrender themselves to "a camp to render possible police verifications in an appropriate manner."⁴⁵ However, neither Camp Valka (which was

---

40 Asylum-seekers from other countries could be recognised on the basis of Article 16 of the West German Constitution.
41 Only a handful of restrictions remained, mainly in relation to legal cases. These were lifted by the Allied High Commission through its introduction of Law No. A-37, 5 May 1955. See Official Gazette of the Allied High Commission for Germany, 3267–70, at 3269.
42 See Sections II and III of the Asylum Decree (Asylverordnung), 6 January 1953, BGBl. I, 3–6, at 3f.
43 This right was guaranteed by Article 19 of the West German Constitution.
44 See the memorandum of the Federal Agency from the beginning of 1954, BArch, B106/47454. Around 28,900 refugees were recognised between 1953 and 1964. In that period, no fewer than 15 per cent and no more than 55 per cent of applicants were granted recognition each year. See Regina Heine, "Ein Grundrecht wird verwaltet. Die Asylpraxis des Bundesamtes," in Bewährungsprobe für ein Grundrecht, edited by Amnesty International (Baden-Baden: Nomos, 1978), 407–47, at 408, 416.
45 Memorandum from Deputy Assistant Under-Secretary Herbert Freiherr von Wolff (Federal Ministry of the Interior) for the minister, BArch, B106/47453. See also para. 4 of the Asylum Decree, 6 January 1953, BGBl. I, 3–6, at 3. This was in accordance with Article 31, para. 2 of the Geneva Convention, 28 July 1951. See BGBl. II, 560–89, at 571.

closed in 1960)⁴⁶ nor Camp Zirndorf (which was established close to the Bavarian city of Fürth close to Nuremberg in 1955 and still functions as a refugee camp today)⁴⁷ wasn't a secure institution. Residents received a permit that guaranteed free movement not only within the confines of the camp but also in the city of Nuremberg (Camp Valka) or Fürth County (Camp Zirndorf).⁴⁸ Therefore, it is not surprising that some 46 per cent of them slipped away from the camps between 1953 and 1959. In general, those who left in this way either emigrated or relocated to other parts of the Federal Republic that granted them residence without feeling the need to inform the camp authorities. Very few refugees remained illegally in West Germany after a claim for asylum was rejected.⁴⁹

The authorities' loose enforcement of the Asylum Decree's requirement that every asylum-seeker should remain in a camp for the duration of the application process can be traced back to the first few weeks of the new system. On 5 February 1953, the head of the Federal Agency, Eduard Kramer, informed the Federal Ministry of the Interior that there was no need to oblige every asylum seeker to be admitted to the camp. He continued: "[T]he persons concerned are accommodated by their relatives or friends or are employed by American agencies or companies. Understandably, they don't want to be admitted to a camp." Moreover, he suggested that the obligation to remain within the confines of a camp could have "political implications" because the US occupying administration, in particular, employed many foreign refugees in its "labor service units," often as security guards.⁵⁰

In light of these concerns, and the high cost of strict enforcement, the Federal Agency soon became the chief advocate for a less rigid approach. It argued that administration, subsistence and welfare costs would all be substantially reduced if asylum-seekers were allowed to remain outside the camp.⁵¹ Moreover, it had evidence that mandatory residence within the camp would impose a significant financial burden on certain municipalities. For example, in February 1953, the town clerk of Solingen in northwest Germany, Gerhard Berting, contacted the Federal Agency with respect to a Belgian citizen who was living with his (German) family in the city. He

---

46   See circular of the Bavarian Ministry of the Interior, 30 May 1960, Ministerialamtsblatt der bayerischen inneren Verwaltung, 439.
47   Camp Zirndorf was founded by a decision of the Federal Cabinet during a meeting of 22 June 1955. See Die Kabinettsprotokolle der Bundesregierung 1955, edited by the Bundesarchiv (Boppard: Bundesanzeiger Verlag 1997), 376–87, at 387.
48   See circular from Federal Minister of the Interior Gerhard Schröder to Ministers of the Interior of the West German Länder, 18 March 1959, Gemeinsames Ministerialblatt, 166.
49   See Schoeppe, "Die Sammellager," 60.
50   Letter from the Federal Agency to the Federal Ministry of the Interior, 5 February 1953, BArch, B106/47454.
51   Ibid. Para. 4 of the Asylum Decree of 1953 facilitated the release of refugees in certain circumstances (e.g. if they had found a job in the Federal Republic). See BGBl. I, 3–6, at 3.

felt he was unable to return to his home country due to his collaboration with the German forces during the war, so he had claimed asylum on the grounds of "persecution" by the Belgian state.[52] However, Berting argued against the Belgian's transfer to Camp Valka as this would mean his "pregnant wife and his three children would have to be assisted by the public welfare system." In addition, he asked the Federal Agency if other asylum-seekers in similar situations could be exempted from the obligation to reside in the camp as this would enable them to hold down a job and continue to support themselves and their families.[53]

Before long, the federal authorities bowed to the inevitable and took the pragmatic decision not to insist on the obligation that had been written into the Asylum Decree. In practice, this meant that they also abandoned the plan to review the cases of the 5,000 asylum-seekers who had entered West Germany under the previous IRO regime. By the latter half of the 1950s, initial screenings of new asylum-seekers, which were still conducted in one of the two camps, were normally completed within three months of arrival. Then, in 1960, the exception became the rule as all asylum-seekers were henceforth required "to make use of any possibility for accommodation outside the federal reception camp as soon as their presence in the camp is no longer necessary for their recognition process."[54] Seven years later, on 27 July 1967, the Ministry of the Interior announced that "the majority of foreigners respect law and order in the Federal Republic,"[55] so West Germany no longer needed to exert control over refugees by incarcerating them in camps. Consistent economic growth, the gradual cementing of the new republic and greater respect for human rights throughout society all contributed to this significant shift in the country's refugee policy.[56]

---

52 In general, the Federal Agency dealt only with claims for asylum based on the Geneva Convention, which normally involved refugees from the Soviet sphere of influence. "Western" citizens could usually apply for asylum under the terms of Article 16 of the West German Constitution.

53 Cited in letter from the Federal Agency to the Federal Ministry of the Interior, 5 February 1953, BArch, B106/47454.

54 Para. 11 of the "Lagerordnung des Bayerischen Staatsministeriums für Arbeit und soziale Fürsorge für die Sammellager für Ausländer," Bayerischer Staatsanzeiger No. 4, 22 January 1960, 4.

55 Letter from Federal Ministry of the Interior Secretary of State Karl Gumbel to the Federal Parliament, Deutscher Bundestag, printed paper 5/2046.

56 See, for instance, Ulrich Herbert, "Liberalisierung als Lernprozess. Die Bundesrepublik in der deutschen Geschichte – eine Skizze," in Wandlungsprozesse in Westdeutschland. Belastung, Integration, Liberalisierung 1945–1980, edited by Ulrich Herbert (Göttingen: Wallstein, 2002), 7–49.

The recognition process in federal reception camps for foreign refugees after 1953

When the Federal Agency was founded in 1953, one of its first tasks was to decide which types of persecution were sufficiently serious to warrant the granting of asylum. The West German courts, which had the final say over Federal Agency decisions during the appeals procedure, assisted with this process. For instance, as early as 21 January 1953, the Federal Court of Justice ruled that "considerable persecution measures are only those which directly emanate from the administration of the home country."[57] So it was only forms of persecution which were inflicted by a state on its own citizens which were deemed worthy for recognition. The Federal Agency did not define minor restrictions on personal liberty, such police surveillance or a requirement to report to the local authorities at regular intervals, as persecution. By contrast, repeated questioning by the police, imprisonment without trial or deportation might be reasonable grounds for claiming persecution.[58] Such claims were only ever taken into consideration if the asylum-seeker could provide evidence of "a persecution measure directly aimed against the foreigner […] where the state refuses to provide protection."[59] Then the West German authorities would need to decide whether the persecution had been sufficiently serious to merit official recognition of the victim. Judge Lothar Schmitt, of the administrative court in Ansbach (which heard all asylum-seekers' first appeals against negative decisions by the Federal Agency), stated: "The asylum-seeker who faces harm due to his political opinion needs to provide evidence of serious conflict. It is insufficient for him merely to differ from the politics of the day without fundamentally rejecting the political system."[60]

The Federal Agency rejected the Yugoslav Dane L.'s application for asylum on 7 July 1958 on the grounds that he had failed to provide concrete evidence of persecution. Specifically, the decision stated:

> It certainly can be presumed that he is an anti-communist and that life in communist Yugoslavia seemed unbearable to him. However, he shares this opinion

---

57 Entscheidungen des Bundesgerichtshofes in Strafsachen, Vol. 3, 392–5, at 395.
58 See various judgements of the first level of the administrative court in Ansbach in the 1950s in Karl Friedrich Zink, "Das Asylrecht in der Bundesrepublik Deutschland nach dem Abkommen vom 28. Juli 1951 über die Rechtsstellung der Flüchtlinge unter besonderer Berücksichtigung der Rechtsprechung der Verwaltungsgerichte," Ph.D. thesis, published by Nuremberg University, 1963, 77.
59 Undated memorandum annexed to letter from the Federal Agency to the Federal Ministry of the Interior, 1 March 1966, BArch, B106/81067.
60 Lothar Schmitt, "Das Asylrecht des Grundgesetzes," in Bayerische Verwaltungsblätter, 1964, 33–6, at 36.

with many of his fellow countrymen, just as the difficulties linked to this are a common fate. It would have been a precondition for his recognition that he was personally threatened by persecution because of his opinion, or at least that he had well-founded fear of persecution.[61]

Similarly, in the case of Milan L., another Yugoslav, the Bavarian Administrative Court in Munich – the second tier of the appeals process – decreed on 25 November 1959: "Mere opposition to the communist regime does not justify recognition as a foreign refugee. The crucial point is the attitude of the home country towards the claimant, not the attitude of the claimant towards the communist regime of his home country."[62] Eight months earlier, the same court had ruled that the purpose of the Geneva Convention was not "to provide shelter for proven fighters in the Cold War against communism to support their resistance" and that antipathy towards communism should not be equated with persecution, even though "owing to the present political situation most asylum-seekers in the Federal Republic come from communist-ruled countries." The judges' conclusion was that any asylum-seeker who had suffered genuine persecution should be granted recognition "regardless of the political system from which it emanates," whereas the mere fact "that someone has fought against communism" should have no bearing on that decision.[63]

Notwithstanding occasional disagreements with the Federal Agency, in general the UNHCR approved of the West German recognition process. For instance, on 5 May 1955, the organisation's representative in Camp Valka, K. C. Elliot, stated:

> Although we ourselves have our own ideas one must be just and admit that the procedure and basic policy is in accordance with the [Geneva] Convention. Each case is individually considered and when a refugee has fair grounds, is <u>honest</u> (so many I am afraid, are not) and explains his case without frills, he has decent chances of recognition.[64]

So, even though the Federal Agency's recognition process was markedly different from the IRO's, the local UN representative raised no fundamental objections to the new procedures.

---

61 Notice of the Federal Agency, 7 July 1958, ITS Document 79402424.
62 ITS Document 79417046.
63 Judgement of the Bavarian Administrative Court in Dane L.'s asylum case, ITS Document 79402442.
64 Letter to the UNHCR office in Bonn, ITS Document 79658148 (original emphasis).

Conclusion

The IRO and the West German authorities adopted very different approaches to the processing of asylum-seekers because they had very different objectives and perspectives. The IRO was founded primarily to provide social benefits to foreign refugees and – if possible – prepare them for resettlement abroad. It saw no need to investigate whether those refugees' claims of persecution were authentic. As long as it concerned bona fide refugees the vast majority was automatically placed under IRO mandate. If subsequent resettlement failed the refugees were left to the West Germany administration because the Western Allies insisted that it must grant asylum to each and every mandated refugee.

By contrast, the West German authorities felt that the arrival of ever more refugees was placing an intolerable burden on their war-stricken country that had to be mitigated as soon as possible. As a result, in the early years of the Federal Republic, foreign refugees were often perceived and represented as a security issue. However, the Federal Agency and the courts eventually developed a practical and, crucially, fair system for dealing with asylum-seekers based on the West German Constitution and the Geneva Convention.

These divergent perspectives were epitomised by the two systems' attitudes towards refugee camps. For the IRO, camps were simply a means to accommodate refugees who would otherwise lack shelter. By contrast, the West German authorities viewed them as an effective control mechanism. Yet, over time, the Federal Republic gradually realised that the disadvantages of enforcing mandatory stays in a camp outweighed the supposed security "benefits." This eventually led to a change of policy that not only allowed but encouraged refugees to find alternative accommodation.

The treatment of foreign refugees in West Germany in the 1950s and 1960s is symbolic of the country's gradual retrieval of its national sovereignty after the war. In the immediate post-war era, the Western Allies and the United Nations exerted complete control over any foreign refugees who crossed the border into West Germany. This was followed by a short period when the country's own institutions and agents wanted to challenge some of the IRO's decisions and practices, yet any refugee who had been placed under IRO mandate still had, from 1951 on, the right to remain in the Federal Republic as a "homeless foreigner." Refugees who arrived after June 1950 were treated differently. For most of them, the IRO was no longer responsible. Initially, the Federal Republic planned to reassess and potentially deport those refugees. However, following the introduction of its own recognition system in 1953, it eventually abandoned that idea and instead adopted what would become a rather liberal approach to asylum-seekers.

Can camp life create a common world?

Michel Agier

This paper addresses the question "Can camp life create a common world?" It considers camps as places of socialisation and politics, or what anthropology terms "common life" (*"vie commune"*). I will attempt to clarify this phrase throughout the text.

Various processes of urban formation take root nowadays in informal migrants' encampments, refugee camps and all kinds of *out-places* (places outside, on the margins), which initially function as places of refuge, when they are created. The empirical starting point of my reflection, then, is the urban encampment – that is to say the encampment insofar as it has an urban future (*"devenir urbain"*) – which is also a social world for the individuals who are casually gathered there. I will first identify three dualisms – or ambiguities – that explain the dynamics of these places.

First, as they are on borders – or kinds of borderlands – can these spaces be considered as *heterotopias* or places of refuge that are internally or externally produced? Or can they be a mixture of both a *heterotopia* and a place of refuge?

According to Foucault, *heterotopias* are "places of this kind that are outside of all places, even though it may be possible to indicate their location in reality."[1] They are any kind of "other" space – places of death, illness, deviation or crisis. They create a real or fictional entity, which allows us to locate an otherness that we may contrast with own self or "us." In this mirror effect, *heterotopia* is the term for an "outside" of thought, reason or society. But in the same process, there is also a "duality," and we can identify the emergence and later consolidation of an urban form (camp-city or ghetto, for example) as it is directly linked to this outside or *heterotopia* in its concrete form – as self-settlement, encampment and camp.

The second duality or ambiguity relates to the relationship – and sometimes the confusion – between securitarian and humanitarian logics. Our knowledge and understanding of contemporary camps developed significantly at the end of the 1990s, and the relative importance of this field of study today reflects not only the significance of encampment around the world but also the political concerns it raises. Two

---

1   See Michel Foucault, "Des Espaces autres. Hétérotopies" (1967), in Dits et écrits 1954–1988, vol. 4: 1980–1988 (Paris: Gallimard, 1994), 752–762, at 755.

themes have been central to academic research into camps and related controversies: a *securitarian* theme that links the general concept of encampment to the colonial era; and a *humanitarian* theme that encompasses moral denunciation as well as political or biopolitical analysis.

It is important to mention here the trailblazing work of sociologists Pierre Bourdieu and Abdelmalek Sayad in Algeria in the 1960s, even though their book was written and published after Algeria's independence in 1962. *Le Déracinement* (or "Uprooting") focuses on the displacement of rural populations by the French colonial administration in Algeria between 1957 and 1960 – "one of the most brutal [displacements] ever to take place in history," according to the authors.[2] The aim of this strategy was to diminish the "rebels' influence" by removing people from their traditional social settings by dispersing and resettling them in "regroupment camps" near military strongholds. Bourdieu and Sayad's study shows how encampment introduces the totalitarian model (including confinement and discipline) within the colonial rationale. It also highlights the social and economic dislocations that rural agricultural areas suffer following the eviction of their inhabitants. Finally, it demonstrates how humanitarian intervention – traditionally aimed at regrouping and controlling populations – can become "a weapon of war."[3] The colonial and post-colonial dimension of camps has since been one of the major focuses of mainly political and socio-historical approaches to camps, which in Europe are tackled from the angle of immigrant control policies.[4]

In the early 1980s the anthropologist Barbara Harrell-Bond was the first to take an interest in this type of confinement and the violence that occurred within so-called "humanitarian" camps: that is, those established and managed by the UNHCR.[5] According to Harrell-Bond, such camps were characterised by a "deprivation of liberty" even though they were ostensibly established in the name of emergency and rescue.

---

2   Pierre Bourdieu and Abdelmalek Sayad, Le Déracinement. La Crise de l'agriculture traditionnelle en Algérie (Paris: Editions de minuit, 1964), back cover. Translated and republished as: Uprooting: The Crisis of Traditional Agriculture in Algeria (Cambridge: Polity Press, 2020).

3   Ibid., 25.

4   See Emile Temime and Nathalie Deguigné, Le Camp du Grand Arénas, Marseille, 1944–1966 (Paris: Éditions Autrement, 2001); Marc Bernardot, Camps d'étrangers (Bellecombe-en-Bauges: Éditions du Croquant, 2008); Jérôme Valluy (ed.), "L'Europe des camps : La Mise à l'écart des étrangers," special issue of Cultures & Conflits 57 (2005); Olivier Le Cour Grandmaison et al. (eds), Le Retour des camps? Sangatte, Lampedusa, Guantanamo ... (Paris: Autrement, 2007); Carolina Kobelinsky and Chowra Makaremi, Enfermés dehors. Enquêtes sur le confinement des étrangers (Paris: Editions du Croquant, collection Terra, 2009).

5   Barbara Harrell-Bond, Imposing Aid: Emergency Assistance to Refugees (Oxford – New York: Oxford University Press, 1986); Barbara Harrell-Bond and Guglielmo Verdirame, Rights in Exile: Janus-Faced Humanitarianism (New York: Berghahn Books, 2005).

Therefore, camps are political places, and even sites of enduring "biopolitics." Analysis of the contradictions, ambiguities and limits of humanitarian confinement developed considerably from the 1980s onwards through a critique of the separate management of bodies, spaces and populations by ambiguous systems that can be jointly or alternatively securitarian and humanitarian – be they governmental or non-governmental, national or global, public or private – through approaches where a dialogue was established between philosophy, social sciences and (sometimes) law.[6] In this way, as I have argued elsewhere, the management of the vulnerable is simultaneously a government of undesirables.[7]

Ethnographic enquiry is a tool that helps to criticize the philosophical conception of camps as "exceptional" (as developed in Giorgio Agamben's view and by followers).[8] Ethnography denaturalises and recontextualises the camp in all its forms. It uncovers capacities for transformations in the humanitarian or securitarian situation of the camp. Even if the ambiguity persists, one can observe in these situations and places what is usually called "agency" in English – a term that corresponds to what the French anthropologist George Balandier referred to as *"reprise d'initiative"* ("regaining initiative") in the 1950s in the context of the end of the colonial era and the struggle for independence in Africa.[9] Basically, this is the issue of the formation and the manifestation of a subject, or more precisely that of a subjectivation that can be tackled from a social science perspective in relation to the questions of power and social relations as they exist in places of encampment.

---

6   Hannah Arendt, Les Origines du totalitarisme. L'Impérialisme (Paris: Fayard, 1951); Michel Foucault, "Des espaces autres. Hétérotopies"; Giorgio Agamben, Homo Sacer, I: Le Pouvoir souverain et la vie nue (Paris: Seuil, 1997); Mariella Pandolfi, "Une Souveraineté mouvante et supracoloniale," Multitudes 3 (2000): 97–105; Marie-Claire Caloz-Tschopp, Les Étrangers aux frontières de l'Europe et le spectre des camps (Paris: La Dispute, 2004); Bulent Diken and Carsten B. Laustsen, The Culture of Exception: Sociology Facing the Camp (London – New York: Routledge, 2005); Peter Nyers, Rethinking Refugees: Beyond States of Emergency (London – New York: Routledge, 2006); Federico Rahola, "La Forme-camp. Pour une généalogie des lieux de transit et d'internement du présent," Cultures and Conflits 68 (2007): 32–50; Didier Fassin and Mariella Pandolfi (eds), Contemporary States of Emergency: The Politics of Military and Humanitarian Interventions (New York: Zone Books, 2010); Illana Feldman and Miriam Ticktin (eds), In the Name of Humanity: The Government of Threat and Care (Durham, NC: Duke University Press, 2010); Eyal Weizman, The Least of All Possible Evils: Humanitarian Violence from Arendt to Gaza (London: Verso, 2011); Maja Janmir, Protecting Civilians in Refugee Camps: Issues of Responsibility and Lessons from Uganda (Bergen: University of Bergen, 2012).
7   Michel Agier, Managing the Undesirables: Refugee Camps and Humanitarian Government (Cambridge – Malden, MA: Polity, 2011).
8   See Giorgio Agamben, Means without End: Notes on Politics (Minneapolis: University of Minnesota Press, 2000) and, among others, Diken and Laustsen, The Culture of Exception.
9   George Balandier, Sociologie actuelle de l'Afrique noire (Paris: PUF, 1955).

Liisa Malkki's fieldwork in the 1980s with Hutu refugees from Burundi who had settled fifteen years earlier in the Mishamo camp or the small town of Kigoma, Tanzania, shed unprecedented light on the subject of political socialisation in refugee camps.[10] Malkki demonstrated that such camps are political places where identities are reconstructed, partly because regrouping facilitates the rehashing – and sometimes even the strengthening – of national memory. She highlighted the main benchmarks for questioning the relation of refugees in their representations, and of scholars in their analysis, to the norm of the "national order of things" as well as, more generally, the cultural implications of social life in the context of camps and forced displacements. I have previously discussed the distinction she established between refugees in camps (imprisoned in a memory of national identity) and those in cities (described as open, nomadic).[11] These places are actually hybrid and often cosmopolitan living environments, as is typical of many other border landscapes in the contemporary world.[12]

It is now possible to discuss the different kinds of camps – not only refugee camps and internally Displaced Persons' settlements but also makeshift migrant camps and, to a certain extent, detention centres, accommodation centres, transit shelters and so on – and to focus on the relations between mobility and immobility without denying the immobilising power of relative confinement: that is, without forgetting that camps, including humanitarian ones, generally and effectively represent a form of deprivation of liberty, as Barbara Harrell-Bond explained decades ago. Many investigations, Ph.D. theses, detailed monographs and collective works have been published over the last fifteen years.[13] I am unable to comment on all of

---

10   Liisa H. Malkki, Purity and Exile: Violence, Memory, and National Cosmology among Hutu Refugees in Tanzania (London – Chicago: University of Chicago Press, 1995); Liisa H. Malkki, "Refugees and Exile: From 'Refugee Studies' to the National Order of Things," Annual Review of Anthropology 24 (1995): 495–523.
11   See Michel Agier, "Between War and City. Towards an Urban Anthropology of Refugee Camps" (followed by a discussion with Liisa H. Malkki and Zygmunt Bauman), Ethnography 3 (2002) 3: 317–41.
12   See Michel Agier, Borderlands: Towards an Anthropology of the Cosmopolitan Condition (Cambridge: Polity Press, 2016).
13   Cindy Horst, Transnational Nomads: How Somalis Cope with Refugee Life in the Dadaab Camps of Kenya (New York: Berghahn Books, 2006); Simon Turner, Politics of Innocence: Hutu Identity, Conflict and Camp Life (Oxford – New York: Berghahn, 2010); Amanda S. A. Dias, Aux Marges de la ville et de l'état. Camps palestiniens au Liban et favelas cariocas, preface by Michel Agier (Paris: Karthala/IFPO, 2013); Alexander Horstmann, "Ethical Dilemmas and Identifications of Faith-Based Humanitarian Organizations in the Karen Refugee Crisis," Journal of Refugee Studies 24 (2011) 3: 513–32; Bram J. Jansen, Kakuma Refugee Camp: Humanitarian Urbanism in Kenya's Accidental City, Zed Books, 2018; Tristan Bruslé, "What Kind of Place is This? Daily Life, Privacy and the Inmate Metaphor in a Nepalese Workers' Labour Camp (Qatar)," in South Asia Multidisciplinary Academic Journal 6 (2012), <https://journals.o

these often brilliant and rich works here, but it is worth mentioning that they focus on the many inherent tensions of camps, which are described as violent and possibly political, cultural and urban spaces, conceptualising hybridity, resilience or agency. Camps for refugees, internally Displaced Persons and so-called "illegal aliens" all bear witness to a strong and relentless tension between two theoretical designs: that of "confinement outside," defined from the perspective of an analysis focused on state power (as we have just seen when discussing the outside *heterotopia*); and that of cultural, ethnic, national and social diversity (that is, the camp viewed as a global crossroads and a place for banal cosmopolitanism, as ethnographic fieldwork conducted at the heart of everyday life within the camp environment has shown). Mobility and immobility intersect within the very places of confinement that act as borders – state or city borders that can act as either "airlocks" (e.g., the camps for Displaced Persons on the outskirts of Monrovia and Khartoum) or "ghettos" (e.g., the numerous Palestinian camps that keep growing vertically because of the lack of space to expand horizontally).

The third duality or ambiguity that I wish to address relates to the conception of time in camps. The refuge is a shelter created by people moving in a hostile context, whether embodied in war, violence or xenophobic or racist rejection. It takes the form of an urban encampment that can be described in several ways – camp-city, clandestine encampment or *invasione* (shanty town). As time goes by, and under certain circumstances, it may become another type of urban form: a ghetto.

Faced with precarious lives and situations, the sensitive measure of reality takes as its main criterion the possibility of duration. In this context, the lives of refugees and the situations in camps comprise a model of uncertainty. These are spaces and populations that are administered as strictly urgent and exceptional situations (*urgentiste* and *exceptionnaliste*), and time may stand still within them for indefinite periods. In theory, a camp is an emergency intervention that can be placed on "standby" for months or even years: ten to fifteen years for Sudanese, Liberian and Guinean camps; thirty years in the case of Somali refugees in Kenya; nearly forty years for the Sahrawi refugee camps in Algeria and Angolan refugees in Zambia; and more than seventy years for the Palestinian refugees living in city-camps in the Middle East, on the margins of which other refugees – including Iraqis, Syrians and Sudanese – have recently settled. Waiting becomes an endless present. All of these spaces could be characterised as "waiting zones."

---

penedition.org/samaj/3446> (19 October 2021); Hala Abou Zaki, "Revisiting Politics in Spaces 'Beyond the Center': The Shātīlā Palestinian Refugee Camp in Lebanon," in Malika Bouziane et al. (eds), Local Politics and Contemporary Transformations in the Arab World: Revisiting Governance beyond the Center (London and New York: Palgrave, 2014), 178–95. See also the collection of articles in Humanity 7 (2016) 3 on camps as "hybrid spaces." (Are Knudsen and Maja Janmyr eds.).

There are two opposing attitudes with regard to the temporality of refugee camps. According to the first, the refugees are awaiting some sort of return. Time seems configured by waiting to return to a lost place whose memory their exile maintains, even if each refugee's biography makes any return to the past impossible. In this framework, what is experienced in the camp has no personal or common, general meaning, if not as a suffering which is the justification to ask for the return – like a personal complaint or a collective demand. From this perspective, the refugee is entirely "absent" from both the lost land and the present.[14] Expectation and absence fill the imagination in the current reality of the camp, where all of this happens.

The second conception of the camp's temporality is more pragmatic: it supposes that the exiles live, survive, meet and organise their existence. Real time sets in when the present grows longer, even more so without a sense of the past or a clear expectation of the future – come back home, stay or go to another place. It is a concrete presence, as opposed to the imaginary of the absence felt in exile, but a presence of bodies and material installations that has none of its own spatio-temporal marks to situate what this space means for the duration. Thereby, the camp is a model for ephemeral architecture, with temporary constructions built out of light, plastic materials that can be swiftly dismantled and rebuilt somewhere else, much like the 1960s notion of "instant cities," which advocated urban areas that could be relocated from one place to another. To some extent, camps may be considered as displaceable cities. In some recent camps, the caravan, the container and/or the mobile home have started to take the place of the tent or the rudimentary shelter with a plastic roof. For instance, many of those left homeless by Hurricane Katrina formed regroupment camps of caravans and mobile homes, and shipping containers provide accommodation for Syrian refugees in Jordan's Zaatari camp, asylum-seekers in Calais and the residents of a number of UNHCR camps. The so-called "emergency architecture" – or "architecture without borders"[15] – of these places is becoming ever more complex, substantial, professional and permanent. There is a certain stability in the materiality of these camps, even if the people are in a state of permanent temporariness. As technology and competence develop, new ephemeral, disposable and/or transposable shelters, construction materials, roads, supplies, sanitary systems and medical equipment will continue to emerge and confirm the expansion of the humanitarian logistics market.

The two temporalities that intersect in the daily life of the camps illustrate the ambiguous nature of these spaces. The first requires international NGO workers always to have something urgent to do: 4×4s crisscross the few drivable thoroughfares; walkie-talkies are always crackling; and "expat" volunteers bemoan their inability to

---

14   See Elias Sanbar, Le Bien des absents (Arles: Actes Sud, 2001).
15   A French NGO called Architectes sans frontières (ASF) was created in 1979.

linger longer in conversation with the refugees. All of this hectic activity contrasts with the slowness that characterises the second temporality – the rhythm of the encamped people themselves. Thus, in a single space, humanitarian workers who are busy tackling an emergency for the duration of their "mission" (usually three to six months) intersect with refugees who are trying to find their way in these hybrid places, and in the inevitable slowness, over the course of years.

The pragmatism that is born in this situation – a temporal and spatial border in the refugees' lives – is characterised by new and "other" learning experiences. Life on the border encourages coping strategies, muddling through, self-transformation, mastering the art of "making do" and "living with it," as people deal with middlemen and smugglers, adversity, resilience and rebirth. Can this everyday pragmatism help to transform these places of confinement into places of mobility by making them more liveable and open, by scratching at their walls until they crumble, by drilling through doors or putting up ladders? We may well think so if we look at how some camp inhabitants have managed to cope: Karen refugees in Thailand; Sudanese and Somali refugees in Kenya; Palestinian refugees on the West Bank; migrants in northern Morocco and on the fringes of Europe. All of these examples demonstrate the vitality as well as the tensions and conflicts that characterise contemporary camps.

How to live a long and even a "good" life in a camp is a significant political question that has come to the fore due to the contemporary policy of excluding undesirables. Camps are created by a policy of humanitarian and securitarian confinement and sidelining, and although the encamped people are in a waiting zone, in a waiting condition, they are able to reorganise their lives, change the space and their shelters, turn those shelters into houses and even lead good lives. For instance, Palestinian refugees are often very attached to their camps, in much the same way as anyone else can be attached to their neighbourhood. Indeed, the most well-established Palestinian camps, as well as a number of African and Asian camps for refugees and internally Displaced Persons, have been urbanised to such an extent that they have become attractive urban hubs. This has led other migrants and refugees to settle either within the camps or on their peripheries, creating new urban configurations that are both poor and cosmopolitan, so that some of them now illustrate what has been termed a "centrality of the margins."[16] Furthermore, the fact that the Palestinian settlements retain their original categorisation as "camps" in the eyes of both the authorities and the inhabitants, even though they now more closely resemble densely populated, working-class suburbs, sheds light on the relationship between urbanisation and political marginality in a whole array of *heterotopias* – such as fave-

---

16   Mohamed Kamel Doraï and Nicolas Puig, L'Urbanité des marges. Migrants et réfugiés dans les villes du Proche-Orient (Paris: Téraèdre/IFPO, 2012).

las, *barrios*, slums, ghettos and townships – around the world today.[17] As all of these settlements develop and urbanise, they never completely lose the characteristics of the camp because they remain exceptional, extra-territorial, places of exclusion.

Camps continue to be characterised by uncertainty, undesirability and precariousness – three traits that must inform any speculation about their future. With that in mind, three possible scenarios may be considered. The first of these is eradication, as happened with the destruction of the migrant settlements in Patras in 2009 and Calais in 2009 and 2016. However, removing well-established camps is a much more difficult task, as the Zambian authorities discovered with regard to the Meheba camp, which was established in 1971 to house refugees fleeing from the civil war in neighbouring Angola. The first attempts to close the camp were made in 2002, following the signing of a peace accord in Angola, but these failed, and it was still home to more than 20,000 people in 2018. By then, the population included some of the original Angolan refugees and two generations of their descendants who had been born and raised in the camp, but also refugees from other central African countries, such as the Democratic Republic of the Congo, Rwanda and Burundi. The arrival of these newcomers resulted in a reorganisation of the camp within the regional context, as a hybrid but stabilised space.

This case leads us to the second possible scenario – the gradual, long-term transformation of refugee camps, which can go as far as granting them recognition and what Henri Lefebvre termed a "right to the city."[18] This is evident in the slow integration of internally Displaced Persons from South Sudan on the periphery of Khartoum and the transformation of their camps into permanent neighbourhoods.

The third potential scenario is simply waiting, which is particularly widespread at the moment. This results from compromises reached between the various forces acting with roles to play in each camp's present and future: the inhabitants, international organisations and their agents, and representatives of the national state.

Neither monstrous nor pitiful, these separate places will be perceived in a new light once they have been contextualized in the perspective of the world space and society to come. In this respect, we can observe what happens when refugees oppose the closure of their camp and refuse to move, or when communities of peasants or forest-dwellers are expelled from their land and establish a new camp in a nearby city. For instance, camps in Colombia or in Paraguay in the middle of the capital city

---

17   Loïc Wacquant, "Designing Urban Seclusion in the 21st Century," *Perspecta: The Yale Architectural Journal* 43 (2010): 165–78; Agnès de Geoffroy, "Fleeing War and Relocating to the Urban Fringe – Issues and Actors: The Cases of Khartoum and Bogotá," International Review of the Red Cross 91 (2009) 875: 509–26; Michel Agier, "Camps, Encampments, and Occupations: From the Heterotopia to the Urban Subject," Ethnos: Journal of Anthropology 84 (2019) 1: 14–26.
18   Henri Lefebvre, Le Droit à la ville (Paris: Anthropos, 1968).

Asuncion, have persisted for years as both a survival strategy and a form of political protest.

Something similar developed in the so-called "Jungle of Calais" between April 2015 and October 2016 as its number of residents increased to some 10,000 occupants. Relegated to the outskirts of the town, the Jungle emerged, in the end, as a political fact. Many organisations and individuals from all over Europe supported the inhabitants as they gradually organised themselves and established a form of autonomous governance over their own space – the Jungle – which therefore faced the control of the local and national authorities and even the NGOs, associations and concerned individuals who provided aid and professed solidarity. It is my contention that this was the real reason why the camp, which had become a political subject, was violently destroyed and the residents dispersed by force.[19]

The history of camps and encampments can therefore be considered not only as the banishment and consequent invisibility of "undesirables" but also as the presence and agency of urban, political subjects in a common world, local as well as global – a response to the demand for a place for politics beyond existing national frameworks.

---

19   See M. Agier et al., The Jungle: Calais's Camps and Migrants (Cambridge: Polity Press, 2018).

Part II
(Dis)empowering role of humanitarian intervention

Interventions by non-governmental organisations in state-run internment camps in France
The rescue of Jewish children from Rivesaltes as told through the example of Vivette Hermann

Lilly Maier

Towards the end of May 1942, Vivette Hermann wrote a letter to her fiancé Julien Samuel. Hermann was a young Jewish woman who had spent the last seven months as a social worker in the French camp Rivesaltes, where she had worked to free all of the Jewish children interned there. In the letter, which was sent shortly before her departure from the camp, she wrote: "If you only knew what it costs me to leave Rivesaltes. It's kind of a part of me that I leave there."[1]

In this quote, we can see Hermann's reluctance to abandon a place that most of the other people staying there would have done almost anything to escape. She was not the only Jewish woman to venture voluntarily into an internment camp in Vichy France, but she merits special attention because of the crucial role she played in the liberation of over 400 Jewish children from Rivesaltes.

This paper is based on extensive archival research I conducted in France and the United States for my ongoing doctoral research into Jewish women in France who rescued or helped other Jews during the Shoah.[2]

Vivette Hermann's background

Vivette Hermann was a young Jewish woman who studied philosophy at the Sorbonne in Paris. In 1939, towards the end of the Spanish Civil War, she spent a short time as a volunteer in Barcelona, where she provided milk to local children. This was

---

1   "Si tu savais ce qu'il m'en coûte de quitter Rivesaltes. C'est un peu une partie de moi que j'y laisse": Vivette Hermann to Julien Samuel, 22 May 1942, Samuel Family Private Archive, copy in possession of the author.
2   Dissertation at the University of Munich, working title: "Between Rescue and Self-help: Jewish Female Rescuers in France during the Shoah."

her first experience of relief work.³ With the approaching fall of Paris, she fled to the south of France in May 1940 to join her family. There she continued her studies in Toulouse.⁴ The following summer, Andrée Salomon recruited her to work for the *Œuvre de Secours aux Enfants* (OSE; Children's Aid Society). Although French, Hermann spoke fluent German, which was one of the reasons why the OSE was interested in hiring her.⁵ A few months later, at the age of just twenty-two, she voluntarily went into Rivesaltes to actively organise the liberation of the children on site. (Most of them were subsequently housed in French children's homes, although some were sent to the United States.) In 1942, the young woman married Julien Samuel, another OSE official, which is why she is known as Vivette Samuel in most scholarly research and her own published writings. However, she was still Vivette Hermann throughout her time in Rivesaltes, so I will refer to her as such.

Throughout this paper, I will put emphasis on Hermann's experience by quoting from her memoir *Sauver les enfants* (subsequently published in English as *Rescuing the Children*, with an additional foreword by Elie Wiesel), her unpublished 1948 report *Comme des brebis ... (Like Sheep ...)*, which is partly based on a diary she kept inside the camp, a more polished version of the same diary that she published as a journal article in 1950, monthly reports she wrote for the OSE as well as her private letters that were made available for research by the family for the first time.⁶

History of the Rivesaltes internment camp

The *Camp de Rivesaltes* was located in the commune of Rivesaltes, near Perpignan, in the south of France. Founded in 1938 as a military base due to its strategic location close to the Spanish border, its official name was Camp Maréchal Joffre, in honour of the commander-in-chief of the French forces in the First World War.⁷ The camp housed very different groups consecutively: initially, soldiers en route to the French

---

3 OSE France, "Histoire de l'OSE – les présidents et directeurs généraux: Vivette Samuel" <https://www.ose-france.org/je-decouvre/histoire/presidents-et-directeurs-generaux> (3 May 2021).
4 Ibid.
5 Vivette Samuel, Rescuing the Children: A Holocaust Memoir (Madison: University of Wisconsin Press, 2002), 29.
6 Vivette Samuel, Sauver les enfants (Paris: Levi, 1995); Samuel, Rescuing the Children; Samuel, Comme des brebis ... (Chatou: 1947–8), Mémorial de la Shoah, 3.18216; Vivette Samuel, "Journal d'une internée volontaire," Evidences 14 (1950): 6–12. Many thanks to the Samuel family for their generosity in granting access to Vivette's correspondence.
7 Joël Mettay, L'Archipel du Mépris. Histoire du Camp de Rivesaltes de 1939 à nos jours (Canet: Editions Trabucaire, 2001), 33.

colonies, then refugees from the Spanish Civil War.⁸ From 1941 on, Rivesaltes served the new Vichy government as a state-run internment camp for refugees, political opponents such as freemasons, communists and trade unionists as well as Sinti and Roma, and Jews, many of whom were deportees from Baden and the Palatinate.⁹ At first, the new arrivals were still outnumbered by the Spanish, but from July 1942 onwards (non-French) Jews were in the majority.¹⁰

Officially classified as a *Centre d'hébergement* – which loosely translates as "shelter" – the camp has usually been described as an internment camp in post-war France.¹¹ However, many historians have taken issue with this classification and have repeatedly pointed out the similarities of the Vichy camps to concentration camps run by the National Socialists.¹² For instance, the French historian Joël Mettay went so far as to call Rivesaltes "an antechamber of Auschwitz."¹³

Within the camp system in the south of France, Rivesaltes was considered a "model camp" as well as the "family camp," and the majority of children interned in Vichy France were sent there with their parents.¹⁴ It spanned 600 hectares and could accommodate up to 20,000 people in barracks that were constructed in a much more permanent way than the barracks in other French camps.¹⁵ Yet, the supply situation and the level of hygiene were catastrophic from the very beginning, and many of the internees died. In November 1940, a report by the International Red Cross described widespread malnutrition, an "invasion of rats" and an unusually high mortality rate for children and the elderly.¹⁶ (In theory, the internees should have received the same rations as the civilian population in the south of France, but reality showed a different picture.) Follow-up visits in 1941 and 1942 found that conditions had deteriorated, despite the best efforts of several relief organisations to alleviate the internees' suffering.¹⁷

---

8   Roger Barrié, Mémento chronologique du Camp de Rivesaltes, 1923–1965 (Perpignan: Musée Mémorial du Camp de Rivesaltes, 2010), 27.
9   Charles B. Paul, "Introduction," in Samuel, Rescuing the Children, xxiv; Christian Eggers, Unerwünschte Ausländer: Juden aus Deutschland und Mitteleuropa in Französischen Internierungslagern 1940–1942 (Berlin: Metropol, 2002), 14.
10 Mettay, L'Archipel du Mépris, 39–40.
11 See, for example, the official website of the Rivesaltes Camp Memorial: <https://www.memorialcamprivesaltes.eu/en/history-rivesaltes-camp-memorial> (3 May 2021).
12 Eggers, Unerwünschte Ausländer, 14–15; Paul, "Introduction," xx; Mettay, L'Archipel du Mépris, 26.
13 Mettay, L'Archipel du Mépris, 26.
14 Stephanie Corazza, "The Routine of Rescue: Child Welfare Workers and the Holocaust in France," unpublished Ph.D. thesis, University of Toronto (2017), 41; Eggers, Unerwünschte Ausländer, 92–3.
15 Eggers, Unerwünschte Ausländer, 92.
16 Mettay, L'Archipel du Mépris, 21, 45.
17 Ibid., 45; Eggers, Unerwünschte Ausländer, 442.

The Jewish internees (refugees and deportees alike) initially lived within the main camp, but in April 1941 most of them were transferred to a separate section (Îlot B) on the pretext that this would allow them to celebrate Passover in accordance with Jewish dietary laws.[18] This newly created "camp within the camp" was in a poor structural condition compared to the rest of the camp, had no electric light and was furnished with unhygienic double bunk beds.[19] Moreover, no milk was dispensed there, so the children had to walk a kilometre to Îlot J, wait in line for hours for their daily rations, then trek back to Îlot B. Many of them decided it was not worth the effort, which led to dangerous numbers of severely undernourished children in the camp.[20]

NGOs at Rivesaltes

International non-governmental aid organisations, such as the Red Cross, tried to alleviate the internees' suffering by sending *internés volontaires* ("voluntary internees") or *assistants résidents* ("resident social workers") to the camps in the south of France: doctors, nurses and social workers who lived inside the camps to offer assistance to the interned.[21] All of these voluntary internees were paid, and they enjoyed certain privileges within the camps; most importantly, they were free to leave at any time.[22]

Another NGO that was active within the camps was the OSE. Originally a Russian Jewish-relief organisation, it now ran several children's homes for Jewish refugee children in France.[23] For the Jewish social workers sent by the OSE, the situation was much more uncertain and dangerous than for those from other (foreign) organisations. After all, American or Swiss relief workers could be confident that they would be allowed to leave the camps whenever they wished, irrespective of political developments in Vichy, but for the French Jewish volunteers, it was like going into the proverbial lion's den. Who could say what would happen to them if the Vichy government, with its increasingly anti-Semitic tendencies, suddenly changed course?

---

18   Mettay, L'Archipel du Mépris, 63–5; Eggers, Unerwünschte Ausländer, 93–4.
19   Ibid.
20   Eggers, Unerwünschte Ausländer, 16–17.
21   Corazza, "Routine of Rescue," 109.
22   For example, the OSE instructed its workers to leave the camp every five weeks, and rented a room in the city of Rivesaltes so that they could occasionally wash themselves properly and sleep in a real bed. See Samuel, Rescuing the Children, 49.
23   For more about the OSE's work, see: Lilly Maier, Arthur und Lilly. Das Mädchen und der Holocaust-Überlebende (München: Heyne, 2018), 55–131.

In 1941, the German authorities requested the Vichy government to force all Jewish organisations to join the newly created *Union Générale des Israélites de France* (UGIF; General Union of French Jews), which was, in effect, a single *Judenrat* (Jewish Council) for the whole of the south – and later all – of France.²⁴ So, in 1941, the OSE had to disassemble and was forced to join the UGIF. Within the UGIF, the OSE took over the third section, *Santé* (health); they organised food distribution and medical programmes and continued running children's homes.²⁵ At the same time, the OSE was a member of the Nîmes Coordinating Committee, a coalition of twenty-five French and international NGOs that the American Donald A. Lowrie of the Young Men's Christian Association (YMCA) had founded in 1940 with the aim of boosting relief efforts in the French camps.²⁶ Other members included the Quakers (American Friends Service Committee), the Unitarian Service Committee, *Secours Suisse aux Enfants* (Swiss Relief for Children; the children's aid branch of the Swiss Red Cross) and the *Comité Inter Mouvements auprès des Évacués* (Cimade; Committee for the Movement of Refugees).²⁷ The Nîmes Committee was able to focus the efforts of its member organisations and negotiated on their behalf with the Vichy authorities to gain access to the camps.²⁸ Once inside, the NGOs fought against hunger by distributing milk and food, worked to improve sanitary and health conditions, started kindergartens and schools, and provided psychological as well as medical assistance. Even more importantly, they worked to secure the liberation of as many internees as possible, especially minors.²⁹

At the beginning of 1941, over 3,000 children – 300 of whom were under the age of three – were interned in Rivesaltes alongside their parents.³⁰ About 350 of these children were Jewish.³¹ The Nîmes Committee's *Commission des Enfants et des Vieillards* (Commission for Children and the Elderly) reported that the children in the Rivesaltes camp were both malnourished and suffering from a range of diseases and other medical conditions, including skin fungi, mucosal anaemia, protruding eyeballs, tooth decay, swollen lymph nodes and rickets.³²

After intensive lobbying, the Nîmes Committee received permission from the Vichy government to liberate children under the age of fifteen from the internment

---

24 Corazza, "Routine of Rescue," 6.
25 Samuel, Rescuing the Children, 32–5.
26 Ibid., 34.
27 Mettay, L'Archipel du Mépris, 53.
28 Ibid.
29 Ibid.
30 Eggers, Unerwünschte Ausländer, 298. OSE reports from February 1941 and 17 March 1941, Mémorial de la Shoah, CMXXI-12.
31 Eggers, Unerwünschte Ausländer, 298.
32 Ibid., 299.

camps, as long as the committee bore all costs.[33] I want to stress that this was a legal way of liberating the children. The organisations had to seek and receive the parents' permission, provide and pay for shelter for the liberated children (usually in children's homes) and, most importantly, obtain authorisation from whichever local prefecture was the intended destination for each child.[34] At first, the Vichy authorities only sporadically granted release, but their attitude changed after most of the infants interned in Rivesaltes died in an epidemic in September 1941, and the conditions in the camp continued to deteriorate.[35]

The liberation operation was extremely expensive: Vivette Hermann writes that it cost the OSE 5,000 francs to pay for lodging and food for three months, which was the required guarantee sum to liberate a child.[36] By way of comparison, just two years earlier (before the German occupation), the cost of a whole year's care in one of the OSE's children's homes had been 5,600 francs.[37] Another report by the OSE states that it was also quite expensive for the receiving children's homes because they were obliged to quarantine every new arrival.[38] Within the Nîmes Committee there were often discussions if liberating the children was worth it or if they should focus their energies on helping the internees within the compounds of the camp. The money needed to free one child could be used to help at least four inside.[39] The OSE and Swiss Aid were the two NGOs that most strongly believed that the liberation of the children had to be the priority of the Nîmes Committee. Joseph Weill, the OSE's representative on the Nîmes Committee, argued that the operation benefited not only the freed children but also their interned parents, as the latter would be able to take better care of themselves (and maybe even escape) once relieved of the responsibility of looking after their children.[40]

All of the NGOs understood the importance of maintaining good working relationships with both camp officials and the Vichy government. The camp authorities had the power to revoke access to the camps, so the relief organisations instructed their workers to abide by the rules and work within the system.[41] In fact, Vivette Hermann's predecessor, Charles Lederman, was ordered to leave Rivesaltes follow-

---

33 Samuel, Rescuing the Children, 34.
34 Ibid.; Eggers, Unerwünschte Ausländer, 447–8.
35 Eggers, Unerwünschte Ausländer, 447.
36 Samuel, Rescuing the Children, 49.
37 Ernst Papanek, "Financial Report 1939," in One Year Children's Houses, New York Public Library, Ernst Papanek Papers, Box 41.
38 "Rapport sur les conditions d'internement et de vie des enfants juifs," Mémorial de la Shoah, Fonds Lublin, CMXXI-12.
39 Samuel, Rescuing the Children, 34.
40 Ibid.
41 Corazza, "Routine of Rescue," 116.

ing reports that he had overstepped his duties and encouraged internees to escape.[42] The OSE felt that replacing him with a young woman would help to appease the camp officials.

Vivette Hermann in Rivesaltes

Vivette Hermann entered Rivesaltes on 3 November 1941 at the age of twenty-two. Her first impressions are recorded in her memoir:

> The gates went up as we showed our passes. A French flag waved at the entrance of the vast camp. […] The paths between the blocks were deserted when suddenly some children came to meet us. Dirty and in rags, they painfully advanced on the stony soil, wrapped in gray blankets. They carried rusty cans – they were going over to Swiss Aid to get a warm drink. This was the reality of the camp. Two worlds faced each other: I, well dressed, wearing a red, close-fitting garment I had knitted during the summer […], good shoes with crepe soles […]; the children all bent over and shivering in their dirty blankets. What a contrast from the very beginning between the places I came from and the destitution of the camp![43]

Hermann was acutely aware of her position as a "voluntary internee," which at once allowed her access to the camp administration, but also brought her to a position of trust and respect among the regular internees. "The internees trust us because we share their hard life," she wrote to her parents less than a week after her arrival.[44] At the same time, Hermann often felt ashamed for her privileged situation. For example, just ten relief workers shared a barrack that housed sixty internees anywhere else in the camp:

> There certainly was no comfort in that place. There was but a single source of water, most often frozen, a washbasin, and a pitcher. But we were given the opportunity of taking care of our needs in a bucket, while the internees were obliged, day and night, to go to the sanitary tubs rattling in the wind. Very quickly, I thought of myself as privileged.[45]

Hermann was often overcome by a sense of shame as she reflected on these disparities and struggled to define her place within the camp system. Hermann's main ob-

---

42 Samuel, Rescuing the Children, 29.
43 Ibid., 36. The date of her arrival is given as 3 November 1941 in her memoir but 4 November in her journal. See Samuel, Comme des brebis, 24.
44 Vivette Hermann to her parents, Rivesaltes, 8 November 1941, in Samuel, Rescuing the Children, 38–9.
45 Ibid., 37.

jective was to help the internees and it seems that she believed being seen as "one of them" would create a feeling of trust that would help her do her work. However, in many ways, it was the fact that she was *not* a regular internee, but instead a representative of an outside NGO, that put her in a position where she had the power to help. In her memoir, written decades after the letter to her parents, Hermann comes to a more nuanced description, both in regards of seeing herself as a part of the group of resident social workers in Rivesaltes as well as in the group's relation to the internees: "We were the link between them and the camp's administration, and also between them and the outside. Our function as intermediaries reassured them. Moreover, they saw us live with them and share their hard existence to some extent. This solidarity brought us closer."[46]

Hermann was shocked by the appalling conditions she encountered in Rivesaltes: "The supply of water was inadequate, and there was no central sewer for drainage. The smell of human decay pervaded everything. Clothing was shredding into rags. Rodents lived in the camp, and malaria had become endemic."[47] With no formal training as a social worker, her very first day in the camp left her feeling powerless and overwhelmed: "Nothing prepared me for this task except a sincere desire to help the men, women and children who are suffering behind the barbed wire."[48] To help her cope, she often reflected on a piece of advice from the OSE physician Joseph Weill: "Look into misery the way a doctor looks into a patient's illness."[49] This maxim features prominently in all her writings.

While in Rivesaltes, Hermann coordinated the liberation of the camp's interned children. Her responsibilities included convincing the parents to grant permission for their children's removal from the camp, preparing the children for the separation and overcoming a host of administrative hurdles during negotiations with the camp authorities.[50] Preliminary discussions with the parents revealed a sharp contrast in attitudes towards the programme depending on the background of the internees: whereas the majority of Spanish parents were against it, the Jewish parents – especially the German and Austrian deportees – jumped at the chance to save their children.[51] In her diary, Hermann quotes "all the [Jewish] women" in her packed waiting room pleading, *"Nehmen Sie mein Kind weg"* ("Take my child away").[52] Every parent

---

46   Ibid., 46–7.
47   Ibid.
48   "Rien ne m'a préparée à cette tâche, si ce n'est un désir sincère de venir en aide à des hommes, des femmes et des enfants qui souffrent derrière les barbelés": Vivette Hermann diary entry, 3 November 1941, in Samuel, Comme des brebis, 24.
49   Samuel, Rescuing the Children, 38, 47.
50   Ibid., 44.
51   Ibid., 46.
52   Samuel, "Journal d'une internée volontaire," 8.

who enrolled in the scheme had to sign an official declaration that they were entrusting their child to the care of the OSE or the UGIF to be placed in a children's home or to allow emigration to the United States on a *Kindertransport* (children's transport).[53]

Hermann had regular meetings with the camp commander David-Gustave Humbert, whom she described as very friendly and "always correct" in his dealings with the relief workers: "His qualities as a human could not be denied […] yet he appeared to be indifferent to the drama taking place around him."[54] The camp commander's office had to send all the applications for liberations, transfers, visas, etc. to the prefectural office handling the case, usually in Perpignan. The entire process was very lengthy and arduous – beds in children's homes often had the be reserved for months until all the papers arrived. By the time the liberation orders finally came, children had oftentimes been sent to other camps or had fallen ill and were not allowed to leave the camp for quarantine reasons, so the whole process had to be started all over again.[55]

Nevertheless, Vivette Hermann eventually managed to evacuate all of the Jewish children from Rivesaltes. Several convoys left the camp in the autumn of 1941, and a further fifty-five children were liberated in January and February 1942. Seven more had been granted permission to leave but were too ill to travel. A census taking shortly after showed that a total of ninety-eight Jewish children remained in the camp.[56] In a later report, Hermann explained that three groups of children were still to be liberated because the OSE had yet to receive authorisation for their release or had not submitted the requisite forms. Additionally, "some children […] for the moment still refuse to leave."[57] Interestingly, Hermann writes that the children refused to go and not that their parents refused to give permission. This speaks to a larger problem and typified the parents' and children's contrasting attitudes to their separation. In the beginning, Hermann and the OSE organised reunions and visits of the liberated children to the camp, but these were often traumatic for all parties. Oftentimes children did not want to leave again or could not handle how their parents had deteriorated since their departure.[58] So, the OSE soon stopped these visits. Instead, Vivette Hermann was able to negotiate with the camp authorities that the parents of the liberated children receive passes to visit them in the children's homes or to say

---

53   Parental forms, Dossiers 01589 and 01255, OSE Archives. For more on the French–American Kindertransport, see: Maier, Arthur und Lilly, 150–208.
54   Samuel, Rescuing the Children, 40.
55   Ibid., 43.
56   Centre d'hébergement de Rivesaltes, Bureau OSE, K 43, "Rapport d'activité du mois de Février 1942," Mémorial de la Shoah, OSE (II)-47.
57   "quelques enfants qui pour le moment refusent encore de partir" (original emphasis): report by Vivette Hermann, 1942, Mémorial de la Shoah, OSE (II)-55.
58   Samuel, Rescuing the Children, 51–2.

goodbye to them at the train station if they were on their way to the United States.[59] This proved to be much less distressing for all concerned.

Hermann was usually meticulous about following every rule to the letter. However, in February 1942, she inadvertently liberated a child over the age of fifteen. Her perspective on this incident changed over the years: In her published diary, she writes of a cunning fifteen-year-old named Joseph J. who made himself a year younger when she talked to him (thereby taking the matter of his rescue into his own hands); in her memoir, she puts the blame on herself.[60] Either way, the OSE was furious and concerned that Hermann might have jeopardised the whole operation. Fortunately, though, neither the camp authorities nor the local prefecture noticed the error. As a result, Hermann – with the blessing of the OSE – started to falsify ages deliberately, which enabled her to liberate about a dozen extra adolescents.[61]

By the end of May 1942, Vivette Hermann's work at Rivesaltes was finally done. The OSE's next report from the camp declared: "There are no more children who want to leave."[62] Over the course of just seven months, Hermann had managed to free all 400 willing Jewish children from Rivesaltes.[63] Shortly before her own departure from the camp, the OSE organised a party for the mothers of the liberated children, which happened to fall on Vivette Hermann's birthday. I want to close with a longer passage from the letter to Hermann's fiancé that I quoted before:

> Miss Mazour [sic] was at the camp, coming to pick up our last convoy of children. To mark the occasion, a party was organised last in the synagogue for all parents who have children in OSE houses … The turnout was impressive […] [Dr Malkin said:] "I don't want to forget to tell you that today is Miss Hermann's birthday. Let us wish her to marry and to be as good to her children as she was to your children." There was such thunderous applause that I started to cry.[64]

---

59 Ibid., 56. See also: "Rapport d'activité du mois de Février 1942," Mémorial de la Shoah, OSE (II)-47.

60 Samuel, Rescuing the Children, 55; Vivette Hermann, journal entry, 10 February 1942, in Samuel, "Journal d'une internée volontaire."

61 Samuel, Rescuing the Children, 55.

62 "Il ne reste plus d'enfants qui veuillent partir": Centre d'hébergement de Rivesaltes, "Rapport du mois de Juin [1942]," Mémorial de la Shoah, OSE (II)-54.

63 Samuel, Rescuing the Children, 44.

64 "Mme Mazour [sic] était au camp, venue chercher notre dernier convoi d'enfants. En cet honneur une fête avait été organisée hier soir dans la synagogue pour tous les parents qui ont des enfants dans les maisons OSE … Le nombre fut imposant […] « Je ne veux pas oublier de vous dire qu'aujourd'hui est aussi l'anniversaire de Melle Hermann. Souhaitons-lui de se marier, et d'être aussi bonne pour ses enfants qu'elle le fut pour vos enfants ». Ce fut un tel tonnerre d'applaudissements que je me suis mise à pleurer": Vivette Hermann to Julien Samuel, 22 May 1942, Samuel Family Private Archive, copy in possession of the author. "Miss Mazour" was Germaine (Jenny) Masour.

Outlook

Notwithstanding Vivette Hermann's departure, the OSE's work in the camp was far from over. In the summer of 1942, mere months after Hermann had left the camp, Rivesaltes did indeed become an "antechamber of Auschwitz" when the Vichy authorities started arresting Jewish families and deporting them to the German-run Drancy internment camp, from where they were sent to Auschwitz.[65] Following the internment of scores of Jewish children at Rivesaltes – often under the pretext of family reunification – the OSE and other NGOs stopped abiding by the rules and resorted to increasingly desperate and usually illegal tactics to save the children from deportation.[66] At the same time, the OSE clandestinely started to close its children's homes. With the help of the Jewish Résistance in France, they hid around 2,000 children under false names in French families, on farms and in monasteries. Some of the older teenagers subsequently joined the Résistance themselves. A further 1,000 children were smuggled over the border to Switzerland by the OSE.[67]

Vivette Hermann – after her marriage to Julien Samuel in an OSE children's home in Couret in October 1942 now Vivette Samuel – went to work for the OSE in Limoges and later Chambéry and was involved in organising these illegal rescue attempts. After the war, Samuel earned her diploma in social work and remained with the OSE for the rest of her working life. She oversaw the organisation's successful implementation of many modern social work practices, such as case work, and became the OSE's director general in 1979.[68]

---

65 Samuel, Rescuing the Children, 76; Eggers, Unerwünschte Ausländer, 447–9.
66 Samuel, Rescuing the Children, 84–96.
67 Katy Hazan and Serge Klarsfeld, Le Sauvetage des enfants juifs pendant l'occupation, dans les maisons de l'OSE, 1938–1945 / Rescuing Jewish Children during the Nazi Occupation: OSE Children's Homes, 1938–1945 (Paris: OSE / Somogy Éd. d'Art, 2009), 32–6; Katy Hazan and Georges Weill, "The OSE and the Rescue of Jewish Children, from the Postwar to the Prewar Period," in Resisting Genocide: The Multiple Forms of Rescue, edited by Jacques Semelin et al. (New York: Columbia University Press, 2011), 256.
68 OSE France, "Vivette Samuel" <https://www.ose-france.org/je-decouvre/histoire/presidents-et-directeurs-generaux> (3 May 2021).

Figure 1: Vivette Hermann

Source: Fonds OSE/CDJC, Mémorial de la Shoah, Fonds Vivette Samuel.

Reconstructing Lives, Creating Citizens[1]
The role of the American Jewish Joint Distribution Committee (JDC) in the rehabilitation of detainees on Cyprus, 1946-49

Anat Kutner

> Cyprus, to romantics, is the legendary island of Aphrodite Goddess of love [...] Here in Cyprus, threshold to them of their Promised Land, the refugees wait until time turns them from "illegal" into "legal" immigrants. The official army term for them is I.J.I.s – illegal Jewish Immigrants.[2]

In these words, Maurice Pearlman describes the self-perception of the post-Second World War deportees to Cyprus. Pearlman, a British-Jewish journalist, joined the Ma'apilim (illegal immigrants) ship *Theodor Herzl*[3] to give a first-hand account of its journey, and found himself arrested upon arrival in Haifa and deported to Cyprus. Before securing his release by identifying himself to the British authorities as a British reporter, he took advantage of his time in Cyprus to gather impressions in order to convey to the world the experiences of those attempting to enter Palestine. In addition, he wrote a detailed report on the activities of the JDC (American Jewish Joint Distribution Committee) in Cyprus.[4]

During the summer of 1946, the British Mandate government officials in Palestine faced an increasing number of illegal immigrants. The previously insignificant

---

1 I would like to thank my team – Ayala Levin-Kruss, Elisheva Friedlander and Ori Krausher – for all their help and good work.
2 Maurice Pearlman, A.J.D.C and the Cyprus Camps, February 1948, Cyprus Collection 1945–1949 173530, JDC Archives.
3 The ship Theodor Herzl, named after the "Father of Modern Zionism," set sail on 2 April 1947 from France, carrying 2,641 illegal immigrants. Eleven days later it was blocked by the British Navy, and its passengers were sent to Cyprus.
4 Maurice Pearlman was later the first Israeli military spokesman and the Israeli ambassador to the Congo. He wrote several books and published numerous articles. Sources on the Cyprus camps are mostly in Hebrew. My research is based largely on the JDC Archives in Jerusalem, the Cyprus Collection and the Jerusalem Collection, as well as Morris Laub's oral history. All are available on the JDC website: <https://archives.jdc.org>.

illegal immigration had begun primarily as an act of protest against restrictions the British authorities had imposed on Jewish entry to the region. This had grown to such an extent that it now threatened to overwhelm Mandate Palestine (Eretz Israel – the land of Israel – in the minds of the refugees).[5] A large number of refugees from Europe and North Africa were expressing a desire to start a new life in a Jewish state that they would help to establish in the land of Israel.[6]

The migration of refugees by sea to Palestine started a few months after the end of the Second World War. Between August 1945 and July 1946, the British authorities tried to address this issue by holding the refugees at the Atlit detention camp near Haifa and in Latrun Prison near Jerusalem before eventually releasing them according to existing immigration quotas.[7] However, conditions worsened for both the inmates and the authorities as these holding areas continued to fill, so the authorities began drafting plans to send the would-be immigrants elsewhere. The first idea was to send the immigrants back to Europe, but this failed both practically and – more importantly – in the eyes of the international media.[8]

---

5 For more about Displaced Persons in Europe, see, for example: Françoise Ouzan, "Rebuilding Jewish Identities in Displaced Persons Camps in Germany," Bulletin du Centre de Recherche Français à Jérusalem 14 (2004): 98–111; Avinoam Patt, Finding Home and Homeland: Jewish DP Youth and Zionism in the Aftermath of the Holocaust (Detroit, MI: Wayne State University Press, 2009); Avinoam Patt and Michael Berkowitz (eds), "We Are Here": New Approaches to Jewish Displaced Persons in Postwar Germany (Detroit, MI: Wayne State University Press, 2010); Yehuda Bauer, "Jewish Survivors in DP Camps and She'erith Hapletah," in The Nazi Holocaust, Part 9: The End of the Holocaust, edited by Michael R. Marrus (Berlin – New York: K. G. Saur, 2011), 526–38; Atina Grossmann, "Remapping Relief and Rescue: Flight, Displacement, and International Aid for Jewish Refugees during World War II," New German Critique 117 (2012): 61–79.

6 For more about British anti-immigration policies, see: Nahum Bogner, The Resistance Boats: The Jewish Illegal Immigration 1945–1948 (Tel Aviv: Ministry of Defense, 1993 [Hebrew]); Steven Wagner, "British Intelligence and the 'Fifth' Occupying Power: The Secret Struggle to Prevent Jewish Illegal Immigration to Palestine," Intelligence and National Security 29 (2014): 698–726.

7 For more about Atlit and Latrun, see: Yehoshua Caspi, "Prisons in Eretz Yisra'el during the British Mandate," Cathedra 32 (1984): 141–74 [Hebrew]; Mordechai Naor, Atlit Ma'apilim Camp (Atlit: Ministry of Education, 1990 [Hebrew]); Tal Misgav, Story of Latrun Internment Camp in the Mandate Period (Jerusalem: Ariav, 2008 [Hebrew]).

8 This policy was most famously implemented when refugees on the Exodus were disembarked in Haifa, loaded onto three other ships, and transported back to Marseilles. See, for example: Aviva Halamish, The Exodus Affair: Holocaust Survivors and the Struggle for Palestine (London: Syracuse University Press, 1998); Ruth Gruber, Exodus: The Ship that Launched a Nation (New York: Crown, 1999); Shai Horev, Sailors who Had Knowledge of the Sea (Haifa: Duchifat, 2015 [Hebrew]).

Figure 1: Men aboard the SS Galilah, which is flying the Israeli flag

Source: JDC Archives, Photograph Collection, NY_62672.

The decision to send illegal immigrants to Cyprus was a third blow to the Yishuv (Jewish population in Palestine) after the arrest of many of their leaders and the confiscation of weapons, including those used in self-defence. In part, this was an act of revenge by the British authorities in response to the Etzel underground's bombing of the King David Hotel on 22 July 1946, but there was also a practical aspect to the new policy: if they were in Cyprus, the illegal immigrants would be unable to elude guards and slip through barbed-wire fences into Mandate Palestine. In addition, the British hoped that ejecting those who had managed to reach the shores of Palestine might dissuade other prospective illegal immigrants from making the trip. However, the deportation of the first shiploads of refugees to Cyprus was delayed because the British were insufficiently prepared to handle uncooperative passengers, and construction of the detention centres (on the sites of former POW camps, beyond the outskirts of towns) proved to be a slow process.[9] The illegal immigrants' resistance was improvised but highly effective and continued for several days. In the

---

9   Dalia Ofer, "Holocaust Survivors as Immigrants: The Case of Israel and the Cyprus Detainees," Modern Judaism 16 (1996) 1: 1–23.

end, though, the Yishuv's leaders realised that they had no choice, so the illegal immigrants were forcibly deported to Cyprus.[10]

This brought the JDC into the picture, because support for the detainees was handled by the organisation's staff in Palestine. Charles Passman, a former member of the advisory committee to the JDC in Palestine and now its director for the Middle East and the Balkans, tried to extend his work into Cyprus's detention camps. He made several trips to the island in a bid to coordinate the JDC's aid operations. British bureaucracy as well as the physical and mental condition of the detainees created a heavy workload. The JDC also recruited Rose Viteles, an American-born social worker and volunteer who had participated in a number of Zionist operations after moving to Palestine in 1925, to undertake social work on Cyprus. She volunteered to assist in managing one camp, but the workload proved to be too much for her.[11] As a result, the JDC's leaders hired US-born and -educated Morris Laub, who had already worked with refugees as a member of the United Nations Relief and Works Agency for Refugees in the Near East (UNRRA) delegation to Greece and later as the JDC's director in northern Italy.[12] He agreed to oversee the organisation's operations on Cyprus for three months, on the assumption that the camps would not last long. Upon arrival, though, he realised that the task was far greater than he had imagined, so he offered to extend his tenure by another year, if necessary. In the spring of 1947, he brought his wife and two young children to the city of Famagusta. They would remain there until February 1949, when the last of the detainees finally immigrated to Israel.[13]

Laub's first task was to professionalise and expand the JDC's activities on the island. Shortly after his arrival, the British opened the winter camps, which increased Laub's workload, so he hired Joshua Leibner – another American who was a representative of the Kibbutz movement but only wanted to be a shepherd – as his senior

---

10 See Nahum Bogner, The Deportation Island: Jewish Illegal Immigration Camps (Tel Aviv: Am Oved, 1991 [Hebrew]), 33; Arieh J. Kochavi, "The Struggle against Jewish Immigration to Palestine," Middle Eastern Studies 34 (1998) 3: 146–67. There were limited relations with the local Cypriots, mostly in the hospitals, as well as some forms of help and the sale of food to the JDC.

11 Bogner, Deportation Island, 57.

12 During his work in Italy, Laub worked with members of the Bricha and the Mossad for Aliyah B and therefore knew the needs of the illegal immigrants and the problems of the Displaced Persons. According to Bricha people, they asked him to come. See Bogner, Deportation Island, 81.

13 For more about Laub, see his memoirs: Morris Laub, Last Barrier to Freedom: Internment of Jewish Holocaust Survivors on Cyprus, 1946–1949 (Berkeley, CA: Magnes Museum, 1985).

deputy. Leibner and his family duly moved to Cyprus from Kibbutz Ein Hashofet in Palestine.[14]

Laub's most pressing priority, which continued throughout his tenure, was to increase the budget and scope of the JDC's activities on Cyprus. In addition to improving the detainees' standard of living and addressing their medical needs, he was determined to ensure that the British fulfilled their duty of care.[15] One of the first tasks was to increase the food quota. The British had imposed strict limits on the amount of food provided to the detainees, both because they were considered prisoners-of-war and because of the economic situation back in Britain, so the JDC sought and was eventually granted permission to supplement their meagre rations.[16] The organisation was also put in charge of the detainees' welfare and medical care. Four doctors, one dentist and eight nurses were already serving in the camps by the end of January 1947. JDC staff also ran the nursery and supplemented the supply of medicines with a number of drugs that the British authorities were either unable or unwilling to provide.[17] Detainees with psychiatric problems were transferred to the government psychiatric hospital on the island.[18]

Education and vocational training

Children and teenagers were in Cyprus's camps from the very beginning. Almost every ship that made the journey to the island, starting with the *Henrietta Szold*, which left Greece on 30 July 1946, carried children and youngsters from orphanages and Kfarei No'ar (youth villages, which were actually boarding schools which functioned as kibbutz for youngsters). These passengers comprised a significant proportion of the illegal immigrants to Palestine and some of them even participated in the struggle for the right to settle there. The large number of children, and the need to provide

---

14 Leibner complemented Laub by reducing the latter's workload and especially by maintaining continuous contact with the Yishuv in Eretz Israel, primarily through his network of fellow-Kibbutzniks. See Bogner, Deportation Island, 82; Laub, Last Barrier, 4–5.
15 Ibid., 20.
16 The JDC did so by importing flour, thus providing extra bread. Children up to the age of seventeen, pregnant women and the sick and debilitated received a daily supplement of about 700 calories. The extra food included fresh fruit and vegetables, milk and egg powder, honey and jam. See Bogner, Deportation Island, 84.
17 A shortage of medical staff meant that eighteen detainees worked informally as unpaid physicians for a few hours a week, assisting the physicians and dentists sent from Palestine.
18 However, in 1947, when the Mandate government permitted pregnant and breast-feeding women as well as old and sick inmates to leave the camps and enter Palestine, some mentally ill detainees were sent along with them. See Rakefet Zalashik and Nadav Davidovitch. "Measuring Adaptability: Psychological Examinations of Jewish Detainees in Cyprus Internment Camps," Science in Context 19 (2006) 3: 419–41.

a tailor-made programme for them, led to the decision to establish a youth village in Camp 65 to house orphans who had arrived alone. Youth movement counsellors attempted to recruit any children who were not already members and set about building an orderly and pleasant environment for them, in contrast to the poor living conditions in the adults' camps at this time.[19]

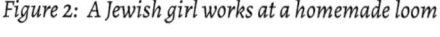
Figure 2: A Jewish girl works at a homemade loom

Source: JDC Archives, Photograph Collection, NY_12071.

Despite approving the separation of youngsters from adults, the British authorities did not grant any special privileges to the children's camp, and it was a struggle to arrange a clean water supply, medicines and beds. Luxuries such as books and classrooms were out of the question. By the end of May 1947, the number of children had increased to over 2,000, which prompted Laub to ask the British authorities to fulfil their humanitarian obligations and take care of them. In response, the British governor insisted that the camps were not his responsibility; instead, he requested

---

19 Bogner, Deportation Island, 122. The teenage girls on the Katriel Yaffe carried explosives on their bodies to try to damage the deportation ship to Cyprus.

military personnel to oversee them. Nevertheless, the JDC was granted permission to import study materials in the interest of providing the children with at least some mental stimulation.[20]

Figure 3: Children in a JDC classroom in one of the detention camps

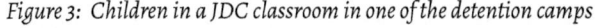

Source: JDC Archives, Photograph Collection, NY_12228.

Many of the children were illiterate because they had failed to receive a proper education during the war years. Now they demanded to be taught solely in Hebrew, so the demand for books in that language was high,[21] as was the need for classrooms. Three separate groups of children were taught by the same teachers, in the same

---

20   Ibid., 128.
21   An example of a list of Hebrew books sent to Cyprus: "List of Hebrew Books with Vowelization," Cyprus Collection 1945–1949 570349, JDC Archives.

classroom, with the same textbooks, each day. Knowledge of Hebrew was the most important factor when deciding which group a new student would join, followed by general knowledge and only then age. In addition to teaching standard lessons, the school promoted Zionist values and celebrated Zionist holidays.[22]

Educational programmes were also established for adults in the other camps, but the teachers were not professionals and there were sometimes no chairs –or even walled classrooms – for the students. Nevertheless, there was a thirst for the Hebrew language and Zionist knowledge,[23] as one of the detainees explained in an impassioned letter that appeared in a magazine published in Cyprus by students of the Gutenberg Teachers' Seminar:

> A few weeks ago, you asked the Yishuv to help the Cyprus detainees by sending cigarettes, packages, clothing etc. I would like to express my opinion, which is not mine only, but every youth's opinion: we do not need gifts. We are fed up with the spoiled bread of the desert and the detention. We do not need any materials. We need teachers! Send us teachers! This is a call of despair. If you do not want youth educated in the diaspora's spirit, if you want us to come with anger and agony, if you want good soldiers, there is only one answer: send us teachers! Teachers!!![24]

The children – as well as their teachers and leaders of the Yishuv – understood the need for more teachers and the importance of education as a tool. They wanted the future state of Israel to have good citizens, which for them meant eradicating the spirit of the diaspora. They expected more teachers to be sent from Palestine to help them prepare for life in Israel.[25]

Many of the young people in Cyprus had spent much of the previous decade in Europe's ghettos and concentration camps, in hiding or on the run. Most were either completely untrained or had received minimal training in skills that would be next to useless in their new homeland. Therefore, it was clear to both the Jewish Agency and the JDC that they would have to organise more practical training in various trades and agricultural work.[26] However, at least initially, the primary purpose of this vocational training was simply to keep the detainees occupied. Once again, Morris Laub

---

22 "Report on Schools in Cyprus Camps," 27 September 1948, Cyprus Collection 1945–1949 562883, JDC Archives.
23 Letter No. 127 from Morris Laub to Paris Education Dept. "Re: Education and Cultural Work in Cyprus Camps," 24 May 1948, Jerusalem Collection 1944–1952 2771397, JDC Archives.
24 Letter from JDC Tel Aviv to Cyprus Refugees Welfare Committee "Regarding Joint Training Seminar in Cyprus," 28 September 1948, Cyprus Collection 1945–1949 562919, JDC Archives [Hebrew; my translation].
25 Shimon Reshef and Yuval Dror, Hebrew Education in the Years of the National Homeland (Jerusalem: Bialik Institute, 1999 [Hebrew]), 125.
26 For more about the Jewish Agency, see: Ernest Stock, "The Reconstitution of the Jewish Agency: A Political Analysis," American Jewish Year Book 73 (1972): 178–93; Adi Pinhas and

requested support in the form of funding, some designated spaces for the workshops and help in building them,[27] but the British authorities were far from enthusiastic about his plans. The JDC staff attributed this reluctance to the fact that the military commander on the island believed that the camps would soon be evacuated, so any investment in new buildings and equipment would go to waste.[28]

Meanwhile, a series of meetings in Palestine debated the important issues of course content and funding. The Jewish Agency's staff devised various professional programmes, including training in printing, construction, shoemaking, sewing, cooking and tailoring, and formulated a work plan and estimated budget for each course.[29] There was agreement in principle that the costs would be shared equally by the JDC and the Jewish Agency. The former would be responsible for implementing the programme, while the latter would bear the costs for the content, which it would coordinate. The JDC's investment would be split into two stages: first, purchase of basic equipment and construction of workshops; then regular monthly payments to cover acquisition of further equipment and instructors' salaries.[30] In Cyprus, as in other places, the JDC was well aware of the Yishuv leadership's views on what detainees en route to Eretz Israel should be taught, and it attempted to implement them.[31]

Cultural integration: Shoshana Damari

The number of detainees on Cyprus started to increase in the months leading up to Passover 1948, so the Yishuv's leaders and the JDC organised a "Passover Package" to boost the spirits of those they considered members of their exiled family. On board the ship, in addition to holiday food and specially printed Haggadot, were the singer Shoshana Damari and the composer Moshe Wilensky. After arriving in Cyprus, the

---

Ori Arbel-Ganz, "Do Institutions Matter in the Age of Governance? The Jewish Agency as a Metaphor," Israel Affairs 25 (2019) 1: 185–203.

27 Memorandum of conversation, 19 June 1947, Cyprus Collection 1945–1949 569402, JDC Archives.

28 "Vocational Training," 22 January 1948, Cyprus Collection 1945–1949 569260, JDC Archives; "Vocational Training," 22 January 1948, Geneva Collection 1945–1954 753696, JDC Archives.

29 "Vocational Training Program Agreement," 22 October 1947, Cyprus Collection 1945–1949 569383, JDC Archives; "Monthly Material Requirements for Workshops under A and Ax," Cyprus Collection 1945–1949 569314, JDC Archives.

30 Boris Joffe, "Education in Europe," 10 March 1947, Geneva Collection 1945–1954 753700, JDC Archives.

31 Meeting summary, 4 July 1947, Cyprus Collection 1945–1949 569392, JDC Archives; meeting summary, Cyprus Collection 1945–1949 569410, JDC Archives; meeting minutes, 6 August 1947, Cyprus Collection 1945–1949 569305, JDC Archives; summary, 21 October 1947, Cyprus Collection 1945–1949 569289, JDC Archives.

duo made their way to the camps and performed a series of concerts – often several in a single day – for the detainees. The set list reflected a deep understanding of the audience's composition, aspirations and tastes as it included holiday songs, Zionist songs, children's songs and even a few Yiddish songs that brought tears to the eyes of many.

After hailing Damari's visit as a cultural highlight for the camps, an article in the *Davar* newspaper quoted Moshe Brachman, director of the Committee for the Exiles of Cyprus, who claimed that the detainees had memorised every word and kept every copy of the 10,000 concert programmes the committee had printed and distributed.[32] Meanwhile, Morris Laub wrote to Charles Malamuth, the JDC's spokesman, to suggest that the organisation should make full use of Damari by sending her on a European tour. He considered the singer and Wilensky as paragons of Israeli culture.[33]

Case study: the National Security Fund

For the leaders of the Yishuv, mobilisation of the people and the economy for the war effort was paramount in a period of escalating violence and the transition from Jewish community to statehood. Financing was provided through the collection of taxes, the sale of government bonds, national loans and fundraising campaigns. For example, the economic committee, a subcommittee of the ad hoc committee founded by the Jewish Agency and the Yishuv's National Council (Va'ad Leumi), conceived a campaign to raise half a million Palestine pounds. The administrators insisted that all members of the Yishuv must participate, regardless of status or political persuasion.[34]

The resulting National Security Fund (Magbit l'Bitahon Ha'Am) targeted specific individuals with substantial capital, such as businessmen, factory-owners and bankers, as well as the general public. Volunteers, mostly youth, went door-to-door collecting between two and six Palestine pounds according to each resident's ability and willingness to contribute. By the end of the campaign, the fund had raised 350,000 pounds from affluent individuals and 150,000 from the general public. David Ben-Gurion (later Israel's first prime minister) perceived the fund's success as a testament to the Yishuv's willingness to commit to the cause following the establishment of the emergency state. Nevertheless, according to an estimate made

---

32 A. Kinarti, "Shoshana Damari in Cyprus," Davar, 28 May 1948.
33 Letter from M. Laub to Mr Ch. Malamuth, "Re: Mrs Shoshana Damari – Singer," 2 May 1948, Jerusalem Collection 1944–1952 2771152, JDC Archives.
34 Yitzhak Greenberg, "Financing the War of Independence," *Studies in Zionism* 19 (1988) 1: 63–80.

by Eliezer Kaplan (a Zionist activist and the Yishuv's treasurer who would later become Israel's first treasury minister), around 63 per cent of his compatriots avoided paying their fair share and therefore shirked what he considered their essential national duty. Consequently, the National Security Fund's executive committee explored several ways in which contributions might be increased in the future.[35]

Although fundraising for security purposes was compulsory only for residents of Mandate Palestine, the detainees on Cyprus took it upon themselves to collect donations in response to a document, written in Yiddish by the Committee for National Security in March 1948, which encouraged people on the island to make contributions in the interest of safeguarding the residents of Eretz Israel. The appeal went on to explain that the only difference between the two groups was that the latter had received a certificate to enter Palestine whereas the former were still waiting for one. It concluded: "Let us be genuine and worthy of being the last generation of prosperity and the first generation of salvation."[36] Although it had no real authority in the camps, the Committee for National Security established strict guidelines for how the donations should be collected, and the social pressure it exerted persuaded many of the detainees to hand over much of the little they had.[37] In addition to money, there were substantial donations of treasured belongings, including silver kiddush goblets, gold wedding rings and other pieces of jewellery. Of course, all of these items would have had great sentimental as well as monetary value, but the detainees were determined to give as much as they could.[38]

The camps' extraordinary generosity attracted the attention of the fundraising coordinators in Palestine, who sent a letter of sincere thanks on the eve of Passover 1948:

> With reverence and tears of gratitude we received your contribution towards the protection of the people and the land. Every penny you saved from bits of sustenance, every dismantled piece of jewellery, brought with them not only encouragement to those standing in battle but something greater than that: strengthened faith in the eternity of Israel. If, after what you have been through, you have found in the depths of your soul the courage for the establishment of a nation,

---

35 Moshe Naor, "From Voluntary Funds to National Loans: The Financing of Israel's 1948 War Effort," Israel Studies 11 (2006) 3: 62–82.
36 Letter from Committee for National Security in Cyprus Camps to Committee for National Security Campaign, "Summer Camps," 1 March 1948, Jerusalem Collection 1944–1952 2771063, JDC Archives.
37 Declaration in Yiddish, 2 March 1948, Jerusalem Collection 1944–1952 2771062, JDC Archives.
38 For example, see: covering letter from Camp 70 Secretariat to Central Fund for National Security, "Regarding Donations from Cyprus Detainees," 17 May 1948, Jerusalem Collection 1944–1952 2770983, JDC Archives; cover letter from I. Yaacobovsky to Magbit Habitachon Management, "Regarding Donations Account," 10 August 1948, Jerusalem Collection 1944–1952 2770938, JDC Archives.

for public organisation and for contributions, you and we shall be blessed. We believe in complete faith: the brand plucked from the fire will be planted in the homeland and will flourish and prosper.[39]

As is clear from this letter, the Yishuv appreciated that the detainees had sacrificed a great deal to make such a substantial contribution to the cause. Moreover, it shows that they knew the camps' generosity was a manifestation of the residents' determination to make their own way to Eretz Israel. The leaders in the camps already saw themselves as integral parts of the Yishuv's institutions, while the detainees saw themselves as citizens of the future state of Israel whose arrival had merely been delayed by a set of unfortunate circumstances.

The camps officially closed in February 1949, whereupon the majority of detainees immediately immigrated to Israel. However, two groups remained on Cyprus: young men of fighting age whom the British wanted to keep away from the conflict in Israel and individuals who were too sick to travel. The British authorities subsequently repurposed most of the camps' building materials, and today only a small museum – housed in a reconstructed hut – remains on one of the sites.

Summary

Life in the tents and huts of Cyprus's detention camps was characterised by significant physical and emotional strain. The lack of privacy and the fact that the detainees were often treated as if they were prisoners-of-war made daily life unpleasant. On the other hand, many of the detainees reassured themselves that they were merely on an extended stopover en route to the Promised Land. This explains why they devoted so much time and effort to learning Hebrew, the customs of the Yishuv and even the songs of Eretz Israel. In some ways, mainly because they knew it was only a matter of time before they would become legal citizens of Israel, they even acted as if they were already residents and donated much of the little they had to the nascent state's coffers.

The refugees on Cyprus were unique because they symbolised a conflict between two opposing forces. On one side were the British authorities in Palestine – and on Cyprus – who had resolved to control the number of people entering the country and thereby its demographic composition. On the other were the illegal immigrants who viewed entering Mandate Palestine as their natural right, especially given all they had endured during the war and were still enduring as refugees in post-war

---

39   Thank-you letter from Magbit Hitgaisut, 19 April 1948, Jerusalem Collection 1944–1952 2770984, [Hebrew; my translation].

Europe. Thus, Cyprus's detainees were important players in an international conflict between pre-war imperialism and post-war self-determination.

Only an organisation without any political affiliation, such as the JDC, could step in to resolve the complex humanitarian crisis that had arisen on Cyprus. On the one hand, it had the means and the organisational ability to provide desperately needed basic humanitarian aid as well as cultural and educational programmes that gave the detainees' current lives some meaning and helped them prepare for their future lives in Israel. On the other hand, it was not perceived as a Zionist organisation, so the British authorities allowed its workers and teachers to enter the camps and provide these services. By operating under the British radar in this way, the JDC was able to help a group of people who had been denied the opportunity to become citizens of Eretz Israel to transform themselves into better citizens of the state of Israel.

Civilian internees, common criminals or dangerous communists?
The International Committee of the Red Cross, the United Nations Command and internment in South Korea, 1950–53

Jean-Michel Turcotte

June 2020 marked the seventieth anniversary of the start of the Korean War, and most of the conflict's social, military and political aspects have now been thoroughly analysed in a substantial scholarly corpus on the subject.[1] However, the internment of civilians in South Korea is still relatively unknown, especially among non-Korean-speaking academics. This is rather intriguing, considering the attention historians usually pay to the issue of prisoners-of-war (POWs).

The repatriation of POWs was a cornerstone of the armistice negotiations and also provoked violence in UN POW camps.[2] In addition to captured enemy soldiers, South Korean police and military forces – with the cooperation of US authorities – interned thousands of non-military captives who were blurrily categorised as "common criminals," "refugees," "internees" or "POWs." In light of the United States' and South Korea's fiercely anti-communist stance at the time, and the fact that many of these civilians were considered communists, traitors, criminals, spies and/or guerrillas, their detention was especially harsh.[3] Nevertheless, their plight remains largely unexplored. This paper aims to rectify this oversight, in part at least, by

---

1   Steven H. Lee, "The Korean War in History and Historiography," Journal of American–East Asian Relations 21 (2014) 2: 185–206.
2   David C. Chang, The Hijacked War: The Story of Chinese POWs in the Korean War (Stanford, CA: Stanford University Press, 2019); Monica Kim, The Interrogation Rooms of the Korean War: The Untold History (Princeton, NJ: Princeton University Press, 2019), 174–216; Charles S. Young, Name, Rank, and Serial Number: Exploiting Korean War POWs at Home and Abroad (New York: Oxford University Press, 2014); and Susan Carruthers, Cold War Captives: Imprisonment, Escape, and Brainwashing (Berkeley: University of California Press, 2009).
3   Sahr Conway-Lanz, "The Struggle to Fight a Humane War: The United States, the Korean War, and the 1949 Geneva Conventions," in Do the Geneva Conventions Matter?, edited by Matthew Evangelista and Nina Tannenwald (Oxford: Oxford University Press, 2017), 69–104.

analysing primary sources relating to the work of the International Committee of the Red Cross (ICRC), a humanitarian organisation that conducted inspections of South Korea's prisons and POW camps between 1950 and 1953.

It is my contention that internment operations in South Korea as well as the work of the ICRC need to be understood through the prism of the political warfare of the early Cold War. Violent anti-communist policy contributed to shaping a perception among US and South Korean authorities that the latter's civilian internees were highly "dangerous individuals." In turn, this perception motivated the South Korean authorities to tighten their internment practices and refuse to recognise the majority of civilian captives as internees or political prisoners, irrespective of the recent adoption of the 1949 Geneva Conventions. Moreover, it prompted the United Nations Command (UNC) to abrogate any responsibility for the prisoners' treatment on the grounds that their internment was a Korean "national" issue. For the ICRC, the complexity of the ideological struggle in Korea, coupled with the work of United Nations' civilian agencies, frustrated its efforts to ensure that all sides abided by international humanitarian law (IHL).[4] By the end of the conflict, countless internees had become victims of international politics and the US and South Korean military and political authorities' deeply subjective, anti-communist interpretations of IHL. As a major consequence, although the ICRC's representatives undertook forty-seven visits to civilian sites between December 1950 and May 1953, they were able to offer only limited humanitarian assistance to individuals who were often in states of abject deprivation.[5]

A difficult humanitarian situation, autumn 1950

On 26 June 1950, a day after North Korean forces invaded the South and thereby started a three-year war, the ICRC in Geneva, in accordance with the 1949 Geneva Conventions, offered its services to all governments involved in military operations

---

4   Geoffrey Best, War and Law since 1945 (Oxford: Oxford University Press, 1994), 350–54; and Suzannah Linton, "Deciphering the Landscape of International Humanitarian Law in the Asia-Pacific," International Review of the Red Cross 101 (2019) 911: 756–8.

5   Catherine Rey-Schyrr, De Yalta à Dien Bien Phu: Histoire du Comité International de la Croix-Rouge 1945–1955 (Geneva: CICR, 2007), 518–87; Jeanne Briand, "Le Travail humanitaire et la guerre de Corée: La Croix Rouge Internationale dans le camp de Kojedo," in La Guerre de Corée et ses enjeux stratégiques de 1950 à de nos jours, edited by Pierre Journaud (Paris: L'Harmattan, 2015), 139–56; Tessa Morris-Suzuki, "Unconventional Warfare: The International Committee of the Red Cross and Humanitarian Dilemmas in Korea 1950–53," History Australia 10 (2013) 2: 15–34; and Caroline Moorehead, Dunant's Dream: War, Switzerland and the History of the Red Cross (New York: Carroll & Graf, 1999), 569–79.

on the Korean peninsula. However, while the US-led UN forces, deployed to support the South Korean regime, accepted the offer, North Korea and China refused to allow any ICRC representatives on their territory. Moreover, while US General Douglas MacArthur, commander-in-chief of the UNC, and South Korean president Syngman Rhee declared that UN forces would respect the 1949 Geneva Conventions, they referred only to the third Convention, which relates to recognised combatant prisoners-of-war, and therefore implicitly excluded civilians.[6]

The plight of civilians was an issue for the ICRC as early as October 1950. Although two of the organisation's delegates in Korea, Frédérick Bieri and Jacques de Reynier, had no official accreditation to visit civilian sites of detention, they witnessed first hand the harsh treatment meted out to civilians arrested on the streets of Seoul for political reasons. For instance, in one report, de Reynier described "lamentable processions of men and women" identified as communists and guards hitting "these unfortunate people with sticks anywhere and for nothing."[7] Two months later, he raised the issue during a personal meeting with South Korea's acting minister of foreign affairs, Chung W. Cho: "[We] witnessed a group of civilian prisoners all tied to a rope, marching towards Westgate Prison. We followed them until they entered the prison, where, by the way, we saw a number of female prisoners (some with infants on their backs) kneeling on the ground with bowed heads."[8] In response, the minister admitted that conditions inside the prison were bad, but claimed that, "contrary to rumours," these individuals were "criminals, suspects, traitors or collaborators" and that "no civilians were ever arrested because of their ideology or belief."[9]

The ICRC in Geneva decided to press the South Korean authorities on this matter, so it requested a meeting between de Reynier and President Rhee. This strategy succeeded, as he eventually obtained official permission to visit two prisons for civilians in Seoul and Taegu. On arrival, he was shocked by the brutal conditions: nearly twenty deaths each day, extra-judicial executions and incarcerated women and children; no medical or washing facilities; more than twenty captives in cells designed for three; no special care for nursing mothers; endemic dysentery and tuberculosis; and, finally, obvious signs of malnutrition, torture and physical mistreatment. According to de Reynier, notwithstanding further South Korean denials, these captives

---

6   Rey-Schyrr, De Yalta à Dien Bien Phu, 526–7.
7   Report by J. de Reynier, 25 September–5 October 1950, cited in ibid., 573.
8   ICRC Delegation to South Korea to President of South Korea, 18 December 1950, in Le Comité International de la Croix-Rouge et le Conflit de Corée: Recueil de documents du CICR I, 26 juin 1950–31 décembre 1951 [Recueil de documents du CICR I] (Geneva: CICR, 1952), 165.
9   South Korean Ministry of Foreign Affairs to ICRC Delegation to South Korea, 18 December 1950, in ibid.

were clearly political prisoners. The jailers treated the prisoners so brutally solely because they were deemed "communist criminals and traitors." None of the captives had faced trial or been found guilty of any common law or other crime.[10]

De Reynier had worked with POWs in the Second World War and during the 1948 Arab–Israeli War, but the conditions in South Korea were the worst he had seen. He counted some fifty dead bodies, and even witnessed with horror a woman giving birth on the floor of a crowded cell:

> We are facing a typical case of abuse of power. 9,200 people are dying slowly just because they are communists. They are dying like dogs, without care, without news, without medication, handcuffed for more than a month [...] all this immense silent suffering and without relief is due exclusively to the wickedness of men. I am sorry, I cannot give an objective report, I myself am sick of it, I have never seen anything worse in my life and I have visited hundreds of camps.[11]

Although de Reynier's reports – including alarming photographs – were sent to the UNC, the United Nations and the South Korean and US governments, the ICRC was in a complex legal position that hampered its efforts to provide humanitarian aid and relief to the internees. Although the US military authorities expressed concern for the prisoners, they refused to accept any responsibility for their welfare because of their civilian status; instead, they simply referred the matter to the South Korean government. Similarly, the UNC did not intervene, even after an internal memorandum had stated that the situation may adversely affect the war effort by demoralising the troops and discrediting the organisation's military operations.[12]

Perhaps because he had seen the deplorable state of the prisons for himself during a series of personal visits, President Rhee was rather more receptive to the ICRC's concerns. He announced his intention to improve living conditions, provide better medical care, reduce the number of captives per cell and the number of death sentences, and release 11,000 of the 27,000 prisoners who were currently in detention. In addition, he granted the ICRC official authorisation to visit all of the prisons. Nevertheless, Chung W. Cho continued to refer to the prisoners as "dangerous criminals" and "common law offenders," claimed that "communists only think of killing" and insisted that it was his duty "to kill them first, before they have an opportunity to kill others."[13] He also declared that, while the South Korean govern-

---

10   Ibid.
11   Report by J. de Reynier, 14 December 1950, C SC, Corée, Vol. 1409, Archives du CICR [ACICR], Geneva.
12   K. B. Bush to State Department, 19 December 1950; and Report by Colonel Chaplin, 22 December 1950, RG554, Entry 217, Box 1, National Archives and Records Administration [NARA], College Park, MD.
13   South Korean Ministry of Foreign Affairs to ICRC Delegation to South Korea, 18 December 1950, in Recueil de documents du CICR I, 166.

ment was doing everything in its power to help the prisoners, it was engaged in "a life and death struggle" against communism.[14] Although the UNC reclassified thousands of individuals captured with North Korean troops as refugees, these captives were still detained in POW camps, albeit in separate compounds. Moreover, US officers concluded that they must be categorised "as persons dangerous to the aims of the United Nations in Korea […] if left at large."[15]

Visiting prisons in 1951

Although some modest improvements had been made by the spring of 1951, leading the ICRC delegates to describe the prison system as a "tolerable regime," they noted that the guards were still violent towards the internees and all of the facilities were still overcrowded and poorly equipped. Similarly, after a visit to a hospital in Taegu, de Reynier described it as "the most awful possible hell: dirty, smelly, messy, people dying without care everywhere."[16] In another report, he turned his attention to the brutality of the South Korean criminal justice system and lamented that "it is difficult to change a culture of bullies" and that "changing the customs of a country takes centuries."[17] His conclusion was that the vast majority of detainees were actually political prisoners, but they were treated as common criminals under South Korean law even if they had not been charged with any offence.[18] Also, the lack of official support from the US authorities meant that it was still difficult to deliver humanitarian aid to interned civilians. Towards the end of December 1950, the UNC had tacitly agreed that the ICRC could visit civilian internees in official POW camps by reasserting its commitment to respect the 1949 Geneva Convention on military prisoners.[19] However, while some individual US officers agreed that steps should also be taken to release some of those held in South Korea's prisons, or at least bring them under the protection of the Geneva Conventions, UNC memorandums recommended taking no action on this "domestic" issue in order to avoid any responsibility for the "inhumane treatment, atrocious conditions and brutal and arbitrary mass executions of political prisoners."[20] The thinking was that any perceived UNC involvement in an international scandal could have a negative impact on public opinion and the morale of UN troops.

---

14   South Korean Ministry of Foreign Affairs to ICRC, 25 January 1951, in ibid., 169.
15   K. B. Bush to Commanding General, 12 January 1951, RG6, Box 3, Folder 5, MacArthur Memorial Archives and Library, Norfolk, VA.
16   Report by J. de Reynier, 2 April 1951, B AG 210 056–001, ACICR.
17   Report by J. de Reynier, 19 January 1951, C SC, Corée, Vol. 1410, ACICR.
18   Report by J. de Reynier, 2 March 1951, B AG 210 056–001, ACICR.
19   Colonel Chaplin to UNC, 22 December 1950, RG554, Entry 217, Box 1, NARA.
20   K. B. Bush to State Department, 19 December 1950, RG554, Entry 217, Box 1, NARA.

Although ICRC delegates were allowed to conduct nine prison visits in 1951, an early resolution of the problem of civilian captives remained highly unlikely not only because the issue was inseparable from South Korean domestic politics but also because Washington and the United Nations had called for an official commission on the treatment of all internees. In addition, the delegates' travel and security throughout Korea and the distribution of relief both depended on the cooperation of the UNC, as humanitarian aid came under the auspices of the United Nations Civil Assistance Corps and the United Nations Korean Reconstruction Agency. In light of the UN forces' advance into North Korea in April 1951, de Reynier suggested that the UNC should open some camps strictly for civilians. He argued that such an approach would clarify the status of the internees and help to solve the problem of South Korea's overcrowded prisons. In addition, any civilians captured in North Korea by UN forces clearly could not be classified as South Korean citizens, so they should remain the legal responsibility of the UNC until their release. De Reynier also noted that prison directors in Taegu and Pusan had disclosed that 80 per cent of their detainees were political prisoners and several individuals claimed to be North Korean citizens. He urged Geneva to make a formal approach to the South Korean government and the UNC to clarify the ICRC's position, discuss these issues, promote the organisation's role and facilitate the delivery of humanitarian aid to the internees.[21]

De Reynier was far from popular with the military authorities in South Korea. For instance, his insistence that US General William Beiderlinden and his deputies must provide aid to the civilian internees prompted the UNC to threaten an official complaint against him for repeated violations of his accreditation. De Reynier responded that he welcomed such a complaint as it would demonstrate both the ICRC's concern for Korean civilians and the deplorable attitude of the UNC.[22] Henry Meyer, a physician with the Danish Red Cross, experienced similar hostility from US officers during his visits to camps in 1951, when he was routinely ordered to "close [his] eyes, mouth and ears, [and told] that it was not [his] business to interfere with political prisoners."[23]

Despite further improvements in the summer of 1951, conditions inside South Korea's prisons remained appalling, with an occupancy rate of 300 per cent on some sites. According to de Reynier, a "dead silence" hung over these institutions. Most importantly, the vast majority of the captives had been detained for political reasons. For example, de Reynier cited the case of a fifteen-year-old girl who had been sentenced to life imprisonment for espionage. He remained understandably pessimistic about such prisoners' prospects and suggested that "only death [is] certain

---

21 Report by J. de Reynier, 2 April 1951, B AG 210 056–001, ACICR.
22 Ibid.
23 H. Meyer to David de Traz, 2 November 1951, B AG 225 056–003, ACIRC.

in the short term."[24] Meanwhile, Henry Meyer reported that South Korea's treatment of political prisoners "constitute[d] one of the most distressing chapters of the war in Korea," not least because of the "disgusting conditions" in which they were held. While he acknowledged that some of these internees were suspected members of the Communist Party or so-called "leftists," he stressed that others were POWs awaiting transfer to other camps, common criminals, victims of personal revenge or simply relatives – including the wives and children – of captives.[25]

Internees and POWs, 1952

The line between POWs and internees was often blurred. In addition to captives held in South Korea's prison system, thousands of internees found themselves in POW camps, especially the most important one at Koje-do, about sixty kilometres from Busan.[26] In the autumn of 1951, the UNC reclassified 37,500 individuals – including 368 refugees – from prisoner-of-war to civilian status on the grounds that they were South Korean citizens who had been forcibly conscripted into the North Korean army.[27] Although the UNC expressed its intention to uphold the Geneva Conventions with regard to these internees, it refused to build specific camps for them; instead, they were held in compounds controlled by the South Korean authorities.[28] In accordance with US policy on non-forcible repatriation, POWs and civilian internees were asked if they wished to be repatriated to North Korea after the armistice. This triggered violence in the compounds as many captives had no faith in the proposed screening process and demanded recategorisation.[29]

The complexity of this issue was especially evident in Koje-do's Section 62. The camp contained some 6,000 internees who unexpectedly requested repatriation to North Korea and recategorisation as POWs, boldly refused any screening and eventually launched a violent revolt. De Reynier's colleague Frédérick Bieri expressed his puzzlement over these captives' "change of heart." During his last visit to the camp in August 1951, the three leaders of Section 62 had been openly anti-communist, yet now they seemed to be ardent communists. For Otto Lehner, newly appointed head of the ICRC in Korea, the main challenge was how to provide aid to these internees

24 Report by J. de Reynier, 5 August 1951, C SC, Corée, Vol. 1411, ACICR.
25 H. Meyer to D. de Traz, 2 November 1951, B AG 225 056–003, ACIRC.
26 Report by F. Bieri, 5–11 December 1951, C SC, Corée, Vol. 1411, ACICR. The camp contained 156,652 captives, including 32,213 civilians.
27 American Consulate General, Geneva, to ICRC, 27 December 1951, B AG 210 056–004, ACICR.
28 General Ridgway to Commanding General, 3 November 1951, RG554, Entry A-1, Box 29, NARA.
29 Rosemary Foot, A Substitute for Victory: The Politics of Peacemaking at the Korean Armistice Talks (Ithaca, NY: Cornell University Press, 1990), 108–29; and Allan R. Millett, "War behind the Wire," Quarterly Journal of Military History 21 (2009) 2: 52.

within the limits of the Geneva Conventions while avoiding instrumentalisation by either pro-communist elements or US officers.[30] Commenting on a violent riot in Section 62 in February 1952 that had left 69 internees dead and 142 injured, the UNC criticised the ICRC for sending its report on the incident[31] to North Korea. According to the UNC, "the ICRC have no legal or moral obligation to supply them [the North Korean authorities] with any information of the incident [...] North Korea have no further interest in them [the internees] and, consequently, have no right to any report concerning them" because the rioters had been classified as civilians.[32]

Elsewhere, the ICRC was still seeking permission to visit many sites, which obviously hindered its attempts to provide humanitarian relief or indeed exert pressure on the authorities to improve conditions. Moreover, the UNC had reclassified some civilians as guerrillas and transferred them to designated camps. After gaining access to these camps, the ICRC delegates noted arbitrary trials and executions as well as the now familiar atrocious living conditions. In response, the South Korean authorities declared their intention to improve the situation in the camps in accordance with the "spirit" of the Geneva Conventions. They also promised impartial trials for captives who had been sentenced to death, even if these "criminals" had already been tried under the Korean penal code, "one of the best in the world."[33] Nevertheless, Lehner remained sceptical and concerned that the plight of the internees would harm the ICRC's reputation as one of the world's leading humanitarian organisations. In the hope of securing better access to the detainees, he and the other delegates decided to refrain from any open criticism of the authorities' treatment of the "guerrillas."

Meanwhile, ICRC delegates Jean Courvoisier and Maurice Piot visited a total of fifteen prisons holding some 15,000 prisoners and noted that 530 of the captives were minors and only 20 per cent were genuine "common criminals." Some of the sites that were housing women and children under the age of twelve had serious structural, sanitation and medical problems. In their reports,[34] Courvoisier and Piot criticised the UN's handling of the official civilian aid and relief operations as well as its apparent lack of interest in South Korea's prisons, despite the urgent need to improve conditions. Moreover, they suggested that the ICRC might face similar accusations of indifference, given its knowledge of the situation and lack of progress in rectifying it. Around the time that he and Piot were compiling their reports, a US judge-advocate whom the UNC had appointed to assess conditions in South Korea's prisons and camps informally admitted to Courvoisier that the Americans had

---

30 Reports by F. Bieri, 4–16 January 1952, C SC, Corée, Vol. 1412, ACICR.
31 Report by Jean F. Munier and G. Hoffmann, 26 February 1952, B AG 210 056–012, ACICR.
32 Major General Bryan Milburn to O. Lehner, 15 March 1952, B AG 210 056–001, ACICR.
33 O. Lehner to Eugène de Weck, 25 March 1952, B AG 210 056–001, ACICR.
34 Reports by J. Courvoisier and M. Piot, 26 February–31 March 1952, C SC, Corée, Vol. 1412, ACICR.

a moral, if not a legal, responsibility towards the internees. He even suggested that it might be worth contacting high-ranking US officers to discuss the situation as the UNC was keen to avoid an international scandal.

After reading Courvoisier and Piot's reports, Lehner pressed the South Korean Under-Minister of Justice to increase the prisons' food rations and medical supplies. He also noted that although the South Korean authorities had pardoned and released a number of detainees (10 per cent of the total, according to President Rhee), further arrests had then been made. Consequently, prison overcrowding was still a serious issue, and it would remain so until at least half of the detainees had been released.[35] In response, the South Korean Ministry of Foreign Affairs stated that "Operation Ratkiller," which aimed to root out North Korean communists and guerrillas among the civilian population, would soon be over, at which point a large number of internees would be released.[36]

The end of internment

In Koje-do, which was still housing 37,390 internees as late as February 1953, civilian detainees' living conditions were similar to those of official POWs, although ICRC delegates noted that they endured especially strict enforcement of security rules because they were considered "fanatics and communists."[37] Nevertheless, according to one UNC officer, tensions between guards and captives eventually eased, due in part to the presence of the ICRC, which had helped to calm the atmosphere in the camp.[38] In South Korea's prisons, by contrast, the internees' living conditions were still appalling due to the lack of relief and the brutal and arbitrary treatment they received at the hands of their captors.

Otto Lehner remained sceptical about the ICRC's capacity to improve the situation throughout much of his tenure in South Korea. For example, in January 1952, he wrote: "[T]he problem of political prisoners is almost unsolvable. It is not enough to visit inmates to see how they perish if we cannot help them. However, as you know, we are not allowed to take any kind of relief action."[39] Six months later, as he re-

---

35 ICRC Delegation to South Korea to South Korean Ministry of Foreign Affairs, 6 March 1952, in Le Comité International de la Croix-Rouge et le Conflit de Corée: Recueil de documents du CICR II, 1 janvier–30 juin 1952 [Recueil de documents du CICR II] (Geneva: CICR, 1952), 57.
36 South Korean Ministry of Foreign Affairs to ICRC Delegation to South Korea, 13 May 1952, in Recueil de documents du CICR II, 50.
37 As reported by Colonel Claudius O. Wolfe to Commanding General, 2 February 1953, RG554, Entry UD-UP 127-C, Box 509, NARA.
38 Report Lieutenant Colonel Alanson T. Leland, 21 February 1953, RG554, Entry A-1 1332, Box 141, NARA.
39 O. Lehner to ICRC, 31 January 1952, cited in Rey-Schyrr, De Yalta à Dien Bien Phu, 575.

flected on sixteen inspections the ICRC had conducted between February and May 1952, he concluded that further visits could be justified only if they resulted in concrete aid and relief for the internees. With a view to securing that relief, he advised the South Korean government to submit an official request for medical supplies and nutritional supplements to ICRC headquarters in Geneva. Moreover, according to Lehner, such an approach might have the added benefit of persuading the UNC to change its position on civilian aid. In the meantime, he and the delegates decided to suspend their prison visits in order to preserve the international reputation of the ICRC, exert pressure on the UN authorities and forestall accusations that the delegates always returned "empty-handed."[40]

Although the South Korean government acted on Lehner's advice and accepted the ICRC's offer of aid, it was months before the UNC altered its position, which delayed the delivery of vital supplies to thousands of imprisoned Koreans. In October 1952, Geneva asked Lehner to remind UN authorities in Tokyo and South Korea of the importance of the ICRC's mission, as there had been no prison visits for five months.[41] The visits resumed at the end of the month after the UN's civilian agencies belatedly authorised the distribution of the ICRC's material and medical aid packages. In the months that followed, the organisation's delegates persuaded the South Koreans to isolate all captives with tuberculous in a single camp and commute all death sentences. However, the purchase, transport and distribution of medicinal and food relief remained sluggish because of poor coordination between the ICRC, the UN and local authorities.[42] Lehner made two final visits to South Korea's prisons after the signing of the armistice in July 1953. He noted some medical, dietary and accommodation improvements, especially in relation to the treatment of minors and tuberculous patients.[43]

Although a large majority of South Korea's civilian internees were released during the summer of 1953, those identified as communists remained in prison, sometimes for decades. Moreover, their situation was not helped by the fact that the ICRC ceased operations on the peninsula at the end of the year.[44]

---

40 List of visits, February–May 1952, and O. Lehner to South Korean Ministry of Foreign Affairs, 24 June 1952, in Recueil de documents du CICR II, 53 and 55, respectively.
41 E. de Weck to O. Lehner, 30 October 1952, B AG 210 056–004, ACICR.
42 Report by ICRC Delegation to Korea, May 1953, B AG 210 056–001, ACICR.
43 Rey-Schirr, p. 576.
44 Amnesty International, South Korea: Prisoners of Conscience Held for over 40 Years (London: Amnesty International, 1993) <https://www.amnesty.org/en/wp-content/uploads/2021/06/asa250411993en.pdf> (14 November 2021).

Conclusion

In the context of the early Cold War, the ICRC's efforts to provide relief to non-military captives in South Korea were frustrated by deep-rooted hostility towards the detainees' alleged political ideology as well as the complexity of an internment system in which the South Korean government, the UNC and UN aid agencies all played significant and often overlapping roles. Throughout the conflict, the organisation's attempts to deliver assistance to internees, refugees, political prisoners and guerrillas were hampered by the UNC's and South Koreans' fiercely anti-communist policies, many captives' violent refusal to accept their officially designated status and the UN authorities' unwillingness to adhere to the Geneva Convention on the treatment of civilians. The lack of any clear recognition of the internees' legal status under the terms of that Convention was reflected in the UNC's and South Koreans' determination to label them "common criminals." Finally, the ICRC was reluctant to exert pressure on the UN authorities after the spring of 1953 because, by then, negotiations for an armistice between the UNC and the North Koreans had reached a critical and very delicate stage. These factors meant that civilians were held captive in South Korea's prisons and POW camps – and remained prisoners of the Cold War – until the very end of the Korean War and sometimes far beyond.

Vicious circles of disempowerment
The social dynamics of contemporary German refugee shelters

Birgit Behrensen

Introduction

In Germany, refugees seeking protection are often obliged to live under highly controlled and disempowering conditions – not for a short time, but for years. This is particularly evident in their housing.

After applying for asylum, all refugees in Germany are first required to live in one of several central reception centres. Resettlement in an assigned municipality usually follows, but in some cases, the initial reception centre or another large camp may remain the only legal place of residence.

As long as an asylum case is pending, the assigned municipality decides where the asylum-seeking person is allowed to reside. Only a minority of municipalities in Germany offers private apartments for asylum-seekers prior to their recognition. Most of the others provide shared, supervised accommodation in smaller or larger refugee shelters for most of their assigned refugees. Legal changes in 2019 have meant that municipalities now have the power to keep a large number of refugees in these shelters for far longer than was previously the case. Thus far, there has not been a comprehensive survey of refugees' accommodation. Nevertheless, there are statistical indications that the number of asylum-seekers in shelters has grown disproportionately compared to that in private housing since 2008.[1]

Concisely, many refugees in Germany are forced to live in some form of centralised refugee shelter for many years. While living there, they experience a lack of privacy and restricted opportunities to live an independent life.

The aim of this paper is to shed light on how the organisation of refugee shelters affects the self-determination of people who are seeking protection. This will

---

1   Kay Wendel, Unterbringung von Flüchtlingen in Deutschland: Regelungen und Praxis der Bundesländer im Vergleich (Frankfurt a. M.: Pro Asyl, 2014), 70ff.

provide clues as to how the logic of refugee shelters contributes to the incapacitation and disempowerment. The focus is on Brandenburg, a federal state in the east of Germany.

Empirical approach

The thoughts and investigations presented here comprise the first findings of an ongoing content-analytical evaluation of documents, semi-structured expert interviews, participatory observation, and unstructured expert conversations in Brandenburg and elsewhere. The evaluated documents include those pertaining to the municipal implementation of the Admission Act in Brandenburg, published transcripts of political debates, publications by refugee organisations and supporting networks, newspaper articles and scientific studies that discuss the situation in Brandenburg's refugee shelters and elsewhere. Expert conversations and interviews have been conducted with former and current residents of refugee shelters, representatives of refugee organisations and supporting networks, trained social workers, semi-skilled workers in the field and other employees who are involved in the organisation and administration of Brandenburg's refugee shelters. All but one of the expert interviews were audio-recorded and transcribed, with due consideration paid to maintaining the contributors' anonymity and adhering to data protection legislation. The expert conversations were summarised in bullet points. Thus far, this research has elicited statements from thirty-two people.

In addition to her core activity as a university lecturer, the author has been working on this study since 2019, with some help for the interviews from her team. The data collection and analysis remain incomplete at the time of writing. Analysis of the material that has been collected began with defining deductive and inductive categories according to the concept of qualitative content analysis.[2] In addition, the author has utilised some grounded theory methodologies.[3] She is currently exploring the notions of minimum and maximum comparisons as well as axial coding. Informed by her concept of inequality-reflecting social research,[4] the author will discuss her findings in various communities in Brandenburg. However, as mentioned, the processes of data collection, analysis, interpretation, and discussion

---

2   Philipp Mayring, Qualitative Inhaltsanalyse: Grundlagen und Techniken, 12th ed. (Weinheim: Beltz, 2015).
3   Anselm Strauss and Barney Glaser, The Discovery of Grounded Theory: Strategies for Qualitative Research (Mill Valley, CA: Sociology Press, 1967).
4   Birgit Behrensen, "Umrisse einer ungleichheitsreflektierenden Sozialforschung," in Fluchtmigrationsforschung im Aufbruch: Methodologische und Methodische Reflexionen, edited by Birgit Behrensen and Manuela Westphal (Wiesbaden: Springer VS, 2019), 51–63.

were still ongoing at the time of writing. Therefore, the following thoughts and findings should be considered as preliminary and interim results.

Overall structures of refugee shelters in Germany

The lives of refugees during the asylum-seeking process in Germany are characterised by financial constraints, limited freedom of movement, and restricted access to all forms of economic and social participation. Assignment to a refugee shelter adds cramped housing, a lack of privacy and living in an involuntary community with people of different origins and languages to this already disempowering situation.[5] Moreover, compared to those living in private apartments, asylum-seekers in shelters have to contend with far less security and higher noise levels.[6]

Nearly all of Germany's refugee shelters have entry-control systems managed by private companies. Residents frequently report that their presence within and their time away from the shelter are monitored. Many shelters ban overnight visits. More often than not, communal spaces, such as libraries, leisure areas and computer rooms, have restricted opening hours. Refugees usually have to share sanitary facilities. Some shelters are situated in remote areas with limited public transport, such as industrial zones or former military bases. Others offer only limited or fee-based access to Wi-Fi. Sometimes, there are no opportunities for private cooking, but only canteen food is available three times a day.

Differences in the organisation of refugee shelters both across Germany and within Brandenburg broadly reflect the specific legal requirements of the federal province or municipality that houses each institution and the standards of the public or private organisation that runs it. However, individual managers and employees may implement these heterogeneous requirements and standards in very different ways. As a result, opportunities for participation and thus the well-being of residents can vary considerably from one shelter to another.

Institutionally determined structures of disempowerment

One might say that all the essential aspects of life are covered within Germany's large reception centres. Indeed, an employee of one such reception centre in Brandenburg

---

5   Birgit Behrensen, Was bedeutet Fluchtmigration? Soziologische Erkundungen für die psychosoziale Praxis (Göttingen: Vandenhoeck & Ruprecht, 2017), 68f.
6   Andreea Baier and Manuel Siegert, Die Wohnsituation Geflüchteter: BAMF-Kurzanalyse (Nürnberg: Bundesamt für Migration und Flüchtlinge (BAMF) Forschungszentrum Migration, Integration und Asyl (FZ), 2018).

linked life within the shelter to an all-inclusive holiday. However, this interpretation neglects to consider that involuntary all-around service can incapacitate people if the service goals are set by the facility rather than framed by the needs of the residents. For example, one such resident, a single mother, reported that she would like the centre's crèche to look after her children for a few hours each afternoon as that would allow her to rest. She explained that she fled from her home country with her children, took a dangerous route to Germany and is now exhausted. However, the childcare workers in the crèche expect her and the other mothers to always remain with their children. One of those childcare workers suggested that the mothers should learn how to play and do handicrafts with their children as they currently lack parenting and educational skills. The single mother we interviewed dismissed these accusations as nonsense and reiterated her need for at least a short time away from the children each day. However, the childcare workers rejected her request and continued to adhere to the crèche's strict rules regarding mothers' attendance.

Another former resident recalled the following incident at the reception centre: "We were outside and we had to wait in line for our names to be called. [...] We then got [a number of items]. For example, we got – how do you say? – pyjamas."[7] The administrative character of mass accommodation is obvious in this memory of waiting in line for something to happen. This is just one of several characteristics that Germany's reception centres share with other "total institutions,"[8] including:

- restrictions on and control of external contacts;
- interlinking sleeping, working and leisure in one place under the same authorities;
- involuntary participation;
- constant structuring of the daily routine by the authorities in accordance with established rules; and
- ensuring all activities conform to a common plan with goals determined by the institution rather than the residents.

The longer people remain at the mercy of a total institution's employees, the more their way of life is impaired by institutional control. This is especially true if inhabitants of institutions are exhausted. For them, there is a risk that they will become ever more dependent on the care and services the institution provides. For example, if a member of staff calls himself a social worker, residents may come to rely on his support and network, even if the employee is only semi-skilled, which is quite often

---

7 Interview with former resident of refugee shelter, slightly amended for sense and translated by the author.
8 Erving Goffman, Asylums: Essays on the Social Situation of Mental Patients and Other Inmates (New York: Anchor Books, 1961).

the case in Brandenburg. Likewise, if a particular doctor works closely with the management team of the institution, residents often have to go to considerable lengths to enforce their right to a second opinion, even if the doctor in the institution does not speak their language or has little experience of trauma. Similarly, if the shelter provides schooling, it can be extremely difficult for parents to negotiate a transfer to an alternative school, even if the on-site education fails to meet their children's requirements. In addition, it requires a lot of effort to secure free, objective advice about asylum applications if this is not provided by the shelter itself. Finally, the remote locations of many shelters exacerbate the refugees' dependency.

The residents of German shelters may be viewed as relatively fortunate, especially when compared with other refugees around the world. The problem is, however, that their incapacitation impedes their integration within German society. One remedy would be to house them in private accommodation, with support provided by the decentralised social work system. This would be far cheaper than maintaining the existing refugee shelters, each with its own complex organisation, and would have the added benefit of mitigating the long-term costs of incapacitation. In the meantime, however, the shelters' residents seem destined to remain excluded from German society and all aspects of the country's social life. They are simply kept waiting,[9] often for many years.

The vicious circle of incapacitation

For an earlier study, the author identified some of the problems associated with centralised refugee shelters.[10] More than ten years later, three of these issues remain all too prevalent in many of Brandenburg's shelters:

- Inadequate advice provided by poorly educated staff on how to manage the multi-dimensional and complex problems associated with seeking asylum and integrating within German society exacerbates the refugees' sense of insecurity.
- Social workers within the shelters often lack well-defined roles. Where the staff take care of supply, control and sanctions at the same time, refugees are often forced into the position of powerless victims.
- This opaque system in which members of staff have ambiguous, multiple responsibilities often seems arbitrary to the residents.

---

9   Jan-Paul Brekke, While We Are Waiting: Uncertainty and Empowerment among Asylum-Seekers in Sweden (Oslo: Institute for Social Research, 2004).
10 Birgit Behrensen and Verena Groß, Auf dem Weg in ein "Normales Leben"? Eine Analyse der Gesundheitlichen Situation von Asylsuchenden in der Region Osnabrück (Osnabrück: Self-published, 2004).

As a result of these issues, many refugees experience a great deal of disempowerment and a lack of self-determination. Their living conditions in the shelters are a stark contrast to how they imagined a life would be in such democratic state as Germany. Moreover, they are very different from what the majority of German citizens perceive to be normal.

Most refugees arrive in Germany with all the attributes they need to take care of their own well-being.[11] However, these skills tend to wither in conditions of incapacitation. Exhausted refugees, in particular, are likely to lose their sense of coherence,[12] which makes them more susceptible to falling ill.[13] In consequence, the incapacitation that the refugee shelter system engenders increases the need for support. This need cannot be adequately met by a few employees who are expected to undertake both social and administrative tasks. The following outcome is that the residents' ever-greater dependency creates even more stress for the employees. This can be illustrated as a vicious circle of incapacitation (see Figure 1).

When looking at the internal dynamics of refugee shelters, it could be said that many refugees are at the mercy of the institutions' assistance and structures. Quite a lot of employees seem to make subjective decisions about how and whom they will support. Similar to the earlier study, the collected data reveals that a small number of residents receive a great deal of support, even to the point of rather inappropriate care, while the vast majority are given little more than minimal administrative advice. Employees are much more inclined to help refugees whom they perceive as humble, quiet, and unobtrusive, rather than those they consider active, loud, and demanding. However, given that members of the former group tend to be reluctant to ask for assistance, it may be the case that no refugees receive the help they need.[14]

Additionally, the residents in most shelters have few self-determined opportunities to shape their own lives, regardless of whether they receive a great deal of attention or very little support. To put it bluntly, it could be said that centralisation erodes autonomy because the residents' lives are determined by the shelters' institutional logic.

---

11   Louis H. Seukwa, Der Habitus der Überlebenskunst: Zum Verhältnis von Kompetenz und Migration im Spiegel von Flüchtlingsbiographien (Münster: Waxmann, 2006).
12   Aaron Antonovsky, Unraveling the Mystery of Health: How People Manage Stress and Stay Well (San Francisco: Jossey-Bass, 1988).
13   Behrensen and Groß, Auf dem Weg in ein "Normales Leben"? Eine Analyse der Gesundheitlichen Situation von Asylsuchenden in der Region Osnabrück (Osnabrück: Self-published, 2004).
14   Ibid.

Figure 1: Vicious circle of incapacitation

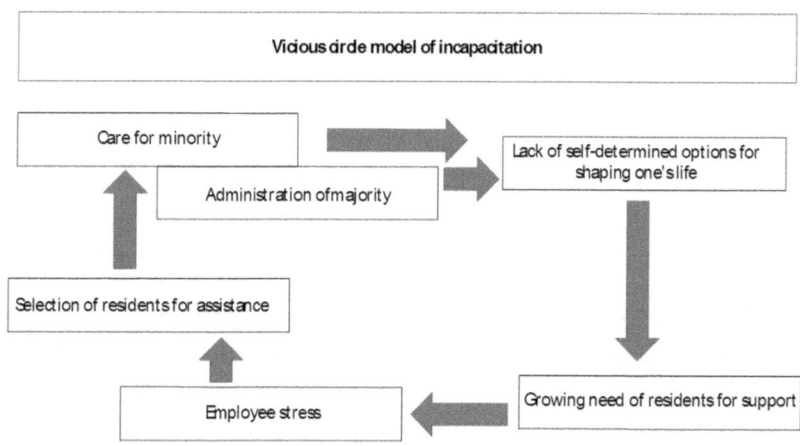

Data collected for the ongoing research project confirms these findings from the earlier study. Again, during both formal interviews and casual conversations, employees routinely differentiate between allegedly "good" and allegedly "bad" refugees. Some members of staff openly disparage the latter (much larger) group's demands, yet also raise concerns about a handful of supposedly outstanding but helpless residents. In addition, little has been done to empower refugees. For example, they have strictly limited prospects in terms of education, work, societal participation and indeed any kind of meaningfulness due to a lack networking opportunities. Finally, the ongoing study has revealed quite a lot about the logic of control within several refugee shelters.

Instrumentalising social work in refugee shelters to establish cultures of control

The issue of control is a long-discussed challenge in social work as it forms half of the profession's "double mandate"[15] along with providing help to those in need. On the one hand, the core of the profession is to enhance clients' autonomy and self-determination. On the other, it is sometimes necessary for social workers to exercise control. This is especially true in the context of protecting against violence and in

---

15   Lothar Böhnisch and Hans Lösch, "Das Handlungsverständnis des Sozialarbeiters und seine institutionelle Determination," in Gesellschaftliche Perspektiven der Sozialarbeit, edited by Hans-Uwe Otto and Siegfried Schneider, 3rd ed. (Neuwied: Luchterhand, 1979), 27.

child welfare. Therefore, the development of a professional attitude requires social workers to remain aware of – and sometimes endure – the dilemma of helping while simultaneously exercising control.

The control side of the double mandate is rather different in the field of refugee immigration, however. In this context, it largely relates to monitoring the regulations established by immigration law, which form the internal political part of the logic of the border regime. The data collected and analysed so far highlights how the logic of the border regime influences the work of some employees in refugee shelters. It should be emphasised that these are far from typical individual cases. Nevertheless, they demonstrate how the logic of the border regime can be incorporated through power asymmetry.

In one interview, a semi-skilled social worker in a refugee shelter explained that she wished to inform the Federal Office for Migration and Refugees (BAMF) about rule violations committed by individual residents. She suggested that these should be taken into consideration whenever BAMF considers applications for asylum. Specifically, she mentioned petty criminal offences and absence from German classes. In general, she expressed a desire to report "whether a client is behaving well" as she believed that such a control function would encourage more refugees to obey the shelter's rules. It should be emphasised that she had never attempted to put these ideas into practice. Rather, they comprised a power fantasy that unfolded during the course of the interview.

In another interview, a fully trained social worker recalled noticing different dates of birth on a young refugee's birth certificate and school certificate, which obliged him to conduct a further investigation. However, in retrospect, he was exasperated that he had been forced to take on this control task simply because an administrative authority had failed to properly fulfil its responsibility. This was not control for the purpose of protecting against violence, but merely to fulfil the logic of Germany's border regime. As Scherr has pointed out,[16] it could be said that such activities help to perpetuate global inequality.

Locked doors

The Covid-19 pandemic turned refugee shelters into highly dangerous places. People were living in close proximity so the virus could spread easily, especially as the shelters' hygiene regimes consisted of little more than routine disinfection. Consequently, a number of collective quarantines were enforced in response to Covid-19 outbreaks, including in Brandenburg. It is still too early to assess the full impact

---

16   Albert Scherr, "Rassismus, Post-Rassismus und Nationalismus: Erfordernisse einer differenzierten Kritik," PERIPHERIE 37 (2017) 2: 232–49.

of these quarantines, but Bozorgmehr *et al*. published some preliminary findings in May 2020.[17] They reported that the inhabitants of refugee shelters have a heightened risk of contracting Covid-19 from fellow residents due to the limited living space and inadequate infection-protection procedures within the facilities. However, they felt that the widespread use of quarantine was unwarranted for two important reasons. First, there was no evidence of an increased risk to the general population if the usual protective measures were observed. Second, people who are confined in collective quarantine often suffer severe psycho-social consequences.

Conclusion

When refugee immigration to Germany started to increase in 2015, there was an urgent need to find accommodation for tens of thousands of people throughout the country, including in Brandenburg. After a short period of chaos, it was decided to house the majority of refugees in large shelters while their applications for asylum were processed. Unfortunately, this decision has meant that most refugees have been forced to live in restrictive and controlling environments, often for many years. Moreover, it has been needlessly expensive as private housing would have been much cheaper, and would have provided far more opportunities for integration and participation in wider German society.

The refugees' outsider status was reinforced with the onset of the Covid-19 pandemic, as many shelters were put into quarantine. This isolation of entire communities – supposedly as a protective measure, but in some cases without any attempt to separate infected from uninfected residents – demonstrates the deep roots of Germany's border regime logic. Transferring the refugees to decentralised, private accommodation would have provided much better protection from the pandemic.

---

17   Kayvan Bozorgmehr et al., SARS-CoV-2 in Aufnahmeeinrichtungen und Gemeinschaftsunterkünften für Geflüchtete: Epidemiologische und normativ-rechtliche Aspekte (Bielefeld: Kompetenznetz Public Health COVID-19, 2020).

Enhancing agency and empowerment in refugee camps as total institutions – real or illusory?

Maximiliane Brandmaier

> "In the heim, there are people that are dirty, they are staying with you in the same room. there are people that doesn't want to talk; they stay with you the same room. there are people that, even before you look for a trouble, he just want to look for a trouble. //mhm// they stay with you in the same room. maybe you want to sleep. they disturbs you. what you have to do? you just have to run away. but if you want to run away, the money they give to you to pay for your house, it will not be enough. even though you want to […] i just endure. every time."[1]

Introduction

The above quotation reflects a feeling of having no choice, the necessity of enduring aversive living conditions and being accommodated with strangers, to follow the house rules every day, month after month, year after year. For refugees with an insecure permit status – not only in Austria – the restrictions to personal agency are huge: limited access to education or to working permits, limited freedom of movement or of choosing one's place of residence, to name just a few. As international research on post-migration stressors has shown for many years, serious risk factors for mental health disorders include long periods of insecurity, accommodation in collective reception centres or refugee camps, limited economic opportunities due to unemployment or low-paid jobs, fear of deportation, loss of socio-economic and/or socio-cultural status, lack of social support, insufficient knowledge of the host country's language, insufficient medical and/or psychological care, as well

---

1   Interviewee quoted in Maximiliane Brandmaier, Angepasstes und widerständiges Handeln in der Lebensführung geflüchteter Menschen. Handlungsfähigkeit im Verhältnis zu Anerkennung und (psycho-)sozialer Unterstützung in österreichischen Sammelunterkünften (Weinheim: Beltz Juventa, 2019), 265.

as racism and other forms of discrimination.[2] In everyday life, the prospect of an uncertain future and the sense of "doing nothing" every day contribute to the development and maintenance of anxiety, depression, psychosomatic disorders and/or post-traumatic stress disorder.

Refugees and asylum-seekers have endured restrictions on their agency for decades, especially since the tightening of European migration and asylum laws and policies in the 1990s. For many years, psychological and sociological research in German-speaking countries focused almost exclusively on the limited (or even nonexistent) agency of asylum-seekers due to the fierce restrictions they face in their everyday lives. More recently, though, several social scientists, perhaps inspired by a rise in the number of refugee protests since 2012, have turned their attention to the possibility of maintaining or even expanding agency. Self-determination and agency are important factors for mental health and as such play a significant role in helping refugees to cope with post-migration stressors.

This article is based on sections of a social-psychological study that analysed the roles of agency,[3] recognition[4] and social support in the everyday lives of asylum-seekers and refugees who were housed in reception centres in three of Austria's federal states: Vienna, Carinthia and Tyrol. The research comprised qualitative interviews with the refugees and asylum-seekers themselves as well as their counsellors, psychotherapists, volunteers and social/care workers. The article will first outline the specific characteristics and dynamics of communal reception centres, which can be understood as "total institutions" in the sense of Erving Goffman's sociological

---

2   For example, see Matthew Porter and Nick Haslam, "Predisplacement and Postdisplacement Factors Associated with Mental Health of Refugees and Internally Displaced Persons – A Meta-analysis," JAMA: Journal of the American Medical Association 294 (2005) 5: 602–12; Howard Johnson and Andrew Thompson, "The Development and Maintenance of Post-Traumatic Stress Disorder (PTSD) in Civilian Adult Survivors of War Trauma and Torture: A Review," Clinical Psychology Review 28 (2008) 1: 36–47.

3   The question of human agency has been discussed for more than four decades now, and in sociology as well as psychology various theories have been developed. In the present study, sociological approaches (Mustafa Emirbayer's and Ann Mische's relational approach, and Anthony Giddens's and Pierre Bourdieu's structural approaches) and psychological theories of learned helplessness (Martin Seligman and colleagues), internal and external control (Julian B. Rotter and colleagues), agency (Albert Bandura) and the Berlin school of critical psychology's concept of agency (Klaus Holzkamp and colleagues) have been taken into account. See Brandmaier, Angepasstes und widerständiges Handeln, 91–106 for further details.

4   In this article, the understanding of recognition is based on: Axel Honneth, Kampf um Anerkennung. Zur moralischen Grammatik sozialer Konflikte, 7th ed. (Frankfurt am Main: Suhrkamp, 2012); Klaus Ottomeyer, Ökonomische Zwänge und menschliche Beziehungen. Soziales Verhalten und Identität im Kapitalismus und Neoliberalismus, 2nd ed. (Berlin – Münster: Lit, 2014).

concept.⁵ Next, it will explore the various forms of agency that were analysed in the study. Finally, it will consider whether increasing social support might help refugees and asylum-seekers to achieve greater empowerment and agency.

The structures and dynamics of total institutions in communal centres for refugees

Refugee's placement on the borders of Europe (for example, in Greece) clearly merit the term "camps", sometimes even "internment". However, if and when those refugees reach the wealthier countries of Central Europe, such as Austria or Germany, such a description may – from the outside – seem inappropriate for the places where they are housed. For example, this study focuses on Austrian communal centres that range in size from small former guesthouses in rural areas, each of which can house no more than thirty residents, to former military barracks on the outskirts of large cities that can accommodate up to 250 inhabitants.

Irrespective of the size of the facility, though, recent research into refugee camps in Austria and Germany has demonstrated that they function as total institutions because they are embedded in an excluding architectural structure and perpetuate a system of exclusion and organised disintegration.⁶ Although the term is often applied only to *closed* environments, such as prisons, all of Austria's communal centres for refugees display at least some of the characteristics of total institutions. Thus, the dynamics and hierarchies of total institutions were found in every research location.

First, all of the central aspects of life, including sleeping, (care) work and leisure time, occur in a single place. Many individuals in similar or identical circumstances are housed together and segregated from the rest of the society to live separate, formally regulated lives. They have no say in where they are accommodated, and their length of stay is usually unknown. Social contact with the outside world is regulated to varying degrees but always very limited. There are symbolic and sometimes even physical barriers to entry and exit: for example, both visitors and residents may have to pass a control post at the entrance and show their identity cards; and those who wish to visit may have to apply for permission from the local authorities or the management, as was the case in Carinthia during the research for this study. Control,

---

5   Erving Goffman, Asylums: Essays on the Social Situation of Mental Patients and Other Inmates (New York: Doubleday, 1961).
6   Tobias Pieper, Die Gegenwart der Lager. Zur Mikrophysik der Herrschaft in der deutschen Flüchtlingspolitik (Münster: Westfälisches Dampfboot, 2008); Vicki Täubig, Totale Institution Asyl. Empirische Befunde zu alltäglichen Lebensführungen in der organisierten Desintegration (Weinheim: Juventa, 2009).

discipline and sanctions are enforced by strict adherence to a lengthy list of house rules that regulate every aspect of communal life.[7] For instance, if a resident was absent from the centre for more than three nights per month, they risk losing their monthly benefits; "pocket money" may be withheld if residents fail to fulfil their cleaning duties; and the inhabitants of some Carinthian camps were not even allowed to prepare their own meals.

Goffman postulated that the declared aims of total institutions are contradictory to what these organisations actually do. In case social workers' ultimate aim is to enable their clients to live independent lives in exile – a task that is usually framed as a combination of welfare and empowerment – they inadvertently help to perpetuate an image of clients who are not *yet* able to care for themselves in the host country. The official goal of empowerment and supporting integration is contradictory to the actual "organised disintegration"[8] of asylum-seekers, the ongoing erosion of their agency and the demoralisation that is generated by multiple legal restrictions and the (communal) character of placement itself. There are parallels here with Goffman's notion of "disculturation", in which inhabitants lose societal habits and capacities in total institutions.

One unofficial but undeniable function of the communal centres is the administration and control of asylum-seekers, which reflects the conflict between help and control within social workers' "dual mandate"[9] to serve both the (welfare) state and the recipients of its support simultaneously. Indeed, one of the main tasks of care workers in the centres – besides providing help and social support – is to control the inhabitants.[10] This is apparent in obligatory controlling visits to the residents' rooms, the presence of security services, the enforcement of the house rules and the implementation of sanctions. Care workers have the power and authority to discipline and sanction any irregular activities, but control is also exercised, for example, by the way in which medical appointments are organised. Moreover, supposedly educational interventions, such as advice about how to raise children and lessons on the host country's cultural norms and values, may influence the conduct of everyday life and reinforce adaptation.

---

7   Birgit Behrensen and Verena Groß, Auf dem Weg in ein "normales Leben"? Eine Analyse der gesundheitlichen Situation von Asylsuchenden in der Region Osnabrück. Forschungsergebnisse des Teilprojekts "Regionalanalyse" im Rahmen der EQUAL-Entwicklungspartnerschaft (Osnabrück: Universität Osnabrück, 2004).
8   Täubig, Totale Institution Asyl.
9   Peter Erath, Sozialarbeitswissenschaft. Eine Einführung (Stuttgart: Kohlhammer, 2006); Gisela Hauss and Dagmar Schulte (eds), Amid Social Contradictions: Towards a History of Social Work in Europe (Opladen – Farmington Hills, MI: Barbara Budrich Publishers, 2009).
10 Maximiliane Brandmaier and Lisa Friedmann, Menschenrechtsbasierte Soziale Arbeit in Sammelunterkünften. Widersprüche – Handlungsgrenzen – Handlungsmöglichkeiten (Göttingen: Vandenhoeck & Ruprecht, 2019), 57–62.

Members of staff, as well as external social and care workers, can't help but act as part of these total institutions. Even if they are motivated to be supportive and try to stand in solidarity with the residents, the distance between the two groups is maintained by the asymmetrical dynamics of power and the fact that one group is free while the other is dependent.[11] Almost all of the decision-making power and most of the access to information remain with members of staff. They are free to leave the institution as soon as the working day is over, whereas the refugees and asylum-seekers have to remain. Therefore, two discrete "worlds," each with its own stereotypical views and prejudices, start to develop in every centre. Social distance is maintained by a variety of mechanisms, including the sanctions and privileges that Goffman described. Social and care workers act within this system and also take advantage of the "underlife," as Goffman termed it. As the research for this project demonstrated, residents with some knowledge of the host country's language and/or good networking capabilities tend to gain access to the management team, secure jobs or some sort of special status within the centre and receive rewards such as useful information or other privileges. For example, one manager admitted that only a few privileged residents knew that he was willing to overlook infringements of the three nights away from the centre per month rule.

While Goffman suggested that desirable behaviour is reinforced in total institutions by the aforementioned system of privileges and sanctions, the research for this study revealed that establishing trustful relationships between care workers and clients can be equally effective. Members of staff can foster considerable gratitude and loyalty among the residents, as well as greater adherence to the house rules, simply by adopting a more respectful and appreciative approach. Such an approach is illustrated in the following case-study.

Case-study of a communal centre in Tyrol

The centre was located in a tourist region of the Alps. It was a former guest house with a few separate units for families and couples, some with cooking facilities, and a couple of shared rooms for single men and women. All of the residents emphasised that they were satisfied with the living conditions within the centre, especially the quiet surroundings, the cleanliness and the support they received from members of staff. The management had attempted to create a friendly atmosphere of mutual support and solidarity among the inhabitants, which included allocating space for festivities and meetings. Residents who were housed in the family units could invite their neighbours to visit, but this was not so easy for those in the shared rooms,

---

11   Goffman, Asylums.

unless they got along very well with their roommates. Thus, it was clear that even a small private space helped to facilitate closer social relationships.

The care workers were perceived as very committed, and the manager was described as cordial and helpful: for example, she arranged the return of a pregnant resident from hospital in the middle of the night. The care workers provided practical support – such as scheduling appointments with physicians, lawyers or the authorities, establishing German language courses, finding places for children and youths in the education system and organising community service or work placements – that served to boost the residents' agency. They achieved this by taking full advantage of Tyrolean state regulations that helped the residents to play more active roles in local society, especially compared to their counterparts in Carinthia. For example, the care workers distributed free tickets for public transport that gave the residents much better access to social and cultural events and encouraged them to work in so-called "charitable" ventures, with rewards provided in the form of vouchers. As a result, many of the disadvantages of the centre's remote location were mitigated by the care workers' commitment to finding practical solutions. It should be pointed out that a number of residents appeared to depend on the care workers' assistance and felt that they could achieve nothing without it, which could diminish their self-efficacy. Nevertheless, overall, the needs-oriented practical and psychosocial support of the staff permitted all residents some freedom to organise their everyday lives and tasks.

With respect to the second component of the double mandate – control – the Tyrolean centre demonstrated that the cultivation of strong personal relationships and loyalty can be just as important as house rules and the consistent implementation of privileges and sanctions. The manager emphasised that the centre's small size not only helped them to spot any non-residents in the compound but also allowed them to create a familial atmosphere. This was reinforced by the manager's obvious commitment to the residents, which ensured that they felt appreciated and were confident that their basic needs would be met. Nevertheless, the residents still felt that they had been placed in the centre under duress and struggled with being obliged to live with strangers in the same room and in a sparsely populated rural area with limited employment and educational opportunities. Therefore, it is perhaps unsurprising that the manager framed interventions also as strategies to prevent arguments and violence. Indeed, the social workers seemed to view prevention as one of their core tasks.

Refugees' and asylum-seekers' forms of agency in everyday life

Multiple legal restrictions on agency, as well as disrespect and a lack of recognition, can be detrimental to refugees' and asylum-seekers' self-image and often leave them feeling imprisoned and powerless. Moreover, such responses are reinforced by a lack of information on how applications for asylum are processed, limited access to society, work and education, and the enforcement of strict house rules in reception centres. All of these factors can have a detrimental effect on agency, self-determination and mental health, especially when the application process is protracted.[12]

The research for this study showed that the length of time spent in a reception centre influences agency and autonomy among the residents. Although this may be attributed to care workers assuming much of the responsibility for the fulfilment of everyday tasks, a similar pattern was evident even when the residents were left to their own devices because there were no social workers in the centres. Therefore, it seems that restricted spheres of action and limited self-efficacy[13] may be sufficient, in themselves, to cause a decline in personal agency.

A theoretical understanding of agency is essential if we are to address this problem. Based on concepts of agency and the conduct of everyday life developed in critical psychology,[14] it is possible to identify three forms of agency in the everyday lives of refugees and asylum-seekers in Austria:

- **Adaptation** encompasses coping strategies such as religious activities, positive thinking and pastimes that help to fill days that would otherwise be characterised by inactivity and boredom. Adaptation does not increase the residents' scope of action, but it can help them to regain strength and accept situations that cannot be changed.
- **Meaningful action** includes creating "highlights" or setting and achieving goals each day, adhering to a daily routine, such as attending a language class, performing tasks within the centre, volunteer work and so on. Like adaptation, it helps residents to cope with the monotony and mental strain of institutional life because it gives some meaning to their everyday activities and may even allow them to enjoy a few hours of freedom outside the centre.

---

12   Brandmaier, Angepasstes und widerständiges Handeln, 419–20; Susanne Johansson, Was wir über Flüchtlinge (nicht) wissen. Der wissenschaftliche Erkenntnisstand zur Lebenssituation von Flüchtlingen in Deutschland. Eine Expertise im Auftrag der Robert Bosch Stiftung und des SVR-Forschungsbereichs (Berlin: Robert Bosch Stiftung, 2016).
13   Albert Bandura, "Self-efficacy Mechanism in Human Agency," American Psychologist 37 (1982) 2: 122–47; Albert Bandura, "Social Cognitive Theory: An Agentic Perspective," Annual Review of Psychology 52 (2001) 1: 1–26.
14   Klaus Holzkamp, "Alltägliche Lebensführung als subjektwissenschaftliches Grundkonzept," Das Argument 212 (1995): 817–46; Josef Held et al., Was bewegt junge Menschen? Lebensführung und solidarisches Handeln junger Beschäftigter im Dienstleistungsbereich (Wiesbaden: VS Verlag für Sozialwissenschaften, 2011); Ernst Schraube and Charlotte Højholt (eds), Psychology and the Conduct of Everyday Life (Hove – New York: Routledge, 2015).

- **Transgressions and acts of resistance**, such as protests against degrading living conditions and discrimination. These acts are often triggered by an imagination of having more agency in the future, including maintaining hopes and dreams, and they can help to alleviate a sense of futility. They form part of everyday life for almost all asylum-seekers, not just political activists, as they struggle to obtain residence permits and better access to education and whenever they raise complaints and suggestions with members of staff.

The meaningful action of learning German seemed to be a particularly effective means of increasing personal agency. Similarly, the few residents who managed to secure paid employment were able to send financial support to their families in their countries of origin, others who fulfilled tasks within the centres were rewarded with extra privileges, and those who participated in charitable work expanded their social networks, all of which may be considered as boosts to agency. Given the difficulty of acquiring a work permit as asylum-seeker, it may be assumed that other residents were working in the irregular sector (another form of agency), but there was an understandable reluctance to acknowledge this.

Collective forms of agency that are based on solidarity, such as campaigns for greater recognition, may be classified as resistant action, but there was little evidence of this in the sample centres due to the residents' fear of the consequences of transgressing rules. Indeed, none of the interviewed residents had participated in any sort of organised migrant or refugee movement. On the other hand, solidarity – such as showing respect and understanding for fellow-residents, being considerate, taking care of each other and passing on important information, such as how to enrol in free German language courses – was a key form of agency in every communal centre.

Helping while controlling? The possibilities and limitations of social support and increasing agency

A number of researchers have investigated whether social support enhances agency.[15] For example, Edge et al. found that the provision of social support (especially by peers) played a role in boosting their agency, self-determination and empowerment.[16] Similarly, the research for the present study showed that social support for refugees helped expanding their personal agency although there was a risk of creating new dependencies and reduced self-efficacy. In addition, family

---

15 Brandmaier, Angepasstes und widerständiges Handeln, 108–16.
16 Sara Edge et al., "Exploring Socio-cultural Factors that Mediate, Facilitate, & Constrain the Health and Empowerment of Refugee Youth," Social Science & Medicine 117 (2014): 34–41.

members or co-residents frequently demonstrated solidarity by providing practical support in the organisation of everyday life. Social support networks consisting of peers and family members were often reciprocal, which enabled the recipients of help to assuage feelings of inferiority and dependency because they were assisting others, too. Recalling Pierre Bourdieu's concept of social, cultural and economic capital,[17] the supporting person's resources were crucial to the efficacy of social support and any consequent increases in agency. Unsurprisingly, friends and relatives provided emotional support, but it has to be considered that familial relationships can be broken or impacted by trauma, guilt or grief. Moreover, many of the refugees were alone in the centres, with no relatives or close friends, and mistrust, which is a natural reaction to prolonged exposure to danger, persecution and trauma, can complicate the process of forging new relationships and maintaining existing ones.

Two-thirds of the refugees who were interviewed for this study expressed appreciation for the practical support they received (e.g. childcare, help in times of illness and translation services). However, in general, they characterised their social relationships as ambivalent, superficial and uncommitted. There was not a widespread sense of solidarity, notwithstanding some individual displays of solidarity. Indeed, most of the interviewees admitted suffering from loneliness and complained about a lack of social support. Sometimes volunteers or social workers in the centres, or from NGOs, attempted to provide alternative social networks for the residents. And the residents routinely turned to social workers if they needed practical support with work-permit or job applications, access to education, or legal advice. Unfortunately, though, the social workers' efforts to boost the residents' agency were constrained by a lack of funding and the narrow legal framework in which they had to operate. They could empower the refugees by facilitating participation, for example by organising German language classes, social contacts with the local population and access to community services; and they could use their own proxy agency[18] to improve the refugees' access to education, ease communication with the authorities and gather information. However, they sometimes expressed ambivalent mindsets because of a sense of disappointment in their clients and frustration over their lack of initiative. The paradox is that the most caring and committed care workers can have a detrimental effect on their clients' agency if they see themselves as the latter's saviours.

Moreover, there is always the risk of care workers abusing their power, especially if they have insufficient understanding of the dual mandate and the dynamics of power within total institutions, and/or inadequate strategies to cope with conflict and stress. Interviews with both refugees and members of staff in the Austrian communal centres revealed a tendency among some care workers to belittle their clients'

---

17   Pierre Bourdieu, "Ökonomisches Kapital, kulturelles Kapital, soziales Kapital," in Soziale Ungleichheiten, edited by Reinhard Kreckel (Göttingen: Schwartz, 1983), 183–98.
18   Bandura, "Social Cognitive Theory," 13.

concerns and either infantilise or culturalise non-desirable behaviour. These were interpreted as subconscious coping mechanism to establish and maintain distance between themselves and the residents and thereby protect themselves against overburdening. Structural factors, such as remote locations that make it difficult for independent organisations and regulatory bodies to conduct regular inspections, also increase the likelihood of power abuse by both care workers and security staff (although the latter were not included in this study). Residents' dependency on members of staff – and consequently the latter's power – was greatest in remote locations. Perhaps unsurprisingly, communal centres in these areas also displayed the most disregard for their residents' well-being, as manifested in living conditions that were hazardous to health and the provision of low quality of food in a number of small, remote Carinthian facilities where the owners (entrepreneurs or former landlords with no background in social work) functioned as the residents' primary contact. Of course, such disrespect exacerbated the residents' pre-existing sense of futility and powerlessness.

The dual mandate of help and control also narrows care workers' scope of action as they are unlikely to support any enhancement of agency that might lead to transgression or resistance, not least because they are bound to the terms of their employers' contracts with the federal state. While many social work studies have discussed the inherent contradictions of the dual mandate, care workers themselves should reflect on the complex interplay of power, privilege and dependency as well as their clients' experiences of non-recognition and disrespect as part of their everyday practice. Developing an appreciation of the residents' lack of agency will help to avert individualising or pathologising reactions to discrimination, inequality and contradictions. Moreover, only care workers with a deep understanding of the characteristics of total institutions, the dynamics of relationships between staff and residents and the different forms of agency will have any chance of empowering their clients. It creates a completely different attitude towards residents who ask for daily updates on their asylum applications or criticise conditions within the reception centre for they will not be perceived as troublesome, as motivated individuals with a justifiable determination to increase their agency. In summary, critical self-reflection, transparency during counselling, avoiding culturalisation and infantilisation, and promoting autonomy are key factors in boosting agency and contribute to recognition.

Many of the Austrian care workers expressed their aim to empower the residents step-by-step and enable them to take care of their own affairs. However, particularly vulnerable people, such as single parents or the survivors of extreme violence with complex trauma-reactive symptoms, need ongoing practical and emotional support over a long period of time.[19] Unfortunately, there has been a distinct lack of psychological support and specialist trauma-sensitive psychotherapy for refugees and

---

19   Brandmaier, Angepasstes und widerständiges Handeln, 455–9.

asylum-seekers in Austria and Germany for many years.[20] For instance, of all the Austrian centres analysed in this study, only one in Vienna – designated a specialist integration house – offered psychological support from staff who were trained to work with clients with severe mental health issues. Although the authorities in Tyrol claimed that their centres were equipped to provide psycho-social support and had systems to identify residents with mental health problems, they had been unable to perform either of these functions for some time due to a shortage of staff.

Residents' attitude towards the social support they received depended on if they perceived an authentic interest in their well-being or their plans for the future, and reliable advocacy for their concern, if they felt recognized as a person and being treated as respected members of society with the same human rights as everyone else. It also encompasses being recognized and supported even in situations of mental crisis and breakdowns. This sort of intersubjective recognition was a positive counter-experience to everyday racism, discrimination and non-recognition. As a result, it reinforced their sense of self-worth, which was crucial as the self is under constant attack in the total institutions of societies that mainly disapprove of asylum-seekers and refugees.[21]

Conclusion

Despite long-term demands and campaigns for abolishment of communal placement or internment of refugees, most states, including Austria, have persisted with – or even expanded – the communal centre model. These centres' social and care workers often share a sense of helplessness with their clients as they struggle to cope with the inherent contradictions of organised disintegration and the dual mandate of help and control. While the research for this study found that many of these care workers had a strong personal commitment to and sense of solidarity with their clients that enabled them to forge trustful relationships and work in a needs- and resource-oriented way, their counterparts in independent NGOs that were not bound to the state's control mandate had much more scope to confront the authorities and help their clients to assert their rights. That said, every social worker who works with asylum-seekers or refugees, be they employed by an NGO, a welfare organisation or the state, is bound by a core feature of all humanitarian

---

20   An overview of specialist psycho-social treatment centres for traumatised refugees and asylum-seekers can be found on the websites of umbrella organisations: for Germany, BAfF (Bundesweite Arbeitsgemeinschaft der psychosozialen Zentren für Flüchtlinge und Folteropfer; https://www.baff-zentren.org); and for Austria, NIPE (Netzwerk für Interkulturelle Psychotherapie nach Extremtraumatisierung; https://www.nipe.or.at).
21   Brandmaier, Angepasstes und widerständiges Handeln, 468–74.

interventions – the dual mandate. In addition, any intervention that aims to expand social networks and increase social support should not focus solely on the individual but should also address societal structures that perpetuate marginalisation and exclusion. Finally, considering social work as a human rights profession, social workers should be sensitive to the experiences of trauma and racism that many of their clients suffer, and they should embrace critical self-reflection, as this will help them to cope with the contradictory dual mandate of help and control.

Many of the structural issues that are risk factors for impaired mental health demand political- and societal-level intervention. For example, refugees' and asylum-seekers' self-determination and agency – at least on a very basic level in the conduct of everyday lives – could be improved by offering them forms of housing that are better suited to their individual needs, such as private rented flats, rooms in shared houses or apartments in integration facilities with psycho-social support, along with various forms of mobile support from social and care workers. Many of the problems in the current communal centre system are caused by the system itself, resulting in a vicious circle for residents and staff alike. By prioritising control, discipline and exclusion, this system not only reduces the residents' personal agency but also forces the care workers to enforce restrictions on the very people they are trying to help, which leads to stress on both sides.[22]

Most of the interviewed refugees and care workers expressed a strong preference for private rather than communal living. This is hardly surprising, as refugees could experience their agentic selves at least on the basic level of private life. They would have to be provided with support structures oriented towards their individual needs, including low-threshold counselling services and, ideally, regular (psycho-)social and mental health counselling services. But such a system would be far preferable to the current reception centre model, which creates structural dependencies that reinforce the residents' sense of helplessness.

---

22   Ibid., 485–8.

Part III
Strategies of coping and resistance

Undesirable asylum-seekers from National Socialist Germany in France
Horst Rosenthals' comics in Gurs Camp

Pnina Rosenberg

German immigrants in interwar France

Horst Rosenthal (b. 1915, Breslau; d. 1942, Auschwitz) was among the German-Jewish asylum-seekers who fled to France following the rise of National Socialism in Germany. By 1939, France was hosting an estimated 30,000–35,000 legal or clandestine refugees of German and Austrian origin.[1] Despite help from relief organisations, their situation was extremely arduous,[2] as insufficient economic resources were compounded by increasing hostility and mistrust from the French.[3] Even so, most of the refugees saw the "cradle of human rights" as a safe haven. With the beginning of the Second World War, their expectations were shattered.

On 4 September 1939, a day after its declaration of war, the Third Republic, alarmed by the prospect of a "fifth column," proclaimed that all male refugees aged seventeen to fifty (later extended to sixty-five) of the "Third Reich" were to be placed under strict police surveillance. Thus, thousands of stateless exiles were ironically and tragically defined as *"indésirables"* and "enemy aliens" and interned in various southern French camps, such as Les Milles, Gurs, Rieucros and Le Vernet.[4]

---

1 Rita Thalmann, "Jewish Women Exiled in France after 1933," in Between Sorrow and Strength: Women Refugees of the Nazi Period, edited by Sibylle Quack (Cambridge: Cambridge University Press, 1995), 52–3; Vicki Caron, "Unwilling Refuge: France and the Dilemma of Illegal Immigration, 1933–1939," in Refugees from Nazi Germany and the Liberal European States, edited by Frank Caestecker and Bob Moore (Oxford: Berghahn Books, 2010), 57–80; Greg Burgess, The League of Nations and the Refugees from Nazi Germany: James G. McDonald and Hitler's Victims (London: Bloomsbury, 2016), 18–19.
2 Greg Burgess, Refuge in the Land of Liberty: France and its Refugees, from the Revolution to the End of Asylum 1787–1939 (New York: Palgrave Macmillan, 2008), 165–85.
3 Hanna Schramm and Barbara Vormeier, Vivre à Gurs: Un Camp de conçentration français 1940–1941, translated by Irène Petit (Paris: Maspero, 1979), 197.
4 Michael Marrus and Robert O. Paxton, Vichy France and the Jews (New York: Basic Books, 1981), 3–4. Caron, "Unwilling Refuge," 76.

Following its defeat in 1940, France was divided into the Occupied Zone and the Non-occupied – or Free – Zone. The latter was headed by Marshal Philippe Pétain and established its seat of government in the town of Vichy. The Vichy regime saw the defeat not as the result of a series of political and military blunders, but as the consequence of a degenerate, sick society that had lost its French character. "Anti-French" groups such as communists, Jews, freemasons and foreigners were identified as the main culprits and became the targets of vicious propaganda. It was seen as essential to rid France of these supposedly negative forces and emphasise the traditional French qualities of *travail, famille, patrie* (work, family, homeland) – the three principles of Pétain's "National Revolution."[5] The camps were therefore an important component of this new regime, as they could be used to segregate antisocial elements who could not be re-educated and were considered the root of all evil from mainstream, wholesome French society.

The xenophobic and anti-Semitic Vichy regime not only collaborated with the German occupiers but exceeded National Socialist directives. The peak came on 16 July 1942, when the French police arrested nearly 13,000 Jewish men, women and children at their homes or on the streets of Paris. The victims were taken to the Winter Stadium (Vélodrome d'hiver or Vel d'Hiv) and later deported to the death camps. As Prime Minister Pierre Laval explained with chilling cynicism, "out of humane consideration, the Head of State determined, contrary to German demands, that children under the age of 16 should be accompanied by their parents."[6] There were only few survivors among the 3,900 children who were taken to the Vel d'Hiv that day.

Gurs Camp

Gurs Camp, near the Pyrenees, was the largest Free Zone internment camp. From March 1939 to November 1943, a rich and diverse population of some 21,790 men, women and children were imprisoned there, most of them of German origin.[7] The first inmates were refugees from the Spanish Civil War or International Brigade fighters who had fled over France's southern border.[8] However, in October 1940, the German regime rounded up some 7,000 Jews in the provinces of Baden and the

---

5   Henri Michel, "La Révolution Nationale latitude d'action du gouvernement de Vichy," Revue d'histoire de la Deuxième Guerre mondiale 21 (1971) 81: 3–22.
6   Réunion du Conseil des Ministres, 10 July 1942, cited in Serge Klarsfeld, Vichy Auschwitz: Le Rôle de Vichy dans la solution finale de la question juive en France 1942 (Paris: Fayard. 1983), 244.
7   Claude Laharie, Le Camp de Gurs 1939–1945: Un Aspect méconnu de l'histoire de Vichy (Pau: Infocompo, 1993), 219.
8   Ibid., 103–35.

Palatinate and sent them to Gurs.⁹ In addition, some 7,000 male refugees from Germany, Austria and Poland had been sent to the French camp of Saint-Cyprien on the Mediterranean coast following the German invasion of Belgium in May 1940, but the camp flooded that October and more than 3,000 of the inmates were transferred to Gurs.¹⁰ Consequently, many of the Gurs internees were persecuted German or Austrian Jews, anti-National Socialist militants or left-wing intellectuals whom the French regime absurdly regarded as a "threat to national security."¹¹

Daily life demanded constant improvisation, as the camp lacked even the most basic necessities. A lack of food and water led to widespread sickness and outbreaks of disease. The camp had been built on non-porous soil, so rain turned the whole site into a mudbath, making movement between the barracks extremely difficult.¹² The inmates' deterioration was ironically but accurately summarised in Heini Walfisch's poem "Le Monsieur élégant dans la boue" ("The Elegant Gentleman in the Mud"), written during his internment in Gurs:

> Once I used to be an elegant monsieur
> I had a sharp crease in my trousers, a tie and a white collar
> I knew by heart the tunes of Figaro and of Tristan
> And I had a vision of the world that was almost mine
> (Meanwhile it all crumbled)
> [...]
> In the meantime many things have happened
> The elegant monsieur has slipped in the mud
> And the worldview, Tristan, the tie and the collar
> (I say without exaggeration)
> Are a little wrinkled, as is the crease of my trousers.¹³

---

9   Ibid., 171–3; Erhard Roy Wiehn (ed.), Oktoberdeportation 1940 (Konstanz: Harting-Gorre, 1990).
10 Sybil H. Milton, "Culture under Duress: Art and the Holocaust," in The Holocaust's Ghost: Writing on Art, Politics, Law and Education, edited by Bernard Schwartz and F. C. DeCoste (Edmonton: University of Alberta Press, 2000), 92; Laharie, Le Camp de Gurs, 173–4.
11 Denis Peschanski, "1939–1946, les camps français d'internement," Hommes et Migration 1175 (1994): 12.
12 Laharie, Le Camp de Gurs, 326–34.
13 Heini Walfisch, "Le Monsieur élégant dans la boue," in Schramm and Vormeier, Vivre à Gurs, 146.

L'École de Gurs[14]

"We did not realise just how extensive was the art produced in the camp [at Gurs,] which was so isolated from the rest of the world, until the spring of 1941, when an art exhibition was held of paintings, drawings, sculpture and graphics in the 'cultural centre,'"[15] wrote Hanna Schramm in her memoir *Vivre à Gurs*.[16] From March 1941, one barracks in each block became a "cultural centre" (*foyer culturel/maison de la culture*) where lectures were held and inmates' visual arts exhibited. Schramm was especially impressed by Julius Collen Turner's[17] portraits, which were "faithful representations of their models, as he refused to improve on the reality of his subjects." Despite this refusal to embellish or flatter the models, as was customary in the camps' commissioned portraits, which often became goods for barter,[18] demand for Turner's work was so great that he could scarcely keep up with it.[19] One of his portraits features Elsbeth Kasser (Figure 1), a Swiss nurse who worked in Gurs on behalf of the Red Cross's *Secours Suisse* and formed close friendships with many of the camp's artists, including Turner and Horst Rosenthal. In addition to purchasing some of the artists' drawings and paintings herself, Kasser encouraged her Swiss colleagues to do the same, which helped the inmates to supplement their paltry food rations. These works and others donated to her by the artists as tokens of their appreciation (including Rosen-

---

14   Borrowed from Mary Felstiner, To Paint her Life: Charlotte Salomon in the Nazi Era (New York: HarperCollins, 1994), 122.
15   Schramm and Vormeier, Vivre à Gurs, 143.
16   Hanna Schramm (b. 1891, Berlin; d. 1978, Paris), an active socialist (SPD) in Germany, moved to Paris where she worked as an educator. She was incarcerated in Gurs in June 1940. She was rescued through the intervention of Abbé Alexander Glasberg in summer 1941, then lived in an absorption centre near Lyon. She remained in France after the Liberation, and is best known for her memoir, Vivre à Gurs. See Ruth Schwertfeger, In Transit: Narratives of German Jews in Exile, Flight, and Internment during "The Dark Years" of France (Berlin: Frank & Timme, 2012), 80–82. On Abbé Glasberg, see Lucien Lazar, L'Abbé Glasberg (Paris: Cerf, 1990); Nina Gourfinkel, L'Autre Patrie (Paris: Seuil, 1953), 231–308.
17   Julius Collen Turner (b. 1881, Schievelbein; d. 1948, Ostend) was a German artist who married a Belgian woman and moved to Ostend in 1936. Following the German occupation of Belgium in May 1940, he was sent to Saint-Cyprien Camp, then transferred to Gurs in October 1940, where he was active in cultural activities. He was released through the efforts of Abbé Glasberg in March 1943 and returned to Belgium three years later. See Norbert Hostyn, Julius Collen Turner 1881–1948: Kunstschilder, Graficus, Portrettist (Ostend: Museum voor Schone Kunsten, Bernd Collen, 1994).
18   Pnina Rosenberg, L'Art des indésirables: L'Art dans les camps d'internement français 1939–1944 (Paris: L'Harmattan, 2003), 83–106.
19   Schramm and Vormeier, Vivre à Gurs, 143.

thal's *Petit Guide à travers le camp de Gurs*), now part of the Elsbeth Kasser Collection, Archive for Contemporary History, Zurich (*Archiv für Zeitgeschichte der ETH Zürich*).[20]

Figure 1: Julius Collen Turner, Portrait of Elsbeth Kasser, 1942, sanguine on paper

Source: Archives of Contemporary History, ETH Zurich / Elsbeth Kasser-Stiftung: BA Elsbeth Kasser / 97.

---

20 Elsbeth Kasser (b. 1910, Niederscherli; d. 1992, Steffisburg) served as a nurse in Gurs Camp from 1940 to 1943. See Therese Schmid-Ackeret, "Elsbeth Kasser (1910–1992): Engagement für Verfolgte und Leidende," in Vergessene Frauen: Humanitäre Kinderhilfe und offizielle Flüchtlingspolitik 1917–1948, edited by Helena Kanyar Becker (Basel: Schwabe, 2010), 130–51; Elsbeth Kasser, "Kunstnere i Gurs-lejren," in Gurs: En interneringslejr Sydfranking, 1939–1942, Tegninger, Akvareller, Fotografier, Samling Elsbeth Kasser (Viborg: Skovgaard Museets Forlag, 1989), 10–11.

Alongside the artists, talented actors, musicians and dancers staged plays from the classical canon as well as cabarets that were highly popular with both their fellow inmates and the camp's French staff (see Figure 5, below).[21] Heini Walfisch's "Théâtre à Gurs" provides an insight into the breadth of the performers' repertoires as well as the meagre rewards they received for their efforts:

> We act for our miserable living,
> Nobody knows what that means
> For Ibsen, a chunk of bread,
> For Shakespeare, an egg
> And maybe a pinch of semolina.[22]

This rich and diverse cultural activity ceased in the summer of 1942 with the onset of deportations to the death camps, where many of Gurs's gifted artists were ruthlessly annihilated.

Gurs through the prism of comics

Horst Rosenthal emigrated to France in 1933 at the age of eighteen and settled in Paris. According to forms he filled in while interned in Gurs, he had worked as an artistic designer, although no other documentation was found to confirm this. With France's declaration of war in early September 1939, Rosenthal, as a "German citizen," was sent to the Parisian Colombes Stadium and from there transferred to various camps, including Gurs. Two months later, he was freed and returned to Paris. However, on 20 May 1940, as the German Wehrmacht attacked France, he was summoned to the Parisian reassembly centre at the Buffalo Stadium and subsequently interned as a "political refugee of German origin" in several camps before ending up in Gurs on 28 October 1940. In July 1942, Rosenthal was transferred to Barcarès, Rivesaltes[23] and finally Drancy prior to his deportation, in Convoy No. 31, to Auschwitz-Birkenau on 11 September 1942.[24]

---

21 On cabarets in Gurs, see Pnina Rosenberg, "Resistance on Stage: Theatrical Performances in French Internment Camps," in Theater unter NS-Herrschaft/Theatre under Pressure, edited by Brigitte Dalinger and Veronika Zang (Vienna: V&R unipress, Vienna University Press, 2018), 291–5.
22 Heini Walfisch, "Théâtre à Gurs," in Schramm and Vormeier, Vivre à Gurs, 139.
23 See Mayer, this volume.
24 See Pnina Rosenberg, "Mickey orphelin: La Courte vie de Horst Rosenthal / Das Waisenkind Mickey Maus, oder: das kurze Leben des Horst Rosenthal," in L'Irréparable itinéraires d'artistes et d'amateurs d'art juifs réfugiés du "Troisième Reich" en France, edited by Anne Grynberg and Johanna Linsler (Magdeburg: Herausgegeben von der Koordinierungsstelle für Kulturgutverluste, 2013), 349–83.

Towards the end of his time in Gurs, Rosenthal produced three small (8 × 14 centimetres each) satirical comic-book critiques of the Vichy regime: *Mickey Mouse in Gurs Camp*; *A Day in the Life of a Resident: Gurs Camp 1942*; and *A Little Guide through Gurs Camp 1942*.[25] These graphic novels depict life in Gurs through the eyes of three different protagonists and from diverse perspectives. In *Mickey Mouse in Gurs*, the narrator is Walt Disney's fictional mouse, who, while strolling somewhere in France, encounters a gendarme. Mickey is unable to present his documents, so the gendarme interns him in Gurs. In contrast to *Mickey*'s first-person narration, *A Day in the Life of a Resident* and *A Little Guide through Gurs Camp* are mostly narrated by all-knowing third persons. However, despite their supposed familiarity with the camp's daily routine, these are unreliable narrators, as is evident in gaps between the images and the text, which serves to heighten the critical irony. The scarcity of information about the artist poses a number of unanswered questions, including the order of the booklets' production. I suspect that *Mickey*, which tells the story of the protagonist's incarceration, came first, followed by *A Day in the Life*, while the hint of an unhappy ending on the final page of *A Little Guide* (see below) suggests that it was the final part of the trilogy.

A Little Guide through Gurs Camp 1942

Visit Gurs

A Little Guide follows the familiar pattern of a guidebook by presenting the marvels of the camp and highlighting its uniqueness. The title page depicts an idyllic scene in which a figure with outstretched arms both welcomes visitors and seems to praise the beauty of this touristic gem (Figure 2). In the middle ground is a typical Gurs barracks, albeit with its windows transformed into two happy eyes and its door a large, smiling mouth, against a backdrop of the snowy Pyrenees.[26] Although there is also a depiction of the camp's fence, it seems unthreatening and far too flimsy to enclose thousands of "undesirables." However, the graphic design of title text, which almost surrounds the image, subtly implies the true nature of Gurs as a place of imprisonment. Thus, the tension between the text and the image is key to deciphering the multi-layered meaning of *A Little Guide*.

---

25 Mickey au camp de Gurs (Mickey Mouse in Gurs Camp) and La Journée d'un héberge: Camp de Gurs 1942 (A Day in the Life of a Resident: Gurs Camp 1942) are in the archives of the Mémorial de la Shoah, Paris (DL xvi-92 and DL xvi-91, respectively); Petit Guide à travers le camp de Gurs 1942 (A Little Guide through Gurs Camp 1942) is in the Archives of Contemporary History, ETH Zurich and Elsbeth Kasser-Stiftung / BA Elsbeth Kasser (122).
26 On the Gurs's "Adrian-type" barracks, see Laharie, Le Camp de Gurs, 35–7.

Figure 2: Horst Rosenthal, A Little Guide through Gurs Camp 1942, title page, ink and watercolour on paper

Source: Archives of Contemporary History, ETH Zurich and Elsbeth Kasser-Stiftung / BA Elsbeth Kasser (122).

On the next page, the invisible narrator uses first person plural when explaining the reason for the guide's publication:

> For some time, posters praising Gurs Camp and inviting travellers to vacation there have been seen at all the railway stations and travel agencies. What is it about this famous camp? In order to satisfy your curiosity, we have prepared this brochure.

This explanatory text appears below a drawing of a couple standing under a railway station clock and reading a poster with the headline "VISIT GURS" (Figure 3). The poster, which depicts two barracks in knee-high water through which a man is wading, again against the backdrop of the Pyrenees, includes the following text:

> If you would like to lose weight
> Go to Gurs!
> Its cuisine is renowned!
> For all information, please visit your police station!

Figure 3: Horst Rosenthal, A Little Guide through Gurs Camp 1942, p. 2, ink and watercolour on paper

Source: Archives of Contemporary History, ETH Zurich and Elsbeth Kasser-Stiftung / BA Elsbeth Kasser (122).

The final line alludes to posters that appeared throughout France in May 1940. German and Austrian émigrés – by then regarded as enemy aliens – were summoned to designated places prior to transportation to various camps, including Gurs. Failure to appear led to imprisonment.[27] Thus, a xenophobic and intimidating government command and subsequent internment on meagre rations in a prison camp are here transformed into a polite invitation to lose some weight at a health spa.[28]

---

27   The posters summoned all Germans and foreigners of undetermined nationalities of German origin aged seventeen to sixty-five to present themselves at designated assembly centres. See Schramm and Vormeier, Vivre à Gurs, 271–3; and Republique Français, Ordre concernant les ressortissants allemands et étrangers de nationalité indéterminée mais d'origin allemande in ibid., facing 64; Rosenberg, "Mickey orphelin," 355, 374–5.

28   The daily allowance in 1942 consisted (theoretically) of 350–400 grams of bread, 100 grams of dried vegetables or rice and 11 grams of margarine, plus 125 grams of meat (or meat substitute) per week and cheese once a month. The actual portions were usually smaller. See Laharie, Le Camp de Gurs, 301–14.

As on the title page, and throughout the rest of the booklet, page two's text and image contradict and challenge each other: while the former describes "inviting" posters, the latter shows two unwelcoming barracks and an inmate trudging forlornly along a flooded path – a familiar practice for internees whenever it rained and the camp became a sea of mud. Close reading of the image/text reveals that the couple with suitcases are not vacationing tourists. Rather, they are émigrés who are adhering to the summons of 23 May 1940 in which "all foreigners mentioned above may, at their expense, take the railway, or any other means of public transport, to reach the assigned assembling centre [...] Their baggage should not be over thirty kilos."[29] By juxtaposing the smart couple with the downtrodden internee, Rosenthal visualises the degradation the travellers are about to suffer – from normal citizens to shabby prisoners deprived of all dignity and freedom of movement, as symbolised by the wading inmate's struggle to move.

Homo pyrénensis

On the next page, the narrator gives the floor to a distinguished academic, who explains to his students – the camp's exotic residents – that "*L'hébergé*, in Latin, is '*homo pyrénensis*'" (Figure 4). Aided by an image of a typical Gurs barracks set against the backdrop of the Pyrenees, the professor outlines the residents' whereabouts ("they live in the southern regions of France [...] in strange habitats, the 'camps'"), diet ("turnips, artichokes, pumpkins and grey tobacco") and living conditions ("males and females are strictly separated," which prevents them from breeding). Through the lecture, Rosenthal presents a largely accurate description of various aspects of life in the camp (several of which are elaborated later in the booklet). However, the pseudo-anthropological terminology endows the text with a sarcastic and satirical dimension.

The lecture begins with a definition of camp's residents – *hébergés* – meaning those who are hosted, guests. This is an allusion to the French Ministry of the Interior's preferred term for the country's detention facilities: *camps d'hébergément* (lit., "accommodation camps").[30]

---

29   Schramm and Vormeier, Vivre à Gurs, 271–2.
30   Anne Grynberg, Les Camps de la honte: Les Internes juifs des camps français 1939–1944 (Paris: La Découverte, 1991), 94. This euphemistic and "laundered" term is deconstructed in Rosenthal's A Day in the Life of a Resident, which portrays a Gurs inmate as a hotel guest. See Pnina Rosenberg, "Mickey Mouse in Gurs: Humour, Irony and Criticism in Works of Art Produced in the Gurs Internment Camp," Rethinking History: The Journal of Theory and Practice 6 (2002) 3: 283–6.

Figure 4: Horst Rosenthal, A Little Guide through Gurs Camp 1942, p. 3, ink and watercolour on paper

Source: Archives of Contemporary History, ETH Zurich and Elsbeth Kasser-Stiftung / BA Elsbeth Kasser (122).

The "anthropological" introduction, tempered with pseudo-scientific Latin to emphasise its supposedly irrefutable validity, evokes an incident in the camp at Le Vernet, which was notorious for its deplorable conditions and brutal punishments.[31] The Hungarian-British author and journalist Arthur Koestler recalled the camp's celebration of New Year's Eve 1941:

> The "politicals" put on an excellent satirical review about the conditions in the camp, culminating in the scene in which a man, after escaping from the camp, preaches to a South Sea tribe about the blessings of real primitive life in Le Vernet. *We have no fire to warm us and no light to see at night and that is real happiness,*

31　Christian Eggers, "Internement sous toutes ses formes: approche d'une vue d'ensemble du système d'internement dans la zone de Vichy," Le Monde Juif 153 (1995): 15–16.

he explains to them until they get angry, kill him, stuff him and put him in their museum with the label: **Homo Verniensis** (Europe 1940).[32]

The inmates are clearly no longer members of normative human society; instead, they belong to a species whose unique characteristics and behaviour will be studied by anthropologists. Such thinking was evident in the anti-Semitic propaganda of Occupied France and the Vichy regime. The notorious *The Jew and France (Le Juif et la France)* exhibition, financed by the Germans and held at the Parisian Berlitz Palace between September 1941 and January 1942, and later in other cities, displayed this attitude, which was echoed in the exhibition catalogue written by Jean Marquès-Rivière, one of the organisers.[33] Marquès-Rivière – a French journalist, author and playwright who headed the police service during the war – stated flatly that Jews were not French, since "the Jews are of a different race [...] and should never mix with the others."[34]

In *A Little Guide*, the professor speaks from behind a lectern that bears the inscription "*Le prof est un âne*" ("The prof is an ass"). This is probably a reference to a common punishment for disobedient French schoolchildren, who were made to don a *bonnet d'âne* (a dunce's cap with two ears like those of a donkey) and stand in the corner.[35] Thus, the inscription not only ridicules the professor and the pseudo-scientific racial theory promulgated by the Vichy and National Socialist regimes but also hints at a reversal of roles: "The teacher is an ass" was no doubt written by his "ignorant" pupils, his captive audience. Moreover, the professor's long white beard, which cascades over the edge of the lectern, resembles an inverted dunce's cap. If the professor traditionally has the power to humiliate and punish, in a kind of poetic justice he himself is now on the receiving end.

The swan song

After illustrating various aspects of camp life, such as the poor sanitation, the black market, censorship and the physical and spiritual confinement and isolation, the booklet concludes with a depiction of a cabaret show (Figure 5). As most of

---

32   Arthur Koestler, Scum of the Earth, translated by Daphne Hardy (London: Victor Gollancz, 1941), 187; bold emphasis added.
33   André Kaspi, "Le Juif et la France: Une Exposition à Paris en 1941," Le Monde Juif 79 (1975): 8–20; André Kaspi, Les Juifs pendant l'Occupation (Paris: Seuil, 1991), 104–10.
34   Jean Marquès-Rivière, Exposition: Le Juif et la France au Palais Berlitz (Paris: Institut d'études des questions juives, 1941), 8.
35   "Bonnet d'âne, oreilles d'âne," in Larousse French Dictionary <https://www.larousse.fr/diction naires/francais/%c3%a2ne/3392/locution?q=bonnet+d%27%C3%A2ne#16000635> (23 May 2021).

the artist–inmates were of German origin, it is not surprising that the final page alludes to Berlin's interwar cabarets and subtly predicts the tragic fate of many of the performers:

> But do you think we were bored? Far from it! We have a permanent theatrical group, whose director is called Nathan. For a year and a half he has presented the same programme, changing only the titles. He enables the French people in the camp to see the true Parisian spirit. As we say in German, "***Schall und Rauch***" [bold emphasis added].

The "Nathan" in question is Alfred Nathan, also known as Peter Pan,[36] who staged the camp's cabaret shows, as Hanna Schramm recalled: "We owe the first soirée to Fred Nathan, who produced a cabaret [...] There was real scenery with a curtain, a small orchestra pit and some rudimentary lighting [...] Nathan wrote most of the scripts."[37]

While the image shows the performer on stage in front of an appreciative audience, the accompanying text praises, albeit somewhat ironically, Nathan's rather repetitive programme before adding that the shows enable the French administrators and others in the camp "to see the true Parisian spirit." Although this might be a reference to one particular cabaret – *Folies (He) Bergère*[38] – there is no doubt that Rosenthal also wanted to highlight the troupe's cultural and artistic roots: "As we say in German, '*Schall und Rauch* [sound and smoke].'" This, the final sentence in *A Little Guide*, is a reference to a famous Berlin cabaret founded in 1901 by the actor and director Max Reinhardt, and probably also to Margot Ruth Rauch (b. 1922, Berlin; d. 1942, Auschwitz), a young musician and dancer from Berlin who featured in a number of Gurs Camp productions.[39] This gifted performer, who had delighted her fellow inmates throughout her time in the camp, was loaded onto the first convoy out of Gurs on 6 August 1942,[40] transferred to Drancy, then, four days later, deported to

---

36 Alfred Nathan (b. 1909, Berlin; d. 1976, East Berlin), stage name Peter Pan, was a Jewish cabaret performer associated with the political left who fled to Paris in 1933. He escaped across the Spanish border on 31 December 1942. See Klaus Budzinski and Reinhard Hippen, Metzler-Kabarett-Lexikon (Stuttgart: J. B. Metzler, 2000), 294; André Fontaine, Le Camp d'étrangers des Milles, 1939–1943 (Aix-en-Provence: Ebisud, 1989), 95–6, 109.
37 Schramm and Vormeier, Vivre à Gurs, 136.
38 The title, Folies (He) Bergère, is an ironic pun: hébergés = inmates and Folies Bergère is a famous Parisian cabaret music-hall. See Folies (He) Bergère, edited and mise-en-scène by Alfred Nathan, music by Kurt Leval, Center for Holocaust and Genocide Studies, University of Minnesota.
39 Rauch played the main role – a Disney-esque cartoon character – in Shmok's Scornful Newsreel (Schmocks hoehnende Wochenschau), and in Folies (He) Bergère. See Shmok's Scornful Newsreel, edited and mise-en-scène by Alfred Nathan, music by Kurt Leval, Center for Holocaust and Genocide Studies, University of Minnesota.
40 Laharie, Le Camp de Gurs, 217.

Auschwitz on Transport no. 17, never to return.[41] Rosenthal's pun on her name may be read as an ominous prediction of the young dancer's tragic fate.

Figure 5: Horst Rosenthal, A Little Guide through Gurs Camp 1942, p. 12, ink and watercolour on paper

Source: Archives of Contemporary History, ETH Zurich and Elsbeth Kasser-Stiftung/BA Elsbeth Kasser (122).

The final curtain fell in Gurs as the deportations began, as one of the remaining inmates recalled: "The convoy of 6 August included almost all our artistic individuals, all those young people who tried to maintain, with great effort, the cultural activities in the camp [...] the dancers Ruth Rauch and Steffi Smith."[42]

Many of these deportees, including Rosenthal, were sent to the gas chambers of Auschwitz. Thus, their rich artistic activities in Gurs were their "swan song."

---

41   Serge Klarsfeld, Memorial to the Jews Deported from France 1942–1944: Documentation of the Deportation of the Victims of the Final Solution in France (New York: Beate Klarsfeld Foundation, 1983), 140, 145.
42   Heini Walfisch, quoted in Schramm and Vormeier, Vivre à Gurs, 160.

Conclusion: removal of the mask

There are two narrators in the twelve pages of A Little Guide. Throughout most of the booklet, the omnipresent guide (or his spokesman – the professor) presents facts and figures "to satisfy" his readers' "curiosity" about the hébergés, whom he describes as "them." Yet, a different narrator – an insider – suddenly and unexpectedly steps forward on the final page. He refers to some of his fellow-inmates by name, acts as a spokesman for the rest of the hébergés and not only uses first (as opposed to third) person plural but specifies all of the residents' – including his own – collective national and cultural origins: "**As we say in German**" (bold emphasis added). In this way, the artist finally unveils the main narrator's true identity: the omnipresent and supposedly objective narrator is actually an inmate, one of the German-Jewish émigrés who are now the camp's hébergés. Although derided as a sub-human homo pyrénensis, it is one of this group who enables the camp's French residents to see "true Parisian spirit." Rosenthal employed a similar artistic device in the final panel of Mickey Mouse in Gurs, in which the protagonist and narrator, Mickey, escapes. Below Mickey's signature, added as a postscript, the artist not only signed his own name but also specified the location and the date – "Gurs Camp 1942." As a result, in addition to revealing himself as the "father" of Mickey, Rosenthal subtly hinted that, in contrast to his fictional creation, he had no means of escape.[43] Thus, we see that one of Rosenthal's artistic strategies was to hide his own persona behind a mask – Mickey Mouse or the impartial narrator – prior to revealing his true self at a crucial moment.

Graphic novels juxtapose images and text to tell a story, with each medium supporting and reinforcing the other, either directly or in a confrontational contrast, by means of irony, satire and other devices. Sometimes the text explains the picture, sometimes it contradicts it, and sometimes the image and the text speak in two voices at once.[44] As we have seen, the panels with a third-person narrator highlight the discrepancies between the "official" semi-bureaucratic textual information and the visual reality. However, this dichotomy is blurred in the final panel (Figure 5). The text describes the image quite accurately, yet only those who share the artist's background and experiences will fully grasp the connotations and allusions that expand and enrich the visualisation.

This poignant final panel, despite its frivolous character, underlines not only the Gurs inmates' heroic attempts to maintain a semblance of normality by recreating

---

43   Pnina Rosenberg, "From Mice to Mickey to Maus: The Metaphor of Evil and its Metamorphosis in the Holocaust," in Critical Insights: Good and Evil, edited by Margaret Sönser Breen (Ipswich, MA: Salem Press, 2013), 201–2.
44   Hugo Frey and Benjamin Noys, "History in the Graphic Novel," Rethinking History 6 (2002) 3: 255.

their pre-war activities but also encapsulates the crucial role that cultural activities such as performing and painting can play by reinforcing spiritual resistance in "The Concentrationary Universe" (*l'univers Concentrationnaire*).[45]

Acknowledgement

I would like to extend my thanks to the Archiv für Zeitgeschichte der ETH Zürich, Elsbeth Kasser-Stiftung (Archive for Contemporary History at ETH in Zurich, Elsbeth Kasser Foundation) for their permission to use Horst Rosenthal's and Julius Collen Turner's images in this article.

---

45 Borrowed from David Rousset, L'univers Concentrationnaire. (Paris: Éditions du Pavois, 1946).

Singing and dancing for freedom of movement[1]
Enacting citizenship and resisting forced confinement in "hotspot" refugee camps in Thessaloniki, Greece 2016

Ioannis Christidis

Introduction

When the Balkan migration route was blocked in March 2016, many of the people trying to cross the Greek–North Macedonian border were trapped in the border area close to the Greek village of Idomeni. Despite the mass struggle for freedom of movement that followed, the border remained closed. In May 2016, the Greek police forcibly transferred 15,000 people from Idomeni into twelve run-down refugee camps, consisting of abandoned military facilities and industrial warehouses in the suburbs of Thessaloniki, Greece's second-largest city, some 70 km from the border. The refugees' attempts to move forward had been thwarted and, furthermore, the living conditions in these state- and EU-run camps were unimaginably grim. Soon, these so-called "hotspot" camps became places of resistance. Backed by an extensive solidarity movement, residents of the camps started to organise protests both inside the camps themselves and in the centre of the city.

In much of the trans-disciplinary literature on refugee camps, individuals labelled "refugees" are often seen as people "out of place,"[2] as depoliticised "bared lives"[3] who "on the way to the camps […] are stripped of every single element of their identities, except one: that of stateless, placeless and functionless refugees."[4] Such approaches overlook the fact that refugees still have their own agency, but they

---

[1] This article forms part of the author's Ph.D. project in ethnomusicology, entitled "Music in the Experience of Forced Migration from Syria to European Borderland." Since 2020, this project has been conducted within the Music and Minorities Research Center of the University of Music and Performing Arts, Vienna, funded by the Austrian Science Fund (FWF): Z 352-G26.
[2] Cathrine Brun, "Reterritorializing the Relationship between People and Place in Refugee Studies," Geografiska Annaler. Series B, Human Geography 83 (2001) 1: 15–25.
[3] Giorgio Agamben, Homo Sacer: Sovereign Power and Bare Life (Stanford, CA: Stanford University Press, 1998).
[4] Zygmunt Bauman, Wasted Lives: Modernity and Its Outcasts (Oxford: Malden, 2004), 76.

do shed some light on the impact of certain policies on refugees' lives. Particularly in Greece, the refugee experience is usually associated with forced immobility in camps, imposed by EU and Greek migration-control policies, and by grinding asylum procedures.[5] Forced migrants are forced into a state of limbo where the absence of basic human, civil and political rights renders them completely subject to state power and often turns them into victims of unaccountable institutional violence.[6] Still, however appalling, this victimisation and dehumanisation constitutes only one side of the complex experience of forced migration and immobilisation of refugees in camps.[7]

This article examines the role of music in the everyday lives of Syrian refugees in the hotspot camps of the EU. It demonstrates music's capacity to evoke collective empathy, mobilise participation and foster acts of citizenship, shifting the imaginaries surrounding refugees from victimisation to agency and strength. Empirical research conducted in Thessaloniki, Greece, in 2016 included audiovisual and digital documentation of music and dance performances in refugee camps and during protests in the city centre as well as exploratory interviews with the main protagonists, who were mainly young men of Syrian origin.[8] This was then supplemented with online research.

The opening section of the article provides a general description of the sociopolitical and historical context of the music. The next section presents an overview of the musical expressions documented in Thessaloniki; the actors and functions; musical genres and prominent songs and dances; the musical instruments; and the means of amplifying, circulating and reproducing music. The third section offers a theoretical approach to music in the context of forced migration via a framework that considers the various stages of the refugee experience – from pre-departure contexts to those relating to the refugee journey and finally confinement in refugee camps – as crucial factors in the transforming and transformative meaning of refugees' music. The fourth section presents direct accounts from the field, particularly those of two protest singers of Syrian origin. Finally, the last section theorises

---

5   Nadina Leivaditi et al., Refugee Protection: Greece – Country Report (Multilevel Governance of Mass Migration in Europe and Beyond Project #770564, Horizon, Report Series, 2020).
6   Jihane Ben Farhat et al., "Syrian Refugees in Greece: Experience with Violence, Mental Health Status, and Access to Information during the Journey and while in Greece," BMC Medicine 16 (2018): 40.
7   Jonathan Darling, "Becoming Bare Life: Asylum, Hospitality, and the Politics of Encampment," Environment and Planning D: Society and Space 27 (August 2009) 4: 649–665; Adam Ramadan, "Spatialising the Refugee Camp," Transactions of the Institute of British Geographers 38 (2013) 1: 65–77; Simon Turner, "What Is a Refugee Camp? Explorations of the Limits and Effects of the Camp," *Journal of Refugee Studies* 29 (2016): 139–148.
8   To avoid potentially harmful consequences, all of the interviewees are unnamed.

the musical expressions of young Syrian men in Thessaloniki as *musical acts of citizenship*, acts that "claim rights and impose obligations in emotionally charged tones."[9] The main conclusion is that Syrian refugees' music-making in Thessaloniki in 2016 was a means by which they recreated a community of struggle with reference to past experiences in Syria but also articulated new objectives connected to the context of their confinement in hotspot camps. Music and dance then became key elements in their goals of escaping from the camps; connecting with the social life of the city and "acting as being citizens" and, finally, advancing their struggle for greater freedom of movement.

The socio-political and historical context of the hotspot camps

The years 2015 and 2016 were marked by an unprecedented increase in the number of people who reached European countries and sought protection under the international framework for refugees. These people travelled by any possible and often risky means. In 2015 alone, of those who tried to cross from Turkey to Europe on boats, 806 people were reported as dead or missing.[10] This mass migration was triggered by a series of conflicts in the Middle East, South Asia and Africa, the most prominent of which was the civil war in Syria[11] which erupted in 2011 after the regime's deadly repression of a mass popular protest movement that many Syrians termed the "Syrian Revolution."[12]

The ongoing conflict in Syria had disastrous effects on human lives (about 600,000 deaths since 2011).[13] In addition, according to the UNHCR, it forced more than the half of the population to abandon their homes.[14] In 2018, the population of dispersed Syrians outside Syria was estimated at 5,629,700, primarily shared among Turkey (63.8%), Lebanon (16.9%), Jordan (11.9%) and Iraq (4.4%).[15] In addition, it is thought that about one million Syrians (18%) have migrated to Europe

---

9   Engin F. Isin and Greg M. Nielsen, Acts of Citizenship (London: Zed Books, 2008), 10.
10 Duvell H. Crawley et al., Unpacking a Rapidly Changing Scenario: Migration Flows, Routes and Trajectories across the Mediterranean: Unravelling the Mediterranean Migration Crisis (MEDMIG Research Brief No. 1, 2016), 5.
11 UNHCR, Global Trends: Forced Displacement in 2014 (Geneva: UNHCR, 2015).
12 Robin Yassin-Kassab and Leila Al-Shami, *Burning Country* (London: Pluto Press, 2016).
13 Syrian Observatory for Human Rights, "Total Death Toll," June 1, 2021 <https://www.syriahr.com/en/217360/> (13 June 2021).
14 The estimated population of Syria was 21.1 million before the war. According to the UNCHR, today there are 6.7 million internally displaced persons in Syria and 6.6 million Syrian refugees. See UNHCR, "Syria Emergency" <https://www.unhcr.org/syria-emergency.html> (13 June 2021).
15 UNHCR, "Refugees Operational Portal (2018)" <https://data2.unhcr.org/en/situations/syria> (13 June 2021).

since 2011, including Palestinian and Iraqi refugees who were living in Syria before the war and Kurdish Syrians who have long been a discriminated group in their home country. Forced migrants from Afghanistan, Iraq, Iran, Pakistan, Somalia, Eritrea, Sudan, Cameroon and other countries have also made their way to Europe over the last decade, albeit in smaller numbers than the Syrians.[16] For instance, in 2015 alone, a total of about 850,000 migrants crossed the border from Turkey to Greece, then made their way to Central Europe along the so-called "Balkan route."[17]

The scale of this movement of people made it an important topic in the media and in EU political discourse. Usually termed the "refugee crisis," it mostly constituted a crisis of the Common European Asylum System, as developed within several EU directives and the Dublin III Regulation of 2013.[18] These migration and asylum control mechanisms are manifestations of the EU's trend towards the securitisation of migration, which seeks to develop a "strong security system to compensate for the 'security lost' by the free movement of persons."[19] In practice, this implies stricter control of the EU's external borders as well as specific measures that will render migrants immobile in entry countries or even non-EU neighbouring states. Dublin III, in particular, allocated the tasks of receiving and processing applications for international protection to specific member states, including all of those with external EU borders.[20]

Greece faced problems implementing Dublin III from the very beginning, so it was little surprise that the system collapsed completely under the increased pressure of the mass migration movement. This triggered controversial reactions within individual EU states. On the one hand, Germany's temporary suspension of the Dublin regulations was welcomed by many actors, including refugees, as a progressive humanitarian response. On the other hand, the European Commission's announcement of a new "Agenda on Migration," published in May 2015, which contained guidelines on how the crisis should be managed, not only aligned with the existing trend of securitisation but aimed to make it even stringent. Specifically, the Agenda advocated early identification of those migrants with a right to asylum and their separation from those with no such right. The former – after long bureaucratic procedures – would then be permitted to proceed to other EU countries,

---

16 Leivaditi et al., "Refugee Protection: Greece," 13.
17 Ibid., 5.
18 Arne Niemann and Natascha Zaun, "EU Refugee Policies and Politics in Times of Crisis: Theoretical and Empirical Perspectives," Journal of Common Market Studies 56 (2017): 1, 3–22.
19 Philippe Bourbeau, The Securitization of Migration: A Study of Movement and Order (London: Routledge, 2011), 27.
20 See in EUR-Lex, "Regulation (EU) No 604/2013 of the European Parliament and of the Council of 26 June 2013," Article 13 <https://eur-lex.europa.eu/legal-content/EN/TXT/?uri=CELEX%3A02013R0604-20130629> (13 June 2021).

whereas the latter would be returned to their countries of origin.²¹ This strategy was subsequently implemented through the so-called "hotspot" approach. To reinforce the border regime and ensure that all migrants who entered Europe irregularly would be registered, identified and processed for either relocation or return, the EU designated hotspot areas in all "frontline" countries where entries were increasing and launched "fast-track" legal and political measures. As part of this "hotspot" mechanism, a number of "Reception and Identification Camps" (commonly known as "hotspot camps") were established in Greek border zones, such as the islands of the northwestern Aegean. These were managed by a variety of different agencies, including the Greek police and army, the European Asylum Support Office (EASO), the European Border and Coast Guard Agency (Frontex), Interpol, the UNHCR, the Red Cross and other humanitarian organisations.

In March 2016, with the closure of the Balkan route and the signing of an agreement between the EU and Turkey that facilitated returns, Greece was transformed from a transit stop into a host country with a growing population of asylum-seekers. Ever more poorly equipped and badly maintained hotspot camps were erected to accommodate refugees arriving from the Greek islands and others who were forcibly relocated from the border zones. For instance, between February and June 2016, twelve hotspot camps were established in the greater urban area of Thessaloniki alone.²² The Greek government simply rented abandoned warehouses, old military facilities and factories, usually in the city's highly polluted western industrial zone and close to the neglected rubbish dumps, then installed tents and containers provided by the UNHCR.

The four largest camps were located on the old Diavata military base, in the abandoned Softex factory and in warehouses in Oreokastro and Vassilika – each provided basic accommodation for between 1,000 and 2,000 people. Some of the camps were ethnically orientated (e.g. for Kurdish Syrians), although the majority were not. There was a constant influx of new residents, so it may be assumed that the ethnic composition of the mixed camps approximated the proportions of migrants who were arriving in Greece at the time. According to UNHCR data, 48 per cent of new arrivals in the camps between January and June 2016 were Syrians, 25 per cent were

---

21   See European Commission, "Communication from the Commission to the European Parliament, the Council, the European Economic and Social Committee and the Committee of the Regions: A European Agenda on Migration," May 2015 <https://ec.europa.eu/home-affairs/sites/default/files/what-we-do/policies/european-agenda-migration/background-information/docs/communication_on_the_european_agenda_on_migration_en.pdf> (13 June 2021).
22   During that period, the "Moving Europe" political initiative created a very well-informed interactive map that shows the exact locations of the refugee camps in northern Greece <http://moving-europe.org/mapping-of-refugee-camps-in-northern-greece/> (13 June 2021).

Afghans and 15 per cent were Iraqis, of whom 41 per cent were adult men, 21 per cent were adult women and 37 per cent were children.[23]

At first, all of the camps looked more like public spaces of imposed socialisation rather than havens of safety and privacy, but this started to change when some of them started to replace the tents with container houses. Besides the forced migrants themselves, Greek police, military and other security personnel, employees of asylum services, Greek and foreign NGOs, UNHCR staff and volunteers and caterers were all on site on a daily basis.

The Greek state probably envisioned that it would be able to maintain firm control over access to and exit from these camps, but the wire fences and checkpoints it erected proved totally inadequate.[24] Residents could enter and exit freely – sometimes through holes made in the fence -, although there was nothing for them to do in the desolate surrounding areas. Inside, the living conditions were equally harsh and inhumane. Due to a lack of space under roofed facilities, tents were erected outdoors, where the temperature could reach 40°C in the summer months. Insects and rodents caused skin infections, especially among the children, and there were fires and accidents on a regular basis. Rain resulted in extensive flooding and the destruction of tents and the residents' possessions. Although NGOs offered some activities for the children, the adults were left with nothing to do during the day other than wait for the results of their relocation applications, which always took months. To highlight the appalling conditions inside the Oreokastro camp, some of the residents painted the word "Tomb" on their tents.[25] Nevertheless, some of the residents managed to keep themselves busy by engaging in financial activities, selling freshly cooked food or cigarettes, providing barbering services, or helping with the children's activities.

Although the international media reported on conditions in the camps, the voices and opinions of the residents were seldom heard in the local media. The refugees' segregation became newsworthy only when fights broke out between residents or accidents occurred. The imposed uncertainty and the migrants' loss of control over their own movement soon triggered protests and several acts of resistance. From the very beginning, local activists organised visits to the camps

---

23 UNHCR, "Greece Factsheet," 1–30 June 2016 <https://data2.unhcr.org/en/documents/details/49749> (13 June 2021).

24 In 2021, the Greek government started to build concrete walls around migrant camps in mainland Greece. See Marion MacGregor, "Greece: Migrant Camps Surrounded by Concrete Walls," INFOMIGRANTS, 9 June 2021 <https://www.infomigrants.net/en/post/32834/greece-migrant-camps-surrounded-by-concrete-walls> (13 June 2021).

25 Aryn Baker, "Syrian Refugees in Greece Are Moving out of Camps, and into a New Kind of Limbo," *Time*, 6 February 2017 <https://time.com/4659464/greeces-refugee-hotels-limbo-finding-home/> (13 June 2021).

with the aim of breaking their isolation and supporting the refugees' demands for better living conditions and more freedom of movement.[26]

During the first such visit, in June 2016, after the activists had installed a sound system for announcements, a group of young residents with their mobile phones in their hands asked if they could connect them to the speakers and play some music. The planned announcements were postponed and a kind of mini-festival began, with ever more people gathering around the speakers and some starting to dance in a huge circle. Many of those present soon became very emotional. Thereafter, this type of musical protest became a common feature of daily life in the camps and during demonstrations in the city centre, with some events uploaded onto the internet or even live-streamed on activists' websites.

I held a threefold position in these events as an active citizen of Thessaloniki involved in solidarity initiatives, a student of musicology and a player of the Middle Eastern oud. The performances were so unique that I was motivated first to start documenting them and later to try to understand what they meant for their actors. Bridging potential gaps in understanding between refugees and local communities, due to language barriers, certain expectations and a variety of class, gender, cultural and other factors, became one of my research goals. Ethnomusicological scholarship on music and forced migration, as well as on music and minorities, provided the theory and method I needed to examine more closely the role of music in these particular experiences of the Syrian refugees I encountered in Thessaloniki.

An overview of documented musical expressions

Before long, every protest featured music, singing or dancing. The main protagonists in these musical protests were young Syrian-Arab men who mainly sang modern Arabic pop songs, with topics relating to the Syrian uprising and their ongoing experiences as refugees, and danced to a popular Syrian genre known as *dabke*. The singing and dancing usually preceded the protests. Two young men would often approach a microphone connected to the speakers and simply start to sing, without any background music to accompany them. Their singing was inspirational, and sometimes punctuated by slogans, but the main reaction was often bewilderment among the mixed audiences of refugees and local activists who could not understand Arabic.

---

26   An example of this mobilisation was the organisation of an international "No Border Camp" in Thessaloniki in July 2016. The initiative running this project published a multilingual newspaper to facilitate communication between the refugees and local society <https://noborder2016.espivblogs.net/noborder-newspaper/> (13 June 2021).

If the singing was mainly directed towards other members of the Syrian-Arab camp community, the *dabke* dance routines soon became popular with other nationalities in addition to the Syrians. *Dabke* is best described as a genre stemming from folk Middle Eastern dance music, which developed during the 1990s into a modern genre of popular music, namely *musiqa sha'biyya*.[27] It features lively electronic beats combined with emulations of traditional instruments like the mijwiz generated by synthesisers and vocals with lyrics in colloquial Arabic. *Dabke* is commonly broadcast – or played live – in Syria and danced during weddings and other festivals.

In Thessaloniki, the participants in dabke – most of whom were young men – generally assembled in a circular or linear formation with their hands clasped together, then performed a variety of steps, although most of the dances were characterised by repetitive stamping of the left foot. The lead performer, whose dance moves tended to be more elaborate and sophisticated, would decide when it was time to move from one routine to the next and then signal this to the other participants. Children would often join the end of the line and attempt to emulate the more basic moves. In one party at the campus of Aristotle University, Thessaloniki, camp residents, students and activists danced in huge concentric circles and spirals.

Speakers, mobile phones, digital networks and the internet all played key roles in these musical expressions. First, most of the tracks were downloaded from YouTube or other online platforms. Second, refugees and activists would often record and/or live-stream performances on Facebook pages they had created to raise awareness of living conditions within the camps, to organise acts of resistance and to establish lines of communication between the residents and potential supporters. Third, the refugees used mobile devices to maintain an emotional connection with their former lives in Syria, whether by listening to and singing their favourite songs or by practising religious rituals. Fourth, participatory aspects of networks such as Facebook helped to provide some relief from the monotonous daily routine of life in the camps. With that in mind, the activist group Refugee TV organised a talent show – *Refugees Got Talent* – in the Oreokastro camp.[28] Contestants performed a wide variety of musical genres on a range of instruments. For

---

27 Shayna Silverstein, "The Stars of Musiqa Sha'biyya," 6 August 2020 <https://norient.com/academic/new-wave-dabke> (13 June 2021).

28 An interview with members of the Refugee TV team can be found in Charalampos Tsavdaroglou, "'Refugee TV' and 'Refugees Got Talent' Projects Affective and Decolonial Geographies of Invisible Common Spaces," in Contested Borderscapes: Transnational Geographies vis-à-vis Fortress Europe, edited by Dionysios Gouvia et al. (Thessaloniki and Mytilene: Invisible Cities Research Group, 2019), 177–194. <https://aoratspoleis.files.wordpress.com/2019/05/contested-borderscapes-4.pdf> (13.06.2021).

instance, an oud player and his son sang "Safarna Al Euroba"²⁹ ("On Our Journey to Europe"); a young man from Raqqa sang in a style that was popular in his home city; and two young girls sang a rap song. Votes were cast online, and the organisers reported that the camp residents' enthusiasm for the event exceeded their expectations.³⁰

Besides the protests, there was more casual, less organised music-making in private tents – which, given the lack of space and the close proximity to neighbouring tents, often became more or less public events too – and in cafés and private apartments in the centre of Thessaloniki. In these contexts, the preference was usually for old popular Arabic songs that the singers identified as *"tarab."* This music had the power to drive some singers and/or audiences to something approaching individual or collective ecstasy – the literal definition of the word *"tarab."* Meanwhile, international and Arabic pop music, hip hop and even heavy metal were played at children's parties and group activities in the camps and the city centre. In at least two of the camps, larger tents were converted into makeshift mosques from which the daily call to prayer – the *adhan* – was broadcast through loudspeakers.³¹ And, finally, some residents played their own musical instruments, including ouds, guitars, darbukes (a type of drum) and sazes.

Music and forced migration

There is a saying among those who study music in the context of migration: music goes where people go. Nevertheless, ethnomusicology's main premise is that music becomes meaningful within specific social and cultural contexts. If these con-

---

29 Original title in Arabic: سافرنا ع اوربا . Written by the Syrian pop singer Nidal Karam (now resident in the Netherlands) to describe his own refugee experience, "Safarna Al Euroba" was widely circulated among Syrian refugees on the internet in 2015 and 2016.

30 There is a documentary about this contest, "Refugees Got Talent," directed by Theopi Skarlatos for Al-Jazeera, which provides valuable information about the situation in Thessaloniki's camps and the roles of music and mobile technologies in the refugees' daily routine and resistance, specifically in the camp of Oreokastro. It is available online at <https://www.aljazeera.com/programmes/witness/2017/03/refugees-talent-170323115635234.html> (13 June 2021).

31 According to Michael Frishkopf, although melodic recitation is an important feature of Islamic religious practice, the Arabic terms mūsīqa and ghinā' (singing) have secular connotations and do not correspond to religious performances of melodic chants. Thus, even though, acoustically, the adhan sounds like what is commonly termed "music," it is not necessarily experienced in the same way by individuals from different cultural backgrounds. See Michael Frishkopf, "Islamic Hymnody in Egypt: Al-Inshād al-Dīnī," in Garland Encyclopedia of World Music, Volume 6: The Middle East, edited by Virginia Danielson et al. (London – New York: Routledge, 2002), 165–176.

texts are rapidly transformed due to social, financial or environmental crises, or indeed forced migration, then consequent transformations might be expected in the music itself and the ways in which it is meaningful. As Adelaida Reyes suggested, in addition to being an expression of cultural traits relating to their homeland, the music of a migrant group is likely to constitute a response to shifting realities and emerging social conditions in their new environment.[32] Drawing on refugee and forced migration studies, Reyes also suggested that every possible aspect of forced migration should be taken into consideration when studying the music of migrants, particularly those designated as refugees. Hence, researchers should pay close attention to pre-departure circumstances, encounters with conflict, the migratory journey itself, institutional labelling and control, and finally the conditions refugees face when reaching their final destination.[33] In addition to revealing how migrant groups adjust themselves – and their music – to new environments, this approach highlights the importance of social, political and cultural interactions, as well as the power dynamics that develop between migrant groups and wider society, in the development of music.

Of course, it should be noted that this is a very general approach. Identifying tens of thousands of people with a variety of cultural, political, social, gender and other experiences solely as "refugees" simply because they happen to originate in one country and move to another runs the risk of neglecting their individual and collective diversity and the power dynamics of their interactions with one another. To take the case of Syrian forced migrants, it is imperative to consider the intersecting categories of ethnicity, class, gender, religion and political affiliation that were key features of pre-war Syria's heterogeneous society. Within a total population of roughly 21.1 million,[34] 80–85 per cent were Arabs, 10 per cent were Kurds (mainly Sunni with a Yazidi minority, all of whom suffered cultural and political discrimination for many years), 4–5 per cent were Turkmens, 3–4 per cent were Assyrians (mainly Christians) and 1 per cent were Armenians.[35] In terms of religion, 74 per cent of Syrians were Sunni Muslims, while 13 per cent were from other branches of Islam (e.g. Ismailis, Shiites, Alawites and Druze), 8–10 per cent were Christians (Eastern Orthodox, Catholic or Maronite) and there were small Yazidi

---

32   Adelaida Reyes, "Music and Tradition: From Native to Adopted Land through the Refugee Experience," Yearbook for Traditional Music 21 (1989): 25–35.
33   Adelaida Reyes, "Music and the Refugee Experience," World of Music 32 (1990) 3: 3–21.
34   World Bank, "Population, Total – Syrian Arab Republic" <https://data.worldbank.org/indicator/SP.POP.TOTL?locations=SY> (13 June 2021).
35   Mustafa Khalifa, "The Impossible Partition of Syria" (2013) <https://s3.eu-central-1.amazonaws.com/storage.arab-reform.net/ari/2013/10/02101305/Arab_Reform_Initiative_2013-10_Research_Paper_en_the_impossible_partition_of_syria.pdf> (13 June 2021).

and Jewish communities.[36] The country also hosted approximately 500,000 Palestinian and 1.2 million Iraqi refugees.[37] Half of the population lived in cities, and there were deep urban–rural class and educational divides.[38] Entrenched patriarchal values, coupled with political, religious and legal constraints, rendered Syria's women significantly less powerful than their male counterparts.[39] Finally, the authoritarian Assad regime has held power for more than half a century, during which time it has restricted freedom of speech and artistic expression, outlawed unionisation, banned independent political parties and ruthlessly suppressed all forms of anti-government protest with deadly violence. For instance, in 2011, when Syrian protesters joined the Arab Spring movement and started to demand democratic reforms, the authorities reacted by ordering snipers to shoot into the crowds. The violence rapidly escalated into civil war and then a proxy war in which a number of states and armed militias attempted to assert control over the region. The carnage not only drove almost half of the Syrian population to leave their homes but also created polarised groups of migrants. After realising that the progressive demands of the Syrian uprising in the domain of civil and political rights would remain unfulfilled, the young organisers of the musical protests in Thessaloniki explained that they had been forced to flee Syria because they refused to join any of the remaining warring factions. This was a decision that left them vulnerable to attack from both the government and Islamist militias, with the latter playing an increasingly dominant role in the conflict, especially after 2013.

Although the complexity and heterogeneity of pre-war Syrian society and the individual characteristics and personalities of the migrants themselves mean there is no such thing as a uniform experience of forced migration from Syria, a number of commonalities may be identified: the high-risk nature of the journey due to strict border controls; the migrants' loss of control over many aspects of their own lives, including their security, especially if they end up in refugee camps; temporary or permanent deprivation of basic human rights due to the migrants' categorisation as "stateless"; and ill-treatment at the hands of particular EU member states and often hostile local societies. Even though forced migrants from Syria who make their way to Europe are entitled to protection under international law, all the above fac-

---

36   Bureau of Democracy – Human Rights and Labor, United States Department of State, "International Religious Freedom Report, 2011" <https://2009-2017.state.gov/j/drl/rls/irf/2011religiousfreedom/index.htm?dlid=192907#> (13 June 2021).
37   Heritage for Peace, "Demographics" <http://www.heritageforpeace.org/syria-country-information/geography/> (13 June 2021).
38   Jo-Anne Dillabough et al., The State of Higher Education in Syria Pre-2011. (London: Council for At-Risk Academics, British Council and University of Cambridge, 2019).
39   Freedom House, "Women's Rights in the Middle East and North Africa 2010 – Syria" <https://www.refworld.org/docid/4b99011dc.html> (13 June 2021).

tors render them relatively powerless. Thus, Syrian refugees may be perceived as socially, politically and legally delineated minorities.

Ethnomusicological research has found that power asymmetries between dominant and weaker groups – such as those that prevail due to the spatial, political and social segregation of refugees from mainstream society in Thessaloniki – can play a determinative role in minorities' musical expressions and responses.[40] It is my contention that the musical expressions of Syrian refugees in Thessaloniki are linked to both their pre-departure circumstances and their experiences during their journeys. In particular, they resonate not only with the political conflict back in Syria but also, following adaptation to a new context of confrontation, with the closure of borders and the EU's hotspot approach to the accommodation of refugees.

Accounts from the field

During my time in Thessaloniki, "Janna, Janna" ("Paradise, Paradise") was one of the most popular songs in the city's refugee camps.[41] When asked about it, one of the protest singers immediately associated it with the start of the Syrian revolution, the protest movement and the ensuing violence and repression, and explained that all of the songs they performed in Thessaloniki were sad.[42] I asked him to sing it for me, but he said that only a large group could convey the true depth of the song's sentiments by singing – and indeed dancing – in unison. He stressed that singing was psychologically beneficial because the music connected him to his past but also allayed some of his harsher memories. In addition, he believed that the protests would help him achieve his ultimate goal – to leave the camp and move to another part of Europe.

Another protest singer revealed that he had started singing in public during the anti-regime protests back in Syria.[43] He insisted that singing could play a key role in any protest movement because of music's power "to create feelings." Moreover, it enabled the protesters to attract more support and to subvert their representation as terrorists or foreign provocateurs in the government-backed media. Music had always been a central feature of everyday life in his home town, especially during social events and local festivals, because "without music and singing [any gathering of a large group of people] has no meaning." As he classified protests as social events,

---

40   Ursula Hemetek, "History, Theory and Methods of Minority Research in Ethnomusicology: The Past, the Present and Visions for the Future," in World Music Studies, edited by Regine Allgayer Kaufmann (Berlin: Logos Verlag, 2016), 93–112.
41   Original title in Arabic: جنة جنة
42   Based on an interview conducted by the author in Thessaloniki on 25 October 2016.
43   Based on an interview conducted by the author online on 13 July 2020.

he suggested that they would be similarly "cold" and "soulless" without musical accompaniment. Singing, for him, was a means to create and maintain a sense of collectivity and common purpose among the young protesters in Thessaloniki and to stir emotions among their audiences, including non-Arab speakers who could not understand the precise meaning of the words. However, in non-protest contexts, he preferred to sing old popular or improvisational love songs, or even *tarab* songs, to evoke memories and create a sense of relief for himself and his companions.

Musical acts of citizenship

Rather than being a tool to promote a specific political agenda in the narrow sphere of institutionalised politics, young Syrian refugees' musical performances in Thessaloniki became political in the sense of what Engin Isin and Greg Nielsen term "acts of citizenship":

> [D]eeds that [...] disrupt habitus, create new possibilities, claim rights and impose obligations in emotionally charged tones; pose their claims in enduring and creative expressions; and, most of all, are the actual moments that shift established practices, status and order.[44]

In a similar vein, the ethnomusicologist Thomas Turino insists:

> The arts are founded on the interplay of the Possible and the Actual and can awaken us from habit. The arts [...] are a type of framed activity where it is expected that the imagination and new possibilities will be given special license.[45]

Moreover, he suggests that certain types of music-making, such as group dancing and singing, foster collectivity, voluntary engagement and direct pleasure, and therefore contribute to the "fundamental habit change" that "is required to forge lasting alternative forms of citizenship."[46] Following this line of thinking, it is worth considering that participatory musical expressions might be the best means of articulating and empowering values linked to social change, especially in contexts where citizens' rights are either unprotected or simply ignored.

In March 2011, the Assad regime's "Kingdom of Silence" was disrupted by mass protests that often included performances of *dabke* music and dance routines, collo-

---

44 Isin and Nielsen, Acts of Citizenship, 10.
45 Thomas Turino, Music as Social Life: The Politics of Participation (Chicago: University of Chicago Press, 2008), 17–18.
46 Thomas Turino, "Music, Social Change, and Alternative Forms of Citizenship," in The Handbook of Artistic Citizenship, edited by David J. Elliott et al. (New York: Oxford University Press, 2016), 298.

quial-Arabic or local-dialect pop music and reworkings of folk wedding songs with modified lyrics.[47] These empowering musical choices reflected the social importance of the protests, while their dissemination on social media encouraged further participation and counterbalanced state-backed propaganda.[48] Although the demonstrations were violently repressed, they may be seen as public acts of citizenship that ruptured Syria's socio-political habitus, created new citizens and used music to articulate and renegotiate the values of freedom (*al-hurriye*) and dignity (*al-karama*).[49]

Conclusion

The musical protests in the hotspot camps of Thessaloniki illustrate how musical meaning can be transformed during refugees' journeys in response to depoliticising and dehumanising external factors. Moreover, they highlight the importance of refugees' individual and collective creativity and agency in the process of turning camps into "hyper-politicized spaces."[50] Young Syrian men performed their songs and dances in the midst of a stringent European border regime and its harsh local implementation in Greece to create visible and audible communities of reference in the struggle for greater freedom of movement across borders and greater respect for their basic human rights. Although most of their songs owed a large debt to Syria's musical traditions, the performers also made full use of innovative tactics that had first emerged in the anti-Assad protests of 2011. Therefore, it could be said that the musical performances in Thessaloniki's refugee camps echoed the earlier struggle for freedom and dignity in Syria, albeit amended in response to a new context of repression. The young protesters used their songs and dances to transform themselves and the other residents of the camps from "stateless" individuals into "active citizens" and thereby issued a powerful challenge to conventional notions of statehood and citizenship and indeed to the EU's refugee regime. Hence, their musical performances – first in Syria and then in Greece's hotspot refugee camps – could

---

47   Robin Yassin-Kassab and Leila Al-Shami, *Burning Country* (London: Pluto Press, 2016); Shayna Silverstein, "Syria's Radical *Dabka*," *Middle East Report* 42 (2012) 263: 33–37; Sadam Issa, "Ibrahim Qashoush's Revolutionary Popular Songs: Resistance Music in the 2011 Syrian Revolution," *Popular Music and Society* 41 (2018) 3: 283–301.

48   Miriam Cooke, Dancing in Damascus: Creativity, Resilience, and the Syrian Revolution (New York: Routledge, 2017).

49   The Syrian Revolution is often termed the "Revolution of Freedom and Dignity." See Malu Halasa et al. (eds), Syria Speaks: Art and Culture from the Frontline (London: Saqi Books, 2014).

50   Simon Turner, "What is a Refugee Camp? Explorations of the Limits and Effects of the Camp," *Journal of Refugee Studies* 29 (2016): 139–148.

be interpreted as acts of citizenship that the singers employed not only to recreate a sense of belonging to a community of shared values but also to influence political decisions that would have a profound effect on their lives in a context where the right to be political had been withheld.

Room(s) for children?
Children's everyday practices in a "community shelter" in Switzerland today

Clara Bombach

Introduction

For now, in Central Europe at least, accommodating refugees in gyms, former airport buildings, exhibition halls and underground bunkers seems to be a thing of the past. New construction projects have emerged over recent years, but the structures are often built quickly, with limited financial and spatial resources, and they tend to be container-like in an architectural and spatial language of transition. Consequently, the difficult living conditions of refugees during the processing of their applications for asylum – as well as their future prospects – have remained depressingly unchanged, despite heavy criticism from, among others, the UNHCR.[1] For an undefined period of time, they are forced to live in cramped, transitional spaces that often fail meet minimum living standards, far from urban centres, in industrial areas on the peripheries of cities. Forced migration/refugee studies assess this reality as a (historically longstanding) strategy of deterrence and sanctioning that aims to immobilise individuals and control them while simultaneously guaranteeing the state's administrative bodies unrestricted access.[2]

---

1 UNHCR, Global Trends: Forced Displacement in 2019 (Geneva: UNHCR, 2020).
2 Thomas Berthold, In erster Linie Kinder. Flüchtlingskinder in Deutschland (Berlin: Bundesfachverband Unbegleitete Minderjährige Flüchtlinge e.V., 2014); Benjamin Etzold, Auf der Flucht: (Im)Mobilisierung und (Im)Mobilität von Schutzsuchenden (Bonn: International Center for Conversation, Institut für Migrationsforschung und Interkulturelle Studien, 2019); Rose Jaji, "Social Technology and Refugee Encampment in Kenya," Journal of Refugee Studies 25 (2012) 2: 221–38; Ronald Lutz, "Der Flüchtling woanders. Verletzliche Orte des Ungewissen: Ein Leben in Lagern," in Flüchtlinge. Multiperspektivische Zugänge, edited by Cinur Ghaderi and Thomas Eppenstein (Wiesbaden: Springer Fachmedien, 2017), 367–80; David Werdermann, "Rechtliche Grundlagen der Teilhabe und Ausgrenzung von Flüchtlingen," Neue Praxis. Zeitschrift für Sozialarbeit, Sozialpädagogik und Sozialpolitik Special Issue 13 (2016): 86–95.

In Switzerland, thousands of people who apply for asylum are centrally housed until official decisions are reached regarding their status. They are not permitted to choose their place of residence, and they sometimes live for several years in temporary facilities that were not designed for the long-term accommodation of people.

How do accompanied children experience everyday life as refugees in Switzerland today? This question is at the centre of my ethnographic dissertation. Using participant observation, I met and studied children in a so-called "asylum shelter." They were invited to discuss their lives, how they lived, what worried them and what made them happy. What do the words "room" and "space" mean to them? Which rooms can they access? Which remain closed to them? Are some rooms specifically for children? This article addresses these questions.

Following this brief introduction, the study outlines its conceptual framework then presents empirical data relating to the children's everyday practices and the spatial organisation of the asylum shelter, following Muchow and Muchow's distinction between spaces *in which* children live, spaces they *experience* and spaces they live.[3] Finally, it asks whether the asylum centre should be described as an "activity space," given the children's everyday practices in relation to where they live.[4]

It is important to note that the children refer to the house where they live not as "shelter" or "centre" but the "camp," which is why the latter term is preferred for the remainder of this article. "Camp" implies that the children are unhappy about their confinement in an administered and temporary place of transit, yet hopeful that their stay will soon be over and that they will "finally live in a private home."

Everyday practices of children in camps

The ethnographic study has a multi-method design. This article presents results from participant observation and ero-epic conversations that were transcribed immediately on site, whenever children spontaneously addressed me and wished to share something.[5] All citations are from these ero-epic transcripts.

---

3   Martha Muchow and Hans Heinrich Muchow, "Recherchen zum Lebensraum des Großstadtkindes" [1935], in Der Lebensraum des Großstadtkindes, edited by Imbke Behnken and Michael-Sebastian Honig (Weinheim – Basel: Beltz Juventa, 2012), 75–156.
4   Baldo Blinkert, Aktionsräume von Kindern in der Stadt. Eine Untersuchung im Auftrag der Stadt Freiburg (Pfaffenweiler: Centaurus Verlag & Media, 1993).
5   Ero-epic interviews are conversations that arise spontaneously, in my case during participant observation on site in the camp, for example when a child feels comfortable and seeks a conversation with me on topics that interest her/him and that she/he wishes to discuss. In childhood sociology, this form of conversation with children is considered particularly useful as the children can play, draw, and decide for or against the conversation, which should arise as naturally and "along the way" as possible. See: Roland Girtler, Methoden der Feldforschung

The study was reviewed and approved by the Ethics Committee of the University of Zurich. In addition to the usual complexities of undertaking research with children, in this particular context of coercion, the question of what constitutes voluntary participation was at the centre of the committee's discussions about research ethics. These and related questions have been intensively debated in refugee studies, so I shall address them only briefly here.[6] Particular dimensions of power asymmetries may be repeated in research contexts; dependencies, hopes and fears may impact participation; and there may be insecurities about the consequences of sharing information. I asked children and adults who had expressed an interest in participating to watch me first, see what I was doing and assess my involvement in everyday practices prior to making a final decision and signing the consent form. From the outset, many of the children and adults were keen to share their experiences and let the "outside world" know about their experiences of camp life. Written consent forms (in Arabic, Dari/Farsi, English, French, German, Tigrinya and Turkish) outlined the process, methodology and aims of the study, how data would be protected, the rights of the participants and the obligations of the researcher, including contact information for a member of the Ethics Committee with whom participants could share any concerns about my work and behaviour in the field. In addition to signing forms prior to the start of the study, as stipulated by Ethics Committee guidelines, all of the participants were asked if they were willing to continue throughout the research process as an ongoing process of consent.

I negotiated a contract with the responsible authorities that allowed me to conduct wholly independent and unrestricted research. For example, I was able to move freely around the house and its surroundings, which enabled me to gain insights into the activities that the families and children wanted to share with me. The study was conducted in a camp where up to ninety people may live at any given time, based on its proximity to the city centre. Staff were on site throughout the daytime and conducted regular checks during the night. Residents had unrestricted access

---

(Wien – Köln – Weimar: Böhlau Verlag, 2001); James P. Spradley, Participant Observation (New York – Chicago – San Francisco: Holt, Rinehart and Winston, 1980).

6   For further details, see, for example: Christina Clark-Kazak, "Ethical Considerations: Research with People in Situations of Forced Migration," Refuge: Canada's Journal on Refugees 33 (2017) 2: 11–17; Peter Hopkins, "Ethical Issues in Research with Unaccompanied Asylum-Seeking Children," Children's Geographies 6 (2008) 1: 37–48; Richard Hugman et al., "When 'Do No Harm' is not Enough: The Ethics of Research with Refugees and Other Vulnerable Groups," British Journal of Social Work 41 (2011) 7: 1271–87; Ulrike Krause, "Researching Forced Migration: Critical Reflections on Research Ethics during Fieldwork," Working Paper Series 123 (2017): 1–36; Refugees Studies Centre, "Ethical Guidelines for Good Research Practice," Refugee Survey Quarterly 26 (2007) 3: 162–72; Hella von Unger, "Ethische Reflexivität in der Fluchtforschung. Erfahrungen aus einem soziologischen Lehrforschungsprojekt," Forum Qualitative Sozialforschung / Forum: Qualitative Social Research 19 (2018) 3: Article 6.

to the camp and their rooms; adults had keys to the house and the family room. Bathrooms, communal areas and the kitchen were shared and most of the families occupied a single room, although an extra room was sometimes provided if a family had a large number of children.

Forty-four children, with ages ranging from a few months to eighteen years, from twenty different families agreed to participate in the study. The field research took place between July 2019 and July 2020 on weekends, weekdays, in school hours and during school vacations and holidays. I was on site for a total of 356 hours spread across 42 daytime and 8 night-time visits. The resulting data were analysed sequentially and reconstructively in an abductive analysis procedure.[7]

This paper presents preliminary results and is only an excerpt of the comprehensive ethnography that remains ongoing.

Childhood in a non-place camp

This study is informed by the social and cultural anthropologist Marc Augé's notion of "non-places"[8] – that is, places that defy people's attempts to form any sort of relationship with them. Camps are often prime examples of this concept: "In the non-place, the functionality of the local is the centre of attention; the individual is successively reduced to the purpose of the place."[9] In addition, the concept is relevant to the struggles that families and children face as they try to settle and introduce daily routines in a place they have not chosen, where they have been forced to stay. During my research, I witnessed numerous children laying claim to a particular room, trying to create favourite or private areas and attempting to appropriate the little space that had been offered to them. Yet, they continued to insist that they did not belong, that the place where they were living was not – and never would be – a home, so they wanted to leave as soon as possible.[10]

Children employ three main strategies to cope with camp life: a) distraction and staying active; b) withdrawal and immersion in another world (dreams, sleep, fantasy and online games); and c) running away. They may use one or more of these cop-

---

7   Gabriele Rosenthal, Interpretative Sozialforschung. Eine Einführung, 5th ed. (Weinheim – Basel: Beltz Juventa, 2015).
8   Marc Augé, Non-places: Introduction to an Anthropology of Supermodernity (London – New York: Verso, 1995).
9   Daniel Göler, "Das Lager als Nicht-Ort. Anmerkungen zum Bamberger Ankerzentrum," in Praktiken der (Im-)Mobilisierung. Lager, Sammelunterkünfte und Ankerzentren im Kontext von Asylregimen, edited by Julia Devlin et al. (Bielefeld: Transcript, 2021), 281–300.
10 Clara Bombach, "'Come to My House': Children's Homing in Swiss Asylum Centres," in Migration and Social Work: Approaches, Visions and Challenges, edited by Emilio J. Gómez-Ciriano et al. (Bristol: Policy Press, forthcoming).

ing mechanisms to varying degrees depending on their age and personal resources. Due to space limitations, this paper will focus primarily on the first strategy – distraction and staying active.

Childhood studies have demonstrated the importance of power and order relations in children's development. Adults have the power to increase or decrease children's access to resources, so children rely on adults making spaces available to them.[11] However, children are also competent social actors: they "actively create spaces and are not victims of their circumstances!"[12] In her research into children's lives and play in Hamburg between the late 1920s and the early 1930s, Martha Muchow identified three distinct categories of space that children inhabit, shape and appropriate.[13] In the next three sections, I use this categorisation as a framework to present some of the empirical data I have collected in the course of my own research.

Spaces in which children live ...

can be objectified in cartographic sketches and recorded accordingly. In her study, Muchow explored not only where children resided but also "where they played and roamed," and drew maps of their neighbourhoods.[14]

Children in the camp had contrasting attitudes to its internal and external spaces, family rooms and communal areas. Outside, there is a terrace, a courtyard, a rather derelict playground and a grassy area where they sometimes play soccer. They like to ride their bicycles in the courtyard and sometimes incorporate natural features (blossom and leaves, stones, soil, etc.) in their play. Children's and adults' bikes are stored alongside dustbins. Weeds are growing in the potholed, uneven ground, and some rubbish is usually lying around. The lower windows of the camp are secured with metal grilles to shield them from the children's enthusiastic ball games. Meanwhile, metal railings on the slightly elevated terrace are designed to protect the children themselves from falling over the edge. A flight of steps and a single wooden bench are the only seating areas. Both are usually occupied by adults

---

11   Burkhard Fuhs, "Mediale Räume von Kindern," in Kindheit und Raum, edited by Rita Braches-Chyrek and Charlotte Röhner (Opladen – Berlin – Toronto: Barbara Budrich, 2016), 328–53.
12   Christian Reutlinger and Bettina Brüschweiler, "Sozialgeographien der Kinder – eine Spurensuche in mehrdeutigem, offenen Gelände," in Kindheit und Raum, edited by Braches-Chyrek and Röhner, 37–64, at 58. See also: Leena Alanen, "Rethinking Childhood," Acta Sociologica 31 (1988) 1: 53–67; Doris Bühler-Niederberger, "Intergenerational Solidarities: Towards a Structural Approach in Childhood Sociology," in The Future of Childhood Studies, edited by Rita Braches-Chyrek (Leverkusen: Barbara Budrich, 2020), 54–69.
13   Muchow and Muchow, "Recherchen zum Lebensraum."
14   Ibid.

while they watch their children play. However, the bench lacks a slat, which makes it uncomfortable or even painful.

The interior space consists of two main sections that can be further subdivided according to function. First, there are communal areas that can be used by all residents and staff, including a large common room equipped with sofas and a foosball table as well as staircases, kitchens and bathrooms. In addition, this part of the camp has three children's rooms: a schoolroom, a playroom and a homework room. Second, there are the individual family rooms, to which only members of the resident family have access. These are furnished with metal-framed beds, cabinets and fridges. Infants have access to cribs, strollers and nappies. Bedding, cleaning products, bin-bags, soap and toilet paper are provided by the camp administration.

Spaces that children experience ...

are reflected in their memories and in how they talk and think about particular places.[15] Muchow encouraged the children she was studying to write essays about "typical" Sundays to learn more about these aspects of their lives.[16]

As mentioned above, at the time of my research, the camp's playground was in a state of disrepair: sometimes there was a swing set in need of renovation, but at other times there were just ropes hanging from a frame. Children often pointed in the direction of the playground, mentioned how important it was to them and complained that the equipment was usually broken. There was a general reluctance to draw pictures of the camp, but any images the children did produce tended to focus on the playground. These could be either positive or negative: while some children incorporated depictions of spiders, smelly toilets and dirty, broken equipment in their drawings, others drew fully functioning swings and suggested that it would be lovely to have a larger playground with a slide, too. Many fights broke out among the children because the most popular items were always scarce, and too many of them wanted to sit on the swing at the same time.

The yard could be an exciting place for the younger children. They used sticks to draw patterns in the dusty sand and splashed in the muddy puddles when it rained. Sometimes the puddles would freeze in the winter, to the great delight of the children, who slithered across them in pyjamas and flip-flops. While playing in the mud, six-year-old Madihah recalled playing in the yellow sand of her country of origin, which was "much more fun than the dusty soil" of the camp garden. She also

---

15 Rita Braches-Chyrek and Charlotte Röhner, "Kindheit und Raum," in Kindheit und Raum, edited by Braches-Chyrek and Röhner, 7–33.
16 Muchow and Muchow, "Recherchen zum Lebensraum."

found the small brown birds in the trees quite disappointing in comparison with the "beautiful, big, colourful birds" of her homeland.

Nevertheless, there were all kinds of interesting items between the trees and the lawn – mainly stones and sticks that were either fashioned into weapons or cherished like holy relics. Three-year-old Abia celebrated her brother's birthday by offering him several objects she had found in the yard and singing "Happy Birthday." Her brother happily mimed opening his presents as the other children joined in the song. The celebrations attracted the attention of a member of staff, who asked whose birthday it was. The children ignored him, continued singing, then set about blowing out imaginary candles on an imaginary cake.

The yard's sandbox was always covered and occasionally served as a makeshift seat for the children and their parents. Five-year-old Saafia shared her greatest wish with me while she was sitting there, watching the father of one of her friends grilling meat on the fire: "You know, I have a father too. I don't know where he is, but he will be here soon."

The children spent most of their time outside the family rooms, in the camp's internal and external common areas, looking for friends, distractions, something to do, play or discover, away from their parents' prying eyes. For example, nine-year-old Ena pretended to be busy on TikTok (an activity her parents allowed), when in reality she was playing online games with some of the older boys (an activity they had banned).

Inevitably, all of the children were especially fond of the three rooms that had been earmarked for their use (the schoolroom, the playroom and the homework room), which meant these rooms' gatekeepers – who could be members of staff, teachers or volunteers – possessed considerable key power. The children's excitement intensified whenever they realised that one of the rooms was about to be opened. They would knock constantly on the door if they saw adults preparing games or lessons inside, and would get up early in the morning to take advantage of opportunities to draw, play or even bake cookies. However, adults not only locked and unlocked the rooms but determined how the children should behave once they were inside. For instance, as they entered the schoolroom, the teacher would stand at the door and demand an appropriate greeting for the time of day: "Good afternoon, *not* good morning." After school, once the teachers had ensured that the room was properly locked, the children would watch them leave and scream goodbyes in their direction until they disappeared from view. In the long hours before the next lesson, some children would repeatedly try the locked door handles or jump up to the height of the windows to make sure that nobody had managed to sneak inside without them noticing.

En route back to the family rooms, the children had to pass through two heavy fire doors that would slam shut behind them with a loud bang. The doors' weight made them difficult to open, especially for the younger children, who sometimes found themselves trapped in the passageway between them. For instance, after waiting patiently in the corridor for several minutes, three-year-old Sada was grateful when her slightly older but much stronger friend came along and opened the second door for her. She slipped straight through and ran to her family room, where she was able to open the much lighter door herself and enter. At its best, the family room could be a haven for a child like Sada, provided there was good communication between the family members. It was generally a quiet environment where family activities took place in a confined space.[17]

Spaces that children live ...

are related to how children behave in particular environments and how they access and moderate the spatial realities they face.[18] Long-term observations can shed light on these processes.[19] The "sociology of space" describes the interactions between those who inhabit particular spaces and the structures they encounter within them. "Spacing" conceptualises the individual construction of space and demonstrates that spaces are created by the actors who act (in) them.[20]

In the camp courtyard, the children sometimes discovered small treasures that had fallen out of the windows, such as colourful hairclips. They also watched butterflies and birds in the fields and trees outside the confines of the camp. Eight-year-old Karima's favourite spot was the wall that surrounded the camp, as this gave her a good view of passing cars. She would sit on a rough woollen blanket, invite her friends to join her, then they would all play "market." Karima explained that she enjoyed "gossiping with my girls and selling stuff, looking at the things other people sell."

Although the children were confined within relatively small spaces, they laid claim to them and used them creatively. For example, the communal room was their indoor playground: they would swing back and forth on the side panels of an old chalkboard and use the sofas as makeshift trampolines. They invented communal games, devised their own vernacular for use during interactions with their peers (e.g. "Du not meine friend" [You are not my friend], "You crazy," "She said fuck you stupid bitch"), engaged in physical competitions (e.g. fastest runner, furthest jumper, coolest dancer) and sometimes – although not always – shared their favourite snacks (e.g. ice-cream, chips, soft drinks). A child could be befriended, unfriended and befriended again within the space of a few minutes.

---

17 Bombach, "'Come to My House.'"
18 Muchow and Muchow, "Recherchen zum Lebensraum."
19 Braches-Chyrek and Röhner, "Kindheit und Raum."
20 Ibid.

Most of the children were ambivalent about life in the camp: they liked the fact that there were plenty of other kids around and lots of distractions both inside and outside the house, but this meant they never had a break and it was loud all the time, with doors banging throughout the day and night. If it became too loud – or the play became too boisterous – in the communal areas, some of the children would retreat to their respective family rooms and hide behind curtains, under blankets or even under beds to give themselves a few minutes of peace and quiet. A number of them had turned the upper bunk beds in their family rooms into play corners or erected homemade tents so they could relax and play on their own without being disturbed. Most of them regarded the clothes they wore and the toys they played with as their own, cherished possessions. When I enquired about their favourite things, they would often show me free gifts from the pharmacy or balloons advertising the opening of a new store. Toddlers slept or sat in car seats for hours on end during the day, and sometimes slept in their strollers at night. Younger children were often reluctant to sleep on the upper bunk bed because they were afraid of falling off and wanted to be close to their parents. When I moved into the camp, five-year-old Bader "checked" my bed by lying on it and warned me, with wide eyes, that I might fall out, especially as my mum wasn't there to prevent me from falling.

As mentioned earlier, the family rooms were discrete spaces, isolated from the rest of the camp. The doors could be locked from the inside, and visitors were allowed to enter only if it suited the residents. Otherwise, knocking tended to be ignored. This was fine with the other residents, but not with the staff, who argued that they had to have unrestricted access. Windows were often covered with curtains and blinds were kept closed, so light in the family rooms could be scarce. One member of each family always seemed to be asleep or at least in bed and about to fall asleep. On one occasion, five-year-old Saafia invited me to visit her family room when it became too noisy and raucous for her in the communal area. We drank tea and ate some nuts with her mother for a few minutes until Saafia crawled into bed, put her thumb in her mouth and fell asleep.

By and large, the children's spheres of activity increased as they aged. Infants and toddlers up to the age of three tended to spend most of the day inside their respective family rooms, especially when the family consisted of a single mother with one or more children. The toddlers would scream and cry until they were finally permitted to go outside, usually in the company of an older sibling. Others would try to escape the moment the door was opened. For example, two-year-old Laela would routinely run into the corridor, but she could not get any further as she did not have the strength to push open the heavy fire door in front of the staircase. She would stand there, helpless, and burst into tears when her mother told her she had to return to the family room. On one occasion, her brother, Bader, left the room shortly after one of these incidents to play with the other kids downstairs and ride his bike in the courtyard, which made Laela cry even more.

Bader and some of the other children would occasionally leave the confines of the camp and ride their bikes in a parking lot behind the house or even along the public roads and pavements, towards the city centre or the local shopping mall. Their parents usually accompanied them on these outings, for instance to buy groceries, although they were sometimes trusted to run these errands alone. Older children, especially teenage boys, left the camp much more frequently. For example, they would visit local sports clubs, go (window) shopping, sit in the parks or the train station or just walk around to give themselves a break from camp life. Some families made trips to the city specifically to use the (clean) public toilets, where soap and toilet paper were provided, as opposed to inside the camp, where each family had to use their own supplies.

Conclusion

For every resident, whether young or old, the reality of life inside the camp was that they did not want to be there but knew that they had to stay for an indefinite period until a decision was reached about their future. Inevitably, there was a universal desire for that indefinite period to end as soon as possible. For instance, nine-year-old Lida insisted, "I hate it here," and explained that she took every opportunity to join after-school programmes or accompany her parents when they left the camp to attend doctor's appointments. However, she sometimes grew tired of these excursions and simply stayed in the family room, watching cartoons for hours on end, hoping that a friend would visit so that they could play with their favourite dolls.

The children brought life and movement into the dreary daily routine and gloom of the camp. Adults – volunteers, staff and residents alike – frequently described them as "so sweet," "lovely" and "positive" and suggested that they were a valued, lively distraction from an otherwise depressing situation. On the other hand, they were also characterised as "too loud," "disturbing," "dirty" and "annoying."

The children had very limited access to the outside world, which meant their withdrawal and distraction strategies were strictly limited, too. When I asked what they knew of the outside world and where they went most often when they left camp, the most common answer was: "Aldi." They longed for volunteers to visit the camp and take them out on day trips, hoped that the school holidays would soon be over and yearned for the weekend to pass as quickly as possible. Their greatest wish – besides leaving the camp for good – was to attend "normal school."

The camp was a waiting room full of people who had no clear idea about what they were waiting for and who would decide about their future. In this parallel universe, the children lived with a blurred perspective and felt isolated from the world outside, which they observed wistfully but also sometimes quite fearfully. They suspected kidnappers and evil spirits were lurking, and worried about anyone – including myself – who left the camp in the evening. For instance, nine-year-old Ena looked at me in disbelief when I explained that I had to leave. She pointed through the window to the dark winter night and asked: "Are you not scared?" Yet, they also experienced a lot of beauty and variety whenever they came into contact with the outside world, especially in "normal school" or when volunteers or their parents took them to the communal swimming pool. They also talked with great joy about excursions to the forest and discoveries in the museum, and longed to return to these places.

In addition to describing the Swiss asylum centre as a "camp," the children used the same term when discussing previous refugee accommodation (e.g. in Greece, Hungary or Turkey) and the experiences associated with it: countless people coming and going; noise; language barriers; conflicts; very limited space; and a lack of understanding about what is happening and what will happen in the future. In Switzerland, the media and especially politicians tend to prefer alternative terms for this type of accommodation, such as "community housing," "integration centre" and "family housing." But all of these euphemisms are misleading. Camps are not integrated communities; they are non-places. The reality of life in a camp is very different from all asylum-seekers' – and especially the youngsters' – conceptions of "home."[21]

Many of the children I met had spent much of their lives in a camp environment. Nine-year-old Lida had been a resident in the Swiss camp for six years. Although some rooms had supposedly been allocated for her and the other children's exclusive use, adults decided when they should be locked and therefore when all exploration must cease. The children respected this and did not question it; at most, they merely expressed regret that the doors remained closed even when they had nothing to do. They knew the rules and abided by them because misbehaving always had consequences. Nevertheless, they did sometimes assert themselves and push the boundaries, such as when calling the communal room "*our* children's room" and demanding preferential access. Some of the older children even had the audacity to remind adults that they always had the option of retiring to their family rooms if the volume became too loud for them. Most of the adults were quite understanding, but if the children were still screaming in the common areas at 1:00 a.m., they would chase them away with shouts of "That's enough! Go to bed!"

Finally, I wish to present a brief assessment of the camp with regard to four important aspects of children's "action spaces": 1) opportunities for interaction; 2) accessibility; 3) flexibility; and 4) safety.[22]

---

21 Bombach, "'Come to My House.'"
22 Baldo Blinkert, Aktionsräume von Kindern in der Stadt. Eine Untersuchung im Auftrag der Stadt Freiburg (Pfaffenweiler: Centaurus Verlag & Media, 1993); Baldo Blinkert, "Urbane Kindheit und Räume," in Kindheit und Raum, edited by Braches-Chyrek and Röhner, 65–83.

1) The children in the camp had ample opportunities to interact with their peers.[23] It was easy for them to meet, play and spend time with numerous other children, given the confined space in which they all lived. However, this also meant that it was quite difficult for them to avoid unwelcome contact or have any time to themselves. The children played relatively autonomously and unobserved by adults for long periods of time in the common areas, sometimes until late at night. However, these play sessions were not always harmonious. There were frequent quarrels, arguments and even violent fights in which, inevitably, the stronger or better-integrated children would prevail over their weaker opponents.

2) There are many barriers for children in camp life, such as heavy doors they cannot open or rooms that remain closed to them. For older children, there was usually unrestricted access to both the common room and the playground, but adults exerted total control over access to other areas, including the three rooms that had been designated for the children's exclusive use.

3) Children are able to adapt and shape flexible action spaces to suit their specific requirements and alleviate boredom.[24] In the camp, the children were highly creative in their use of and engagement with their environment. For example, they slid down the staircase banisters, breathed on the windows and wrote messages on the fogged-up glass, popped blossoms between their fingers and jumped up and down on a warped manhole cover to make it clang. Nevertheless, there were repeated complaints of boredom, especially during the school holidays, exasperation over the lack of organised activities, and annoyance when other children copied a game or made an unpopular suggestion for a new one. These frustrations sometimes escalated into wilful destruction of personal possessions, older children holding the toilet door shut so that younger ones were trapped inside, jumping on sofas until they collapsed or even violent confrontations that ended in serious injury because no adults were present to break up the fights.

4) Clearly, then, the camp could be a dangerous place, especially for the younger children. In addition to the risk of physical attack, they were exposed to a host of spatial dangers, including heavy fire doors that might slam shut on their fingers or

---

23 Unfortunately, this article cannot outline the specific challenges for children with mental or physical disabilities growing up in camps. For further information, see, for example: Clara Straimer, "Between Protection and Assistance: Is There Refuge for Asylum Seekers with Disabilities in Europe?" Disability and Society 26 (2011) 5: 537–51. Also, measures introduced during the Covid pandemic have changed children's interactions dramatically. Families were asked – and wanted – to reduce children's contact to a minimum. As a consequence, families withdrew to their family rooms even more.

24 Blinkert, "Urbane Kindheit und Räume."

trap them in the corridor, windows from which they might fall, and ropes that could twist around an ankle or, even worse, a neck.²⁵

The various spaces of the camp were enlivened by their inhabitants, not just filled by them. The children dealt proficiently with their circumstances and negotiated the theme of their stay: current limbo but also great hope of a decision that would enable them to leave the camp and finally "arrive." Nevertheless, none of those I met after they had left wished to return. Rather, they expressed sympathy for those who were still living there, especially during the Covid lockdown, and were eager to know how friends and foes alike were coping. My replies were news to them as they often had ceased all contact with the camp and its remaining residents after moving out.

---

25   Additionally, I would like to draw attention to some recent studies that have found evidence of discrimination and violation of refugee children's rights in camps. See, for example: Berthold, In erster Linie Kinder; Franziska Eisenhuth, Strukturelle Diskriminierung von Kindern mit unsicheren Aufenthaltsstatus. Subjekte der Gerechtigkeit zwischen Fremd- und Selbstpositionierungen (Wiesbaden: Springer VS, 2015); UNICEF, Uprooted: The Growing Crisis for Refugee and Migrant Children: Executive Summary and Key Findings (New York: UNICEF, 2016); Sarah Fichtner and Hoa Mai Trân, "Lived Citizenship between the Sandpit and Deportation: Young Children's Spaces for Agency, Play and Belonging in Collective Accommodation for Refugees," Childhood 27 (2020) 2: 158–72. In addition, there is evidence of a lack of opportunities for play and retreat. See, for example: Susanne Johansson and David Schiefer, "Die Lebenssituation von Flüchtlingen in Deutschland. Überblick über ein (bisheriges) Randgebiet der Migrationsforschung," Neue Praxis. Zeitschrift für Sozialarbeit, Sozialpädagogik und Sozialpolitik Special Issue 13 (2016): 73–85; Christine Rehklau, "Flüchtlinge als Adressat_innen Sozialer Arbeit? Sozialarbeitswissenschaftlicher Zugang," in Flüchtlinge. Multiperspektivische Zugänge, edited by Cinur Ghaderi and Thomas Eppenstein (Wiesbaden: Springer Fachmedien, 2017), 305–22. Similarly, Berthold, "In erster Linie Kinder" highlighted barriers in the education system. Finally, several studies have explored refugee children's health burdens and the inadequate medical and psychological care they receive. See, for example: James Reavell and Qulsom Fazil, "The Epidemiology of PTSD and Depression in Refugee Minors who Have Resettled in Developed Countries," Journal of Mental Health 26 (2017) 1: 74–83.

Part IV
Pathways and transitions

Cycles of incarceration
From the "Third Reich" through British Mandatory Palestine to Mauritius

Roni Mikel-Arieli

In recent years, research on refugees from territories under the German "Third Reich" (1939–45) has become more focused on the Global South. [1],[2] A growing interest in case studies of refugees in British imperial territories is particularly pronounced in the field of exile studies, with some focusing on places of refuge and others on places of forced internment.[3] This article concentrates on a less known case study of 1,581 Jewish men, women and children who fled German-occupied territories,

---

1   The author would like to thank Tali Nates for her helpful suggestions regarding this paper. This work was made possible thanks to the author's tenure as a Junior Post-Doctoral Fellow at the Center for Holocaust Studies at the Institute for Contemporary History, Munich, Germany; a Phyllis Greenberg Heideman and Richard D. Heideman Fellow at the Jack, Joseph and Morton Mandel Center for Advanced Holocaust Studies, United States Holocaust Memorial Museum; a Research Fellow at the International Institute for Holocaust Research, Yad Vashem, Jerusalem; a Rosa Luxemburg Research Fellow at the Johannesburg Holocaust & Genocide Centre; and a Research Fellow of the Fondation pour la Mémoire de la Shoah, at the Institute of Contemporary Jewry, The Hebrew University of Jerusalem.
2   Monica Bohm-Duchen (ed.), Insiders/Outsiders: Refugees from Nazi Europe and Their Contribution to British Visual Culture (London: Lund Humphries, 2019); Monica Bohm-Duchen and Judith Wassiltschenko (eds), Literatur im skandinavischen Exil, 1933 bis heute (Hannover: Wehrhahn, 2019); Swen Steinberg and Anthony Grenville (eds), Refugees from Nazi-Occupied Europe in British Overseas Territories (Leiden – Boston: Brill Rodopi, 2020); Irene Eber, Jewish Refugees in Shanghai 1933–1947: A Selection of Documents (Göttingen: Vandenhoeck & Ruprecht, 2018).
3   Among others, see: Natalie Eppelsheimer, Roads Less Traveled: German Jewish Exile Experiences in Kenya (Oxford: Peter Lang, 2019); Joan G. Roland, The Jewish Communities of India: Identity in a Colonial Era (New York: Routledge, 2018); Alexis Rappas, "Jewish Refugees in Cyprus and British Imperial Sovereignty in the Eastern Mediterranean, 1933–1949," Journal of Imperial and Commonwealth History 47 (2019) 1: 138–66; Steven Robins, Letters of Stone: From Nazi Germany to South Africa (Cape Town: Penguin Random House, 2016); Shirli Gilbert, From Things Lost: Forgotten Letters and the Legacy of the Holocaust (Detroit, MI: Wayne State University Press, 2017).

survived a long journey to Haifa and were then deported by the British Mandate authorities in Palestine to the British colony of Mauritius. The deportees spent four years and seven months in the Beau-Bassin Camp before their release and departure from the island in August 1945. Although there have been some commemoration efforts since the 1990s,[4] the Jewish deportation to Mauritius has been largely neglected in most accounts of the Second World War and the Holocaust.

There was no comprehensive research into this deportation prior to the late 1990s. For instance, Dalia Ofer mentioned it only briefly in her prominent historical account of Aliyah Bet, *Escaping the Holocaust: Illegal Immigration to the Land of Israel, 1939–1944* (1990),[5] and her article "The Rescue of European Jewry and Illegal Immigration to Palestine in 1940: Prospects and Reality: Berthold Storfer and the Mossad le'Aliya Bet" (1984).[6] Indeed, for many years, the only detailed account of the deportation was a publication by Aaron Zwergbaum – a young lawyer from Brno with Zionist leanings who served as a leader of the detainees in Mauritius – that appeared in *Yad Vashem Studies* in 1960.[7] It was only in 1998, with the publication of *The Mauritian Shekel* by Geneviève Pitot – a native Mauritian who lived in Germany but formed a close relationship with one of the Jewish detainees on the island – that the first significant research into the deportation finally appeared in print.[8] More recently, Gabriele Anderl's "Auf dem Weg nach Palästina: Interniert auf Mauritius" was included in a comprehensive anthology edited by Margit Franz and Heimo

---

4   In 2001, Mauritian author Alain Gordon Gentil published his novel Le Voyage de Delcourt about a fictional romance between a young Jewish detainee and a Mauritian boy. The novel was adapted into a play titled Marika est partie in 2014 and performed in Mauritius, France and Germany. In 2007, Mauritian-French author Nathacha Appanah published her novel Le Dernier Frère about a fictional friendship between a Creole boy and a Jewish refugee from Czechoslovakia. A touring exhibition titled Boarding Pass to Paradise curated by Israeli curator Elena Makarova visited several European and Israeli venues between 2005 and 2008. A documentary entitled The Atlantic Drift was made by the Austrian producer Michel Daëron in 2002, and another entitled In the Shadows of Beau Bassin was produced by the South African independent filmmaker Kevin Harris in 2007. An archival collection containing photographs, documents, memoirs, letters and artwork was deposited in the Ghetto Fighters' House Archives, Israel, in 2008. Geneviève Pitot's book The Mauritian Shekel (see note 7, below, for full reference) was translated into Hebrew in 2014, and the same year the African Jewish Congress established a memorial centre and exhibition in the Mauritian Jewish cemetery garden to commemorate the Mauritian story.

5   Dalia Ofer, Escaping the Holocaust: Illegal Immigration to the Land of Israel, 1939–1944 (Oxford – New York – Toronto: Oxford University Press, 1990).

6   Dalia Ofer, "The Rescue of European Jewry and Illegal Immigration to Palestine in 1940: Prospects and Reality: Berthold Storfer and the Mossad le'Aliya Bet," Modern Judaism 4 (1984) 2: 159–81.

7   Aaron Zwergbaum, "Exile in Mauritius," Yad Vashem Studies 4 (1960): 191–257.

8   Geneviève Pitot, The Mauritian Shekel: The Story of the Jewish Detainees in Mauritius 1940–1945 (Port Louis: VIZAVI, 2017 [1998]).

Halbrainer – *Going East – Going South. Österreichisches Exil in Asien und Afrika* (2014)[9] – and Ronit Frenkel and Kirk B. Sides's article "Exile in Mauritius: Colonial Violence and Indian Ocean Archives" (2016)[10] was published in *Critical Art*. The latter text focuses on the Indian Ocean archive as a lens for thinking about the history of the Holocaust from the Indian Ocean perspective.[11]

This article focuses on the incarceration experiences of a hundred Viennese deportees who were imprisoned in the Dachau concentration camp for a few months in 1938–9 and released by the authorities on condition that they would leave German-controlled territory immediately. Therefore, they had already experienced the hardships of racial persecution and internment prior to the voyage that would eventually transport them to an island in the Indian Ocean. However, their escape from National Socialism did not mean their ordeal was over. For now, it was the turn of the British authorities to confine the deportees in squalid conditions behind barbed-wired fences, first in Mandatory Palestine and then in the colony of Mauritius.

It is important to stress that it is not my intention to compare German concentration camps with British internment camps, or National Socialist anti-Semitic policies with British colonial policies. Instead, by recounting in detail the story of this group of refugees, I wish to give a human face to impersonal historical processes that are often addressed as histories of the Holocaust, Jewish displacement, British imperialism, Palestine, and the Second World War. Using a micro-historical approach that incorporates detailed archival documents together with individual memories, testimonies, letters, and diaries, I tease out the deportees' varied experiences during incarceration to shed light on this under-studied episode by exploring the complex nexus of historical processes that played into, and were shaped by, the group's fate.

---

9   Gabriele Anderl, "Auf dem Weg nach Palästina: Interniert auf Mauritius," in Margit Franz and Heimo Halbrainer (eds), *Going East – Going South. Österreichisches Exil in Asien und Afrika* (Graz: Clio, 2014), 323–34.

10 Ronit Frenkel and Kirk B. Sides, "Exile in Mauritius: Colonial Violence and Indian Ocean Archives," Critical Arts 30 (2016) 2: 282–94.

11 It is important to stress that many memoirs have been published by ex-detainees in German, English, French and Hebrew since the early 1990s. See, for example: Karl Lenk, *The Mauritius Affair: The Boat People of 1940/1941* (Brighton: R. Lenk, 1993); Rachel Springmann-Ribak, *Sweet Lemons: Memories from an Internment Camp on Mauritius, 1940–1945* (Tucson, AZ: Wheatmark, 2011); Alfred Heller, *Dr Seligmanns Auswanderung: Der schwierige Weg nach Israel* (Munich: Beck, 1990).

From Austria to British Mandate Palestine

In 1934, one year after Hitler's rise to power in Germany, the Jewish community in Austria numbered 191,458. Thereafter, over the course of the four years leading up to the National Socialist annexation on 11 March 1938, only 1,739 left the country. More than 90 per cent of those who remained were concentrated in the capital city, Vienna, which meant they constituted the largest Jewish community in the German-speaking world.[12]

Historian Bruce Pauley argues that between the years 1933 and 1938, most of the Jews in Austria perceived National Socialism as a passing phenomenon: "Six decades of anti-Semitic agitation accompanied by next to nothing in the way of concrete anti-Semitic legislation played a central role in giving Austrian Jews a false sense of security."[13] Nevertheless, the persecution of Germany's Jews had a direct impact on Viennese Jewry as the former fled to the city in search of refuge, which forced the community's leaders to make arrangements to support them. Moreover, the Austro-Fascist government implemented its own anti-Semitic policies, including excluding Jews from government positions, banks and insurance companies, and restricting their access to academia. Finally, in 1936, the Austrian authorities started to suppress anti-National Socialist propaganda and granted amnesties to all of the country's imprisoned National Socialists.[14] Therefore, as Doron Rabinovici argues, "during the Austro-Fascist period, the Jewish community had already learned to cooperate with an authoritarian state as a means of protecting its interests."[15]

There were mass celebrations in Vienna following the 1938 "Anschluss," reflecting widespread support for Hitler and National Socialism.[16] Thereafter, the Gestapo oversaw the implementation of anti-Jewish policies in the city, and mass arrests became commonplace. In April 1938, the first transport left for the Dachau concentration camp, near Munich, with 151 deportees, 60 of whom were Jews. Over the next two months, the number of Jews deported to Dachau increased dramatically to 5,000.[17] As anti-Jewish oppression escalated rapidly, the November Pogrom – *Kristallnacht* – was merely one of several peaks in the ongoing brutal destruction of

---

12 Ilana Fritz Offenberger, The Jews of Nazi Vienna, 1938–1945: Rescue and Destruction (London: Palgrave Macmillan, 2017), 2; Doron Rabinovici, Eichmann's Jews: The Jewish Administration of Holocaust Vienna, 1938–1945 (Cambridge: Polity Press, 2011), 17.
13 Bruce F. Pauley, From Prejudice to Persecution: A History of Austrian Anti-Semitism (Chapel Hill – London: University of North Carolina Press, 1992), 326.
14 Rabinovici, Eichmann's Jews, 22–4.
15 Ibid., 25.
16 Offenberger, The Jews of Nazi Vienna, 16.
17 Rabinovici, Eichmann's Jews, 24, 45.

Austrian Jewry. Following the pogrom, the police arrested a further 6,000 Austrian Jewish men and deported them to Dachau.[18]

Research in the Dachau Concentration Camp Memorial Site archive reveals that at least 100 of the men who were deported to Mauritius in December 1940 had been imprisoned in Dachau for several months in 1938–9. Most of them were originally from Vienna and aged between forty and sixty.[19] Some were Zionists, but others were ignorant of both Zionism and indeed Judaism.[20]

Describing his first impressions of Dachau, twenty-six-year-old Simon Thieberg recalled, "The camp was surrounded with wires which were electrified and watch towers with machine guns on the top [...] I was given a red and yellow star and a number, officially becoming a prisoner, not a person."[21] Rabbi Bela Fischer, who was deported to the camp on 23 June 1938 and later became one of the deportees to Mauritius, sarcastically recalled in his memoir:

> I admired the organization that was able to provide accommodation for such a large number of newcomers. The hut-prefects, Aryan prisoners themselves, took charge of a certain number of us. First, they gave us water to drink and a "one-pot-dish" which was not too bad after our long fast. Then they led us to the barbers' where they shaved us and cut our hair quite short [...] Then we got a number and a Jew's distinctive mark i.e. a red and yellow David-Star, fixed both at the left side of the breast and on the trousers at the left knee.[22]

In addition to the hair-shaving, many memoirs and testimonies mention Dachau's daily roll-call. For instance, Chava Eva Guez, who was three years old when her father was released from the camp and returned to Vienna, recalled:

> I remember that when my father came back from Dachau, he was very bloated. My grandmother couldn't recognize him, and when she opened the door, she said: "Sir, what do you need?" I stood aside and said, "Dad, where's your hair?" because they shaved his head. In those days, the Red Cross was still allowed to visit the camps, so they put Brom[ide] into the food, which inflated them greatly [...] He didn't say much about Dachau, however, he told us that it was snowing,

---

18   Pauley, From Prejudice to Persecution, 286–8.
19   All personal information, including full name, date of birth, hometown, date of imprisonment in Dachau and date of release, was extracted from the Prisoners Database at the archive of the Dachau Concentration Camp Memorial Site.
20   Zwergbaum, "Exile in Mauritius," 3–4.
21   Testimony of Simon Thieberg, USC Shoah Foundation Institute, 23 April 1995.
22   Bela Fischer, "My Memories of Nazism," KZ-Gedenkstätte Dachau, Aktennummer 956, p. 5.

and that he had to stand for hours in line, and he suffered from it as his feet and hands froze, and it greatly damaged his health.²³

Rabbi Fischer similarly recalled, "They often kept us standing rigidly at attention five and more hours on the roll-call-square in any weather, when the 'Fuhrer' held one of his speeches, and at that time he was very fond of speaking and he spoke for hours without end."²⁴

Thirty-three-year-old Hans Klein was also deported to Dachau in early June 1938. More than three months later, he was transferred to Buchenwald, where he was imprisoned for almost a year. He recalled:

> On 1 September 1939, I was taken [from Buchenwald] to the Gestapo, the office that had requested me. I was held in the Gestapo prison [sic!] in Rossauerlände for several more weeks, during which I had neither the opportunity to wash nor to shave. I was finally released on 19 October. However, I had to report continuously to the Gestapo office in Prinz-Eugen-Strasse [sic!]. When I was asked there when I would be leaving the country, I explained that I hoped to be ready in four weeks [...] I remained free in Vienna, but, as before, had to report regularly to the Gestapo office, which continued to plague me with threats if I did not manage to leave the country as quickly as possible.²⁵

Indeed, many of the Viennese Jews who were imprisoned in German concentration camps in 1938–9 had already secured emigration papers for themselves and their families. Therefore, to encourage Jewish emigration, Adolf Eichmann, who founded the Central Office for Jewish Emigration in Vienna in August 1938, approved their release on condition that they could – and would – leave immediately.²⁶ Furthermore, in 1939, Eichmann recruited the Austrian-Jewish financial advisor Berthold Storfer to head the Committee for Jewish Overseas Transports. By March 1940, Storfer was organising and coordinating all illegal immigration to Palestine.²⁷ He handled the Committee's financial affairs, negotiated with Jewish organisations, the German authorities and local travel agencies across the "Third Reich," and finally became the sole organiser of European Jewry's River Danube escape routes.²⁸

---

23 Testimony of Chava Eva Guez regarding her experiences in Vienna and Mauritius, V.T/4780, Yad Vashem Testimonies.
24 Fischer, "My Memories of Nazism," 7.
25 Hans Klein, "Meine Auswanderung in die Zwangs-Internierung von Mauritius," File 636, Wiener Library Collection, Yad Vashem Archives.
26 Rabinovici, Eichmann's Jews, 60.
27 Ibid., 83; Anderl, "Auf dem Weg nach Palästina," 324.
28 Ofer, "The Rescue of European Jewry," 175.

In the summer of 1940, Storfer chartered four Danube riverboats and three ships to transport 3,500 Jewish refugees to British Mandate Palestine.[29] On 4 September, 820 refugees from Prague and Brno along with 800 from Vienna and elsewhere who had been registered for Storfer's mass evacuation left the Austrian capital on two boats – *Schönbrunn* and *Melk*. A few hours later, they arrived in Bratislava, where another 1,880 refugees and two further boats – *Uranus* and *Helios* – were waiting to join the convoy. The four boats set sail the following day, and a week later they arrived at Tulcea, in Romania, where the refugees were transferred onto three ships – the *Atlantic*, the *Milos* and the *Pacific*.[30]

None of the 3,500 refugees had an entrance visa for Mandatory Palestine – where a strict immigration quota had been in place since the publication of a White Paper on the subject the previous year – so the British authorities regarded them as illegal immigrants.[31] Therefore, upon their arrival in Haifa in early November, the passengers on board the *Milos* and the *Pacific* were forcibly transferred to another ship – the *Patria* – for deportation to the British colony of Mauritius.[32] The *Atlantic* arrived in Haifa a few weeks later, on 24 November, whereupon the authorities started to load its passengers onto the *Patria*, too. However, overnight, the Yishuv's underground military organisation, the Haganah, smuggled a bomb onto the *Patria*, and at 9 a.m. on 25 November, while most of the *Atlantic*'s passengers were still awaiting their transfer, it exploded, killing more than 260 Jewish refugees.[33]

The British authorities permitted those who had been on board the *Patria* to remain in Palestine and transported them to the Atlit detention camp, near Haifa.[34] Meanwhile, some of the *Atlantic*'s younger passengers were sent to a jail in Acre, while the rest were interned in a separate part of the Atlit camp.[35] Years later, Simon Thieberg recalled his arrival in Haifa:

> [T]he British took us in a camp and interrogated us. One of the interrogators made a remark – "We can treat you like the Nazis treat you" because it was war and they thought maybe there were spies among us [...] Some of the youngsters including me were sent to Acre, where members of the Irgun [another Jewish paramilitary organisation] were imprisoned too, under strict conditions. There,

---

29 Anderl, "Auf dem Weg nach Palästina," 324.
30 Moshe Silberhaft and Suzanne Belling, The Traveling Rabbi: My African Tribe (Johannesburg: Jacana Media, 2012), 298.
31 Lauren Elise Apter, "Disorderly Decolonization: The White Paper of 1939 and the End of British Rule in Palestine," unpublished Ph.D. dissertation, University of Texas at Austin, 2008, 136.
32 Anderl, "Auf dem Weg nach Palästina," 324.
33 Ofer, Escaping the Holocaust, 31–2; Arieh J. Kochavi, Displaced Persons and International Politics (Tel Aviv: Am Oved, 1992), 8, 42.
34 Ofer, Escaping the Holocaust, 36; Zwergbaum, "Exile in Mauritius," 203.
35 Anderl, "Auf dem Weg nach Palästina," 325.

we were held for seven days [...] The British Colonial Police treated us like enemies, especially the young ones.[36]

Those who were sent to Atlit reported similar treatment. The camp contained about 100 barracks and tents, and barbed-wire fences were used to divide it into discrete sections, including the one that separated the *Atlantic*'s passengers from their fellow-refugees who had been on the *Patria* at the time of the explosion.[37] Aaron Zwergbaum wrote in his diary:

> All indications are that our stay is going to be a long one. Blankets and cutlery are handed out, interrogations – yet superficial – are conducted, personal details are taken down, and after two days the luggage is handed out [...] Unfortunately it is quite impossible to establish any contact with the people from outside. We can talk across the fence with the *Patria* people and are happy to see many acquaintances.[38]

Contrary to Zwergbaum's prediction, just two weeks later, on 9 December 1940, he and the rest of the camp's 1,580 *Atlantic* refugees were returned to the port of Haifa, where they were loaded onto two ships – the *Johan de Witt* and the *New Zealand* – and deported to Mauritius.[39]

Josef Adler, a refugee from Czechoslovakia, was just twenty years old when he and the other deportees were evacuated from Atlit:

> The police officers took the men one by one and forcibly led them to the cars. Those who tried to resist were violently thrown into trucks. Most of the young men were completely naked. We went out in a convoy of trucks to the port of Haifa, and they divided us to two ships [...] the men were brought down to the bottom of the ships, the heat was unbearable and as we passed through the Red Sea it became even worse.[40]

During their transfer from Atlit to Haifa, the refugees were escorted by a military convoy and forced to undergo what the British authorities termed a "customs examination," in the course of which their watches, glasses, cutlery and other personal belongings were confiscated.[41] Moreover, as Zwergbaum wrote in his diary, "During

---

36 Testimony of Simon Thieberg.
37 Pitot, The Mauritian Shekel, 120.
38 Aaron Zwergbaum, "Aliyah from Bratislava to Mauritius: The Journey from Presburg to Mauritius," US Holocaust Memorial Museum Archive [USHMM].
39 Anderl, "Auf dem Weg nach Palästina," 326.
40 Josef Adler, "Memories of my Life before and during the Deportation to Mauritius," Mauritius Exiles Collection 6501, Ghetto Fighters' House Archives, Israel.
41 Zwergbaum, "Exile in Mauritius," 203.

the first days [at sea,] the refugees were kept in the holds of the ships which were unbearably hot [...] On one of the ships headed to Mauritius the men's hair was cropped close, not for hygienic reasons, but in order to annoy and to humiliate them."[42] This measure was all too traumatically familiar for the ex-prisoners of Dachau.

Moshe Shertok (Sharett), who was secretary of the Jewish Agency's Political Department at the time, described the deportation as "a horrible act that did not exist in the history of the Land of Israel" and the Beau-Bassin Camp on Mauritius as "a British Dachau."[43] It is highly unlikely that Shertok intended to equate the British detention camp with the German concentration camp; rather, it seems his aim was simply to shed light on the British authorities' harsh treatment of the Jewish refugees. As I explain elsewhere, British colonial documents dating from the second half of 1940 suggest that both the Colonial Office and the High Commissioner for Jerusalem considered the ongoing arrival of Jewish refugees as an immediate threat to security in the Middle East as it would increase the likelihood of a fifth column in Palestine, given the Germans' encouragement of – and active involvement in – Jewish emigration from their territories.[44] For instance, in a telegram sent to the governor of Trinidad on 14 November 1940, Lord Lloyd, Britain's secretary of state for the colonies, argued that the government was facing an urgent problem of "disposal of considerable number of Jews from Central Europe who are expected shortly to reach Palestine coast with a view to illegal entry."[45] He continued that the governor of Mauritius had already agreed to provide accommodation for a considerable number of people and asked if Trinidad would be willing to contribute to the war effort by doing the same. He described the refugees as "Jewish internees [who] would have to be kept under restraint and this would involve the camp being surrounded by barbed wire and the provision of guards [...] [because they] might include enemy agents."[46]

Lloyd's stipulation that the camp must be guarded and encircled with barbed wire reflects the perception among some British politicians and officials that the Jewish émigrés might be enemy agents who should be restrained and detained, as opposed to refugees who had escaped brutal persecution. Although Prime Minister

---

42 Ibid., 204.
43 Mapai meeting, 15 December 1940, quoted in Ahuva Malkin and Eli Shaltiel (eds), Making of Policy: The Diaries of Moshe Sharett (Tel Aviv: Am Oved, 1979), Vol. 5: 144–5; Gerald Ziedenberg, Blockade: The Story of Jewish Immigration to Palestine (Bloomington, ID: AuthorHouse, 2011), 67.
44 Roni Mikel-Arieli, "The Jewish Question in the British Colonial Imagination: The Case of the Deportation to Mauritius (1940–1945)," Jewish Social Studies (forthcoming).
45 Telegram from Secretary of State for the Colonies to Governor of Trinidad, 14 November 1940, Prime Minister's Office Papers 1940–1945, R98.210 228, Bavarian State Library, Munich, Germany.
46 Ibid.

Winston Churchill argued that "it is very unlikely that these refugees would include enemy agents," [47] Lloyd insisted:

> There is evidence to show that these voyages are organized and financed by Jewish agencies with the active assistance of the German authorities. Without such assistance the traffic could not be carried on at all. Is it indeed likely that the Nazis would neglect so good an opportunity of getting their agents into the Middle East?[48]

Indeed, as Tony Kushner argues, while the British government's policies were not anti-Semitic, some governmental officials not only held anti-Semitic views but also had sufficient authority to influence the government's response to Jewish immigration to its territories.[49] Thus, the deportation of more than 1,500 Jewish civilians to Mauritius may be considered one example of British colonial officials' racist perceptions driving the distorted implementation of London's colonial policies.

Interned in the Indian Ocean

The island of Mauritius, in the Indian Ocean, was once the capital of French power in the East as well as the base from which corsairs pursued British merchants as they plied their trade between India and Europe.[50] British imperial control of the island was established after an invasion in 1810 and continued until 12 March 1968, when Mauritius achieved independence.[51] During the Second World War, two-thirds of the local population were of Indo-Pakistani origin, primarily descendants of indentured labourers who had been shipped to the island to work on sugar plantations in the nineteenth and early twentieth centuries; a quarter were Creole (mixed French and African descent); a small number were Chinese in origin; and there was a tiny yet powerful Franco-Mauritian elite.[52]

On 20 November 1940, the local daily newspaper, *Advance*, reported an announcement that Sir Bede Clifford, the island's governor, had made during the

---

47 Telegram from Churchill to Lord Lloyd, 20 November 1940, Prime Minister's Office Papers 1940–1945, R98.210 228, Bavarian State Library, Munich, Germany.
48 Telegram from Lord Lloyd to Churchill, 21 November 1940, Prime Minister's Office Papers 1940–1945, R98.210 228, Bavarian State Library, Munich, Germany.
49 Tony Kushner, The Persistence of Prejudice: Anti-Semitism in British Society during the Second World War (Manchester: Manchester University Press, 1989), 160.
50 Ashley Jackson, War and Empire in Mauritius and the Indian Ocean (London: Palgrave, 2001), 325.
51 Richard B. Allen, Selves, Freedmen and Indentured Laborers in Colonial Mauritius (Cambridge: Cambridge University Press, 1999).
52 Anderl, "Auf dem Weg nach Palästina," 326.

previous day's meeting of the Legislative Council: "refugees shall be arriving in Mauritius." The paper clarified that the new arrivals would be "Jews, citizens of Austria, Hungary, Czechoslovakia, and Germany who have been expelled from these countries."[53] However, the report continued, the deportees were "persons with an average or high standard of education and living which is why it was not contemplated to allow them to stay in Mauritius after the war. Thus, they cannot be referred to as refugees or deportees, but rather as 'detainees.'"[54] The following month, on 23 December, the British authorities on Mauritius issued a local ordinance that defined the Jewish refugees as "European Detainees," authorised the governor to detain them in the colony and equipped him with the tools he needed to discourage contact between the local population and the new arrivals.[55] Specifically, any Mauritian who attempted to offer assistance to the "detainees" risked a two-year prison sentence.[56]

On 26 December 1940, after a seventeen-day voyage on two overcrowded ships, 849 men, 635 women and 96 children disembarked at the harbour of Port Louis, the capital of Mauritius.[57] Two days later, they were all transferred to the Beau-Bassin central prison,[58] which had been hastily converted into a detention camp with new boundaries, administration and regulations.[59] The official documents that initiated this process left no room for doubt: the new arrivals would be prisoners, detained in a secure facility and obliged to respect a clear disciplinary code. They were not free people. Thus, Simon Thieberg's first impressions were correct: "It was a jail, a big jail with very high walls […] It wasn't like a German concentration camp, but we had no freedom […] we each got a cell, but the door was open."[60]

---

53 "Le Gouverneur annonce que des refugies viendront à Maurice," Advance, 20 November, 1940, 1.
54 Ibid., 1.
55 "The European Detainees (Control) Ordinance 1940," Ordinance No. 57 of 1940, 23 December 1940, 112–13, The Mauritius Gazette, Mauritius National Archive.
56 "The European Detainees (Control) Ordinance 1940 – Boundaries of Detainment Camp," Government Notice No. 281, 114, The Mauritius Gazette, Mauritius National Archive.
57 To be precise, 1,581 refugees arrived at Port Louis. However, a few days later, Anita Hirschmann, a thirty-year-old woman originally from Germany, died of typhoid. See Pitot, The Mauritian Shekel, 112.
58 Anderl, "Auf dem Weg nach Palästina," 327.
59 "The European Detainees (Control) Ordinance 1940 – Boundaries of Detainment Camp"; "The European Detainees (Organization and Administration) Regulations, 1941," "The European Detainees (Performance of Detainment Area Duties) Regulations, 1941" and "The European Detainees (Discipline) Regulations, 1941," The Mauritius Gazette, Mauritius National Archive.
60 Testimony of Simon Thieberg.

Figure 1: The Beau-Bassin Prison, Mauritius

Source: Mauritius Exiles Collection, Ghetto Fighters' House Archive, Israel.

The high walls of the main prison compound meant that it was a simple matter to segregate one group of prisoners from the other: while the men were accommodated in the original prison cells, the women and children were housed in a compound of recently erected huts.[61] In his first annual report of January 1942, the detainees' designated representative, Aaron Zwergbaum, suggested that "the lack of freedom [...] and the impossibility of leading a normal family and sex life" were the two main hardships of camp life.[62] Only in July of that year, after a long struggle, were wives finally granted permission to visit the men's camp at certain hours of the day.[63]

Two days after the *Johan de Witt* and the *New Zealand* docked in Port Louis, *Advance* published an editorial that stated: "The arrival of the detainees in Mauritius shows the complexity of the problems which have arisen because of the war. The Jewish problem is an example of how the British administration tackles it with efficiency."[64] Here, it is important to stress that the Franco-Mauritian elite were still a powerful minority on the island because a small group of families' pragmatic decision to cooperate with the British Crown after 1810 had enabled them to retain

---

61 "The European Detainees (Organization and Administration) Regulations, 1941," "The European Detainees (Performance of Detainment Area Duties) Regulations, 1941" and "The European Detainees (Discipline) Regulations, 1941," The Mauritius Gazette, Mauritius National Archive.
62 Zwergbaum, "The First Year in Mauritius," USHMM, 24.
63 Zwergbaum, "The Second Year in Mauritius," USHMM, 7–10.
64 "The Detainees," Advance, 30 December 1940, pp. 80–81.

control over the local sugar industry. Therefore, their positions were usually in line with those of the British officials.[65]

The editorial also asserted that the detainees had received a warm welcome from the Mauritian population: "We have seen the detainees as they pass our office. Thousands of Mauritians had gathered to extend to them the love and welcome that are the inevitable characteristics of this island home of ours. They [the detainees] looked cheerful and we could see on their face a glow of hope."[66] This outpouring of affection is confirmed in many of the detainees' own memoirs, diaries and oral testimonies. However, all stressed that this unexpected welcome was primarily extended by the island's Indo-Pakistani and Creole populations, so they interpreted it as an act of colonial resistance. For instance, in his account of the voyage, Zwergbaum wrote, "It was overwhelming to see how friendly, even enthusiastically we were greeted by the Coloured. What a contrast, remembering what we had suffered under Whites in Europe!"[67] Similarly, Amnon Klein, who escaped from Vienna with his mother when he was just twelve years old, recalled,

> The local population threw flowers on the road as we passed on our way to the camp. Apparently, they thought that we were German prisoners, and it turned out that they hated the British so much that they preferred the Germans over them [...] [F]or me, as the son of a former prisoner of the notorious German camp, Dachau, it was an ambivalent feeling to be considered German.[68]

A few weeks later, on 13 January 1941, an official delegation visited Beau-Bassin and subsequently published its report in the local newspaper. According to the article, "the Detainees' camp has been transformed from a prison house into a nice-looking village where every little thing is provided to make these victims of the Nazis as happy as possible. It looks like a miniature official world where nearly every department has its representative."[69] In reality, though, it was anything but "a happy village," as the large number of detainees who were admitted to the island's mental hospital testifies.[70] Zwergbaum's first annual report draws attention to this issue,

---

65 Tijo Salverda, "Sugar, Sea and Power: How Franco-Mauritians Balance Continuity and Creeping Decline of Their Elite Position," unpublished Ph.D. dissertation, VU University Amsterdam, 2010, 1–2.
66 "The Detainees."
67 Zwergbaum, "Aliyah from Bratislava to Mauritius," 20.
68 Testimony of Amnom Klein, 15 July 2003, Record Group 0.3, File 12247, Yad Vashem Testimony Archive.
69 "With the Detainees," Advance, 5 February 1941, pp. 85–9.
70 See, for example: "Grievances," Advance, 7 January 1941; "Au Camp des internes," Cerneen, 13 January 1941; "Les Internes," Le Mauricien, 17 January 1941; "Au Conseil," Advance, 6 February 1941.

particularly among men who had endured periods of imprisonment in German concentration camps:

> If one asks what is worst about the entire detention, it is one's state of mind. Life here stresses and strains one's nerves. Sometimes it is the walls and being locked up that is hard to take, then you are worn out with worry about relatives, you get depressed that you are wasting the best years of your life here, then again it is the uncertainty of the future. For some, particularly among the detainees who had been imprisoned in German concentration camps, this state of mind manifests itself in a state of apathy. Others try to get over it by fooling around, and still others become increasingly nervous and irritable.[71]

During its visit to Beau-Bassin, the official delegation paid a visit to the camp school, where an Austro-Jewish teacher was delivering a Hebrew lesson. The delegation's account stated:

> As we looked into his eyes, we felt how miserable this patriarch must be. Snatched from his house, driven from his country, dispossessed of his wealth, hunted from one place to another, he was a man who to all appearances was a great scholar, and yet undergoing such suffering endured with a fortitude that could move the most indifferent to depths of pity. He was originally from Vienna where life was smiling [on] him and when came Herr von Hitler, he was sent to the brutal Nazi camp which he described as the tragedy of his martyrdom. The sight of that intellectual was itself [...] proof of the tyranny which is let loose on all conquered peoples by the forces of Hitlerism and no wonder that when we ask[ed] a man of age if he was a German, he spat three time[s] on the ground ejaculating each time "German no people."[72]

In its concluding remarks, the article declared, "By providing a shelter to these detainees, Mauritius is helping the Empire's war effort in a manner which should not be underrated. It has more value in one sense than other material contributions, for we are all aware what a great danger [it] is to leave refugees in the war zones."[73] However, while the delegation's report acknowledged the hardships the detainees had suffered in their homelands, including incarceration in German concentration camps, it neglected to mention that these unfortunate people were now incarcerated once again in a camp where they were treated as detainees rather than refugees. They lived in a prison compound, their freedom was highly restricted and their fate was unknown.

---

71 Aaron Zwergbaum, "The First Year in Mauritius," USHMM, 26.
72 "With the Detainees," p. 87.
73 "With the Detainees II," Advance, 6 February 1941, pp. 90–94, at 94.

The captives' plight was amply represented in a letter that Dr Alfred Heller – a detainee from Munich who had spent a month in Dachau in late 1938 – wrote to a Mr Gitlin of Cape Town, South Africa, two months after his arrival on Mauritius:

> We must have a ground to stand on. Nowhere is there a ground, history and destiny which would inspire us more than Palestine. Our brethren there have shown what they are able to achieve on their own ground, even without freedom. We are sitting in the wilderness, dreaming. You don't think, Sir, that telling dreams is useful, do you? And yet, in a dream there is sometimes a spark; something sometimes catches fire. Maybe somebody perceives that there is a spark and somewhere a gleam of hope may flare up.[74]

A comparable sense of despair is evident in an April 1942 report by the South African Sub-committee on Mauritius.[75] After a meeting in Durban with a group of Czech volunteers who had been released from Beau-Bassin in order to join the Allied forces in the Middle East, Mr J. Meyer, the sub-committee's chairman, stated,

> I have come to the conclusion that the greatest mistake committed by the Imperial Government was to transplant indiscriminately a heterogeneous group of people from Central Europe to a tropical island [administered by] a colonial government that could not possibly be expected to understand the mental and physical background of the people who were entrusted to their charge by the accidents of war.[76]

In addition to suffering mental distress, many of the refugees arrived on the island in poor physical health.[77] Thirteen-year-old Arie Leopold Keller, from Danzig, wrote in his diary: "When we arrived in Mauritius, many of us were sick and weak. Every day we had to bury at least one deceased person."[78] The detainees' frailty is

---

74 From a letter by Dr Alfred Heller to Mr Gitlin in Cape Town, South Africa, 20 February 1940, on display in A Brief History with Illustrations, Beau-Bassin Jewish Detainees Memorial & Information Centre, Mauritius.

75 While the Jewish institutions in South Africa were unable to stop the closing of the country's gates to Jewish refugees, they made enormous efforts to assist those refugees who arrived in southern Africa. The South African Jewish Board of Deputies, together with the Council of German Jewry in London, formed a committee in Johannesburg to dispense relief, while the Council for Refugee Settlement was established and eventually extended its activities to Mauritius. On the establishment of the relief committee, see "Notes on Refugee Funds Raised in the Union," 2–3, Austrian and Polish Relief Fund, Report 1941, ARCH 216.1, File 4, SAJBD Archive, Holocaust-Related Records, USHMM.

76 Minutes of Mauritius Sub-committee meeting, Johannesburg, South Africa, 27 May 1942, Rochlin Archive.

77 Anderl, "Auf dem Weg nach Palästina," 328.

78 Arie Leopold Keller, Mauritius diary, File 40284, Mauritius Exiles Collection, Ghetto Fighters' House Archives, Israel.

also reflected in the local authorities' regular reports to the secretary of state for the colonies, which include the names of those who have died over the previous month, cause of death, age and nationality. Close analysis of these lists reveals that the cause of death was usually typhoid, although some died from malaria, with cases of the latter increasing over time.[79]

Notwithstanding their mental and physical suffering, however, it is important to note that the detainees managed to establish and maintain a rich cultural and social routine within the compound. There were two active synagogues, schools, adult education centres, youth movements, theatre groups, a Zionist association, a library, a newspaper, coffee shops and even a soccer team.[80] As Zwergbaum wrote in his January 1942 report, "Many different various events took place here, and one must realize there was no censorship. Furthermore, all religious customs could be observed without any obstacles. The recreation room was very attractive for stage productions, but then the radio redirected a lot of interest away from the theatre."[81]

Detainees' manufactured toys, bags and other goods out of recycled paper and wood in the camp's workshops. These products were then displayed in a showroom in the camp's external office building and sold to locals.[82] Moreover, in late 1941, some of the skilled detainees were granted temporary permits to work outside the camp as electricians and telephone engineers, in cosmetics and toy factories, and as music, art and language teachers in the local primary schools.[83] Thus, the strict segregation of the detainees from the local community, which the imperial authorities had deemed essential less than a year earlier, was partially abandoned to the two groups' mutual benefit.

---

79   See, for example: Letter No. 28 from the Governor of Mauritius to Secretary of State for the Colonies, 10 February 1941; Letter No. 63 from the Governor of Mauritius to Secretary of State for the Colonies, 26 March 1941; Letter No. 92 from the Governor of Mauritius to Secretary of State for the Colonies, 2 May 1941; Letter No. 136 from the Governor of Mauritius to Secretary of State for the Colonies, 6 June 1941; all in Out Correspondence Colonial Section, Mauritius National Archive.
80   Pitot, The Mauritian Shekel, 161, 165–7; Anderl, "Auf dem Weg nach Palästina," 329–30.
81   Zwergbaum, "The First Year in Mauritius," 34.
82   Minutes of Mauritius Sub-committee meeting, 16 February 1942, Johannesburg, South Africa, the Rochlin Archive.
83   "Des Experts," Le Mauricien, 2 February 1942; Anderl, "Auf dem Weg nach Palästina," 327, 330.

Figure 2: A group of men praying at one of the synagogues set up in the Beau-Bassin camp

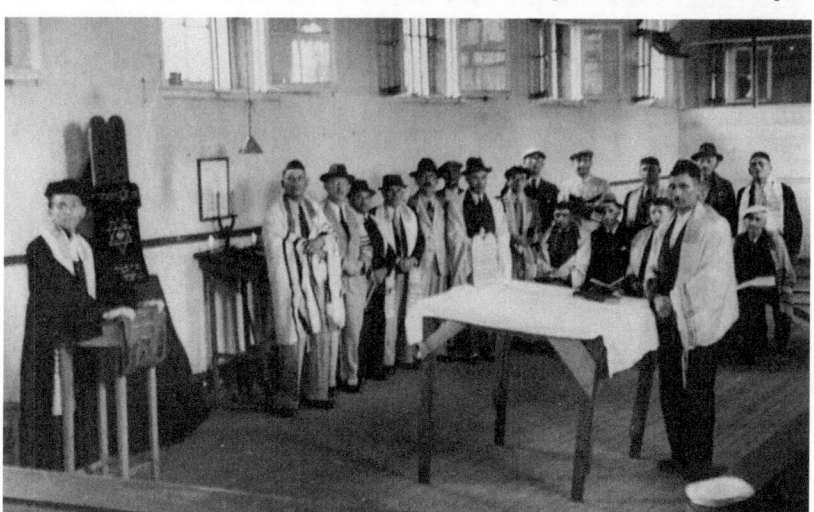

Source: Mauritius Exiles Collection, Ghetto Fighters' House Archive, Israel.

On 21 February 1945, the island's governor informed the detainees that the British authorities had decided to allow them to enter Palestine. However, it was another six months before the refugees finally left Mauritius. The following year, the South African Jewish Board of Deputies acquired Saint Martin Jewish Cemetery, on the outskirts of Beau-Bassin, where 126 of the detainees were buried. Five of the dead were members of the Viennese group who had been imprisoned in Dachau in 1938–9.

Figure 3: Saint Martin Jewish Cemetery, Mauritius, where 126 of the Jewish detainees are buried

Source: Mauritius Exiles Collection, Ghetto Fighters' House Archive, Israel.

Conclusion

More than two years after the deportation of 1,581 Jews to Mauritius, at the opening of the 10th Session of the Assembly of Representatives in Jerusalem on 9 March 1942, Moshe Shertok proclaimed,

> Mauritius and Dachau are completely different, as different as light and darkness. In terms of the regime, the treatment, the public responsibility and, most importantly, in terms of the prospect to stay healthy and alive [...] However, from a Jewish perspective, Mauritius is as oppressive as Dachau! Both in Dachau and on Mauritius we are imprisoned as Jews, we are thrown into these camps and imprisoned there as Jews.[84]

---

84 Moshe Shertok speech at the 10th Session of the Assembly of Representatives, Jerusalem, 9 March 1942, quoted in Moshe Sharett Political Struggle 1942 January–May: An Anthology of Speeches and Documents, edited by Yaakov Sharett (Tel Aviv: The Society to Commemorate Moshe Sharett, 2009), Vol. 1, Part 1: 251.

Indeed, it is impossible to equate the physical conditions in Dachau with those in Beau-Bassin; nor should anyone draw parallels between the two camps' regimens or their treatment of their inhabitants. Nevertheless, as this article has demonstrated, some comparisons are inevitable and justified. The Jews who were deported to Mauritius had already experienced the rise of Hitlerism in Europe, including the National Socialists' occupation of their homelands, the passing of anti-Jewish policies, the November Pogrom and ongoing racial persecution that, in many cases, led to their incarceration in concentration camps. However, because they were fortunate enough to escape anti-Semitic persecution in Central Europe, their stories have been omitted from the vast majority of studies of the Second World War and even the Holocaust. Yet, these Jewish refugees eventually became victims of another form of persecution – colonial persecution in a detention camp on a remote outpost of the British Empire in the Indian Ocean. Of course, most of them still had friends and relatives in German-occupied territories, and the imperial authorities were not averse to implying that they should be grateful that they had ended up in Mauritius instead. As Aaron Zwergbaum astutely pointed out in his account of his time in Beau-Bassin,

> It was perhaps symbolical that the detainees were put into cells where before them criminals had served long terms of imprisonment [...] It was sometimes discreetly suggested to the detainees and at other times they were told quite bluntly, that they ought to compare their position with the fate of the Jews in Nazi-occupied Europe [...] There was undoubtedly an immense difference between the detention camp in Mauritius and a German concentration camp, but such comparison was an insult: it implied that the Jews are not entitled to equal rights like other people but ought to be content with any status that was better than outright persecution.[85]

---

85 Zwergbaum, "Exile in Mauritius," 210–11.

Forced to flee and deemed suspect
Tracing life stories of interned refugees in Canada during and after the Second World War

Andrea Strutz

This paper is based on three case studies of men who fled to Britain from National Socialist Germany – specifically Vienna, Leipzig and Hamburg – and were subsequently deported to Canada as "enemy aliens" in 1940 and interned there for up to three years.[1] Of particular interest is whether and how these refugees were able to build new lives for themselves after their release from the Canadian internment, and in what ways factors such as age, education and agency influenced this process. In this context, a biographical approach seems appropriate,[2] especially to shed more light on the actions and decisions of the persons under investigation.

Agency defines the power of individuals to think for themselves, to make decisions and to act in a way that enables them to shape their experiences and life trajectories.

The scope of agency is dependent on the "human capital" or personal resources and on the "social capital" or networks a person has been encouraged to develop in the process of socialisation and has augmented in adolescents and adult life. "Resources" refer to a person's pool of capabilities, and "capital" suggests a desire to invest such capabilities in achieving goals and life course projects.[3]

---

1   The research for this article was conducted in cooperation with the University of Graz and the city of Graz at the Ludwig Boltzmann Institute for Research on the Consequences of War, Graz – Vienna – Raabs, and was supported by the Future Fund of the Republic of Austria (project: "Flight, Deportation, Internment: Tracing Austrian Refugees from Nazism in Canada," P19-3632), the Provincial Government of Lower Austria and the Stiftung für Kanada-Studien.
2   See Volker Depkat, "Biographieforschung im Kontext transnationaler und globaler Geschichtsschreibung. Einleitung zum Schwerpunkt," in Bios. Zeitschrift für Biographieforschung, Oral History und Lebensverlaufsanalysen 28 (2015) 1, 2: 7–8.
3   Christiane Harzig and Dirk Hoerder, with Donna Gabaccia, What is Migration History? (Cambridge: Polity Press, 2009), 79.

Even though refugees' options for decision-making and action were limited, they are understood as "agents of their own lives."[4] During internment and afterwards, many refugees, including the three people studied here, used their human capital, such as professional skills and expertise, social skills and strategic competences (e.g. to establish a camp school for teenage refugees) as well as their ability to mobilise personal resources, to use structures and to form support networks to cope with and adapt to the new and unexpected social environment in exile and to develop strategies for building a new life in Canada that included utilising support networks (e.g. refugee organisations).

Internment policies in Great Britain and Canada

Great Britain declared war on Germany on 3 September 1939, following the latter's invasion of Poland. For Austrians and Germans living in the United Kingdom, many of whom were refugees with temporary residence permits,[5] this meant that they became "enemy aliens" and were compelled to register with the police. By March 1940, some 73,800 Germans and Austrians residing in the UK had been screened by alien tribunals with regard to possible internment. About 90 per cent (66,200) were deemed "harmless" (Category C) and remained at liberty. The vast majority of this group (55,460) were Jewish refugees or anti-National Socialist exiles who had sought refuge in Britain to escape further persecution in National Socialist Germany. Almost 7,000 of those screened became subject to certain restrictions (e.g. limits on movement and a ban on the ownership of cameras) and were kept under police observation (Category B).[6] About 1 per cent were classified as "dangerous enemy aliens" (Category A) and immediately interned in camps set up in Liverpool, Glasgow, London, on the Isle of Man and elsewhere.[7]

---

4   See Dirk Hoerder, "Individuals and Systems: Agency in Nineteenth and Twentieth Century Labour Migrations," in European Mobility: Internal, International, and Transatlantic Moves in the 19th and Early 20th Centuries, edited by Annemarie Steidl et al. (Göttingen: V&R unipress, 2009), 53–67, at 53.
5   British entry regulations were relaxed after the November pogrom, but the authorities gave preference to those refugees who were willing to migrate further within two years. See Gabriele Anderl, "Flucht und Vertreibung 1938–1945," in Auswanderungen aus Österreich. Von der Mitte des 19. Jahrhunderts bis zur Gegenwart, edited by Traude Horvath and Gerda Neyer (Wien – Köln – Weimar: Böhlau, 1996), 235–75, at 245.
6   See Peter Gillman and Leni Gillman, "Collar the Lot!" How Britain Interned and Expelled its Wartime Refugees (London – Melbourne – New York: Quartet Books, 1980), 44.
7   See ibid.; Francois Lafitte, The Internment of Aliens (London: Penguin, 1940), 36–7, 62; Ronald Stent, A Bespattered Page? The Internment of "His Majesty's Most Loyal Enemy Aliens" (London: André Deutsch, 1980), 30–41.

However, the British government's wartime policy on aliens changed a few months later, when the "speed at which France and the Low Countries fell [...] created panic in Great Britain over the possible existence of 'Fifth Columnists'."[8] The right-wing press became increasingly hostile to the refugees around that time and started spreading rumours that German spies were hiding in Britain.[9] Eventually, the British government "gave way to those who argued that the refugees posed a threat to national security, as potential fifth columnists who might sabotage British defences."[10] At the end of May 1940, the new Churchill government instituted a mass internment policy and started to detain Category B and C males, as well as also Category B females, without distinguishing between refugees or non-refugees.[11] "This measure, to some extent a panic response to the extreme situation of national emergency prevailing in May/June 1940, ultimately caused the internment of some 27,000 enemy aliens, including some 4,000 women, most of whom were Jews who plainly posed no security risk whatsoever."[12]

Memories of arrest and internment show that this was a traumatic experience, especially for those who had been in concentration camps before fleeing. Many of the refugees felt betrayed, as Henry Kreisel, who was forced to flee Vienna at the age of sixteen, stated in his internment diary: "We regarded Britain as the country that had rescued us from Nazi tyranny. To be then incarcerated by our friends seemed almost incomprehensible, a kind of betrayal."[13]

In addition, after Italy's declaration of war on Britain and France on 10 June 1940, some 18,000 Italian residents of Britain had to register with the police and about 4,200 of them were arrested and interned.[14]

In order to relieve the pressure on their own internment system, the British sought to deport male internees to Canada and Australia. Following Canada's assent to a Home Office urgent request, "a bounty of 2,108 German or Austrian Category A, single male internees, including *circa* 1,700 enemy merchant seamen, an

---

8   Rachel Pistol, "Enemy Alien and Refugee: Conflicting Identities in Great Britain during the Second World War," University of Sussex Journal of Contemporary History 16 (2015): 37.
9   See David Cesarani, "An Alien Concept? The Continuity of Anti-alienism in British Society before 1940," in The Internment of Aliens in Twentieth Century Britain, edited by David Cesarani and Tony Kushner (London – Portland OR: Frank Cass, 1993), 24–52, at 45.
10 Anthony Grenville, Jewish Refugees from Germany and Austria in Britain, 1933–1970: Their Image in AJR Information (London: Vallentine Mitchell, 2010), 29.
11 See Gillman and Gillman, "Collar the Lot!," 141–5.
12 Grenville, Jewish Refugees from Germany and Austria, 29.
13 Henry Kreisel, "Diary of an Internment," in Another Country: Writings by and about Henry Kreisel, edited by Shirley C. Neuman (Edmonton: NeWest Press 1985), 18–44, at 20.
14 See Lucio Sponza, "The Internment of Italians in Britain," in Enemies within: Italian and Other Internees in Canada and Abroad, edited by Franca Iacovetta et al. (Toronto – Buffalo – London: University of Toronto Press, 2000), 256–79, at 259.

additional 2,290 Category B and C Germans and Austrians, 407 Italian civilian single male internees and 1,948 genuine prisoners of war"[15] arrived in the Dominion on three ships – the *Duchess of York*, *Ettrick* and *Sobieski*. On the basis of information from London, Canada had been expecting a delivery of dangerous "enemy aliens"; however, it turned out that about 85 per cent of the Austrian and German civilian deportees were refugees.[16] Moreover, about thirty of the 400 Italians were either Jewish or anti-Fascist political refugees.[17]

A fourth ship had set off for Canada, but tragically the *Arandora Star* had been torpedoed and sunk off the west coast of Ireland on 2 July 1940, one day after she had left Liverpool. Over 800 of those on board had lost their lives: two-thirds of about 730 Italians, one-third of about 500 Austrians and Germans, and 79 crew members and army guards.[18] The survivors – a group of about 450 men, including 200 Italian civilian internees, 100 German merchant seamen, German nationals who were known National Socialist sympathisers as well as refugees – were deported to Australia on the *Dunera* just ten days later, along with 2,050 other refugees from Austria, Germany and Czechoslovakia.[19]

Canada declared war on Germany on 10 September 1939. Thereafter, German-Canadians[20] who had immigrated after 1922 but not yet acquired Canadian citizenship were ordered to register with the Royal Canadian Mounted Police (RCMP), which at the time was responsible for the surveillance of individuals and groups

---

15   Ernest Robert Zimmermann, The Little Third Reich on Lake Superior: A History of Canadian Internment Camp R (Edmonton: University of Alberta Press, 2015), 180.
16   See ibid.
17   See Paula J. Draper, "The 'Camp Boys': Interned Refugees from Nazism," in Enemies within, edited by Iacovetta et al., 171–93, at 177.
18   See Gillman and Gillman, "Collar the Lot!," 190–96. There was some confusion over who had died as there was no embarkation list, but it was clear that most of the dead were Italians, and others were refugees from National Socialist Germany.
19   See Ken Inglis et al., Dunera Lives: A Visual History, Clayton (Victoria: Monash University Publishing, 2018), 44; Elisabeth Lebensaft and Christine Kanzler, "Auf der Dunera nach Down Under. Deportationen deutschsprachiger Flüchtlinge nach Australien," in Exil im Krieg 1939–1945, edited by Hiltrud Häntzschel et al. (Göttingen: V&R unipress, 2016), 67–75, at 67–8. Approximately 80 per cent of the refugees deported to Australia were Jewish.
20   The term "German-Canadians" encompasses emigrants from Germany before the First World War and during the interwar period, others from Eastern European countries, including the Tsarist Russia, where German-speaking minorities had settled for centuries prior to migrating to Canada, and yet more from Austria and Switzerland. See Robert H. Keyserlingk, "Breaking the Nazi Plot: Canadian Government Attitudes towards German Canadians, 1939–1945," in On Guard for Thee: War, Ethnicity and Canadian State, 1939–1945, edited by Norman Hillmer et al. (Ottawa: Canadian Government Publishing Centre, 1988), 53–69, at 55.

who were considered dangerous.[21] Out of half a million German-Canadians, about 16,000 were subject to registration, including a number of "refugees of Jewish, Austrian or Czech background."[22] Some 850 of these resident Germans were classified as "disloyal" and interned; a few of them had been members of the National Socialist Workers Party in Canada (NSDAP).[23] After Italy's entry into the war, Italian Fascist organisations and parties were banned, and some 600 Canadian-Italian Fascists were detained.[24] However, by far the largest group of civilian internees in Canada were Japanese-Canadians, who were declared "enemy aliens" after the bombing of Pearl Harbor; some 21,000 of them were deprived of their civil rights and detained in British Columbia alone.[25]

As mentioned above, German refugees who had arrived in Canada before the war had to register with the authorities, but they were not typically interned. Nevertheless, the Canadian government had to deal with the problem of interned refugees when it became apparent that most of the Austrian and German civilians deported from Britain in July 1940 were innocent escapees from National Socialist Germany.[26] Ottawa also had some concerns about the classification of refugees, as the British judgement varied from harmless to dangerous.[27] Since the refugees had arrived in Canada as "enemy aliens," it was decided to hold all of the deported refugees in internment camps in Ontario, Quebec and New Brunswick, and treat them as prisoners of war (POW) under the terms of the 1929 Geneva Convention, until a solution could be found. The Canadian government justified this decision

---

21   The legal basis was the Defence of Canada Regulations (DOCR), effective from 3 September 1939. These regulations entitled the Minister of Justice to arrest and intern without charge any person who was suspected of jeopardising public safety or the security of the state in any way, including Canadian citizens. See ibid., 53.

22   See ibid., 55.

23   There were three main pro-National Socialist organisations in Canada, including the National Socialist Workers Party in Canada, which was open only to German citizens and had approximately 250 members. See Robert H. Keyserlingk, "'Agents within the Gates': The Search for Nazi Subversives in Canada during World War II," in Canadian Historical Review 66 (1985) 2: 221.

24   See Luigi Bruti Liberates, "The Internment of Italian Canadians," in Enemies within, edited by Iacovetta et al., 76–98, at 84.

25   See Pamela Hickman and Masako Fukawa, Righting Canada's Wrongs: Japanese Internment in the Second World War (Toronto: James Lorimer & Company, 2011), 72–123. Overall, the Canadian government interned about 90 per cent of the Japanese-Canadian population.

26   See Draper, "The 'Camp Boys,'" 172; Zimmermann, The Little Third Reich on Lake Superior, 180.

27   Tribunal classifications were sometimes arbitrary and unjustified. For example, some tribunals automatically placed unemployed persons, including refugees, into Category B or applied a political interpretation to the clause "dubious character" and interned socialists and communists. In addition, some 170 Jewish refugees deported to Canada were classified as "pro-Nazi" (Category A). See ibid., 186–7; Gillman and Gillman, "Collar the Lot!," 44–5.

on the grounds that the refugees were still Britain's responsibility, so they could not simply be released on Canadian soil.

Regarding the treatment of aliens and especially refugees, the sinking of the *Arandora Star* caused a shift in British public opinion. Criticism of the mass internment and deportation of refugees grew in both the British Parliament and wider society.[28] In response,

> the Cabinet agreed that the "internal management, though not the safeguarding", of the camps should be transferred from the War Office to the Home Office. Far more important, it concluded that "persons who were known to be actively hostile to the present régime in Germany or Italy, or whom for sufficient reasons it was undesirable to keep in internment, should be released".[29]

This change in Britain's interment policy was confirmed in a White Paper that defined the circumstances under which civilian internees of enemy nationality – including those who had been deported overseas – could apply for release.[30]

However, the cases of all the deported refugees in Canada had to be reviewed before they could apply for a return to the United Kingdom. In light of this, Ottawa requested the physical presence of a British representative "who could help to sort the imported mess of the hapless internees, victims of fear, hysteria and panic."[31] The criminal lawyer and prison reformer Alexander Paterson (1884–1947) duly arrived in Canada and executed his assignment with much foresight and great empathy for the interned refugees' problems. The civilian internees' cases were reviewed in close cooperation with the Canadian authorities to determine whether they posed a security risk, and Paterson then decided which of the criteria outlined in the White Paper might apply if they wished to return to the United Kingdom. Quite a few wanted to remain in Canadian internment for the time being because they had valid visas for the United States. However, these refugees' hopes of direct immigration were soon dashed as Paterson's negotiations with the US State Department failed in the spring of 1941.[32] The Canadian historian Paula J. Draper points out:

---

28 See House of Commons debates on internment camps, treatment of alien refugees, deportation of refugees and release options and procedures: HC Deb 18 July 1940, vol 363, col 408, col 377, col 392, col 435W; HC Deb 22 August 1940, vol 364, cc1475.

29 Gillman and Gillman, "Collar the Lot!," 222.

30 In July 1940, the Home Office presented a first version of the White Paper with eighteen release categories. Another four were added after complaints that many refugees would be unable to apply under the original categories. See Home Office, "Civilian Internees of Enemy Nationality: Categories of Persons Eligible for Release from Internment and Procedure to be Followed in Applying for Release," July 1940, Cmd. 6217; October 1940, Cmd. 6223.

31 Zimmermann, The Little Third Reich on Lake Superior, 187.

32 See Gillman and Gillman, "Collar the Lot!," 267–73.

Not only did internment place a stigma on the refugees which proved impossible to erase, but most were Jews and this did not endear them to US immigration authorities any more than it did to Canadian. Anti-refugee lobbies sprang into action in Washington [DC] and a series of bills were passed expressly to block entrance of the internees. By refusing to release refugees from the camps until the US agreed to accept them, the Canadian government played right into their hands. The CJC [Canadian Jewish Congress] now had to look more closely at pushing government towards wholesale release in Canada.[33]

Canadian Jewish and non-Jewish refugee organisations[34] worked with Paterson to increase the pressure on the Canadian government to release interned refugees and grant them residence in the country, if they so desired. Eventually, in July 1941, the government recognised interned refugees as "friendly aliens" and thereby also accepted the principle of release in Canada.[35]

Characteristics of the group of interned refugees and remarks on how they coped with internment

The group of interned refugees consisted of about two-thirds of expellees from Germany, while about one-third had fled Austria. The majority of them were of Jewish background (according to National Socialist racial definitions), and some of them had fled on political grounds (e.g. social democrats, communists and other opponents of National Socialism). About 90 per cent of the interned refugees who were deported to Canada from the UK in July 1940 were unmarried, and most were young: about a quarter were aged between 16 and 19, two-thirds were younger than 29, and only slightly more than a quarter of the deportees were between 30 and 65. Their social backgrounds were heterogeneous: some were lower or working class, but a larger proportion were (educated) middle class and a few belonged to upper-class families. In terms of religion, many of the interned refugees were of the Jewish faith

---

33 See Paula J. Draper, "Fragmented Loyalties: Canadian Jewry, the King Government and the Refugee Dilemma," in On Guard for Thee, edited by Norman Hillmer et al., 151–77, at 160–61.
34 These were the United Jewish Refugee and War Relief Agencies (UJRA) and the Canadian National Committee on Refugees (CNCR), a non-denominational organisation founded in 1938 that helped interned refugees to find sponsors, places to study and jobs, and compiled individual case files to facilitate the release of internees in Canada. See Valerie Knowles, Strangers at our Gates: Canadian Immigration and Immigration Policy, 1540–2006 (Toronto: Dundurn Press, 2007 rev. ed.), 147–9.
35 See Draper, "The 'Camp Boys,'" 185–9.

(a few were Jewish Orthodox), while others were Protestant, Catholic or non-denominational.[36]

The internment experience imposed a significant psychological burden and considerable mental stress on many refugees. The camps, which were in remote regions of New Brunswick, Ontario and Quebec, were initially under the control of the Canadian army and surrounded by barbed wire. At first, most of the camps housed Jewish refugees, anti-National Socialist political refugees and National Socialist sympathisers together, which inevitably led to conflicts and violence. As a temporary solution, some camps divided their sites into sectors separated by barbed-wire fences, but by October 1940 the Canadian army had reorganised the whole camp system so that almost all of the Jewish and political refugees were now housed in just three locations: Camp N, near Sherbrooke (Quebec); Camp I, Île aux Noix (Quebec); and Camp B, Ripples, near Fredericton (New Brunswick).[37] Living conditions were rudimentary at first: some of the camps were close to derelict and had to be repaired by the refugees themselves before they were habitable. For example, Camp N consisted of just two large sheds – former railway repair workshops that were full of soot, with broken windows and leaking roofs. The federal government had acquired the site just ten days before the arrival of some 700 refugees on 15 October 1940. The refugees complained about the intolerable conditions and even went on hunger strike. However, following negotiations with the camp commander and official representatives of the Canadian government, they agreed to make the camp habitable and winter-proof in return for 20 cents per day per man.[38]

Uncertainty about their own futures and those of relatives left in Europe was a major burden for many of the internees, and depression and neurasthenia were commonplace.[39] A strict daily routine prevailed in all of the camps. Besides compulsory maintenance work, from January 1941 interned refugees could volunteer for

---

36 These are preliminary findings of the ongoing analysis of the personal data of 1,800 deported refugees. See also Andrea Strutz, "Interned as 'Enemy Aliens': Jewish Refugees from Austria, Germany and Italy in Canada," in Refugees from Nazi-occupied Europe in British Overseas Territories: The Yearbook of the Research Centre for German and Austrian Exile Studies 20, edited by Swen Steinberg and Anthony Grenville (Leiden – Amsterdam: Brill | Rodopi, 2020), 46–67.

37 See Draper, "The 'Camp Boys,'" 173–6; Zimmermann, The Little Third Reich on Lake Superior, 110–14.

38 See Eric Koch, Deemed Suspect: A Wartime Blunder (Toronto – New York – London – Sydney: Methuen, 1980), 126–9. Over time, with great help from several aid organisations, camp life became more pleasant: sports were organised; some of the refugees were able to play music; and lessons were scheduled for the young refugees.

39 See Patrick Farges, Bindestrich-Identitäten. Sudetendeutsche Sozialdemokraten und deutsche Juden als Exilanten in Kanada (Bremen: edition lumiere, 2015), 128.

other tasks (e.g. felling trees, growing vegetables and producing knitwear, camouflage nets or wood products) for which they received a small payment.[40] Some of these cheap but skilled workers were even employed by a private company: for instance, the government granted permission for fifteen draughtsmen to work for a shipbuilding firm in a hut outside Camp A in Farnheim, Quebec.[41] Meanwhile, the workshops within the camps proved quite profitable:

> The Ordinance Branch of the Department of the National Defence was very pleased with them, and by June 1941 approximately nine hundred men in four camps were making nets, doing woodwork, sewing, knitting, farming, drafting, shoe-repairing, and manufacturing various wood products including ammunition boxes, kit bags, hold-alls and pillow cases. Profit on sales was $8,036.41. The entire initial investment in these workshops had been written off.[42]

The refugees' participation in such workshops also relieved a little of the monotony and boredom of camp life. Nevertheless, the detainees still had to cope with the stress of separation from their families and friends in an all-male microcosm with no idea of when they might be released.[43]

After Alexander Paterson had completed his reassessment of the refugees' cases, and the US State Department had blocked all onward migration to the United States, more than half of the detainees opted to return to the UK. Meanwhile, about 970 refugees were finally released from internment in Canada between mid-1941 and the end of 1943.[44]

---

40   Earnings and the money that relatives and friends sent to the refugees were deposited in an individual account for each internee and then issued as canteen tickets. In the canteen, which was mostly run by an older internee with some accounting experience, refugees could buy goods such as fresh fruit, cigarettes, toiletries, clothing, magazines and newspapers. See Christine Whitehouse, "'You'll Get Used to It!' The Internment of Jewish Refugees in Canada, 1940–43," unpublished Ph.D. dissertation, Carleton University, Ottawa, 2016, 78–80.
41   See Koch, Deemed Suspect, 240–41.
42   Ibid., 219.
43   See Farges, Bindestrich-Identitäten, 126–32.
44   See Draper, "The 'Camp Boys,'" 189; Strutz, "Interned as 'Enemy Aliens,'" 62. In 1941, some thirty refugees were also released to Cuba and Latin American countries; it was hoped that especially those who were released to Cuba and possessed a valid visa for the United States would be able to enter the country from there.

Building a new life after deportation and internment[45]

Joachim (Jim) Lambek (1922–2014) was released from internment relatively early.[46] According to biographical information on his British alien index card, his Jewish family had roots in Austria-Hungary, but Joachim himself and his younger sister were both born and raised in Leipzig. His mother Charlotte Lambek, née Rosenfeld, was born in Brody (in today's Ukraine) in 1893, while his father Oscar (Osias) Lambek was born in Siary, Gorlice County, southern Poland, in 1890.[47] It is not known when they moved to Leipzig, but the local address book indicates that they were residents of the city by 1914/15; Oscar Lambek was a timber trader.[48] Joachim Lambek attended the local grammar school until he was forced to flee. He and his sister were saved by a *Kindertransport* from Leipzig to England in February 1939; their parents also managed to flee to England some months later.[49] Seventeen-year-old Joachim Lambek and his father were both interned in June 1940. Oscar Lambek was released just two months later, on 23 August 1940,[50] but by then his son had already been deported

---

45   The life histories are presented in sequence according to the dates when certain groups of internees were released; those accepted as students by the Canadian authorities were among the first.

46   The life histories in this chapter were reconstructed primarily on the basis of information gleaned from Canadian and British archives (e.g. files of aid organisations and files of Canadian and British authorities involved in deportation, internment and release), literature, biographical entries, newspaper articles and obituaries. At the time of the research, no comprehensive life history memories were known or accessible. Erich Koch's book (see note 37, above) represents a sort of collective biography that incorporates the experiences and memories of a number of interned refugees. In additions, some diaries, memoirs and autobiographies have been published: for example, those of Henry Kreisel (see note 12) and Josef Eisinger (see note 51) as well as Hans Reichenfeld, On the Fringe: A Sort of Autobiography (Ottawa: Marquardt Printing, 2006).

47   See Home Office (HO) 396/51 and 396/183, *HO 396 WW2 Internees (Aliens) Index Cards 1939–47*, National Archives of the UK [TNA].

48   The first entry for Oscar Lambek appears in the Leipziger Adressbuch, 1915, Vol. 94, part I.

49   See minutes of meeting of the Faculty of Science, McGill University, 21 October 2014, "Resolution on the Death of Emeritus Professor Joachim (Jim) Lambek, Department of Mathematics & Statistics, 2" <https://www.mcgill.ca/science/files/science/facultyagendadocuments-december_2_2014-_one_file_combined_0.pdf> (17 May 2021); Bernie Lambek, "The Way I See It: The Prison Camp, Part 1," The Bridge, 7 April 2021 <https://montpelierbridge.org/2021/04/the-way-i-see-it-the-prison-camp-part-1/> (18 May 2021). Berni Lambek, Joachim Lambek's son, published some essays on the internet about his father's memories and experiences as an interned refugee.

50   HO 396/183, TNA.

as "enemy alien" to Canada on the prison ship *Sobieski* with another 980 civilian internees (Categories B and C) and about 550 German POWs.[51]

Joachim Lambek would spend the next twenty months in Canadian internment until his release on 20 February 1942. Like most of the teenage refugees, he had been unable to finish his schooling because of the racist persecution in and their forced flight from National Socialist Germany. Consequently, some of their fellow-internees – including former teachers and university scholars – worked with external committees and Canadian aid organisations to establish camp schools and vocational training courses in technical professions and agriculture with the intention of preparing their younger counterparts for higher education or careers in essential trades. The students learned mathematics, geometry, chemistry, physics, engineering, agriculture, English language and Latin but also the likes of music and art history. Junior and senior matriculation classes prepared the teenage refugees for the final stages of secondary education and university entrance exams.[52] In addition to participating in voluntary workshops and working as a lumberjack, Lambek attended one of these matriculation classes in Camp B and passed McGill Junior Matriculation in the autumn of 1941.[53] One of his tutors was Fritz Rothberger from Vienna, who gave inspiring lectures in mathematics. These lessons were pivotal for Lambek, as he remembered many years later:

> He also taught advanced mathematics in the camp school, and I took all his courses for about two years. I remember him drawing circles in the sand to illustrate some theorem in analysis. I can safely say that, had it not been for Fritz Rothberger's teaching and friendship at that time, I would never have become a mathematician or entered academia.[54]

It was eventually agreed that refugees "could be released to study at universities if they were sponsored by Canadian families, farmers could request internees to help them, and skilled workers could be released for war work,"[55] but this scheme was laggardly and continued until the end of 1943. The main reason for this was that the director of immigration Frederick Charles Blair – who had the final say over all releases – repeatedly obstructed the process. Furthermore, in this process also age mattered, it was especially difficult for the older men to secure their release in

---

51   Lambek, "The Way I See It"; Koch, Deemed Suspect, 46–50, 262. The Sobieski left England on 4 July and docked at Quebec City eleven days later.
52   See Josef Eisinger, Flight and Refuge: Reminiscences of a Motley Youth (New York: self-published, 2016), 74; Koch, Deemed Suspect, 147–53.
53   See minutes of meeting of the Faculty of Science, McGill University, 21 October 2014, 2.
54   Joachim Lambek, "Reminiscences of Fritz Rothberger," CMS NOTES de la SMC – Canadian Mathematical Society 32 (2000) 5: 29.
55   Draper, "The 'Camp Boys,'" 188–9.

Canada; physically and mentally impaired men were usually sent back to the UK.[56] Lambek, though, was one of the fortunate few who met all the criteria for a student release: he was under twenty-one, had been accepted by McGill University, and a businessman from Montreal and his wife – who were also from Leipzig – had agreed to sponsor him.[57] Consequently, his request was granted, so he was able to enrol at McGill in February 1942 and graduated with an honours degree in mathematics three years later. He acquired a master's degree the following year and immediately started his career as a lecturer in mathematics. McGill was in great need of highly qualified teaching staff like Lambek in these early post-war years as it "had to expand rapidly to make room for returning veterans and one way it dealt with the problem was by opening a satellite campus in St. Jean."[58] Lambek worked on his dissertation under the supervision of Hans Zassenhaus (1912–91) and obtained his Ph.D. in 1950 (the first Ph.D. in mathematics ever awarded by McGill). Following promotion to assistant professor, he became a full professor in 1963. In the course of a remarkable academic career, Lambek made a valuable contribution to the development of computer science both within Canada and internationally in addition to his work as an eminent mathematician. He officially retired in 1992 but remained actively involved with McGill's Mathematics Department until a year before his death in 2014.[59]

Initially at least, interned refugees who were released into Canadian society were granted only temporary residency and lived in limbo as the government was still reluctant to admit and grant them immigrant status. It was only in October 1945 that they were finally permitted to apply for citizenship, when "revelations of the enormity of the Holocaust and growing criticism of Canada's narrow immigration policy tied their hands. The 'camp boys' had become Canadians. They had married, worked hard to contribute to the war effort, and begun to rebuild their lives."[60] Joachim Lambek received his Canadian citizenship in 1947,[61] married Hannah Weiss – who was from a Jewish German-speaking family from Brno (former

---

56   See ibid., 189.
57   See Bernie Lambek, "The Way I See It: The Prison Camp, Part 2," The Bridge, 28 April 2021, <https://montpelierbridge.org/2021/04/the-way-i-see-it-the-prison-camp-part-2/> (18 May 2021).
58   Michael Barr, "An Appreciation of Jim Lambek at McGill: A Talk Given on the Occasion of Jim Lambek's 75th Birthday," Theory and Applications of Categories 6 (1999): 2–4 <http://eudml.org/doc/120199> (19 May 2021).
59   See minutes of meeting of the Faculty of Science, 2.
60   Draper, "The 'Camp Boys,'" 189.
61   See Canada Gazette, 3 April 1948, 1365. Due to his parents' citizenship, Joachim Lambek held Austrian citizenship prior to his expulsion from Leipzig.

Czechoslovakia) – and started a family with her in a Montreal suburb.[62] Meanwhile, his parents and sister were still in London. Oscar and Charlotte Lambek became British citizens in August 1948,[63] which suggests that they planned to stay in the UK. However, the situation changed just six months later when Oscar Lambek died at the age of fifty-eight. By then, Joachim sister was into her second year of marriage to an American whom she had met while studying at the London School of Economics.[64] The couple relocated to Connecticut at the end of the 1940s, and the recently widowed Charlotte Lambek went with them.

The history of these two generations of the Lambek family is characterised by geographical and cultural displacement and transnational experiences. However, Charlotte Lambek and her daughter's immigration to the United States in the postwar period gave the family an opportunity to rebuild social ties that had been interrupted by their flight from National Socialist Germany and especially by Joachim Lambek's deportation to Canada.

Despite the trauma he endured at an early age, Joachim Lambek was able to start a family and to build a personal life as well as a successful career in Canada. This was due in no small part to the education he received in the camp school, which enabled him and many other detainees of his generation to qualify for higher education, start their lives anew and not only integrate within but make valuable contributions to Canadian society in a wide variety of fields.

Fritz (Friedrich) Rothberger (1902–2000) was born in Vienna to Ella and Heinrich Rothberger; his brother Jakob Johann (Hans) Rothberger (1899–1987)[65] was two years older. The Rothbergers were an assimilated, upper-middle-class Viennese Jewish family. Heinrich Rothberger and two of his brothers managed a textile company and a department store on the Stephansplatz in the city centre; he was also an important collector of porcelain art.[66] After high school, Jakob Rothberger

---

62 See Patrick Farges, "Transnational Yekkishkeit from a Canadian Perspective," in Refugees from Nazi-occupied Europe, edited by Steinberg and Grenville, 21–45, at 37; Lambek, "The Way I See It: Part 2."
63 See London Gazette, 19 October 1948, 5542.
64 See Elizabeth Stauderman, "Biography of Joseph Goldstein," Yale Law & Policy Review 19 (2000) 1: 2.
65 The spelling of his first name(s) varies in Austrian, British and Canadian historical sources (Jakob, Jacob, Johann, Hans). For consistency, "Jakob" is used throughout this article.
66 Heinrich Rothberger was born in Vienna in 1868 and, like his father, the founder of the Warenhaus Jacob Rothberger, was a trained men's tailor and merchant by profession. His wife, Ella Rothberger, née Burchardt, born in 1878, was also from Vienna. For the family history, see Ulrike Nimeth and Leonhard Weidinger, "Die Familia Rothberger vom Ende des 19. Jahrhunderts bis 1938," in schneidern und sammeln: die Wiener Familie Rothberger, edited by Christina Gschiel et al. (Wien – Köln –Weimar: Böhlau, 2010), 49–59.

studied at the Vienna Commercial University, trained in men's tailoring, and joined the family business in 1918.[67]

Fritz Rothberger chose a very different career path. He attended the *Akademische Gymnasium*, enrolled at the University of Vienna to study mathematics (major), zoology and philosophy, earned his Ph.D. in 1927, and then lived and worked as an independent scholar in Vienna for the next ten years. He moved to Warsaw in 1937 in order to continue his research in the field of combinatorial set theory, as there was an excellent school of mathematics at the city's university.[68] Following the "Anschluss" of March 1938, Fritz Rothberger decided against returning to Austria and instead sought refuge in the UK: "I arrived in England in June 1939 (coming from Sweden). I obtained my visa through the Society for the Protection of Science and Learning. In autumn of 1939 I went to Oxford, and in January 1940, I settled in Cambridge, where I stayed until May 1940 when I was interned."[69]

The National Socialist regime in Austria forced the Rothberger family to hand over their property, finally the company was "Aryanised" in November 1938 and Heinrich Rothberger's art collection was seized.[70] To increase pressure on the family, Jakob Rothberger was arrested and sent as *Schutzhäftling* to Dachau concentration camp on 31 May 1938, then transferred to Buchenwald on 23 September 1938, where he remained until his release on 14 February 1939.[71] He immediately set about arranging his emigration, which included paying around 27,000 Reichsmarks in *Reichsfluchtsteuer* (Reich Flight Tax).[72] He was issued with a passport in April, and was deregistered as a resident of Vienna on 17 May 1939,[73] so he probably arrived in London later that month, just a few days before his brother Fritz made his own way to England. Shortly after the outbreak of the war, the two brothers were screened by alien tribunals, although the outcomes were different: while a London tribunal classified Jakob Rothberger as Category C, Fritz Rothberger, who was living in a

---

67 See index card for Jakob Johann Rothberger, UJRA Collection "Interned Refugees," Box 6, Alex Dworkin Canadian Jewish Archives [ADCJA].
68 See "Curriculum Vitae," May 1942, Canadian National Committee on Refugees Collection, MG 28-V43, Vol. 2, File 23, Rothberger, Fritz 1942–1943 [Rothberger, File 23], Library and Archives Canada [LAC].
69 Ibid.
70 See Christina Gschiel et al., "Die Familie Rothberger in der NS-Zeit – eine Chronologie," in schneidern und sammeln, edited by Gschiel et al., 167–81, at 168–73.
71 See Häftlingsuntersuchungsbogen/1.1.6/Doc-ID 10271837; Effektenkarte/1.1.5.3/ Doc-ID 6959015/ITS Digital Archive, Arolsen Archives.
72 This sum of 27,000 Reichsmarks in 1939 corresponds to about € 159,000 today. See Historischer Währungsrechner <https://www.eurologisch.at/docroot/waehrungsrechner/#/> (27 September 2021).
73 See index card for Jakob Johann Rothberger, ADJCA; Gschiel et al., "Die Familie Rothberger in der NS-Zeit," 176.

village in Dorset at the time, was classified as Category B.[74] Nevertheless, in May 1940, both were arrested and interned, then, in July, deported as enemy aliens to Canada on the *Sobieski*.

At this point, the brothers' parents were still in Vienna. They were able to flee Austria only on 2 November 1941, by which time the deportation of Jews to ghettos and concentration camps had already begun.[75] According to a surviving family member, the couple intended to travel via Spain and Cuba to Florida.[76] Recently viewed sources show that the escape of Heinrich and Ella Rothberger was organised by the Jewish Transmigration Bureau[77] of the American Jewish Joint Distribution Committee (JDC) and that they arrived in Lisbon on or around 12 November 1941 together with nineteen other emigrants.[78] Apparently, the couple had to wait for several weeks in Lisbon, and it was 8 January 1942 before they finally set sail for Cuba on the SS *Guine*.[79] The ship duly docked in Havana a few days later, but of course the United States was now a combatant in the war, which meant the Rothbergers were unable to complete the final leg of their transcontinental migration to Florida. Instead, they were forced to remain in tropical Cuba until the end of the war.[80]

Meanwhile, in Canada's Camp B, in addition to teaching mathematics in the camp school and working as a lumberjack,[81] their son Fritz was a member of an "elite work party that originally specialized in the hardest jobs like digging post holes and trenches in the solidly frozen ground and later was promoted to perform carpentry work."[82] Nothing is known about his brother Jakob's internment activities, but he was released after nearly two and a half years of internment to Montreal on 22 Oc-

---

74 See HO 396/112; HO 396/138 TNA.
75 See Gschiel et al., "Die Familie Rothberger in der NS-Zeit," 179.
76 See "Interview mit der Tochter von Carl Julius und Leopoldine Rothberger," in schneidern und sammeln, edited by Gschiel et al., 285–92, at 290.
77 The Transmigration Bureau was established by the JDC to help refugees emigrate from Germany, Austria, Czechoslovakia, Holland, Belgium and Luxembourg, primarily to the United States but also to other destinations.
78 See "Incoming Cable Lisbon," 11 November 1941, Immigration, 1941, Dominican Republic Settlement Association Records, 1939–1977, American Jewish Joint Distribution Committee Archives (JDC Archives). It is not possible to reconstruct the escape route from Vienna to Lisbon from the information given in the document.
79 See Jewish Transmigration Bureau Deposit Cards, 1939–1954, Roll 01-Cases 14100–15786, JDC Archives.
80 The Rothbergers were among some 12,000 refugees from National Socialism who arrived in Cuba between 1938 and 1944. See Robert M. Levine, Tropical Diaspora: The Jewish Experience in Cuba (Princeton, NJ: Markus Wieners Publishers, 2010), 79–101, 150–88.
81 See Lambek, "Reminiscences of Fritz Rothberger," 29.
82 Eisinger, Flight and Refuge, 74.

tober 1942 because of his professional qualifications as a men's tailor for work at the Earl Clothing Company.[83]

Fritz Rothberger's release was rather more complicated as he was a highly qualified academic, but too old to be released under the student scheme or as a sponsored researcher. Therefore, the Immigration Department would not allow him to leave internment until he had found a job. The Canadian National Committee on Refugees (CNCR) contacted several Canadian universities and individual sponsors on his behalf, but even though both Toronto University and McGill University were impressed by his previous work,[84] no post could be found for him until January 1943. With the help of individual sponsors, CNCR managed to raise some money to support Rothberger financially and additionally, the committee assisted for getting him accepted as a mathematics instructor at Acadia University in Wolfville, Nova Scotia. But Fritz Rothberger's possible release was far from straightforward, because a number of questions had to be clarified as a letter from CNCR to the president of the university shows:

> I think you know that we have been promised $800.00 for Dr. Rothberger's assistance. If a Carnegie grant should not be forthcoming our Committee would be prepared to make provision for a second year. It would be necessary to advise Mr. Blair [the director of immigration] that there is an opening on the staff at Acadia for Dr. Rothberger and I hope that on this financial basis you will be willing to offer such an appointment.[85]

Eventually an application for release was submitted and granted. After more than three years in internment, Fritz Rothberger was finally released on 2 July 1943. He spent a few days with his brother in Montreal before proceeding to Wolfville,[86] where it seems he adjusted quickly to the new environment and his new career. In letters to the CNCR, he describes Wolfville as a charming little town and suggests that he is finding teaching elementary mathematics rather interesting. He integrated well at the university and was promoted to assistant professor a few years later.[87]

---

83 See "Releases by Date – Farmers & Others 1941–1943," UJRA Collection "Interned Refugees," Box 4, ADCJA.

84 See recommendation letter for Fritz Rothberger from Leopold Infeld, Professor of Applied Mathematics, Toronto University, 6 March 1942, Rothberger, File 23, LAC. Infeld, who did not know Rothberger in person, recommended him on the basis of his publications.

85 Letter to Dr F. W. Patterson, 12 February 1943, ibid.

86 See letter to Constance Hayward, 3 July 1943, Canadian National Committee on Refugees Collection, MG 28-V43, Vol. 2, File 24, Rothberger, Fritz 1943–1947, 1977, Library and Archives Canada [Rothberger, File 24, LAC].

87 See letters to Constance Hayward, 15 July 1943 and 24 March 1944, ibid.

In 1946, in addition to applying for their own Canadian citizenship,[88] Fritz and Jakob Rothberger started the laborious process of arranging their parents' immigration to Canada from Cuba. For instance, the brothers had to provide proof that they could support them financially so that they would not become a burden on the state.[89] After a year of form-filling and letter-writing, and almost a decade of separation, sixty-eight-year-old Ella and seventy-eight-year-old Heinrich Rothberger were finally reunited with their sons in May 1947. They set up home in Montreal and lived a very modest life, having lost all of their personal possessions. Several pieces from Heinrich Rothberger's looted art collection were returned to him under the auspices of the post-war restitution process in 1947/8, but due to his financial situation he could no longer collect art and sold them.[90] Heinrich Rothberger passed away in 1953 and his wife Ella died in 1964.

Very little is known about Jakob Rothberger's life in Canada. He worked as an office clerk for the Wartime Prices and Trade Board (WPTB)[91] between 1943 and 1946/7, but thereafter there is no record of what he did for a living. However, we do know that he never married, and that he continued to live in and around Montreal for the rest of his life. For instance, he spent his retirement years in Greenfield Park, a small suburb to the southwest of the city centre.[92] He passed away at the age of eighty-eight in 1987, and, like his parents, was buried at Montreal's Baron de Hirsch Cemetery.[93]

Although Fritz Rothberger was already over forty by the time he secured his first job in Canada, he was able to build an impressive academic career in the field of mathematics. He continued to teach at Acadia University until 1949, then transferred to the University of New Brunswick at Fredericton to take up a professorship. Later, between 1955 and 1966, he was a professor of mathematics at the Université Laval in Quebec City. He joined the Mathematics Department at the University of Windsor, Ontario, as a full professor in 1967 and remained there until his retirement

---

88   Fritz and Jakob Rothberger received Canadian citizenship in January and February 1947, respectively. See Canada Gazette, 1947, 411 and 416.
89   See admission to Canada application form, 17 July 1946 (copy) and letter from 15 May 1947 to Constance Hayward, Canadian National Committee on Refugees Collection, MG28-V43, Vol. 2, File 24, LAC.
90   For the restitution process, see Christina Gschiel et al., "Rückstellungen nach 1945. Objekte aus der Sammlung Heinrich Rothberger," in schneidern und sammeln, edited by Gschiel et al., 225–40.
91   See Letter to Constance Hayward, 4 July 1946, Rothberger, File 24, LAC.
92   See "Voters Lists 1972 and 1974, Federal Elections, 1935–1980," RG113-B, LAC.
93   See Baron de Hirsch Cemetery, "Find a Grave" <https://barondehirsch.com/en/find-a-grave/?ln=rothberger> (28 May 2021).

three years later.⁹⁴ However, his academic career was far from over. He returned to Wolfville, a place he apparently adored because of its scenic beauty,⁹⁵ and specifically Acadia University, where he continued to teach mathematics as an Honorary Distinguished Professor and Senior Research Fellow until 1981.⁹⁶ He had joined the Canadian Mathematical Society (CMS) in the year of its foundation – 1945 – and was an active participant in several influential academic networks, both within Canada and internationally.⁹⁷ The importance of his pioneering research into combinatorial set theory was "recognized in 1977 when a symposium was held in his honour at the University of Toronto."⁹⁸ He kept in touch with many of his former students, including Joachim Lambek, whom he often met when visiting his parents and brother in Montreal. Students and colleagues alike remembered him as "an outstanding teacher with an inimitable style of lecturing [...] [who] instilled a love for mathematics in numerous young people."⁹⁹ For instance, he inspired the future Nobel laureate Walter Kohn, another pupil in Fritz Rothberger's mathematics classes at the camp school: "Rothberger normally taught us out-of-doors where he wore shorts and boots and nothing else. He used a stick and a sandy area as a blackboard to teach us about the different types of infinities [...] He was a most kind and unassuming man whose love for the intrinsic depth and beauty of mathematics was gradually absorbed by his students."¹⁰⁰ In 2000, Fritz Rothberger died at the age of ninety-eight in his beloved Wolfville. Like his brother, he had never married, so his death marked the end of the direct line of descendants of Heinrich and Ella Rothberger in transatlantic exile.

Gustav Reinhold Jacoby (1875–1965) was born in Mödling, near Vienna, to German-Jewish parents of Protestant faith, so he was one of the oldest interned

---

94 See "Obituary / Avis de décès," CMS NOTES de la SMC – Canadian Mathematical Society 32 (2000) 5: 29.
95 For example, David Poole recalled that Rothberger enjoyed cross-country skiing. See ibid., 31.
96 See ibid., 29.
97 See "Fritz Rothberger," Acadia Archives <https://archives.acadiau.ca/islandora/object/collection%3Afrothberger> (28 May 2021).
98 See "Obituary / Avis de décès," 29.
99 Lambek, "Reminiscences of Fritz Rothberger," 29.
100 Andrew Zangwill, "The Education of Walter Kohn and the Creation of Density Functional Theory," Archive for History of Exact Sciences 68 (2014) 6: 6. Walter Kohn (1923–2016) was saved by a Kindertransport from Vienna to England in 1939. After his release from Canadian internment, he studied physics and mathematics at the University of Toronto and earned a Ph.D. in physics from Harvard University in 1948. Forty years later, he received the Nobel Prize in Chemistry for his work on density functional theory, and mentioned the importance of Rothberger for his education in the camp in his biographical sketch for that prize. See "Walter Kohn – Facts" <https://www.nobelprize.org/prizes/chemistry/1998/kohn/facts/> (6 June 2021).

refugees in Canada.[101] His father Louis Jacoby (1828–1918) was a copperplate engraver and became a professor at the Academy of Fine Arts, Vienna, in 1863.[102] The family moved back to Germany in 1882 and settled in Berlin, where Gustav Jacoby attended the *Joachimsthaler Gymnasium* before going on to study civil engineering at the technical universities of Berlin and Munich. He married Marie Jacoby, née Echte, a Gentile, in 1905. In the course of his career as a government *Regierungsbaumeister* (master builder), he designed, constructed and supervised countless maritime and hydraulic construction projects (e.g. coastal defences, harbours, piers, river crossings and canals) in various parts of Germany, such as Schleswig-Holstein, East and North Frisia and Silesia. He retired in 1934, after thirty-four years of service, and devoted the next four years of his life in Hamburg to researching and publishing articles on the history of engineering and cartography.

However, Jacoby's life dramatically changed on 9–10 November 1938 (the night of the November Pogrom) when he was arrested and imprisoned in the Sachsenhausen concentration camp on account of his Jewish heritage. He was released on 30 November[103] but subsequently expelled from Germany, whereas his wife had to remain in Hamburg. He fled to the UK and eventually arrived in Canterbury in mid-August 1939. Although Jacoby was clearly a refugee from National Socialist Germany, on 5 October 1939 an alien tribunal in Canterbury, Kent, classified him as Category A, which meant immediate internment. The following June, just a month before he turned sixty-five, he was deported to Canada on the *Duchess of York*.[104]

Alexander Paterson reclassified Jacoby as Category C in the course of his case reviews, but Jacoby insisted that he did not want to return to the UK. As soon as his release became feasible in 1941, he started to contact many institutions and individuals in the hope of finding work as a civil engineer, technical assistant, teacher (e.g. German, mathematics, engineering) or even librarian. In addition, he requested support from refugee and welfare organisations such as the CNCR and the Society of Friends. Of course, he was highly qualified and experienced, but his advanced age proved to be a problem. As a result, despite much support from the CNCR, he remained in internment until 23 March 1943, when he was finally released for work

---

101 Personal data, information on education, expertise, persecution and flight were collected from curricula vitae, a Society of Friends questionnaire, a letter to Constance Hayward, 14 November 1941, Canadian National Committee on Refugees Collection, MG 28-V43, Vol. 2, File 11, Jacoby, Gustav 1941–1947 [Jacoby, File 11], LAC.
102 See Hans Vollmer (ed.), Allgemeines Lexikon der Bildenden Künstler von der Antike bis zur Gegenwart (Leipzig: E. A. Seemann 1925), Vol. 18: 260–61.
103 Information on a former prisoner of Sachsenhausen concentration camp, Stiftung Brandenburgische Gedenkstätten / Gedenkstätte und Museum Sachsenhausen, e-mail to the author, 25 June 2021: "Häftlingskategorie: Jude, Meldung: [zu entlassen] am: 30.11.1938, Quellenart: Anweisung der Politischen Abteilung."
104 See HO 396/110, TNA.

as a postal censor in the Dominion Censorship Office in Ottawa. However, this was war-related employment, and Jacoby was made redundant in September 1945 and became unemployed.[105] Shortly thereafter, after a long struggle, he obtained Canadian citizenship[106] in the hope that this would give him a better chance of finding work and might even enable him to bring his wife to Canada.[107] He contacted numerous governmental and technical institutions and told them that he would accept any job offer, anywhere in Canada, but once again his age counted against him and his search proved fruitless.

In the spring of 1946, Jacoby decided on a – from his perspective – temporary return to Great Britain, where his daughter lived. Also, his wife Marie made arrangements for a visit to the UK to meet her daughter and husband again after seven years of separation.[108] His sincere hope was that he and Marie would then be able to travel back to Canada as a couple. However, he was prepared to return on his own, if need be, as he explained in one of several letters he wrote to the CNCR from England, in which he also expressed his opinion about returning to Germany:

> I admire and love Canada and want to be loyal. Thus I would not like to live forever in England (losing the Canadian right [Canadian citizenship]). [...] I have been asked regarding return to Germany, but according to my thoughts and feelings I consider this idea as impossible. Thus in due course I shall go back to Canada maybe within 3 months or one year even if my wife should follow later after I should be settled.[109]

Jacoby diligently continued his search for a job in – and therefore a return to – Canada for more than a year. However, by June 1947, he was close to admitting defeat, as his final letter to the CNCR demonstrates:

> I am between clouds and earth continuing my attempts (fruitless for 15 months) to find in Canada a home, hostel, family, Welfare Association, who might send to me, very soon if possible, a kind invitation for a first accommodation, also small town, countryside, until I might have real work. Did you hear of any chance since your last kind letter about a place throughout Canada? It is so depressing realizing that Canada with space and work for millions of willing people should not help me, a Canadian citizen, a victim of Hitlerism, to grant a modest living.[110]

105　See "Releases," UJRA Collection "Interned Refugees," Box 4, ADCJA; letter to Constance Hayward, 7 September 1945, Jacoby, File 11, LAC.
106　See Canadian Gazette, 1945, 4355.
107　See letter to Constance Hayward, 5 January 1946, Jacoby, File 11, LAC.
108　See letter to Constance Hayward, 27 July 1946, ibid. Jacoby mentioned that he had a daughter living in England for the first time in this letter.
109　Letter to Constance Hayward, 26 August 1946, ibid.
110　Letter to Senator Wilson, 23 June 1947, ibid.

In the end, given that he wished to remain with his wife and needed some income, Gustav Jacoby finally had to accept that they had only one option: he would have to move back to Germany, where at least he was entitled to a pension, even though this had been unthinkable for him for a long time because of the persecution he had endured. Following his return to Hamburg, Gustav Jacoby resumed his scientific research and published further articles in the fields of cartography, geography, coastal structures and dyke construction. He passed away at the age of ninety on 12 May 1965 in Hamburg-Blankenese, just one day after his and Marie's diamond wedding anniversary.[111]

Conclusion

The three case studies examined here demonstrate that factors such as age, education (either pre-existing, acquired during internment or afterwards) and individual agency could have a significant impact on an individual's ability to build a new life in Canada following release from internment. For instance, young adults like Joachim Lambek were able to complete their high school education within the camp school system, gain their freedom under the student release scheme and make the most of opportunities for further education that were subsequently translated into often highly successful lives. Similarly, even though Fritz Rothberger was in middle age by the time he arrived in Canada, his understanding of mathematics and natural aptitude as a teacher, coupled with invaluable support from the CNCR, enabled him to forge an impressive academic career. By contrast, Gustav Jacoby's advanced age was the central reason why he failed to establish a new life for himself in Canada, despite his expertise as a maritime and hydraulic engineer, great personal commitment and individual agency and a willingness to accept any job opportunity. Unfortunately, a lack of information on other elderly detainees means it is currently impossible to judge whether Jacoby's fate was typical for members of his age group or not.

Irrespective of how their lives and careers developed, though, the experience of expulsion, deportation and internment was deeply inscribed into every refugee's biography as a lifelong traumatic burden. "In the years that have passed since internment, none of the refugees have forgotten their experiences. It marked their lives and determined the progress of their adjustment to the Canadian and Jewish communities."[112]

---

111 See Goslar Carstens, "Gustav Jacoby [Zum Gedenken]," in Nordfriesisches Jahrbuch NF 1 (1965): 20–21; Wilhelm Bonacker, "Obituary Notice: Gustav Jacoby," International Journal for the History of Cartography 19 (1965) 1: 117.

112 Paula J. Draper, "The Adjustment of Jewish Refugees from Nazism to Canadian Life," Refuge: Canada's Journal on Refugees 5 (1985) 2: 17.

Filling the gap
Displaced Persons and émigré scholars in the post-slavery society of the US South

Andreas Kranebitter and Peter Pirker

Introduction

Between 1948 and 1952, the US government relocated some 400,000 Displaced Persons from camps in Germany, Austria and Italy to the United States.[1] It was a rather heterogeneous group. Originally, the highly controversial programme implemented by the Displaced Persons Act of 1948 was intended for Holocaust survivors and forced labourers who could not or did not want to be repatriated to their countries of origin. With the beginning of the Cold War, however, the character of the programme changed. The Act brought Displaced Persons and refugees from the now-communist countries of Eastern Europe to the fore, at least in the public debate in the United States, as admission was to be granted primarily to *"Volksdeutsche"* (ethnic Germans) expelled from Eastern Europe and refugees from Soviet communism, including former National Socialist collaborators from the Baltic countries.

Under all previous immigration laws, Eastern Europeans had been granted admission to a very limited extent. The quota system by country of origin had discriminated against them compared to Western Europeans because they were considered less adaptable or less willing to adapt to US society. Anti-Semitism underlay this discrimination.[2] The Displaced Persons Act differed from earlier migration policies not only in regard to the ethnic groups it was designed to address, however. The

---

[1] See Displaced Persons Commission, Memo to America: The DP Story. The Final Report of the United States Displaced Persons Commission (Washington: The US Government Printing Office, 1952), 242–3.
[2] See Carl J. Bon Tempo, Americans at the Gate: The United States and Refugees during Cold War (Princeton, NJ: Princeton University Press, 2009), 24; Haim Genizi, America's Fair Share: The Admission and Resettlement of Displaced Persons, 1945–1952 (Detroit, MI: Wayne State University Press, 1993), 81–3, 209; Ben Shephard, The Long Road Home: The Aftermath of the Second World War (New York: Anchor Books, 2012), 377–8.

strictly regulated allocation – with "sponsors" obliged to guarantee jobs, housing and transportation for the refugees, who were therefore left with very little choice in these matters – was an unprecedented innovation in the history of US immigration, but it also led to several unforeseen difficulties. "Resettlement problems" became a frequently discussed topic in the media discourse, polarising those in favour of resettlement and those against it.[3] Social scientist Gregor Sebba noted that the latter group often accused the new arrivals of being "communists or criminals" and had little interest in addressing Displaced Persons' adjustment problems, while those in favour of the scheme usually tried to avoid mentioning such issues altogether.[4] This left state institutions as well as a number of heavily involved private aid organisations in desperate need of social scientific advice regarding how to tackle these issues.[5]

This was especially true in the southern states, where comparatively few refugees were resettled. To the astonishment of many, some 75 per cent of the approximately 20,000 Displaced Persons from post-war Europe who were initially resettled in southern states had already moved west or north by the end of 1951.[6] The need to understand the reasons for this exodus prompted resettlement agencies to commission social scientists to undertake comprehensive studies into the Displaced Persons' circumstances. As a result, whereas states with long histories of immigration, such as New York and Minnesota, did not even keep accurate records of how many former Displaced Persons had settled in their communities, the likes of Louisiana, Mississippi and Georgia – each of which accepted approximately 1,000 former Displaced Persons – inadvertently became laboratories for detailed social science research and specifically for émigré scholars who were able to make full use of their linguistic skills and cultural backgrounds in the course of their work. Two such scholars were Rudolf Heberle, whose 1949–50 research with Dudley S. Hall was published as *New Americans: A Study of Displaced Persons in Louisiana*

---

[3] According to Shephard, 72 per cent of the population rejected further immigration, arguing that immigrants would drive Americans from their jobs. See ibid., 373.

[4] Gregor Sebba, Displaced Persons in Georgia: Report to the Georgia Displaced Persons Committee (Athens: University of Georgia, 1954), 112.

[5] See Sigrid Wadauer, "Historische Migrationsforschung. Überlegungen zu Möglichkeiten und Hindernissen," Österreichische Zeitschrift für Geschichtswissenschaften 19 (2008) 1: 6–14.

[6] US Displaced Persons Commission, Memo to America, 250.

and Mississippi, and Gregor Sebba, whose *Displaced Persons in Georgia* was based on research conducted between 1952 and 1953.[7]

In this paper, we will compare the methods and findings of these two studies, although the primary focus will be on Sebba's work. After summaries of Heberle's and Sebba's personal experiences earlier in life and accounts of their projects in the Deep South, the paper concludes with a discussion of epistemological breaks and blind spots in the social scientific research into European Displaced Persons after the Second World War.

The two studies had very different impacts: whereas only a handful of academic monographs have ever mentioned Sebba's report, Heberle and Hall's book received much more attention. We argue that these contrasting receptions may be attributed to the studies' respective tones: Heberle and Hall's attitude towards the resettlement scheme was largely positive, while Sebba was much more critical. Both of these attitudes may be traced back to the émigré authors' own immigration experiences: Heberle's arrival in the United States had been followed by a period of smooth, "successful" integration, whereas Sebba never thought of himself as a fully acculturated US citizen. The general air of optimism in the former's study even extended to the title – *New Americans* – and the illustration of a happy female Displaced Person on the front cover.[8] Sebba felt that such positivity was unjustified, not least because Heberle and Hall's methodology was flawed and their research covered only the first year of the resettlement programme. For instance, in a November 1952 letter to Eric Voegelin – who, like Heberle, taught at Louisiana State University – Sebba revealed that his study would challenge many of Heberle's findings: "Then Heberle can look at what could have been done in Louisiana," he added. "My book will raise dust. I come to results that are not at all optimistic."[9] However, unlike Heberle, Sebba was unable to publish his manuscript because he suffered from a distinct lack of funding and support, as his correspondence in the Gregor Sebba Papers at the University of

---

7   See Rudolf Heberle and Dudley S. Hall, *New Americans: A Study of Displaced Persons in Louisiana and Mississippi* (Baton Rouge, LA: Displaced Persons Commission, 1951); Rudolf Heberle, "Displaced Persons in the Deep South," Rural Sociology 16 (1951) 4: 362–77; Sebba, Displaced Persons in Georgia. Research for New Americans was conducted between spring 1949 and summer 1950 for the Institute for Population Research in the Department of Sociology at Louisiana State University. Sebba's study was conducted at the suggestion of the Georgia Displaced Persons Committee, headed by Tom Linder, State Department of Agriculture, in order to develop proposals for future immigration programmes, and was financed by Governor Talmadge. See J. C. Holton (Secretary State Committee) to Tom Linder, 9 July 1952, Gregor Sebba Papers [GSP], Special Collections, University of West Georgia, Box 1, Folder 10, Part 7.
8   Heberle and Hall, New Americans, 1951.
9   Gregor Sebba to Eric Voegelin, 25 November 1952, Eric Voegelin Papers [EVP], Hoover Institution Archives, Stanford.

West Georgia demonstrates. It is our contention that this was due to his epistemological approach and his attitude towards Displaced Persons, both of which were at odds with the views of leading political figures in Georgia who opposed further immigration due to fears that it would undermine their efforts to preserve the state's racially segregated, post-slavery society.

Personal experience as a driving force for research

Both Sebba and Heberle felt that personal experience played an important role in their research, albeit in different ways. Born in the north German town of Lübeck in 1896, Heberle established his reputation within the young discipline of sociology at an early age. After studying under Ferdinand Tönnies and others in Kiel (and eventually marrying Tönnies's daughter Franziska), he held the position of a private lecturer (*Privatdozent*) at the same university from 1929 to 1938.[10] As a Rockefeller scholar, he researched migration and social mobility in the United States from 1926 to 1929 and again in 1936. However, during the second of these research trips, the *Reichsministerium für Wissenschaft, Erziehung und Volksbildung* informed him that he would no longer be employed by the University of Kiel, although he had been supported there earlier under the National Socialist regime. Heberle himself attributed this decision to his studies of German minorities in Lithuania in the 1920s and the election of National Socialists in the province of Schleswig Holstein in 1932[11] – one of very few reports on National Socialism by a German-speaking sociologist at the time.[12] The ultimate reason, however, was that he was descended from a Jewish great-grandfather, which meant that his *Ariernachweis* (Aryan certificate) was insufficiently "spotless" to allow him to advance from lecturer to full professor, a promotion his university had supported until 1937.[13]

---

10 For autobiographical notes and more on the importance of personal experience in his work, see Rudolf Heberle, "Soziologische Lehr- und Wanderjahre," in Geschichte der Soziologie. Studien zur kognitiven, sozialen und historischen Identität einer Disziplin, Volume 1, edited by Wolf Lepenies (Frankfurt am Main: Suhrkamp, 1981), 271–98. For a biographical account, see Rudolf Waßner, Rudolf Heberle. Soziologie in Deutschland zwischen den Weltkriegen (Hamburg: Rolf Fechner Verlag, 1995).

11 See Rudolf Heberle, Landbevölkerung und Nationalsozialismus. Eine soziologische Untersuchung der politischen Willensbildung in Schleswig-Holstein 1918 bis 1932 (Stuttgart: Deutsche Verlags-Anstalt, 1963).

12 See Michaela Christ and Maja Suderland (eds), Soziologie und Nationalsozialismus. Positionen, Debatten, Perspektiven (Berlin: Suhrkamp, 2014); Andreas Kranebitter and Christoph Reinprecht (eds), Die Soziologie und der Nationalsozialismus in Österreich (Bielefeld: transcript, 2019).

13 See Christian Fleck, A Transatlantic History of the Social Sciences: Robber Barons, the Third Reich and the Invention of Empirical Social Research (London – New York: Bloomsbury Aca-

In light of the sudden termination of his career in Germany, Heberle and his family immigrated to the United States in July 1938, whereupon he accepted the offer of a full professorship at Louisiana State University in Baton Rouge. In this new position, he soon embarked on several studies of the state's mostly African-American agricultural labour force.[14] Thus, the Displaced Persons study he conducted with his student Dudley S. Hall at the end of the 1940s was just one in a long series of research projects. Since Heberle was also a consultant for Louisiana's Department of Agriculture and a prominent member of both the Southern Sociological Association and the American Sociological Society, one might say that he was soon fully integrated into the state's administrative and scientific communities. However, this integration was not quite as straightforward as Heberle himself intimated when claiming that the "culture shock" had not been "that great" and that he had swiftly put down roots.[15] His biographer Rudolf Waßner found evidence in Heberle's unpublished diaries that he actually struggled with "Americanization," especially at first, as it meant "the loss of so many things that are dear to us and for which this country cannot offer equivalents."[16] Yet, his integration ultimately developed into what might be termed naturalisation, to such an extent that he decided to remain in the United States rather than accept the University of Kiel's offer of a professorship in 1960.[17]

Regarding the question of the impact of Heberle's personal experiences on his research into Displaced Persons in the Deep South, he never mentioned his emigration from Germany, his research into immigration to and migration within the United States, or his studies of African-American labourers when writing about his own history, although he did allude to his much earlier Lithuanian research.[18] As we will demonstrate, this cultural framing led to a focus on the migrants' need to integrate, with little consideration given to immigration policies or even the Displaced Persons' personal histories – two subjects that Heberle himself had explored in earlier projects. In short, the emphasis was firmly on the "new Americans" – as the Displaced Persons were euphemistically called – and their "adjustment problems," rather than "old Americans" and their attitudes to immigrants. As a result, there was a huge blind spot in Heberle's research.

---

demic, 2011), 62. According to Fleck (ibid.), Heberle had tried to adapt to the National Socialist regime by joining the Sturmabteilung. See also Waßner, Rudolf Heberle, 77–8, 110–15.

14   See Heberle, "Soziologische Lehr- und Wanderjahre," 292.
15   See ibid., 291, 294.
16   Rudolf Heberle, quoted in Waßner, Rudolf Heberle, 39; our translation.
17   Ibid., 118.
18   See Heberle, "Soziologische Lehr- und Wanderjahre," 277–8; Rudolf Heberle, "In Praise of Field Work: An Autobiographical Note," Zeitschrift für Soziologie 11 (1982) 2: 105–12.

Sebba, by contrast, arrived at the University of Georgia as late as 1946.[19] Thus, he was still a relatively new arrival himself when he started to study the state's recent immigrants, and he was certainly sensitive to the difficulties of adapting to a society in which there were hardly any foreign-born people. There had been very little voluntary immigration to Georgia throughout history, and the descendants of African slaves continued to be both legally and informally oppressed. For instance, Sebba's own employer, the University of Georgia, did not allow African-Americans to enrol at the time of his research. It would be 1961, after a ten-year legal battle with the National Association for the Advancement of Colored People (NAACP), before this policy was finally reversed.[20]

Gregor Sebba was born in 1905 in Libau, Latvia, to a Jewish family that emigrated to South Tyrol three years later. The family was evacuated to Linz after Italy declared war on Austria in 1915, and thereafter his parents ran a small cosmetics shop. However, the family was unable to obtain Austrian citizenship following the defeat of the Central Powers in 1918. Consequently, Sebba continued to hold Latvian citizenship until 1930, whereupon he became stateless following his refusal to return to his homeland for military service. He had graduated from the University of Innsbruck the previous year with degrees in political science and law, then worked as a research assistant in the Institute for Statistics of Minority Peoples (*Institut für die Erforschung von Minderheiten*) at the University of Vienna until 1933. As was typical for a Jewish scholar in 1930s Austria, all hope of an academic career soon vanished.[21] For the next five years, Sebba supported himself by working in the advertising department of Julius Meinl AG and for the journal *Wirtschaftliche Rundschau*. However, he continued to participate in scientific debates and organised a sociological working group, through which he met several scholars who would go on to become prominent sociologists and philosophers in the future. Politically, he was much more of a conservative liberal than a leftist. The Gestapo arrested him in March 1938, and he was forced to leave the country six months later.

Following his expulsion, Sebba suffered a year of alienation and deprivation as a hapless exile in New York. He submitted dozens of job applications but failed to gain any sort of foothold in the US scientific or educational community. But then the war against Germany finally presented him – and many other Jewish refugees – with

---

19 Peter Pirker, "'Musst immer tun wie neugeboren.' Zum politischen Denken und zur antinazistischen Praxis des Wiener Sozialwissenschafters Gregor Sebba," Voegeliniana Occasional Papers 91B (2013), 6.
20 Peter Besel, "University of Georgia Desegregation Riot (1961)," BlackPast, 11 March 2018 <https://www.blackpast.org/african-american-history/university-georgia-desegregation-riot-1961/> (15 May 2021).
21 See Pirker, "Musst immer tun wie neugeboren," 15–16.

an opportunity. In 1940, the British secret service – the Special Operations Executive (SOE) – recruited him to generate support for the Allied war effort by founding and leading what would soon become the most active Austrian exile organisation in the United States, Austrian Action.[22] However, he was still a stateless Jew, which prompted a number of political rivals to insist that he had no right to represent the Austrian exile community. For instance, Otto Habsburg pointed out that Sebba was "not even an Austrian, but Lithuanian [sic] of Jewish extraction."[23] In short, Sebba's rivals succeeded in ousting him from Austrian exile politics and he was socially displaced once again. It was the US Army and the Office of Strategic Services (OSS) – which he joined in 1943 – that ultimately aided his naturalisation and acculturation to US society through intensive army life. Sebba himself revealed his increasing use of colloquial language and gradual familiarisation with everyday US culture in letters to friends, among them the aforementioned Eric Voegelin.[24]

The US military also played a key, if less direct, role in Sebba's subsequent integration into post-war society. This was because the 1944 GI Bill of Rights paved the way for a massive expansion of US higher education as it entitled millions of war veterans to generous grants and scholarships. The inevitable influx of new students meant many universities were desperate to recruit more teaching staff. As a result, with a little help from the OSS, and although he had no experience as a lecturer and had published very little, Sebba became Professor of Economics at the University of Georgia in 1946.

Six years later, when he turned his attention to Georgia's Displaced Persons, Sebba drew on his own history of displacement, statelessness, alienation, adaption and acculturation. Shortly after starting his research, he cautiously criticised the dean of his own faculty, Robert Preston-Brooks, and the university for its silence on the "Negro question."[25] Describing himself as a "European observer," he quoted from Preston-Brooks's own work on the history of Georgia to draw attention to the state's tradition of denigrating its African-American citizens. While Sebba referred to Swedish sociologist Gunnar Myrdal's *An American Dilemma* (1944) to classify Preston-Brooks's bias as conservative, he avoided any reference to the work of W. E. B. Du Bois, a professor at the segregated University of Atlanta at the time and the author of two truly groundbreaking books on the history and sociology of African-

---

22 For a detailed account, see Peter Pirker, Subversion deutscher Herrschaft. Der britische Kriegsgeheimdienst SOE und Österreich (Göttingen: Vienna University Press, 2012), 100–11.
23 Otto Habsburg to Col. Donovan [William J. Donovan, Office of Strategic Services], 1 April 1942, National Archives and Records Administration, College Park, Records Group 226, Entry 210, Box 72, Folder 1.
24 See EVP.
25 Gregor Sebba, "Introduction," in Georgia Studies: Selected Writings of Robert Preston-Brooks, edited by Gregor Sebba (Athens: University of Georgia Press, 1952), 1–23.

Americans in Georgia.[26] A similarly ambivalent attitude towards Georgia's structural racism is evident in Sebba's study on Displaced Persons.

However, for a few months at least, the process of observing, meeting and interviewing those Displaced Persons may have prompted Sebba to refer his own experiences to inform his scientific research. Rather than repressing his memories – as was his custom throughout most of his life, according to his wife Helen[27] – he seemingly allowed himself to remember, which in turn shaped his approach to his single scientific engagement with refugees from Europe and the "adjustment problems" they faced in Georgia.

Georgia on their minds: Displaced Persons in the US Deep South

From the very beginning, Sebba's memories of his own flight from Austria gave him a deep understanding of the people he was studying. Against the background of his own experience, he argued that they required not merely "a home and a job, but full resettlement in the full sense of the word. Some of them need rehabilitation."[28]

According to official statistics, only 1,250 Displaced Persons had been resettled in Georgia by 1952.[29] However, they were highly mobile, which meant a traditional statistical survey was unfeasible. Therefore, although his official title was "chairman of statistics," Sebba became increasingly critical of positivist methods and decided to adopt a qualitative approach based on interviews with sponsors as well as the Displaced Persons themselves. He was optimistic that he would be able to interview a significant proportion of this relatively small cohort before "Time has done its work, scattering and obliterating evidence." In addition, he envisaged corresponding with members of recently dissolved state commissions and voluntary organisations while memories of the resettlement programme were still "fresh" in their minds.[30]

Below, we focus on two important aspects of Sebba's study: (1) its structural analysis of the "Displaced Persons problem" within a context of profound macro-sociological and economic change; and (2) its fine cultural sociological analysis.

---

26   Gunnar Myrdal, An American Dilemma: The Negro Problem and Modern Democracy (New York: Harper, 1944); W. E. B. Du Bois, Black Reconstruction: An Essay toward a History of the Part which Black Folk Played in the Attempt to Reconstruct Democracy in America, 1860–1880 (New York: Harcourt Brace & Company, 1935); W. E. B. Du Bois, Black Folk then and now: An Essay in the History of Sociology of the Negro Race (New York: Henry Holt & Co., 1939).
27   Helen Sebba to Willi Schaber, 19 May 1986, Institut für Zeitungsforschung Dortmund, Nachlass Willi Schaber.
28   Sebba, Displaced Persons in Georgia, 12.
29   See ibid., 8.
30   Ibid., ii.

(1) The resettlement of European Displaced Persons in the United States did not take place in a vacuum but rather in the midst of mass rural depopulation due to the ongoing mechanisation of farming and the so-called "Second Great Migration" of African-Americans from the rural South to the urban North.[31] This major demographic shift had a powerful and lasting impact on the nation's history, most notably by galvanising the Civil Rights Movement. Sebba characterised the Displaced Persons programme as a scheme to mitigate this "exodus of the Negro"[32]. Every Displaced Person needed a sponsor to ensure that they did not become a drain on public finances, and many of those sponsors were farmers who "wanted them as a substitute for native labor lost because of low earnings."[33] However, the recently arrived Displaced Persons were attracted by far higher industrial wages just as their African-American predecessors had been, so it is little surprise that many of them soon left their sponsors and relocated to urban areas. As Sebba wrote, "The high mobility of the displaced persons was the result of factors largely beyond their control, rather than individual restlessness."[34]

The problem was compounded by a distinct lack of state planning, irrespective of the fact that the resettlement programme was indeed "a type of planned immigration foreign to the American tradition."[35] This new approach had been prompted by a sharp decline in the number of immigrants to the United States in the inter-war period and a parallel shift in the discourse. Whereas, traditionally, immigrants had been praised for their "rugged individualism," the emphasis was now on their need to adjust and adapt to US values and customs.[36] However, there was no state (let alone federal) plan for how the terms of the Displaced Persons Act should be implemented at the local level. For instance, there were no officials to check that the sponsors were fulfilling their obligations or to resolve any problems that a Displaced Person may face after their initial placement. A small group of sympathetic voluntary organisations provided some assistance, but they could not hope to meet all of

---

31   For recent overviews, see William Collins, "The Great Migration of Black Americans from the US South: A Guide and Interpretation," Explorations in Economic History 80 (2021) <https://www.nber.org/papers/w27268> (2 November 2021); Nicholas Leman, The Promised Land: The Great Black Migration and How It Changed America (New York: Random House, 1991); James N. Gregory, The Southern Diaspora: How the Great Migrations of Black and White Southerners Transformed America (Chapel Hill: University of North Carolina Press, 2005); Isabel Wilkerson, The Warmth of Other Suns: The Epic Story of America's Great Migration (New York: Random House, 2010).
32   Sebba, Displaced Persons in Georgia, 15.
33   Ibid.
34   Ibid., 279.
35   Ibid., 8.
36   See ibid., 118–19.

the new arrivals' requirements on their own. For Sebba, these structural deficiencies were the main reasons for the failure of the Displaced Persons programme, or at least for the widespread perception of its failure: "[I]t is impossible to buck the trend of economic development that produces the current shrinkage of the farm population."[37] In other words, the poorly planned scheme never stood a chance of reversing one of the major macro-sociological trends of US post-war society. It did, however, "[force] an unnatural stability upon the newcomers."[38] Moreover, this "unnatural stability" was not merely economic but psychological, too.

(2) One of the Displaced Persons (Case 69 in Sebba's survey) declared: "We did not come to America to be DPs all our lives."[39] His and others' expectations – in part informed by accounts from friends and relatives who had immigrated to the United States before the war – were soon dashed by the reality of life in Georgia, where their sponsors seemed to expect not only a "normal" business relationship with the new arrivals but also their eternal gratitude.[40] The Displaced Persons' disillusionment and strong desire to transform a status that most of the sponsors were equally determined to perpetuate led to an inevitable revolt against paternalism.

The strength of Sebba's approach lies in the fact that he combined analysis of the problems of interaction and contradictory expectations with socio-cultural analysis of the Displaced Persons' psychological adaptation during a number of discrete phases. After the first shock of displacement from their homes, then the struggle for survival and the "demoralizing wait in the DP camps"[41] of Europe, the gulf between expectations and reality in the United States came as another shock to most "new Americans" during the accommodation phase. This was then followed by phases of adjustment and finally acculturation. The crucial point here is that these phases were often contradictory. For example, what was helpful during accommodation (e.g. regular contact with compatriots) could be a hindrance during acculturation, as Sebba explained with a detailed look at eating habits:

> Accommodation means eating turnip greens and grits because a refusal to eat them may be taken amiss. Adjustment means eating them because this is what Southern people eat, but eating creamed spinach and pumpernickel by preference. Acculturation means eating turnip greens and grits like any other Southerner, and liking it.[42]

---

37   Ibid., 225.
38   Ibid., 101.
39   Ibid., 99.
40   See ibid., 280.
41   Ibid., 93.
42   Ibid., 124.

However, the Displaced Persons' European tastes and customs were deeply embedded and therefore slow to change. This is of course also true for their experiences of imprisonment, since many of them still bore the emotional and psychological scars of detention.

Sebba did not devote much attention to his subjects' experiences in Europe's camps either during or after the war,[43] but it was clear that these ordeals were still having a major impact on their efforts to adjust to life in the United States. For instance, he reported one sponsor's account of a rapid deterioration in his relationship with his allocated Displaced Person, Hans:

> He said that for the first month the family was his idea of a dream come true […] He said that the man was undoubtedly the hardest worker he had ever seen and one of the best […] The only trouble, he said, was that Hans spent half his time daydreaming. And that he would speed past him like crazy only to stop a while a half row or so ahead and lean on his hoe thinking about something and then usually they would stop and he would tell Mr D. all about what he had been thinking about. He said that quite often the thoughts were of things that happened during their days in the concentration camps.[44]

Repeated references to the camps presented a significant challenge to the research team's interview routine, as they were more interested in how the Displaced Persons were coping with their current situation. For example, in his record of an interview with a Jewish immigrant to Atlanta, Sebba wrote:

> In almost every respect outside the English he has adjusted very well. However, he does seem to have a very decided memory of the past years and it seems that these recollections of the years he spent in concentration camps are with him almost constantly. It was very difficult to get him away from that, he kept going back talking about the powers of the concentration camp and the things that happened to them during those years and immediately after.[45]

One can only imagine the trauma that Displaced Persons experienced whenever they applied for a visa or swore the mandatory "employment oath" in which they

---

43 Interestingly, in contrast to Heberle, who in general speaks only of prisoners-of-war and forced labourers (Heberle and Hall, New Americans, 5), Sebba mentions the experience of violence in a variety of National Socialist camps and focuses on this group of Displaced Persons. See Sebba, Displaced Persons in Georgia, 3).
44 Interview with Mr Ditzell, sponsor, White County, GSP, 19 November 1952, ID MS-0051, Box 1, Folder 3. In a very similar way, a Jewish Displaced Person interviewed in Atlanta was obviously haunted by his concentration camp experience. See Case 28 in Sebba, Displaced Persons in Georgia, 94.
45 Interview with Isaac Wise, Atlanta, GSP, 14 November 1952, ID MS-0051, Box 1, Folder 3.

promised to work for their sponsor for a "reasonable" length of time, not least because they were often misled into thinking that they could be detained or even deported if they refused to comply.[46] As Sebba pointed out, all of these procedures must have evoked painful memories of forced labour, coercion and violence during the war.[47] In short, there was probably a direct link between Displaced Persons' allegedly "peculiar" behaviour and their internment camp experiences.

Eventually, many Displaced Persons started to feel more secure in their new environment, which in turn enabled them to begin the process of embracing many aspects of the American way of life, including car ownership. "Moreover the possession of an automobile gave the DP the feeling that he could move, a feeling important to him even if he did not have to move. In this sense the automobile came to be a symbol of freedom to him."[48] In other words, a Displaced Person's first car often symbolised a definite passage from the past world of camps to a life beyond detention and heteronomy.

A comparative view: epistemological breaks and blind spots

Sebba's study went far beyond his declared aim to evaluate the Displaced Persons resettlement programme in Georgia. He swiftly diverged from the state's perspective on the "Displaced Persons problem" and instead started to focus on the Displaced Persons themselves and the dynamics of their "adjustment problems."[49] This epistemological shift was reflected in a proposal Sebba submitted to the University of Georgia's chancellor that his report should be subtitled *A Study in Adjustment*.[50] Moreover, in a brief abstract for the report, he alluded to some "unexpected" results and suggested: "Considerable doubt is cast on the philosophy and provisions of the Displaced Persons Law of 1948."[51] This standpoint put him in direct opposition to the state, which probably explains why his own university refused to provide the funding he needed to publish his study.[52] Similarly, and even more predictably, the State Committee for Displaced Persons in Georgia showed no interest in publishing the report.[53] It also rejected Sebba's proposal to include private aid organisations

---

46 Sebba, Displaced Persons in Georgia, 24.
47 Ibid., 25.
48 Ibid., 168.
49 Gregor Sebba to J. C. Holton, 9 June 1953, GSP, Box 1, Folder 10, Part 37.1.
50 Gregor Sebba to Mr Caldwell (Chancellor, University of Georgia), 20 January 1953, GSP, Box 1, Folder 10, Part 37.1.
51 Displaced Persons in Georgia: A Study in Adjustment, GSP, Box 1, Folder 10, Part 37.1.
52 The lack of support is obvious from his correspondence. See GSP, Box 1, Folder 10.
53 J. C. Holton to Gregor Sebba, 26 February 1953 and Gregor Sebba to J. C. Holton, 3 March 1953, GSP, Box 1, Folder 10, Part 37.1.

in its inquiry into his findings. The Committee was headed by Agricultural Commissioner Tom Linder, one of the most powerful politicians in what was a largely agrarian state. His assistant, J. C. Holton, justified the decision in a February 1953 letter to Sebba by stating that "the proposed hearing [...] would be dominated by representatives of the various agencies who opposed any immigration restrictions."[54] He supported his argument by alluding to a House of Representatives hearing on immigration policy that had been held in Atlanta just four months earlier. At that meeting, in addition to labelling the current selective quota system "racist," organisations such as the Anti-Defamation League suggested that US immigration law reflected the spirit of the Ku Klux Klan. In response, so-called "patriotic" organisations such as the Daughters of the American Revolution, who opposed any further immigration, launched a series of anti-Semitic attacks. Linder's position on the matter was clear: during the hearing, he complained about an existing "imbalance of population" and advocated a complete cessation of immigration.[55] He and other southern Democrats attempted to maintain the existing "racial and ethnonational regime" in two ways: at the state level, they refused to revoke racist segregation laws; and at the federal level, they called for new legislation to prevent the immigration of any more Eastern Europeans, whom they identified as mostly Jewish disseminators of socialism and communism.[56]

In marked contrast to Sebba's study, the few that were undertaken in other states – most notably Heberle and Hall's uncritical analysis of the implementation of the Displaced Persons programme in Mississippi and Louisiana – tended to be basic statistical reports supplemented with occasional discussions of individual shortcomings. Heberle and Hall's use of descriptive statistics, coupled with their preoccupation with Displaced Persons' individual adjustment problems, meant their report was positivist research in the truest sense of the term. They continued to use the state's terminology and answer the state's research questions throughout their fieldwork and seemingly never felt the need to shift the discourse by pursuing new lines of enquiry during interviews. Even published by the Displaced Persons Committee of Louisiana, it was "administrative research" *par excellence*.

---

54 Holton to Sebba, 26 February 1953.
55 Hearings before the President's Commission on Immigration and Naturalization, Friday, 17 October 1952, Atlanta, GA, Twenty-Fourth Session. Linder explicitly stated that Jewish Holocaust survivors did not want to integrate themselves and were a breeding ground for socialism and communism. In 1954, when running for the governorship of Georgia, he called white students who wished to attend mixed schools with black students "mentally ill." See "Georgian Asks Mental Tests for Liberal Whites," Jet, 8 July 1954, 14; Jeff Roche, Restructured Resistance: The Sibley Commission and the Politics of Desegregation in Georgia (Athens: University of Georgia Press, 2010), 27–8.
56 Bon Tempo, Americans at the Gate, 27.

Although their report briefly mentioned that the Displaced Persons Act marked a significant shift in US immigration policy due to its espousal of planned migration, acknowledged that Displaced Persons were different from other immigrant groups and referred to problems with resettlements on sugar-cane (Louisiana) and cotton (Mississippi) plantations, Heberle and Hall clearly believed that most of the blame for any "maladjustment" rested squarely with the Displaced Persons themselves. They were not farmers; were unfamiliar with American crops; could not speak English; had misconceptions of American society based on what they had seen in the movies or heard from GIs; could not cope with the climate, the isolation of farm life and long periods of inactivity (especially on cotton plantations); were demoralised and dissatisfied; and, finally – the only structural critique – received insufficient wages.[57] Nevertheless, they were still perceived as an improvement on their predecessors – African-American plantation workers – who were notable by their almost complete absence from the report, along with any discussion of the racist structures of the Deep South's post-slavery economy. Instead, although the authors acknowledged that the Displaced Persons were recruited specifically to alleviate a "shortage of labor"[58] on the plantations, the only statistical comparison they offered was with "Louisiana and Mississippi Whites,"[59] as if the states' African-American populations did not deserve to be counted.

In short, Heberle and Hall uncritically reflected the views of their main group of interviewees: farm managers and plantation owners. For instance, they termed the exploitative employment contracts between African-American labourers and plantation owners "custom" and suggested that this was a "neighborhood type" relationship.[60] Of course, this perspective is blind not only to the legacy of slavery but also to the reasons for the "Second Great Migration," even though that mass exodus was precisely why the plantation owners now needed a new labour force of immigrants.

Sebba's study could scarcely have been more different. He drew attention to the great waves of social change that were sweeping across America and linked them directly to the shortcomings of the Displaced Persons programme (see Figure 1). The new arrivals could not replace recently departed African-American farm hands and sharecroppers who were fighting against segregation and structural racism, and they had no intention of trying. Before long, they were following in the footsteps of their African-Americans predecessors by fleeing from the farmers' low wages and paternalistic attitudes and making their way to America's industrial heartlands. They were simply not prepared to remain in exploitative patron–client relationships in order to pay off their "debts" through hard agricultural labour – a system that the

---

57   See Heberle and Hall, New Americans, 40, 45–7, 73f.
58   Ibid., 40.
59   Ibid., 39.
60   See ibid., 87.

Supreme Court had condemned as "peonage" in 1942[61] – and fill the gaps in the Deep South's floundering post-slavery economy.

Figure 1: Decline of the Georgia farm population[62]

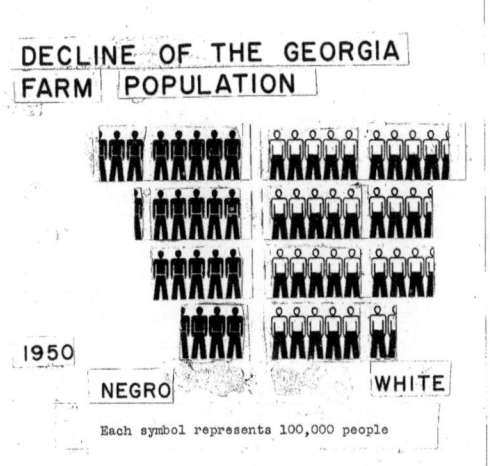

Source: University of West Georgia Collections, Gregor Sebba Papers, Box 1, Folder 13.

Although Sebba covered much more ground – and was far more critical – than even he probably intended, he stopped short of tackling the highly controversial subject of structural racism and anti-Semitism. For instance, he only briefly touched upon the relationship between southern racism and (wartime and post-war) anti-Semitism, and the prevalence of both in attitudes towards Displaced Persons; the emotions felt by refugees who had recently survived Europe's concentration camps when they were put to work in slave-like conditions on their sponsors' farms and

---

61 See ibid., 211. Sebba referred to the 1942 Supreme Court decisions Taylor vs. Georgia 314US15 and Bailey vs. Alabama 219US219.
62 Sebba was familiar with debates in Vienna on the presentation of statistics (see, e.g., Gregor Sebba, "Review of Say It with Figures, by Hans Zeisel," Journal of the American Statistical Association 44 (1949): 332–3) and produced this visualisation of the decline of Georgia's farm population using Otto Neurath's Isotype method. It demonstrates that he was well aware of the significance of macro-sociological shifts, yet, in a decision that symbolised his approach to the whole project, chose to omit it from the final report.

plantations; and the sociological significance of their arrival for the African-American minority who were in the process of migrating to urban centres and the northern states.

Nevertheless, his report can help to inform readings of some major contributions to US social scientific discourse in the immediate post-war era, such as Theodor W. Adorno, Else Frenkel-Brunswik, Daniel J. Levinson and R. Nevitt Sanford's *The Authoritarian Personality*.[63] His study also highlights the connection between anti-Semitism and the "refugee problem" before and immediately after the end of the Second World War. It contains a particularly startling interview with a deeply prejudiced woman who articulates a fantasy of a Jewish uprising to seize power within the United States. The authors justifiably interpret this as a projection of the woman's desire for a pogrom against the Jews, but they seem to overlook the importance of the context in which the interview took place – the fierce debate on Displaced Persons' arrival from Europe and their supposedly preferential treatment in 1945:

> I think there will be bloodshed over it in this country. (Do you think it will be justified?) There's no doubt that they're taking over the business affairs of the nation. I don't think it's right that refugees should be taken care of the way they are. I think they should take care of their own problems.[64]

Clearly, this woman, and many other Americans, now associated *all* Displaced Persons and refugees with "the Jews". They were loathed for both their alleged strength and their alleged weakness: "It is the image of the Jewish refugee who is depicted simultaneously as strong ('He takes jobs away from our American boys') and as weak ('He is a dirty outcast')."[65] According to the authors, even interviewees who were otherwise categorised as "mild" anti-Semites displayed strongly anti-Semitic attitudes towards refugees.[66] In other words, simply identifying "the Jew" with "the refugee" had the effect of boosting prejudice against both groups.

Instead of a conclusion, we want to stress that contemporary social science research into the resettlement of Displaced Persons between 1948 and 1952 not only sheds light on the context of social scientific knowledge production in the past but also provides a wealth of valuable resources for the field of migration studies today. However, a close reading of these studies demands an understanding of biographical interdependencies. As we have demonstrated throughout this paper, Gre-

---

63   Theodor W. Adorno et al., The Authoritarian Personality (New the York: Harper and Brothers, 1950).
64   Ibid., 635.
65   Ibid., 640.
66   See ibid. The traits ascribed to these Jewish Displaced Persons are ingratitude, disregard for the rules of hospitality, loudness and aggression (ibid., 641).

gor Sebba's and Rudolf Heberle's contrasting migration stories exerted a profound influence on their research. Heberle himself was a "new American" who progressed rapidly from adaptation to integration to full naturalisation, but this came at the cost of robbing him of the critical faculties he needed to produce a balanced study of the implementation of the Displaced Persons Act. By contrast, although Sebba was probably the more conservative of the two researchers, he did not shy away from setting his analysis and critique of US immigration policy in the context of simmering anti-Semitism and post-slavery racial segregation, and at least touched upon the crucial issue of intersectional discrimination. As a result, his research went much further than either he or his superiors had expected, but he also paid the price in the form of academic marginalisation.

The life and afterlife
of a twentieth-century French camp: Gurs

Christoph Jahr

It has become a truism to characterise the twentieth century as the "Century of the Camps" and "the camp" as the "nomos of the modern." Likewise, the "concentration camp" is identified as a "site of modernity."[1] However, this broad perspective tends to simplify a complex and contradictory phenomenon by focusing on its radical end. The political agenda behind the establishment of a camp, its various functions and the fate of the internees often changed significantly over time, and sometimes very rapidly. A camp is, figuratively speaking, an institution that has a life – and an afterlife – of its own; sudden turns and unpredictable developments are the rule rather than the exception. The Gurs internment camp in southern France, which was in operation from early 1939 to late 1945, illustrates this point perfectly. Therefore, firstly, I will present the long prehistory of the "modern camp"; secondly, I will discuss how Gurs fits into this broad picture; and, thirdly, I will address some aspects of the commemoration of Gurs from 1945 to the present.[2]

---

1   See Zygmunt Bauman, "Das Jahrhundert der Lager," Neue Gesellschaft, Frankfurter Hefte 41 (1994) 1: 28–37; Joël Kotek and Pierre Rigoulot, Le Siècle des camps: Détention, concentration, extermination: Cent Ans de mal radical (Paris: Lattès, 2000); Giorgio Agamben, Homo Sacer: Sovereign Power and Bare Life (Stanford, CA: Stanford University Press, 1998); Habbo Knoch, "Konzentrationslager", in Orte der Moderne. Erfahrungswelten des 19. und 20. Jahrhunderts, edited by Alexa Geisthövel and Habbo Knoch (Frankfurt a. M.: Campus, 2005), 290–99.

2   A plethora of sources is available thanks to numerous local memorial initiatives in Gurs itself and the internees' regions of origin. The website of the Gurs Memorial – <http://www.campgurs.com> – offers a good introduction, although it is only available in French. An exemplary "camp biography" is John C. Guse, "Polo Beyris: A Forgotten Internment Camp in France, 1939–47," Journal of Contemporary History 54 (2019) 2: 368–400.

The "modern camp" – a brief history of a long-standing institution

The twentieth-century internment camp has a long prehistory.[3] In a broad sense, the *castra* of the Roman Empire are the modern camp's most important antecedents for two reasons. Firstly, they not only fulfilled their obvious military functions but also served as bridgeheads of Romanisation and therefore played a key role in transforming "Barbarians" into "Romans." Secondly, they were in many cases the focal points of cities that flourished along the borders of the Empire from Castra Devana (Chester) in northwest England to Noviomagus (Nijmegen), Moguntiacum (Mainz), Castra Regina (Regensburg), Vindobona (Vienna) and Durostorum (Silistra, Bulgaria). Last but not least, from the sixteenth century onwards, Roman camps were rediscovered and used as blueprints for the accommodation of armies during campaigns. Similarly, "ideal cities" concepts often took their cues from Roman town planning, and the ancient camps' rectangular layout was often mirrored in designs for new cities in the seventeenth and eighteenth centuries. Institutions of separation and confinement that further contributed to the formation of the modern camp include Jewish ghettos, the early modern workhouses, the tsarist system of forced labour (*Katorga*), the forcible "relocation" of Native Americans to reservations during the nineteenth century and the prisoner-of-war camps established during the US Civil War and the Franco-Prussian War of 1870–71.

The "modern camp" finally took shape at the turn of the twentieth century. The Spanish *campos de reconcentración* during the Cuban War, the British concentration camps in South Africa during the Boer War and the camps established by the United States in the Philippines during the war of 1899–1902 gave birth to this "modern" physical, juridical and political institution. The camp, until then closely linked to the military sphere, increasingly became an institution that also affected millions of civilians. It was used to protect and control refugees, to detain people rounded up for political or other reasons, to monitor and punish, to discipline and "educate," to separate the "wanted" from the "unwanted" and, finally, to transform ordinary people into an ideologically determined "new man." In the age of totalitarianism, most ignominiously embodied in the Nazi concentration camps and the Soviet Gulag, "the camp" eventually became synonymous with absolute terror and genocide.[4]

---

3   See Christoph Jahr and Jens Thiel, "Prolegomena zu einer Geschichte der Lager. Eine Einführung," in Lager vor Auschwitz. Gewalt und Integration im 20. Jahrhundert, edited by Christoph Jahr and Jens Thiel (Berlin: Metropol, 2013), 7–19; Christoph Jahr and Jens Thiel, "'Das Lager.' Überlegungen zur Geschichte einer Institution zwischen Herrschaft, Recht und Gewalt," Juridikum – Zeitschrift für Recht und Gesellschaft 31 (2020) 1: 79–88.

4   Christoph Jahr, "'Diese Concentrationen sollten die Pflanzstätten für den militärischen Geist des Heeres bilden …' Fragmente einer Begriffsgeschichte des 'Lagers' in europäischen Konversationslexika," in Lager vor Auschwitz. Gewalt und Integration im 20. Jahrhundert, edited by Christoph Jahr and Jens Thiel (Berlin: Metropol, 2013), 20–37.

Today, at least in a German-speaking context, *"Lager"* is equated with *"Konzentrationslager"* and even *"Vernichtungslager"* to such an extent that *"Lager"* itself is fearfully avoided. Thus, *"Flüchtlingslager"* often becomes *"Flüchtlingscamp"* in contemporary German. This may be comprehensible with regard to German history, but it distracts attention from the fact that "the camp" is an instrument of domination that has been – and continues to be – used by different political systems for different purposes. Therefore, it would be misleading to view "the camp" as an aberration on the road to modernity; rather, it is intrinsic to that journey.

A camp over time

The French Republic established about 100 internment camps for political refugees – mostly members of the International Brigades and anti-fascists – in southern France from February 1939 onwards, following Franco's victory in the Spanish Civil War. These camps accommodated approximately 300,000 civilian refugees and 200,000 Republican Army soldiers. The makeshift facilities were fenced with barbed wire and hastily set up on various beaches (e.g. Argelès-sur-Mer, Saint-Cyprien and Barcarès), often by the internees themselves. Refugees were also housed in school buildings, disused factories, monasteries and even sports stadiums, so that southern France eventually had a total of about 400 places of detention, including pre-existing prisons. The north of the country had about sixty.[5]

The *Centre d'accueil des réfugiés espagnoles de Gurs* (Reception Centre for Spanish Refugees), as it was euphemistically called, was located in the historical province of Béarn (now the département Pyrénées-Atlantiques, then Basses-Pyrénées), about thirty miles from the Spanish border.[6] During the camp's first phase, from April to November 1939, the French government interned almost 19,000 people in Gurs: Basques, former Spanish Republican soldiers, and some 6,000 International

---

5 Christian Eggers, "Gurs – und die anderen. Gedanken zur Erforschung der französischen Internierungslager 1939–1945," Francia 21 (1994) 3: 171–80, at 174. Some 160 are listed in Marcel Bervoets-Tragholz, La Liste de Saint-Cyprien. L'Odyssée de plusieurs milliers de Juifs expulsés le 10 mai 1940 par les autorités belges vers des camps d'internement du sud de la France, antichambre des camps d'extermination (Bruxelles: Alice Éd., 2006), 174–7. See also Emmaline Bennett, "Cities of Defeat: Spanish Civil War Refugees and the French Concentration Camps of 1939," undergraduate thesis, Columbia University <https://drive.google.com/file/d/1Mb16 dM3BvYoeNRRMtkohOYQMroMqc-9X/view?usp=sharing> (10 May 2021).
6 Still the most detailed account of the camp's history is: Claude Laharie, Le Camp de Gurs 1939–1945: Un Aspect méconnu de l'histoire du Béarn (Biarritz: Société Atlantique d'Impression, 1985), 21–72.

Brigade fighters (including 700 Germans), divided into supporters of the Comintern and opponents of Stalinism, who continued to fight factional battles with one another.[7] At this time, the camp was administered by the *Garde Nationale Mobile* (originally a French Army auxiliary force, established in 1866) under the supervision of the War Ministry.

Figure 1: Plan of Gurs

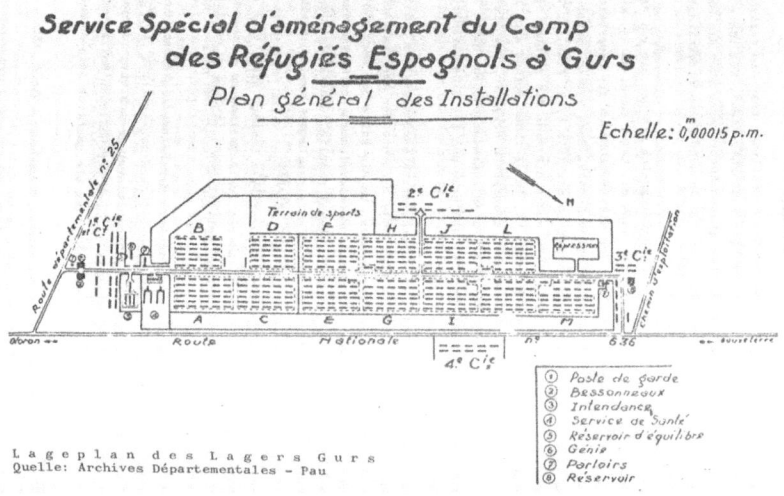

Source: <https://www.wikiwand.com/de/Camp_de_Gurs>.

Although Gurs possessed many of the iconic features of a wartime camp, it could not be described as a "typical" concentration camp. For instance, it was rectangular in layout, rather than square: about 2,000 metres long by 500 metres wide, with a paved road down the middle. The whole camp was enclosed by a barbed-wire fence, but this was only two metres high and it was not electrified. So it was an obstacle

---

7   Dieter Nelles, "Die Unabhängige Antifaschistische Gruppe 9. Kompanie im Lager Gurs. Zur Gruppenspezifischen Interaktion nach dem Spanischen Bürgerkrieg," in Das "andere Deutschland" im Widerstand gegen den Nationalsozialismus. Beiträge zur politischen Überwindung der nationalsozialistischen Diktatur im Exil und im Dritten Reich, edited by Helga Grebing and Christl Wickert (Essen: Klartext, 1994), 56–85. Figures at: <http://www.campgurs.com/le-camp/lhistoire-du-camp/survol-statistique/les-internés-venant-despagne/> (21 April 2021).

for anyone trying to escape, but far from an insurmountable one. Moreover, there were no watchtowers, although the camp was regularly patrolled by armed guards.

Figure 2: Photo of Gurs

Source: <https://collections.ushmm.org/search/catalog/pa1057438>.

The barracks in Gurs betrayed the military origins of the "modern camp." Introduced by the French Army during the First World War, they were constructed out of thin wooden planks that offered little protection from the cold, wind and rain. Jeanne Merle D'Aubigné served the internees on behalf of a Protestant aid organisation.[8] When she entered one of the barracks, the "shutters were closed because there were no windows; everything was dark. Here at least the women had beds (elsewhere they lay on the bare floor)."[9] Each building could accommodate up to sixty people at times of peak occupancy, which allowed less than two square metres per

---

8   Various charities, including the International Committee of the Red Cross, provided humanitarian aid to camp inmates in France. See Christopher R. Browning, "From Humanitarian Relief to Holocaust Rescue: Tracy Strong Jr., Vichy Internment Camps, and the Maison des Roches in Le Chambon," Holocaust and Genocide Studies 30 (2016) 2: 211–46; Luiza Iordache Cârstea, "The Importance of Humanitarian Aid during the Second World War: The Case of the Joint Relief Commission of the International Red Cross in France (1940–1945)," Nação e Defesa 149 (2018): 38–53.

9   Jeanne Merle D'Aubigné, "Lager Gurs," in Befreie, die zum Tode geschleppt werden. Ökumene durch geschlossene Grenzen, 1939–1945, edited by Adolf Freudenberg (München: Kaiser, 1985), 74–110, at 75–6; my translation.

person. The barracks were so primitive because the internees built the whole camp from scratch in just six weeks under the assumption that it would close within the next six months, but it was still operational more than six years later.

Another feature of the "modern camp" is its adaptability, with changes often made to size and structure according to the needs of the camp authorities. Gurs was designed to accommodate about 20,000 internees, but the number fluctuated between 300 and 27,000 at any given time.[10] There were 382 barracks in total, divided into 13 *"îlots"* (islands), each consisting of about 30 buildings and encircled by its own fence. Number 14 was the *"Îlot de représsailles"* (penalty block). These "camps within a camp" allowed the authorities to segregate the internees at will by nationality, politics, religion, class or gender.

The French government's policy towards the various groups of refugees and foreign citizens was rather contradictory.[11] At first, efforts were made to force them to contribute to France's economy by turning them into work brigades (*Compagnies de Travailleurs Étrangers*). By the summer of 1939, the plan was to integrate special foreign units within the French Army, while some other internees joined the existing *Légion Étrangère*. As a consequence, the number of internees in Gurs dropped from almost 19,000 in June 1939 to roughly 2,500 by May 1940, more than 80 per cent of them *"internationaux."*

---

10 All figures at: <http://www.campgurs.com/le-camp/lhistoire-du-camp/survol-statistique/tableau-général/> (21 April 2021).

11 Regina M. Delacor, "From Potential Friends to Potential Enemies: The Internment of 'Hostile Foreigners' in France at the Beginning of the Second World War," Journal of Contemporary History 35 (2000): 361–8; Vicky Caron, "The Missed Opportunity: French Refugee Policy in Wartime, 1939–40," Historical Reflections 22 (1996) 1: 117–58.

Figure 3: Transformation of the camp

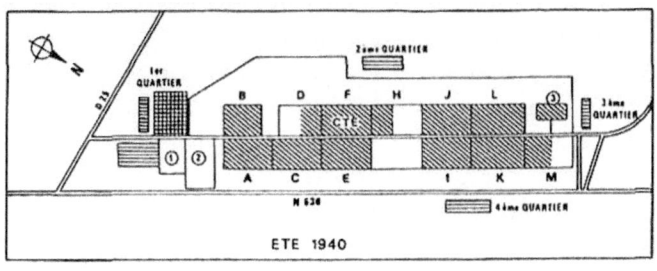

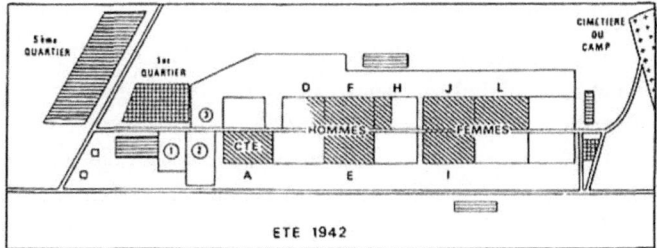

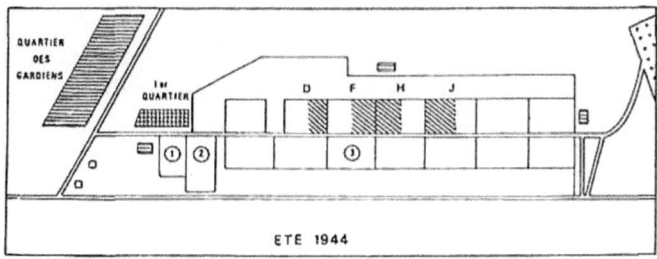

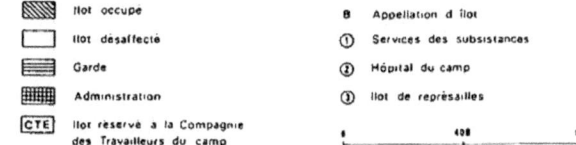

Les transformations du camp de Gurs

Source: <Laharie, Le Camp de Gurs, p. 53 <http://www.campgurs.com/le-ca mp/lhistoire-du-camp/le-camp-installation/lentretien-du-camp/>.

However, the German–Soviet Non-Aggression Pact of August 1939 and the outbreak of war a month later initiated a dramatic reversal that marked the beginning of the camp's second phase. In an atmosphere of anti-communist hysteria, anti-

Semitism and xenophobia, Prime Minister Édouard Daladier ordered the mass internment of political opponents on 18 November 1939. One of these was the French communist Raoul Nolibos (1890–1985), who was sent to Gurs along with about 100 of his comrades.[12] In contrast to the situation in Gurs, the majority of internees in other camps were not French citizens but immigrants, many of whom – some 15,000 in total – had fled "Greater Germany." This indiscriminate mass internment of "enemy aliens" and domestic communists echoed a policy France had pursued in the First World War and meant the Third Republic squandered an opportunity to harness the fighting spirit of thousands of fierce opponents of National Socialism.[13]

Nevertheless, by May 1940, two-thirds of these internees had been released. Following the German invasion, however, the French government interned as many as 15,000 so-called *"indésirables"* – unwanted foreigners as well as actual or perceived domestic political opponents – in Gurs. This mass exchange of prisoner groups marked the start of the camp's third phase. More than 9,000 of the new internees were German or Austrian refugees, mostly women and children, half of them Jewish. As a result, the camp was housing almost 12,000 people by the end of June. Hannah Arendt was among the lucky ones who exploited a "few days of chaos" before "everything became very regular again, and escape was almost impossible."[14] She knew where to go because some of her friends lived relatively close to the camp. Others who did not have contacts in France were too apprehensive to take advantage of this unexpected opportunity, with one explaining: "Considering the dangers – here in Gurs at least I know my way around. Outside is the unknown."[15] Emma Kann, like Arendt, "left the camp alone," then "walked down the road to Oloron [...]. It was a wonderful feeling to leave the barbed wire behind me and walk through this beautiful and fertile French countryside."[16] Arendt reflected on their experiences in her 1943 essay "We Refugees": "Apparently nobody wants to know that contemporary history has created a new kind of human beings – the kind that

---

12   Nolibos's biography is at: https://maitron.fr/spip.php?article124052; List of detainees in Gurs: https://prisons-cherche-midi-mauzac.com/des-camps/transfert-de-96-internes-administratifs-du-camp-de-gurs-vers-le-camps-de-nexon-12027 (21 April 2021).

13   Christian Eggers, Unerwünschte Ausländer. Juden aus Deutschland und Mitteleuropa in französischen Internierungslagern 1940–1942 (Berlin: Metropol, 2002), 50–5; Jean-Claude Farcy, Les Camps de concentration français de la première guerre mondiale (1914–1920) (Paris: Anthropos-Economica, Historiques, 1995).

14   Arendt in a letter to the journal Midstream in 1962, quoted in Elisabeth Young-Bruehl, Hannah Arendt: For the Love of the World (New Haven, CT: Yale University Press, 2004), 155.

15   Lisa Fittko cited a conversation with a fellow inmate. See Fittko, Mein Weg über die Pyrenäen. Erinnerungen 1940/41 (München: Hanser, 1985), 67; my translation.

16   Ottmar Ette, "Von der Normalität des Ausnahmezustands. Lagererfahrung und Über-Lebenswissen in Texten von Emma Kann, Hannah Arendt und Max Aub," in Juden und Judentum in der deutschsprachigen Literatur, edited by Willi Jasper et al. (Wiesbaden: Harrassowitz, 2006), 87–114, at 93; my translation.

are put in concentration camps by their foes and in internment camps by their friends."[17]

After the collapse of the Third Republic, the northern part of France, as well as the entire Atlantic coast, fell under German military administration. Meanwhile, in the unoccupied south, the collaborationist *État Français* established itself in the spa town of Vichy under the leadership of France's greatest First World War hero, Marshal Philippe Pétain. A Foreign Office commission headed by Ernst Kundt was sent to Gurs and other camps at the end of July to weed out any internees who might be sympathetic to the National Socialist regime – a necessary step, given the French authorities' previous lack of interest in the political views of interned foreigners. As a result, 700 inmates were released from Gurs and sent back to Germany. By late October 1940, the camp was home to just 1,920 Spanish refugees, about 700 Germans or Austrians and 600 *"politiques français"* – some 3,500 internees in total. However, the composition changed abruptly following Germany's unexpected decision to use Vichy France as "a convenient dumping ground for at least some of Germany's remaining Jews."[18] On Sukkot (22 October) 1940, some 6,540 Jews were loaded onto trains and deported from Baden and the Palatinate in southwest Germany, with Gurs chosen as their destination point solely because it had enough space to accommodate them.

In addition, Vichy was interning even more "undesirable elements," including nearly 4,000 German Jews who had been granted asylum in Belgium prior to the outbreak of hostilities but had then fled again to escape the invasion and subsequent occupation.[19] Rabbi Yehudah Leo Ansbacher (1907–98), for example, left Germany for Belgium in 1933 but was then captured in Brussels on 10 May 1940 and held "along with a large group of German citizens. The fact that I had left Germany [...] out of fear of the Nazis, and had immigrated to Belgium, did not matter one iota. To the Belgians, I and those like me were collaborating with Hitler's army."[20] After an exhausting train journey, he finally reached Saint-Cyprien in southern France. However, in October 1940, he was rounded up again and transferred to Gurs, where he joined almost 11,000 of his fellow German Jews. Of these, 1,710 were eventually released and allowed to return home, 755 escaped, 1,940 emigrated, 2,820 were drafted into French labour battalions and the remainder stayed in the camp.

In the autumn of 1940, a civilian management team – the *Direction Générale de la Sûreté Nationale* – replaced the camp's original military administration. However,

---

17 Quoted in Young-Bruehl, Hannah Arendt, 152.
18 Charlotte Bonelli, Exit Berlin: How One Woman Saved her Family from Nazi Germany (New Haven, CT: Yale University Press, 2014), 211.
19 See Bervoets-Tragholz, La Liste de Saint-Cyprien.
20 Belah Guṭerman and No'omi Morgenshṭern, The Gurs Haggadah: Passover in Perdition (Jerusalem: Devora, 2003), 15.

living conditions for the 12,000 internees remained very poor. The National Socialists had murdered Elizabeth Marum Lunau's father, Ludwig Marum, a Social Democratic member of the German Reichstag of Jewish descent. Although she had emigrated to France as early as 1936, Elizabeth was interned in Gurs shortly after the German invasion. Fifty years later, she recalled:

> The camp was a desolate place, a vast treeless plain with no grass. [...] There was a latrine. One walked up wooden steps to a row of holes; far below were large metal pots. [...] When it rained, which was often, the ground turned into a sea of mud. One had to walk with feet in mud up to the ankles. Often the mud sucked the shoes off our feet, and we had to fish for the precious shoes.

Moreover, food was scarce and mundane: "One person was given a large pot filled with dark liquid. Bread was distributed at 11:00 A.M. – one pound of French bread for twenty-four hours."[21]

Nevertheless, before long, Gurs had become a vibrant centre of intellectual and artistic activity. Schools, a library, a theatre group and even an orchestra were all established within the confines of the camp;[22] and the inmates were not entirely segregated from the outside world. There were, of course, the residents of the surrounding villages, who interacted with the inmates in many ways. For instance, a thriving black market developed across the camp's barbed-wire fences.[23] Oskar Althausen, who had been deported from Mannheim to Gurs in October 1940, recalled after the war that "a newspaper vendor came every day [...]. So we knew what was going on outside" and although the press was subject to censorship, the internees "were not completely cut off from all information."[24] In fact, Gurs became a postal hub, with between 5,000 and 8,000 mail items leaving or arriving in the camp each

---

21 Elisabeth Marum-Lunau, "Arrival at Camp de Gurs: An Eyewitness Report," in Between Sorrow and Strength: Women Refugees of the Nazi Period, edited by Sibylle Quack (Cambridge: Cambridge University Press, 1995), 63–8, at 65.

22 Due to limited space, I cannot elaborate on these developments here. For further details, see Claudia Nickel, "Kulturbaracken. Kreative Räume in südfranzösischen Lagern," in Die Transformation der Lager. Annäherungen an die Orte nationalsozialistischer Verbrechen, edited by Alexandra Klei et al. (Bielefeld: Transcript, 2011), 119–37; Claude Laharie, Gurs: L'art derrière les barbelés (1939–1944): Les Activités artistiques (sculpture, peinture, musique, artisanat) des internés au camp de Gurs (Biarritz: Atlantica, 2008); <http://www.campgurs.com/le-camp/lhistoire-du-camp/période-vichy-40-44-survivre-à-gurs-sous-vichy/les-activités-artistiques-1940-1943/> (21 May 2021).

23 Sandra Ott, Living with the Enemy: German Occupation, Collaboration, and Justice in the Western Pyrenees, 1940–1948 (Cambridge: Cambridge University Press, 2017).

24 Stefanie Virginia Gerlach et al., "… es geschah am helllichten Tag!" Die Deportation der badischen, pfälzer und saarländischen Juden in das Lager Gurs/Pyrenäen. 20. Tishri 5701, Sukkoth, 22. Oktober 1940, Laubhüttenfest (Stuttgart: Landeszentrale für politische Bildung, 2003), 29; my translation.

day.²⁵ Letters from the inmates were subject to strict censorship, but since thousands of them were sent illegally as well as legally, information about living conditions within the camp soon reached the outside world.

Gurs, like every other camp in southern France, benefited from the activities of a variety of humanitarian aid organisations, including the Quakers, the YMCA, the Swiss Humanitarian Aid Unit, which was led by the so-called "Angel of Gurs," Elsbeth Kasser,²⁶ and the *Oeuvre de Secours aux Enfants*. The latter organisation was credited with saving 409 of the 560 children and juveniles deported to Gurs. News of the deportation of Baden's Jews to Gurs reached Washington via the US Embassy in Berlin as early as 25 October 1940, and an American delegation visited the camp on 28 November.²⁷ Two months later, *Argentinisches Tageblatt*, a distinctly anti-fascist newspaper of the German diaspora, published a report of the American Friends Service Committee. Under the headline "Misery in the French Concentration Camps" the paper informed its readers that "for three years people have been dragged from one concentration camp to another" and that "14000 people" – including "500 children and 1200 people over 70 years of age" – were now living "in a breathtaking atmosphere in Gurs" and dying at a rate of "15 to 25 deaths per day."²⁸

Shortly after his deportation to Gurs in October 1940, Alfred Levi informed his son Richard (who had managed to make his way to England) that the French officials were often rude, but in general "the treatment we are enjoying in Le Camp de Gurs is much better than the treatment accorded us in Dachau two years ago."²⁹ Moreover, some of the internees managed to leave the camp by legal means. For example, although Frieda Strauss was a German citizen through marriage by the time of her deportation from Mannheim, she had been born in Switzerland and was finally al-

---

25 Laharie, Le Camp de Gurs, 64.
26 See Ohne Wenn und Aber dem Gewissen verpflichtet. Flüchtlingspfarrer Paul Vogt, 1900–1984. Rotkreuzschwester Elsbeth Kasser, 1910–1992, edited by Philippe Dätwyler, 3rd ed. (Zürich: Kid, 2000).
27 Michael Dobbs, The Unwanted: America, Auschwitz, and a Village Caught in between (New York: Alfred A. Knopf, 2019), 160–8.
28 Reprint of Argentinisches Tageblatt, 9 February 1941 in Peter Selg, Maria Krehbiel-Darmstädter. Von Gurs nach Auschwitz. Der innere Weg (Arlesheim: Ita-Wegman-Inst. für anthroposophische Grundlagenforschung, 2010), 105; my translation. See also Sebastian Schoepp, Das Argentinische Tageblatt 1933 bis 1945. Ein Forum der antinationalsozialistischen Emigration (Berlin: Wissenschaftlicher Verlag, 1996).
29 98 Briefe ins englische Exil. Die gewaltsame Trennung der jüdischen Familie Levi aus Friesenheim. Zum Gedenken an die Deportation Alfred und Brunhilde Levis nach Gurs, Rivesaltes und Auschwitz, edited by Heidi Beck-Braach and Rosita Dienst-Demuth (Konstanz: Hartung-Gorre, 2010), 161.

lowed to return there in April 1942, after eighteen months in Gurs.[30] Dora Hecht was not so fortunate. Her niece, Luzie Hecht, who had emigrated to the United States in 1938, managed to rescue many of her European relatives, but Dora died of malnutrition in Gurs in November 1941.[31]

The final catastrophe unfolded during the camp's fourth phase, between 6 August 1942 and 3 March 1943, when 3,907 Jewish prisoners were handed over to the Germans. The majority of them were then transported to the death camps, mainly Auschwitz, via the Drancy transit camp, near Paris. So, in the space of just three and a half years, Gurs was transformed from a refugee camp into a "waiting room" for Auschwitz. With most of its prisoners gone, the camp was closed in November 1943 before briefly reopening six months later to intern fewer than 300 political prisoners and members of the French Resistance.

After the Allies liberated France in August 1944, Charles de Gaulle's new provisional government arrested tens of thousands of actual and alleged collaborators, criminals, Italian and German civilians as well as a handful of prisoners-of-war. It seemed only logical to house them in the country's recently evacuated detention centres and internment camps, so Gurs was reopened and duly received 300 German prisoners-of-war, 1,600 French collaborators and 1,500 Spanish anti-fascists. Once again, the level of hygiene was deplorable so there was a constant risk of disease, and both food and basic equipment were lacking.[32] Raoul Nolibos, the communist who had been interned in Gurs in November 1939, was now head of the *Commission d'Épuration* of the *Comité Départemental de Libération*, which meant he was responsible for condemning some of his fellow-countrymen to a similarly miserable fate.[33]

It goes without saying that the camp's fifth and final phase should not be equated with the years 1940 to 1943; nevertheless, the camp was once again a place of profound human suffering and disenfranchisement. At the end of 1945, it was finally closed for good, but its history did not end there.

---

30   Gretl Drexler, Briefe aus Mannheim, Gurs und Grenoble (1939–1942). Das Schicksal einer jüdischen Frau aus Landau in der Pfalz, edited by Roland Paul (Kaiserslautern: Institut für pfälzische Geschichte und Volkskunde, 2014), 309, n. 772.
31   Bonelli, Exit Berlin, 206–35.
32   On the Marseilles region, see: Laurent Duguet, Incarcérer les collaborateur: Dans Les Camps de la Libération 1944–1945 (Paris: Vendémiaire, 2015).
33   See José-Ramón Cubero, Sortir de la guerre. Tumultes, chaos et mises en cause. Les Hautes-Pyrénées (1944–1952) (Morlaàs: Cairn éditions, 2018), 55–6.

Commemoration

Immediately after the war, the *Association des Communautés Juives des Basses-Pyrénées* erected the first memorial to Gurs to highlight the fact that the camp's Jewish inmates, although not the most numerous, suffered the most. Thereafter, though, Gurs soon faded into local, national and international oblivion. Even the cemetery fell into a state of disrepair. However, following the publication of a German newspaper article headlined "Are the Jews of Baden forgotten?" in August 1957,[34] the mayor of Karlsruhe and the leader of the Jewish community in Baden ensured that the answer would be "no" by initiating the cemetery's restoration. They completed the task six years later, and since then the communities of Baden and the Palatinate have continued to care for the site. In addition, delegations from Baden always make the trip to Gurs to participate in the French national *Journée de la Déportation* remembrance day on the last Sunday in April each year and the *Commémoration des Persécutions Racistes et Antisémites* on the third Sunday each July.[35] Finally, many communities in southwestern Germany, including Freiburg, Rastatt, Mannheim, Bruchsal, Neustadt a.d.W. and Saarbrücken, have commemorated their deported Jews with a series of simple but emotive street signs that indicate the distance to Gurs and other camps.

On the French side, the *Amicale du Camp de Gurs*, an association of former prisoners founded in 1979, played a key role in anchoring the camp in French collective memory.[36] In 1994, the Israeli artist Dani Karavan designed a double row of stelae to commemorate the different groups of victims and a large wood and concrete memorial that mirrors the contours of the barracks.[37] A permanent exhibition, opened in 2004, displays documents alongside recollections of life inside the camp. School parties visit on a regular basis.[38]

---

34   Badische Volkszeitung, 10 August 1957, quoted in Stefanie Virginia Gerlach et al., "… es geschah am helllichten Tag!," 80.
35   Ibid., 36–7.
36   See: <http://www.campgurs.com/lamicale/lhistoire-de-lamicale/création-de-lamicale-du-camp-de-gurs/> (3 June 2021).
37   See: <https://www.danikaravan.com/portfolio-item/france-homage-to-the-prisoners-of-gurs/> (3 June 2021).
38   See: <http://www.campgurs.com/offre-p%C3%A9dagogique/commission-%C3%A9ducation/> (3 June 2021). Two educational videos are available at: <http://www.campgurs.com/offre-p%C3%A9dagogique/vid%C3%A9os/> (3 June 2021).

Figure 4: Signpost to Gurs, Freiburg im Breisgau

Source:<https://commons.wikimedia.org/wiki/File:Wegweiser_am_Freiburger_Platz_der_alten_Synagoge_für_die_durch_die_sog._Wagner-Bürckel-Aktion.jpg>.

The camp's first occupants, refugees from the Spanish Civil War, have recently received the recognition they deserve after years of obscurity. Known in National Socialist jargon as *"Rotspanier"* (Red Spaniards), they were pressed into forced labour first by the Vichy regime, then by the German occupiers. Later, thousands of them were deported to concentration camps, especially Mauthausen, where they were forced to work for *Organisation Todt*. Their suffering was belatedly commemorated in an exhibition in Berlin in 2021.³⁹

Figure 5: Mickey Mouse in Gurs

Fig. 1. *Mickey au camp de Gurs*, panel 4.
©*Mémorial de la Shoah*, used with permission.

Source: ©Mémorial de la Shoah, used with permission <https://www.semanticscholar.org/paper/Remediating-the-Documentary%3A-Photography-and-Drawn-Werbe/25e9bf4955c5cc0586b5ab39a72ac0eeafdc2074/figure/0>.

No less significant has been the "Europeanisation" of Holocaust remembrance, epitomised by Jorge Semprún's 2004 play *Gurs: A European Tragedy*. Unlike Semprún, who survived Buchenwald, the aforementioned Emma Kann had personal experience of Gurs, which she later rendered into several poems.⁴⁰ The camp also features prominently in Ken Krimstein's 2018 graphic novel *The Three Escapes of Hannah*

---

39 See: <http://www.campgurs.com/le-camp/lhistoire-du-camp/période-espagnole-1939-les-activités/> (19 April 2021); <http://rotspanier.com/english/> (2 August 2022); Antonio Muñoz Sánchez, "'Rotspanier' vs. Bundesrepublik. Der Kampf der spanischen Zwangsarbeiter der Organisation Todt um ihre Anerkennung als Opfer des Nationalsozialismus (1956–1972), " Zeitschrift für Geschichtswissenschaft 69 (2021) 3: 240–259.
40 Ottmar Ette, "Lager Leben Literatur. Emma Kann und Jorge Semprún in Gurs. Im Spannungsfeld von Erleben und Erfinden," in Raum und Gefühl. Der Spatial Turn und die neue Emotionsforschung, edited by Gertrud Lehnert (Bielefeld: Transcript, 2011), 229–58.

Arendt: A Tyranny of Truth.⁴¹ Finally, Horst Rosenthal's *Mickey au Camp de Gurs* could be seen as a precursor to another graphic novel, Art Spiegelman's phenomenally successful *Maus*.⁴²

Figure 6: Memorial plaque, 1980

Source: <https://de.wikipedia.org/wiki/Camp_de_Gurs#/media/Datei:Camp_de_Gurs_pannea u_mémoriel_1980.jpg>.

There are still blind spots, though. The commemorative plaque at Gurs indicates that it was operational between April 1939 and the end of August 1944, when it was liberated by Allied forces. Therefore, there is no mention of the fact that it subsequently housed prisoners-of-war as well as actual and alleged French collaborators. Should these final inmates be commemorated, or would that be disrespectful to the memory of the earlier internees – the victims of terror, racism and anti-Semitism?

---

41 Ken Krimstein, The Three Escapes of Hannah Arendt: A Tyranny of Truth (New York: Bloomsbury, 2018), 112–13.

42 Philip Smith, "'Un Livre pour enfants': Mickey au Camp de Gurs as Picture Book," Children's Literature 47 (2019) 1: 104–19; Pnina Rosenberg, "Mickey Mouse in Gurs – Humor, Irony and Criticism in Works of Art Produced in the Gurs Internment Camp," Rethinking History: The Journal of Theory and Practice 6 (2002) 3: 273–92.

Whatever the answer may be, there is no doubt that the camp has become a European – and possibly even a global – *lieux de mémoire*.

Conclusion

As the French historian Denis Peschanski wrote in his groundbreaking study *La France des camps*: "Six hundred thousand internees in some two hundred camps: these figures alone say enough about the importance of internment in France during the dark years."[43] For six and a half years, Gurs fulfilled a variety of functions under three very different political regimes, just as countless other internment camps have been repurposed throughout history. By 1945, nearly 65,000 people had been housed in Gurs, and nearly 1,100 of them had died and been buried in the camp cemetery. It was a grimly "cosmopolitan" place, with internees from Spain, France, Italy, Belgium, the Netherlands, Germany, Austria, Poland and Czechoslovakia who often shared nothing save for their common fate of incarceration.

To a large extent, France's internal struggles were fought on the backs of the unfortunate internees of Gurs and the other detention centres. Accordingly, a variety of designations were used for these institutions: *"centre d'accueil," "centre de rassemblement," "centre à caractère répressif," "camp d'hébergés," "camp d'internés"* and even *"camp de concentration."*[44] These were crucial staging posts on the path from Daladier's immigration policies to Vichy's deportation of non-French citizens to the death camps. Moreover, the fact that many of them were established during the democratic Third Republic should finally quash the notion that "the camp" is an exclusively authoritarian phenomenon. On the contrary, "the camp", understood as a "state of exception" that has become a space, "is not least [...] a marginal district within democracy."[45]

The twentieth-century camp was a place of hardship, terror and persecution, but also a hub of humanitarian aid, caring, solidarity and creativity. And, today, it is a place of shared commemoration.

---

43   Denis Peschanski, La France des camps. L'Internement, 1938–1946 (Paris: Gallimard, 2002), 15; my translation.
44   Eggers, "Gurs – und die anderen," 176–7.
45   Cf. Giorgio Agamben, State of exception (Chicago: University of Chicago Press 2005); Quote: Ralf Rother, "Lager in Demokratien," in Auszug aus dem Lager. Zur Überwindung des modernen Raumparadigmas in der politischen Philosophie, edited by Ludger Schwarte (Bielefeld: Transcript, 2007), 144–61, at 147; my translation.

Hard time in the Big Easy
The unique role of New Orleans in Second World War enemy alien internment

Marilyn G. Miller

Camp Algiers and the Enemy Alien Control Program

On 9 November 2016, the day after the election that sent Donald Trump to the White House as the United States' forty-fifth president, I stood with radio producer Laine Kaplan-Levenson outside the locked security gates of a US Customs and Border Patrol Station in the Algiers neighbourhood of New Orleans, Louisiana, on the West Bank of the Mississippi River. Situated just a few miles from the city's historic French Quarter or *Vieux Carré*, the property we stood before was inaugurated in the early twentieth century as a US quarantine station and then repurposed during the Second World War as the Algiers Detention Station, an internment facility used primarily for non-citizen "enemy aliens" (Figure 1). I had seen a few mentions of the New Orleans site and its role in the largely secret Second World War Enemy Alien Control Program in Max Paul Friedman's book-length study *Nazis and Good Neighbors* and Harvey Strum's essay "Jewish Internees in the American South, 1942–1945."[1] But the scope of both those studies was much broader than the New Orleans context, and I was left with a host of questions. How was the New Orleans detention site selected, outfitted and utilised to house these alien enemies? Why was it established in a city known as the "Big Easy," famous for its culinary and carnal pleasures and its year-round carnivalesque atmosphere?[2] What was this detention experience like for those who were held there? Was it better characterised

---

1 Max Paul Friedman, Nazis and Good Neighbors: The United States Campaign against the Germans of Latin America in World War II (Cambridge: Cambridge University Press, 2003); Harvey Strum, "Jewish Internees in the American South, 1942–1945," American Jewish Archives 42 (1990) 1: 27–48.
2 According to Antony Stanonis, the nickname "Big Easy" originated with Black jazz musicians and referenced the city's association with leisure, promiscuity, permissiveness and moral laxity. See Anthony J. Stanonis, Creating the Big Easy: New Orleans and the Emergence of Modern Tourism, 1918–1945 (Athens: University of Georgia Press, 2006), 243–4.

as internment or incarceration? The Big Easy seemed an unlikely setting for doing "hard time" behind bars. And, at a moment when the city was deeply engaged in celebrating its tricentennial, it seemed almost no one was aware of this surprising chapter in its unique 300-year history.

Figure 1: US quarantine station, New Orleans, c. 1930, showing the site's location on the West Bank of the Mississippi River

Source: Photo courtesy the Historic New Orleans Collection.

Signed by President Franklin D. Roosevelt immediately after the bombing of Pearl Harbor and the United States' subsequent entry into the Second World War, Proclamations 2525, 2526 and 2527 activated the Enemy Alien Control Program, authorising the detention of allegedly dangerous enemy aliens of German, Italian or Japanese ancestry living in the United States.[3] Posters prohibited named alien en-

---

3   For an official governmental description, see "World War II Enemy Alien Control Program Overview," <https://www.archives.gov/research/immigration/enemy-aliens/ww2> (8 November 2021).

emies from entering areas deemed sensitive to US security and advised them to register their identity at US post offices (Figure 2). Propaganda generated by the US government warned the populace to "speak American" and not speak "the enemy's language," portraying Germany's Adolf Hitler, Japan's Tojo Hideki and Italy's Benito Mussolini in caricature form voicing anti-democracy slogans in their respective languages (Figure 3).[4] Nonetheless, unlike the wartime domestic "relocation" of more than 100,000 Japanese (two-thirds of whom were US citizens), which was ultimately treated as a shameful and embarrassing chapter of US history, the Alien Control Program's targeting of "enemy" non-citizens during wartime has never been the subject of a sustained national reckoning. Who were these alien enemies and why were they held at this location, so close at hand? What was the connection, if any, between the detention of enemy aliens in New Orleans' "backyard" neighbourhood of Algiers to the more well-known Japanese relocation program?[5]

Figure 2: US Department of Justice "Notice to Enemies of Alien Nationalities," advising them to register their identity at a US post office, printed in German, Italian and Japanese

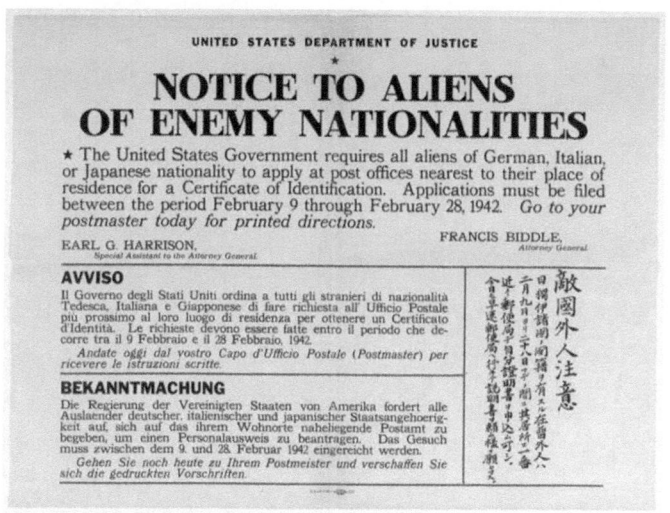

Source: Italian American Historical Society.

---

4   For an interesting discussion of this poster, see blog entry from the University of Pennsylvania language lab <https://languagelog.ldc.upenn.edu/nll/?p=24050> (8 November 2021).

5   For a comprehensive study of Japanese internment, see Greg Robinson, By Order of the President (Cambridge, MA: Harvard University Press, 2009).

When my producer colleague and I met at the former internment camp in 2016 with the idea of featuring its history in a podcast for the public radio series *Tripod: New Orleans at 300*, I had already discovered a 1946 article from a local newspaper that claimed one of those interned there was a member of Hitler's inner circle, bringing high-stakes international wartime tensions into the local frame of New Orleans.[6] The 30 March 1946 piece, titled "Close Pal of Hitler Held in Algiers Detention Unit," ran soon after the camp had been decommissioned (Figure 4).[7] Arrows added to a photo of the site indicated the buildings where the Hitler associate and other internees had been held. How, I wondered, did this unnamed individual come to be interned right across the river at Camp Algiers? Who was interned along with him, before him and after him? Along with the front-page story about Hitler's confidant held at the station, I had found other news stories with dates ranging from 1943 to 1946 that also referred to the Algiers site's use as an internment camp, although they provided few answers to the broader questions regarding who was held there, what the reasons were for their internment, when and for how long they were held, what were their origins or political affiliations, and why they were confined at this specific site.

---

6   Laine Kaplan-Levinson, "The World War II Internment Camp, 'Camp Algiers,' Part I," in WWNO, Tripod: New Orleans at 300, 12 January 2017 <http://wwno.org/post/wwii-internment-camp-camp-algiers-part-i> (8 November 2021). A link to the Part II is also available on the site.

7   Ken Gormin, "Close Pal of Hitler Held in Algiers Detention Unit," Times-Picayune, 30 March 1946, p. 1.

Figure 3: US Second World War propaganda poster discouraging the use of German, Japanese or Italian and encouraging all to "Speak American"

Source: Wikipedia Commons (public domain).

With the 1946 article and photo of the detention unit in hand, Kaplan-Levenson and I could see that, while some of the buildings no longer remained, we were in fact standing at the exact location from which Camp Algiers had been photographed seventy years earlier, at the time of its closure. When we requested entry to the facility, functioning then as an active Border Patrol station, we were denied access. No personnel present in 2016, including the station's information officer, claimed to possess any knowledge of its use as an internment camp during the Second World War, and they responded with substantial scepticism to our enquiries. I soon learned that this response of incredulity was characteristic of the local populace. Even the staff at New Orleans' World War II Museum, the city's number-one tourist attraction in the city, claimed to know nothing about the existence of Camp Algiers or have any materials relevant to its role in wartime internment. It was this general lacuna of awareness at the local level that inspired me to write *Port of No Return: Enemy Alien*

Internment in World War II New Orleans.[8] This essay offers a condensed version of the principal facts and events detailed in that study.

Hiding in plain sight

A central question in my inquiry was how the New Orleans station with its history as a Second World War internment camp was able to hide in plain sight for so long. Why was there this glaring gap in public knowledge? The first reason is likely the most obvious: The Enemy Alien Control Program was, after all, a secret operation, both in its application within the United States and in its later expansion to include some fifteen cooperating countries in Latin America. A second reason, though, is that research on wartime internment in the United States has understandably focused on Japanese internment – a historical episode that internee activists and their descendants' still fight to expose well into the twenty-first century, after a protracted struggle seeking acknowledgement and redress from the US government. By contrast, few Americans know that throughout the period of its participation in the Second World War, "and as late as 1949, the US government operated a nationwide penal complex designed to hold 'dangerous' enemy aliens who were neither criminal nor of Japanese ancestry."[9]

All Second World War internment camps in the United States were operated by either the Immigration and Naturalization Service (INS) or the Department of Justice (DOJ). When I consulted with archivist William Creech at the US National Archives in Washington, DC, where the INS records are located, he warned me that the New Orleans detention facility was admittedly a minor player in a vast matrix of some 400 camps that extended from Hawaii to New York's Ellis Island and from North Dakota to Texas. Some, such as Crystal City, a model "family camp" in Texas, held up to 3,500 men, women and children at any given moment, whereas the Algiers unit probably saw only 2,000 or fewer internees pass through its gates during the years of its operation as a detention facility. With luck, Creech said, I might find a memo of how many potatoes they ordered weekly to feed the internees. Fortunately, I found many kinds of documents in this and other archives related to my "backyard" camp, including architectural plans, a telegram announcing its opening, lists of those detained and held on specific dates, news articles confirming the camp's opening, operation and decommissioning, letters and pleas (often with a censor's stamp) from internees to family members and governmental figures whom

---

8   Marilyn Grace Miller, Port of No Return: Enemy Alien Internment in World War II New Orleans (Baton Rouge: Louisiana State University Press, 2021).
9   Stephen Fox, America's Invisible Gulag: A Biography of German American Internment & Exclusion in World War II: Memory and History (New York: Peter Lang, 2000), xxii.

they hoped might grant them release, and site visit reports from diplomatic, religious and immigrant aid organisation representatives, such as the Swiss Legation, the Young Men's Christian Association and the National Refugee Service, respectively.[10] But I found the most detailed and personal information regarding the individuals who passed through Camp Algiers in their Department of Justice and Department of State "name files," containing the government's own paper trails regarding their suspected status as enemy aliens, apprehension, detention, internment and release, often after several years without even receiving an explanation – much less a hearing – pertaining to their internment.[11]

Debate continues regarding the precise numbers and identities of those held in US internment camps as part of the Alien Enemy Control Program, but "German" enemy aliens undoubtedly constituted the largest group. For the US government, the "German" category included all persons from territories under German control as of December 1941, including Poles, Austrians and Czechs. Historian Arnold Krammer calculated the total number of Germans, German-Americans, and German-Latin Americans incarcerated during the program to be in excess of 25,000 persons.[12]

Due in part to its location near the Gulf of Mexico and shipping routes that connected it to Central American ports, the vast majority of those held at Camp Algiers were German-, Italian- and Japanese-born persons arrested and deported to the United States from Latin America. A few, especially later in the war, were German-born persons apprehended within the United States, including Hitler's "pal" referred to in the 1946 local news article. Camp Algiers also stands out among the dense network of internment facilities nationally, because, at one point, it became an "anti-Nazi" refuge for some sixty Jews from Germany, Austria and elsewhere apprehended in Latin America, deported to the United States and interned in camps elsewhere in the US South before being congregated at the New Orleans site.

---

10   Alien enemy internment camp records and case files are housed in the Records of the Immigration and Naturalization Service, Record Group 85 at National Archives I in Washington, DC <https://www.archives.gov/research/guide-fed-records/groups/085.html#85.4> (8 November 2021).

11   Information on individual enemy aliens is located in the Special War Problems Division records and Central Decimal File records in the General Records of the Department of State, Record Group 59 <https://www.archives.gov/research/foreign-policy/state-dept> (8 November 2021) and in the Alien Enemy Control Unit records and case files in the Records of the Department of Justice, Record Group 60 <https://www.archives.gov/research/guide-fed-records/groups/060.html#60.14> (8 November 2021), both at National Archives II in College Park, MD.

12   Arnold Krammer, Undue Process: The Untold Story of America's German Alien Internees (London: Rowman and Littlefield, 1997), x.

Repurposing the Alien and Sedition Acts

Though the United States' Enemy Alien Control Program was implemented in the Second World War, its precedents date back to 1798, when the Fifth Congress passed the Alien and Sedition Acts, which complicated the path to citizenship and used the terms "alien" and "enemy" in combination. Historian Carol Berkin believes these late eighteenth-century laws can now be seen as the "forerunners of such modern abuses of American rights and liberties as twentieth-century immigration quotas, the Red Scare, Japanese internment camps, and minority voter suppression."[13] Thus, at the moment when the Japanese attacked Pearl Harbor, more than a million immigrants who were citizens of Germany, Italy and Japan – about a quarter of the non-citizen population of the entire country – were quickly classified as "enemy aliens."[14]

After the Enemy Alien Control Program was implemented on the domestic front, President Roosevelt determined that the enemy alien threat exceeded the geography under his leadership. The National Socialists' rapid advance in Europe convinced him of the need to extend the reach of anti-alien policies beyond the United States' national boundaries. He claimed a secret map provided proof of Hitler's plan to control the entire hemisphere (Figure 4). Though the map's validity was questioned, Roosevelt ultimately gained the support of some fifteen Latin American countries in resisting pro-National Socialist and pro-Fascist forces. Paradoxically, in a much-touted "Good Neighbor" policy, implemented less than a decade earlier, the United States had promised non-interference in the other Americas. Guided by the State Department, Federal Bureau of Investigation (FBI), Department of Justice and executive branch, officials in Central and South America collaborated by drawing up lists of potential enemies of the United States, arresting and holding them in detention and eventually helping the US military deport them to the United States. The subsequent selection and detention of those named "enemy aliens" depended on the political environment in the specific Latin American countries, the countries' respective relationships with the United States, levels of corruption, and many other factors. In many cases, European and Japanese-born residents in Latin America were deemed a threat based solely on their country of origin, regardless of any political or criminal activity – or lack of it. Thousands were summarily subjected to US-sponsored surveillance and seizure outside its borders and became part of a new, specious, wartime commerce in which officials in Latin America frequently demanded bribes from those who hoped to avoid internment or deportation, appropriated properties and businesses of those detained, and

---

13   Carol Berkin, A Sovereign People: The Crises of the 1790s and the Birth of American Nationalism (New York: Basic Books, 2017), 202.
14   Paula Branca Santos, "Injustice Ignored: The Internment of Italian-Americans during World War II," Pace International Law Review 13 (2001) 1: 151–82, at 161.

improved their countries' standing with the powerful neighbour to the north by swelling the ranks of potential enemy aliens. In many cases, those detained and named as enemy aliens would not ever know the reason for their detention, and most of those detained in Latin America would not receive any kind of hearing during stays in Camp Algiers and other camps that stretched from months to years.

A 1942 Associated Press photo with the caption "Enemy Aliens Leave Panama for US" shows individuals ascending the gangplank of a US Army Transport vessel in the Canal Zone, guarded by US military police.[15] In many cases, Latin American functionaries decided who to include on these lists based solely on country of origin or surname, rather than on any evidence of criminal or pro-Axis political activity. Just as happened with the Japanese on US soil, persons of German, Italian, and Japanese birth were labelled as dangerous enemies without supporting evidence. Additionally, Austrians, Poles, Hungarians, Czechs and even a Swedish count were classified as "Germans," notwithstanding their protestations to the contrary.

For the small group of Jewish refugees caught up in the Latin American Enemy Alien Control Program, the application of the "German" label was especially bitter, since the National Socialists had only recently stripped Jews and many other non-Aryans of their citizenship condemning them to the stateless condition that prompted their desperate flight to Latin America. At least eleven of those held at Camp Algiers had already spent time in a European labour or death camp before being deported to the United States. Under the guise of identifying alien enemies for the U.S., many Latin American officials also profited by blacklisting businesses, preventing Axis-born persons from owning businesses, and confiscating named enemy aliens' properties and assets. All this occurred even though only about 10 per cent of Axis nationals named as enemy aliens in Latin America actively identified as National Socialists.

---

15   This photo and many other materials relevant to the Latin American component of the Enemy Alien Control Program can be viewed under "Latin American Internment Program" on the German American Internee Coalition site <https://gaic.info/history/the-world-war-ii-latin-american-internment-program/> (8 November 2021).

Figure 4: The "secret map" mentioned by President Franklin Roosevelt in his 1941 "New World Order" speech

Source: Image courtesy the FDR Presidential Library and Museum.

Port of no return

New Orleans was the point of delivery for many of the ships carrying these "enemy aliens" from Latin American ports. Their manifests have much to tell us. For example, the SS *Cuba* left the Panama Canal Zone on 4 October 1942, arriving in New Orleans a few days later (Figure 6). The enemy aliens on board are identified by their names, age, sex, marital status, calling or vocation, nationality, "race or people," birthplace and, finally, last permanent residence. Some passengers on this particular manifest are identified as German on all counts, whereas others are labeled as "Jewish" in the category "race or people." This is important because it shows that in at least some cases, the US government knew at the time of their arrival that certain individuals were Jews, and thus unlikely allies of the German regime; yet, they were interned alongside Germans of all political stripes, and even subjected to pro-National Socialist activities in the US camps. The facing page of this same manifest indicates that the arriving passengers were to be "interned for the duration" for however long the war lasted. Some would remain in US internment until 1946.

Figure 5: Ship's manifest of the SS Cuba, sailing 4 October 1942 from the Canal Zone to New Orleans; some passengers are identified as "Jewish" in the "race or people" category

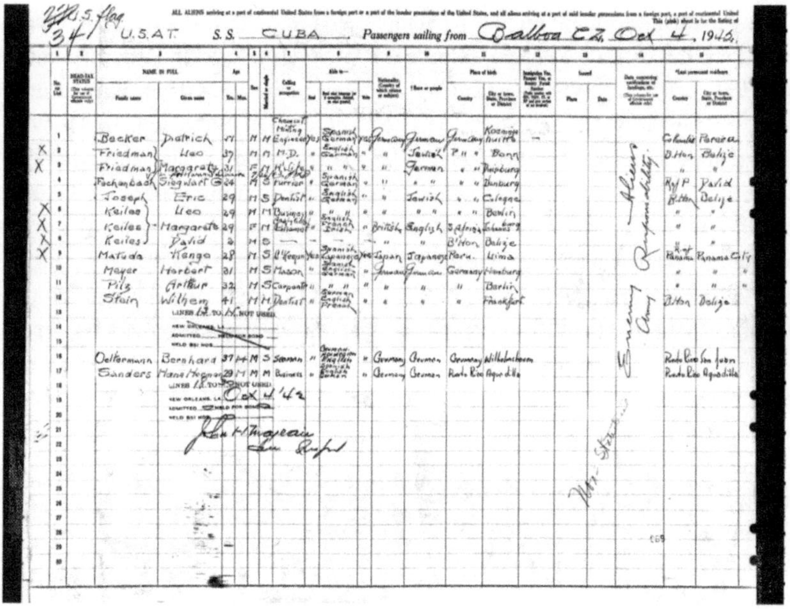

Source: Records of the Immigration and Naturalization Service, National Archives.

The men, women and children who arrived on these vessels rarely proceeded directly to Camp Algiers. Rather, New Orleans functioned as a hub from which named aliens and the family members who "voluntarily" joined them were sent to internment facilities elsewhere by train. Nonetheless, it was in New Orleans that these newly arrived detainees were stripped of their passports and other documentation, and then charged with entering the United States illegally. This tactic, itself illegal, was only used with named enemy aliens arriving from Latin America. It was in New Orleans where these incoming passengers and their luggage were sometimes sprayed with insecticide; some of those arriving were even forced to undress and enter a shower area naked. Thus, even if a small percentage of the people who passed through New Orleans as enemy aliens would finally return to the countries where they were detained, the site symbolically represents a point or "port of no return" from which they could not return to pre-internment life. The internment experience could not be undone, even if most chose to silence or suppress it, even with their own children, upon their eventual release.

Despite constituting a minority, pro-National Socialist contingents assumed dominance among German-identified populations in some US internment camps. Hoping to incur good treatment for their own citizens detained or imprisoned behind enemy lines in German-controlled territories, US officials permitted Nazi supporters in the internment camps to assemble, sing National Socialist songs, display swastikas and celebrate Hitler's birthday. Even at Camp Algiers, at one point labelled an anti-National Socialist facility, someone mowed a swastika into the unit's lawn. An August 1942 bulletin of the Jewish Telegraphic Agency publicized the frictions that inevitably ensued between pro- and anti-National Socialist internees under the headline "Jews, Nazis Fight in U.S. Internment Camps; Separation Asked by Jewish Internees."[16] After many months complaining of such conditions, a group of about sixty Jewish men, women and children were concentrated at Camp Algiers in February of 1943, thanks to the intervention of the Joint Distribution Committee, the National Refugee Service, and other Jewish aid organizations. As I expand on in Chapter 6 of *Port of No Return*, a woman named Cecilia Razovsky worked tirelessly in the "Joint," the NRS, and other organizations to improve the conditions of Jewish internees and secure their ultimate release, even as leadership in these organizations was wary of the way such efforts might call into question Jewish groups' loyalty to the nation and support of the government's national security operations as evidenced in the Enemy Alien Internment Program.[17] Thus, for a brief period after Jews were consolidated at New Orleans's Camp Algiers, it was known as an anti-National Socialist camp and the "Camp of the Innocent."

Classification and release of internees

Although there are only partial records of who was held at the Algiers site during its 1942–1946 run as an internment camp functioning within the city limits of New

---

16 "Jews, Nazis Fight in US Internment Camps: Separation Asked by Jewish Internees," Jewish Telegraphic Agency, 18 August 1942.
17 For further details of Razovsky's work, see: Miller, Port of No Return, chapter 6; and Bat-Ami Zucker, Cecilia Razovsky and the American Jewish Women's Rescue Operation (London: Vallentine Mitchell, 2008).

Orleans, one very interesting list compiled in November 1944 documents the government's attempts to sort out its primarily German internees as "Pro-Nazi," "Anti-Nazi" or "Jew" (Figure 6). The inclusion of several question marks in the classification columns shows that, even in late 1944, officials were still uncertain of many internees' true political postures, however. Thanks to this list and other archival research, I was able to identity the "pal of Hitler" mentioned above in the March 1946 *Times-Picayune* story as Kurt Ludecke, who had represented the National Socialists in the United States in the 1930s, and in 1937 had published a book titled *I Knew Hitler*. Having made the case to US officials that he had repented of his earlier support of Hitler's campaign, Ludecke appears on the November 1944 list as "Anti-Nazi" although with a question mark alongside this classification. The government remained septical of Ludecke's conversion throughout the war and even after it ended; he was released from Camp Algiers but later was detained off and on at Ellis Island in a long-fought battle to avoid repatriation to Germany that ended unsuccessfully in 1948.[18]

Ludecke's case is unique in terms of his protracted detention, his final "removal" to Germany and the legal precedent the case set for subsequent generations.[19] Piecing together the stories of many other individuals, it becomes clear that, despite long confinements, separations from spouses and family members, lack of access to hearings or even explanations for their detention, internment ultimately provided a kind of back door entrance to legal residence in the United States for many apprehended in Latin America who passed through Camp Algiers and other internment facilities. It was without doubt ironic that many of those caught up in the Enemy Alien Control Program were residing in Central or South American countries at the time of their apprehension precisely because their efforts to find refuge in the United States had failed. Panama, Nicaragua, Colombia, Costa Rica, the Dominican Republic and other sites south of the border sometimes offered the only route out of Europe as the National Socialists occupied ever more early escape routes, such as Belgium, France and Italy. Jewish refugees, in particular, traversed incredibly peripatetic routes to "safety" in Latin America, acquiring visas to countries in the region only as the last available option when entry to the United States was denied. Their subsequent arrest, detention, deportation from those countries and internment at the hands of the US government thus seemed to them not only a grave injustice but also a hideous joke.

---

18   Kurt Ludecke's name files in the Department of State (Record Group 59) and Department of Justice (Record Group 60) files at the National Archives both provide details of his long internment saga. See: RG 60 COR 146–13, Enemy Alien Files, Box 318, NA; and RG 59 740.00115, European War 1939 / 5819, Box 2841, NA.
19   See Stephen Vladek, "Ludecke's Lengthening Shadow: The Disturbing Prospect of War without End," Journal of National Security Law and Policy 2 (2006): 53–110.

From the local perspective, however, Jews and other alien enemies who were released from internment after it was finally determined they posed no threat to national or hemispheric ultimately received a message of "welcome" from North America. For example, the 21 August 1943 edition of the *New Orleans Item* celebrated the release from Camp Algiers of a German-Jewish refugee violinist identified only as "Siegfried" together with his mother.[20] Reporter Marjorie Roehl wrote that "Mr Siegfried met America this morning with music in his heart and at his fingertips. With him, her eyes glad, her earrings bobbing, went his mother." Dr David Fichman of the New Orleans Committee for Refugee Services was also on hand to wish the two godspeed as they left for an unidentified city in the country's interior under a parole-type programme called "Internment at Large." Identified in my research as Jeanette and Siegfried Wolff, the smiling and well-attired mother and son were photographed together at New Orleans' Union Station with Fichman, also a rabbi at Touro Synagogue. Roehl's article quoted Siegfried (Wolff) as saying, "Your America is a wonderful place [...] We can live in quiet here where everyone is free."

Other German internees apprehended in Latin America were not so lucky, however, and would remain in internment until much later dates. Hamburg businessman Wolfgang Harten was arrested in Ecuador and interned in a Texan camp in December 1943. Though his wife and children were finally able to join him after a hellish voyage almost a year later, the family was then interned at Crystal City until the camp closed in May 1946, well after the war ended. The Hartens waited several weeks at Camp Algiers before finally boarding a plane back to Panama, from where they eventually were able to travel on to Ecuador. The diaries in which Gertrude Harten described these experiences (providing a female perspective rarely seen in the archival materials) were later compiled and published in Spanish by Karin Schramm, the youngest of the Harten children, only a baby at the time of their internment.[21]

---

20   Marjorie H. Roehl, "Refugee Violinst Fled from Nazis; Finds US: Welcomes Self and Mother," New Orleans Item, 21 August 1943, pp. 1, 5.
21   María Cuvi Sánchez and Karin Harten Ahlers (eds), Gertrudis: Diarios de una mujer alemana sobre el Ecuador, 1937–1956 (Quito: Abya-Yala, 2014). A section of Gertrude Harten's diaries is also available in English on the German American Internee Coalition website <https://gaic.info/the-harten-family-story/> (8 November 2021).

Figure 6: A page of the November 1944 list titled "Aliens at Algiers, LA," with marks indicating classification as "Pro-Nazi," "Anti-Nazi" or "Jew"; question marks indicate doubt about the classification

		Pro-Nazi	Anti-Nazi	Jew
German - Detained				
Steiner, Carl Offerman	39/10518		x	
Germans Interned				
Barber, Harold	56176/788			?
Blumenthal, Annaliese Gaertner	56162/820		x	
Blumenthal, Ernst	56125/317			
Hoffmann, Franz	56176/552	x	x	
HUEPER, Wilhelm L.D.C.	56125/789		x	
Ising, Friedrich Wilhelm Hermann	56176/901			?
Jacobi, Arthur	56125/462			
Jacobi, Erna Frieda	56125/388	x		x
Jacobi, Herta	56125/388			
Jacobi, Manfred	56125/388			
Jacobi, Ursula	56125/388			
Johanning, Friedrich	39/7162		x	
Kaul, Fritz Karl, Dr.	56125/318			x
Kolb, Gertraude Rose	39/7694			
Kolb, Heide Marie	39/7694	x		
Kolb, Karl	39/9042			
Kolb, Klaus Peter	39/7694			
Kuhne, Werner Gerhard Otto	56176/856	x	x	
Loewenthal, Emil	56125/459			
Loewenthal, Hilda	56125/384			
Loewenthal, Joan	56125/384			
Ludecke, Kurt George W.	39/3087		X?	
Meyer, Irmgard Martha	56162/33			x
Meyer, Siegfried Bernhard, Dr.	56125/320			

Source: US National Archives; used with permission.

Reading such accounts from our own era marked by virulent attacks on noncitizens arriving from Latin America and other areas of turmoil and internal conflict suggests that conditions were in fact *better* in some respects for enemy alien internees during the Second World War than they are for non-citizen detainees during today's "peacetime;" this was especially true for German noncitizens who were perceived in the United States to be "white" in contrast to Japanese Americans and border-crossing Mexican migrant workers.[22] In "Aliens Live Well at Algiers Base," a story that ran in a New Orleans newspaper in September 1945, the officer-in-charge, Raymond Bunker, assured readers that he and others at Camp Algiers served more as social workers than prison guards: "The work is much more than surveillance [...] We are more social workers than jailers and have a wonderful opportunity to show these people what the American way of life is."[23] Such a claim is hard to imagine in the context of for-profit detention today. Under Donald Trump, Louisiana became an "epicenter" of Immigration and Customs Enforcement (ICE) detention facilities, with sites located in "old state prisons and local jails [...] several hours away from New Orleans and other major cities in the region, far from most immigrant rights groups and immigration lawyers. Migrants complain of mistreatment and prolonged detention."[24] Just as during wartime more than three quarters of a century ago, governments in the United States and elsewhere claim harsh measures of non-citizen control and deprivation of freedom are necessary to maintain national and hemispheric security in the Second World War.

In hindsight, then, it's clear that the Enemy Alien Control Program – even when administered in a city as driven by pleasure as New Orleans--contributed to contemporary US policies and practices that routinely treat non-citizens arriving from Latin America as dangerous criminals, despite supporting evidence. Our hope is that exposure of the internment programme in contemporary scholarship can serve as a memorial of sorts to the unjustly interned, and that such work will serve as a warning of history's propensity for repeating itself when we fail to sufficiently examine what happened and continues to happen in its shadows.

---

22 See Jessica Ordaz, The Shadow of El Centro: A History of Migrant Incarceration and Solidarity: Justice, Power, and Politics (Chapel Hill: University of North Carolina Press, 2021), 17: "German racial privilege led to treatments and wages, even after the start of World War II, that differed for Japanese Americans and later Mexican migrants."
23 Quoted in "Aliens Live Well at Algiers Base," Times-Picayune, 1 September 1945, p. 13.
24 Nomaan Merchant, "Louisiana Becomes New Hub in Immigrant Detention under Trump," AP News, 9 October 2019.

Annex

Index of Names

A
Adler, Josef, 216
Adorno, Theodor W., 266
Agamben, Giorgio, 10, 89, 269, 285
Althausen, Oskar, 278
Ansbacher, Yehudah Leo, 277
Antonovsky, Aaron, 142
Arendt, Hannah, 10, 89, 276, 277, 284
Augé, Marc, 196

B
Balandier, George, 89
Baltinester, Wilhemina, 52
Bandura, Albert, 148, 153, 155
Behrensen, Birgit, 19, 20, 138, 139, 141, 142, 150
Beiderlinden, William, 130
Bentwich, Norman, 51
Ben-Gurion, David, 120
Berkin, Carol, 294
Berting, Gerhard, 81, 82
Biddle, Francis, 45
Bieri, Frédérick, 127, 131
Böhnisch, Lothar, 144
Bourdieu, Pierre, 88, 148, 155
Brachman, Moshe, 120
Brandmaier, Maximiliane, 20, 147, 148, 150, 153, 154, 156, 157
Brekke, Jan-Paul, 141

Bronner, Wilhelm, 56
Bronner, Alfred, 56
Bronner, Richard, 56
Brooks, Robert Preston, 257
Bunker, Raymond, 302
Butler, Tubal Uriah, 50, 56

C
Calkins, Fay, 67–69
Cho, Chung W., 127
Churchill, Winston, 55, 218, 231
Clifford, Bede, 218
Courvoisier, Jean, 132, 133
Creech, William, 51, 292

D
Daladier, Édouard, 276, 285
Damari, Shoshana, 120
de Gaulle, Charles, 280
de Reynier, Jacques, 127–131
de Traz, David, 130, 131
de Weck, Eugène, 132, 134
Du Bois, W.E.B., 257, 258
D'Aubigné, Jeanne Merle, 273, 274

E
Edge, Sara, 154, 172, 197
Ehard, Hans, 75, 78
Eichmann, Adolf, 212, 214
Elliot, K. C., 84

F

Fichman, David, 300
Fischer, Inge, 53
Fischer, Bela, 213–214
Fischer, Ernst Otto, 53, 56
Fischer, Lucy, 53
Fisher, Leon D., 64, 69
Foucault, Michel, 87, 89
Fox, Stephen, 292
Frenkel-Brunswik, Else, 266
Freud, Gustav, 53
Friedman, Max Paul, 40, 287
Friedmann, Lisa, 150
Frisch, Heinrich, 56
Frisch, Norbert, 56
Frisch, Resi, 56

G

Giboney, Thomas B., 65
Glasberg, Alexander, Abbé, 164
Glaser, Barney, 138
Goffman, Erving, 20, 140, 148–151
Gormin, Ken, 289
Groß, Verena, 141, 142, 150
Guez, Chava Eva, 213, 214
Gumbel, Karl, 82

H

Habsburg, Otto, 31, 36, 52
Hall, Dudley S., 173, 252, 253, 255, 261, 263, 264
Hammerman, Baruch, 53
Hammerman, Esther, 53
Hammerman, Helene, 53
Harrell-Bond, Barbara, 88, 90
Harrison, Earl G., 62
Harten, Gertrude, 300
Harten, Wolfgang, 300
Haslam, Nick, 148
Heberle, Rudolf, 23, 24, 252–255, 261, 263, 264, 267

Hecht, Dora, 280
Hecht, Luzie, 280
Held, Josef, 10, 19, 30, 31, 35, 37, 39–46, 49, 52, 129–131, 134, 135, 153, 164, 172, 183, 187, 214, 216, 218, 246, 254, 263, 277, 287, 289, 292, 293, 295, 298
Hermann, Vivette (= Vivette Samuel), 17, 18, 99, 100, 104–110
Hideki, Tojo, 289
Himmler, Heinrich, 43
Hitler, Adolf, 48, 57, 161, 212, 222, 277, 289, 293, 294, 298, 299
Højholt, Charlotte, 153
Holton, J. C., 253, 262, 263
Holzkamp, Klaus, 148, 153
Honneth, Axel, 148
Horthy, Miklós, 49
Huggins, George, 52
Humbert, David-Gustave, 60, 107

I

Isin, Engin, 179, 189

J

Jacoby, Marie, née Echte, 247–248
Jacoby, Gustav Reinhold, 23, 246–249
Johnson, Howard, 50, 148

K

Kann, Emma, 276, 283
Kaplan, Eliezer, 121
Kaplan-Levenson, Laine, 287–291
Karavan, Dani, 281
Kasser, Elsbeth, 21, 164, 165, 167, 176, 279
Kempner, Robert M. W., 36, 38, 39
Ketchum, John Davidson, 34, 35
Koestler, Arthur, 171, 172
Kramer, Eduard, 12, 14, 31, 36, 41, 81
Krammer, Arnold, 37, 42, 43, 293

L

Lambek, Joachim, 23, 238–241, 243, 246, 249
Lambek, Oscar (Osias), 238, 241
Laub, Morris, 111, 114–116, 118–120
Lederman, Charles, 104
Lehner, Otto, 132–134
Leibner, Joshua, 114, 115
Leval, Kurt, 173
Levi, Alfred, 279
Levi, Richard, 279
Levinson, Daniel J., 266
Levy, David, 59, 69
Linder, Tom, 253, 263
Lloyd, George, 217, 218
Lomazow, Jacob, 63, 67–69
Lösch, Hans, 144
Lowrie, Donald A., 103
Ludecke, Kurt, 299

M

MacArthur, Douglas, 127, 129
Mahler, Bernhard, 56
Malameth, Irene, 53
Malameth, Otto, 53–54
Malamuth, Charles, 120
Malkin, Isia, 108, 217
Malkki, Liisa, 90
Marum Lunau, Elizabeth, 278
Marum, Ludwig, 278
Masour, Germaine (Jenny), 108
Meyer, Henry, 44, 130, 131, 223
Miller, Marilyn Grace, 25, 40, 292, 298
Moser, Oscar, 57
Muchow, Hans Heinrich, 194, 197, 198, 200
Muchow, Martha, 194, 197, 198, 200
Mussolini, Benito, 39, 289
Myrdal, Gunnar, 257, 258

N

Nathan, Alfred, alias Peter Pan, 47, 173
Nielsen, Greg, 179, 189
Nolibos, Raoul, 276, 280

O

Oberländer, Theodor, 76, 78
Otto, Hans-Uwe, 53, 54, 56, 131, 144, 257, 265
Ottomeyer, Klaus, 148

P

Passman, Charles, 114
Paterson, Alexander, 234, 235, 237, 247
Pearlman, Maurice, 111
Peschanski, Denis, 38, 163, 285
Pétain, Philippe, Maréchal, 162, 277
Pieper, Tobias, 149
Piot, Maurice, 132, 133
Pohek, Marguerite, 67
Porter, Matthew, 148

R

Rauch, Margot Ruth, 173, 174
Reinhardt, Max, 173
Resnick, Reuben, 59
Reyes, Adelaida, 186
Rhee, Syngman, 127, 133
Rice, James, 59, 169
Rivière, Jean Marquès, 172
Robinson, Greg, 289
Roehl, Marjorie, 300
Roosevelt, Franklin D., 40, 49, 55, 288, 294, 296
Rosenberg, Alfred, 20, 21, 38, 164, 166, 169, 170, 175, 284
Rosenthal, Horst, 21, 161, 164–171, 173–176, 196, 284
Rothberger, Ella née Burchardt, 241–243, 246
Rothberger, Fritz, 23, 239, 241–246, 249

Rothberger, Heinrich, 241–245
Rothberger, Jakob Johann, 241–245

S

Salomon, Andrée, 100, 164
Samuel, Julien, 99–109
Sanford, R. Nevitt, 266
Sayad, Abdelmalek, 88
Schneider. Siegfried, 144
Schramm, Hanna, 161, 163–164, 166, 169, 170, 173–174
Schramm, Karin Harten, 300
Schraube, Ernst, 153
Schulzer, Johann, 73
Sebba, Gregor, 23–24, 252–254, 256–267
Sebba, Helen, 258
Seinfeld, Kurt, 56
Semprún, Jorge, 283
Seukwa, Louis H., 142
Shertok, Moshe, 217, 226
Shuster, George N., 75, 78
Smith, Steffi, 174, 284
Spiegelman, Art, 284
Stanonis, Antony, 287
Stecher, Hans Bernd, 15, 47, 48, 51–58
Stecher, Siegfried, 53–54
Stecher, Viktor, 52–58
Stecher, Jakob, 47, 54
Stecher, Sophie (née Baltinester)
Stecher, Wilhelm, 53
Storfer, Berthold, 22, 210, 214, 215
Strauss, Anselm L., 138
Strauss, Frieda, 279
Strum, Harvey, 287

T

Talmadge, Eugene, 253
Täubig, Vicki, 149, 150
Tauscher, Alice, 52
Tauscher, Erich, 52–57
Tauscher, Gertrude, 52
Tauscher, Bertha, 52
Taylor, Maxwell D., 59, 265
Thieberg, Simon, 213, 215, 216, 219
Thompson, Andrew, 148
Tönnies, Ferdinand, 254
Truman, Harry S., 62
Trump, Donald, 71, 287, 302
Turino, Thomas, 189
Turner, Julius Collen, 90, 164, 165, 176, 178, 190
Turnour, Edward, 50

V

Viteles, Rose, 114
Vladek, Stephen, 299

W

Walfisch, Heini, 163, 166, 174
Waßner, Rudolf, 254, 255
Weill, Joseph, 104, 106, 109
Welwart, Emil, 56
Wendel, Kay, 137
Wiesel, Elie, 100
Wilensky, Moshe, 120
Wolff, Jeanette, 300
Wolff, Siegfried, 300

Z

Zwergbaum, Aaron, 210, 213, 215, 216, 220--222, 224, 227

Short Biographies of contributors and editors

Michel Agier is an anthropologist at Ecole des Hautes Etudes en Sciences Sociales (EHESS), member of the Centre d'études des mouvements sociaux (CEMS/EHESS-CNRS).

Gabriele Anderl is a freelance researcher and author with the focus on contemporary history and a member of the board (Vice President) of the Austrian Society of Exile Research (öge).

Birgit Behrensen is professor of Sociology for Social Work at the Brandenburg University of Technology (BTU) Cottbus-Senftenberg with the focus on refugee migration in Eastern Germany and one of the founding members of the Network Migration, Conflict and Social Transformation (MIKOWA) in Brandenburg, East Germany.

Rachel Blumenthal, a lawyer and historian of the postwar era, is a fellow of the Avraham Harman Institute of Contemporary Jewry at the Hebrew University of Jerusalem.

Clara Bombach is a social and cultural anthropologist and research associate at the Marie Meierhofer Children's Institute in Zurich, Switzerland. She is currently doing her PhD in Educational Science at the University of Zurich.

Maximiliane Brandmaier is a social psychologist and psychotherapist at the Behandlungszentrum für Folteropfer Ulm (BFU).

Ioannis Christidis is a doctoral student in ethnomusicology at the University of Music and Performing Arts Vienna and a research fellow at the Music and Minorities Research Center (MMRC).

Christian Cwik is a researcher and lecturer at the Center for Inter-American Studies (University of Graz). His focus is on Latin American and Caribbean History. He is Vice-President of the Association of Latin American and Caribbean Historians (ADHILAC).

Linda Erker is a historian of the 20th century at the Department of Contemporary History at the University of Vienna and board member of the Austrian Society of Exile Research (öge).

Christoph Jahr is an author and historian of the 19th and 20th century at the Department of History at the Humboldt-University Berlin.

Andreas Kranebitter is sociologist and acting head of the Archive for the History of Sociology in Austria (AGSO) at the University of Graz.

Anat Kutner is the Director of JDC's Jerusalem Archives. Her research interests include the role of JDC and its work in the contemporary Jewish world and in the history of the State of Israel.

Lilly Maier is a historian and author with a focus on rescue. She has published two books about the *Kindertransport* and is currently a PhD candidate at the University of Munich.

Michael Mayer is an Assistant Professor of History at the Political Academy in Tutzing, Bavaria, and teaches at Augsburg University. His research mainly focuses on Holocaust Studies and Asylum Policy.

Roni Mikel-Arieli is a postdoctoral fellow in cultural history at the Avraham Harman Institute of Contemporary Jewry at the Hebrew University of Jerusalem with the support of the Fondation pour la Mémoire de la Shoah.

Marilyn Grace Miller is Professor in the Department of Spanish and Portuguese and Sizeler Professor in Judaic Studies at Tulane University in New Orleans, Louisiana. Her most recent book is Port of No Return. Enemy Alien Internment in World War II New Orleans (2021, LSU Press).

Peter Pirker is a historian at the Department of Contemporary History at the University of Innsbruck.

Christoph Reinprecht is a Professor of Sociology at the University of Vienna and president of the Austrian Society for Exile Research (öge).

Pnina Rosenberg is an art historian who teaches art and legacy of the Holocaust at the Technion, Israel Institute of Technology, Haifa.

Matthew Stibbe is Professor of Modern European History at Sheffield Hallam University and associate editor of the journal *Immigrants and Minorities*.

Andrea Strutz is a historian at the LBI for Research on the Consequences of War, a lecturer at the University of Graz, speaker of the history section of the Association for Canadian Studies in German-speaking Countries (GKS) and network chair of the Oral History and Life History Network of the European Social Science History Conference (ESSHC).

Jean-Michel Turcotte is postdoctoral research fellow at the Leibniz Institute of European history in Mainz. He is currently working on his second book on the history of the Geneva Conventions.

Kim Wünschmann is the Director of the Institute for the History of the German Jews in Hamburg and teaches modern and contemporary history at University of Hamburg.

Historical Sciences

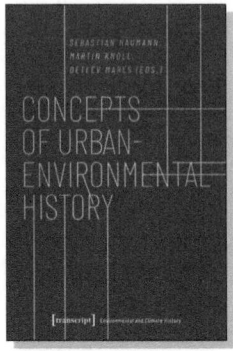

Sebastian Haumann, Martin Knoll, Detlev Mares (eds.)
Concepts of Urban-Environmental History

2020, 294 p., pb., ill.
29,99 € (DE), 978-3-8376-4375-6
E-Book:
PDF: 26,99 € (DE), ISBN 978-3-8394-4375-0

Aurora G. Morcillo
(In)visible Acts of Resistance in the Twilight of the Franco Regime
A Historical Narration

January 2022, 332 p., pb., ill.
50,00 € (DE), 978-3-8376-5257-4
E-Book: available as free open access publication
PDF: ISBN 978-3-8394-5257-8

Jesús Muñoz Morcillo, Caroline Y. Robertson-von Trotha (eds.)
Genealogy of Popular Science
From Ancient Ecphrasis to Virtual Reality

2020, 586 p., pb., col. ill.
49,00 € (DE), 978-3-8376-4835-5
E-Book:
PDF: 48,99 € (DE), ISBN 978-3-8394-4835-9

All print, e-book and open access versions of the titles in our list are available in our online shop www.transcript-verlag.de/en!

Historical Sciences

Monika Ankele, Benoît Majerus (eds.)
Material Cultures of Psychiatry

2020, 416 p., pb., col. ill.
40,00 € (DE), 978-3-8376-4788-4
E-Book: available as free open access publication
PDF: ISBN 978-3-8394-4788-8

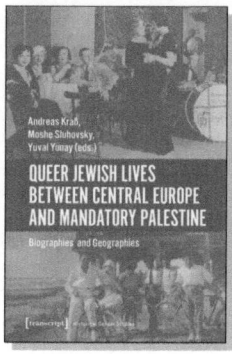

Andreas Kraß, Moshe Sluhovsky, Yuval Yonay (eds.)
Queer Jewish Lives Between Central Europe and Mandatory Palestine
Biographies and Geographies

January 2022, 332 p., pb., ill.
39,99 € (DE), 978-3-8376-5332-8
E-Book:
PDF: 39,99 € (DE), ISBN 978-3-8394-5332-2

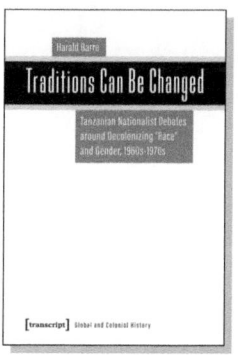

Harald Barre
Traditions Can Be Changed
Tanzanian Nationalist Debates
around Decolonizing »Race« and Gender, 1960s-1970s

2021, 274 p., pb.
45,00 € (DE), 978-3-8376-5950-4
E-Book:
PDF: 44,99 € (DE), ISBN 978-3-8394-5950-8

All print, e-book and open access versions of the titles in our list are available in our online shop www.transcript-verlag.de/en!